ST PAUL'S CATHEDRAL

Archaeology and History

Fig. 1 *The cathedral from the north-west, by Antonio Canaletto in 1754 (Yale Center for British Art)*

ST PAUL'S CATHEDRAL

Archaeology and History

John Schofield

with contributions by

Lyn Blackmore, Robert Bowles, Hazel Forsyth, Damian Goodburn and Azizul Karim, Jackie Keily, Adrian Miles, Jacqueline Pearce, Terence Smith, the late Bill White and Robin Wroe-Brown

OXBOW | books

Oxford & Philadelphia

First published in the United Kingdom in 2016. Reprinted as a paperback in 2022 by
OXBOW BOOKS
The Old Music Hall, 106-108 Cowley Road, Oxford, OX4 1JE

and in the United States by
OXBOW BOOKS
1950 Lawrence Road, Havertown, PA 19083

Paperback Edition: ISBN 978-1-78925-805-9
Digital Edition: ISBN 978-1-78570-276-1

A CIP record for this book is available from the British Library

Library of Congress Cataloging-in-Publication Data

Names: Schofield, John, 1948- author.
Title: St Paul's Cathedral : archaeology and history / John Schofield ; with contributions by Lyn Blackmore, Robert Bowles, Hazel Forsyth, Damian Goodburn and Azizul Karim, Jackie Keily, Adrian Miles, Jacqueline Pearce, Terence Smith, the late Bill White and Robin Wroe-Brown.
Description: Philadelphia : Oxbow Books, 2016. | Includes bibliographical references.
Identifiers: LCCN 2016025723 (print) | LCCN 2016026436 (ebook) | ISBN 9781785702754 (hardback) | ISBN 9781785702761 (epub) | ISBN 9781785702778 (mobi) | ISBN 9781785702785 (pdf)
Subjects: LCSH: St. Paul's Cathedral (London, England)--History. | Wren, Christopher, Sir, 1632-1723--Criticism and interpretation. | Excavations (Archaeology)--England--London. | Cathedrals--England--London. | London (England)--Antiquities. | London (England)--Buildings, structures, etc.
Classification: LCC NA5470.S5 S36 2016 (print) | LCC NA5470.S5 (ebook) | DDC 726.609421--dc23
LC record available at https://lccn.loc.gov/2016025723

Typeset in the United Kingdom by Frabjous Books
Printed in the United Kingdom by Short Run Press

For a complete list of Oxbow titles, please contact:

UNITED KINGDOM
Oxbow Books
Telephone (01865) 241249
Email: oxbow@oxbowbooks.com
www.oxbowbooks.com

UNITED STATES OF AMERICA
Oxbow Books
Telephone (610) 853-9131, Fax (610) 853-9146
Email: queries@casemateacademic.com
www.casemateacademic.com/oxbow

Oxbow Books is part of the Casemate Group

CONTENTS

LIST OF FIGURES

LIST OF TABLES

ACKNOWLEDGEMENTS

I am grateful to the Dean, the Very Reverend David Ison, and the Chapter of St Paul's Cathedral for their support of this publication. The archaeological excavations and surveys of 1994 to 2014 which are reported here were funded by the Cathedral, and I am grateful for the support of the previous deans Eric Evans, John Moses and Graeme Knowles. The Friends of St Paul's have been generous in their assistance, and I thank the previous Registrar, Nicholas Cottam, for his support. This report reflects the work of Martin Stancliffe, Surveyor to the Fabric from 1990 to 2011, his successor Oliver Caroe, and Martin Fletcher, the Clerk of Works. Many others have helped me: at the cathedral, Catherine Angerson, Simon Carter, the late Robert Crayford, Christine Faunch, Graham Lacdao, Sarah Radford, Teresa Heady and Jo Wisdom; at the Museum of London and Museum of London Archaeology, Edwin Baker, Ian Betts, Lyn Blackmore, David Bowsher, Andy Chopping, Maggie Cox, Damian Goodburn, Meriel Jeater, Azizul Karim, Jackie Keily, Carlos Lemos, Adrian Miles, David Sankey, Tracy Wellman and Robin Wroe-Brown. The plans and other site drawings in this work are by Carlos Lemos of MOLA. Kathryn Stubbs of the Department of the Built Environment at the City of London Corporation and Jeremy Smith at London Metropolitan Archives have been most helpful. Gordon Higgott has given helpful criticism at several stages. At Oxbow Books I thank Clare Litt, Julie Gardiner and Katie Allen; and Val Lamb for the design. The publication of this book has been made possible by a grant from the estate of Edwin Schofield.

FOREWORD

Viewed within the great span of architectural history St Paul's is a relatively modern building. Despite its image as the monumental masterpiece of Sir Christopher Wren, the reality is more complex. For much of its first 100 years the masonry structure itself was still settling, and for the greater part of the 18th century the interior was considered unfinished. Although the first part of the 19th century was relatively uneventful for the cathedral, the need to respond to wider changes in churchmanship and church attendance had a significant impact on its interior between 1850 and 1900. The early years of the 20th century were preoccupied by concerns over the building's structural stability, and these had only just been resolved when World War II brought damage and change, involving repair works which extended into the 1960s. Thus it is only in the last 50 years that the building has reached a state when it could be considered to have 'settled down'.

For those initially charged with the care of the building after Wren's withdrawal from the construction process, the job of Surveyor was one of tidying up loose ends and overseeing a number of additions (from several of which Wren is known to have disassociated himself). Accordingly the post of Surveyor to St Paul's was seen by Dean Secker in 1750 as no longer required, and he thus represented to the then Surveyor, Henry Flitcroft, that his position should be terminated. This, perhaps understandably, provoked a passionate response from Flitcroft who produced a 'Humble Memorial' to the trustees of the St Paul's Fund to ask them whether '... the Care of this Great and Noble Fabrick, which has hitherto been under the Inspection of an Able and Experienced Surveyor, ought not still to Continue so'. This appeal resulted in confirmation of Flitcroft's appointment with the new title of Surveyor to the Fabric, and thus started the line of formal appointments for the purpose of the care of the fabric which continue to this day.

Over the years these appointments have broadly reflected the spirit of the times. It is perhaps no surprise that the Surveyor for much of the second half of the 18th century, Robert Mylne, should have been as much an engineer as what we would nowadays consider an architect, and that those who dominated the first half of the 19th century, the Cockerells, father and son, should have been architects with a particularly antiquarian classical interest. But when Francis Cranmer Penrose was appointed to the Surveyorship in 1852 he brought a wide range of interests to the job, including an interest which we today might describe as archaeological. Penrose was Surveyor for 45 years, and made a significant contribution to the care and development of the building; and appreciation of his contribution to the understanding of the cathedral's history is increasingly recognized, not least in this book.

St Paul's has always been a thoroughly studied building: the building accounts and many of the original drawings survive, and were substantially published in the Wren Society volumes, the publication of which marked the bicentenary of the architect's death; recent scholarship has added significantly to the understanding of Wren's design processes and the structure of his office;[1] successive Surveyors and their teams have recorded and drawn the building many times (a remarkable set was independently published by Arthur Poley in 1927); and the relatively recent foundation of the St Paul's Cathedral Architectural Archive (SPCAA) has brought recognition of the wealth of archival and other material which survives at the cathedral. However, the task of subjecting this material to up-to-date archaeological scrutiny has not previously been attempted.

In this context the year 1990 may be seen as a turning point for the cathedral in a number of significant ways. This is primarily due to the fact that this was the year in which the new Care of Cathedrals Measure was brought onto the statute books. Hitherto the Dean and Chapter had been free to determine how best to discharge their duty of care to the fabric, and were subject to no external constraints in doing so; but this Measure introduced a number of important new obligations on the Cathedral Chapter. One of these was the appointment of a Cathedral Archaeologist to join the Cathedral Architect or Surveyor to the Fabric as a statutory professional adviser. In this the Measure reflected the widely held and growing understanding that the archaeological study of historic buildings is an essential component of the proper care of their fabric.

The new Measure also introduced the establishment of a statutory Fabric Advisory Committee (FAC) for each cathedral, and over the succeeding years these bodies have brought a broad range of expertise to bear on the principal issues related to the care of cathedrals' fabric. In the case of St Paul's, the FAC, initially under the chairmanship of Professor Peter Burman and latterly under Sandy Nairne, has been a source of much wisdom and encouragement to all concerned with this part of the cathedral's life. The committee has from the first been supportive of the opportunities for further understanding and scholarship presented by the appointment of a Cathedral Archaeologist.

The fact that I was appointed Surveyor in 1990 also makes that year a significant one for this study since, as John Schofield points out, my initial report on the fabric formed the foundation for an extensive 20-year programme of works which, while primarily addressing the sound preservation of the historic fabric, also comprehended very many other aspects of the cathedral and its mission. A series of works extended from the lantern on the top of the dome down to the crypt, and from a comprehensive liturgical reordering of the interior to the introduction of extensive new facilities for both staff and public. It incorporated works in almost every part of the cathedral, and several of them enabled John Schofield and his colleagues to gain access to some hidden, indeed buried, parts of the cathedral, which in turn provided the basis for the studies which underpin this book.

Sir Bernard Feilden (Surveyor to the Fabric 1969–77) coined the term 'specialist generalist'[2] to describe the job of the Surveyor. Work on a great historic cathedral such as St Paul's now calls for the Surveyor to the Fabric to be supported by teams of specialists for its proper execution: historians, art historians, engineers, quantity surveyors, conservators, conservation scientists, specialist contractors in many different fields, archivists and, of course, archaeologists. St Paul's stands as the first post-Reformation English cathedral, as the most substantial piece of architecture by perhaps England's best known architect, as an icon for London, and as an international tourist destination – but it also represents a huge mass of archaeological evidence. There have been many who have studied and written about the building's form and layout, its structural details, its construction history, its documentation and its message; but only now has a book been devoted to a study from a strictly archaeological viewpoint, drawing together the work of many specialists and setting out the present state of knowledge of this particular dimension of the building. In this it is the logical sequel to the author's study of the pre-Fire cathedral (*St Paul's Cathedral Before Wren*); but it also marks the starting point in what is likely to become an ongoing series of studies as the building (and its fabric archive) gradually yield up those secrets to which an archaeologically trained eye can add significant understanding.

Martin Stancliffe
Surveyor Emeritus to St Paul's Cathedral

SUMMARY

This monograph is an archaeological account of St Paul's Cathedral in the City of London, built in 1675–1711 to the designs of Sir Christopher Wren, and its history as a building from the early 18th century to the early 21st century, as illustrated by recent archaeological recording, documentary research and engineering asssessment.

After an introduction to the project and its many varied sources (Chapter 1) the first part of the text is a detailed account of the construction of the cathedral (Chapter 2). The construction of the cathedral, which started in 1675, was a consequence of the Great Fire of London in 1666. The progress of building, which was officially declared finished in 1711, can be followed by a detailed comparison of the fabric with voluminous building accounts which have survived. Separate parts of the building, that is the crypt and vaulting above the choir, nave and aisles, the roofs, ironwork and statues can be assigned to named masons, craftsmen and artists.

Though faced in Portland stone, the walls of St Paul's contain probably thousands of carved and occasionally painted pieces of stonework from the medieval cathedral and its monuments. Excavation for the Wren crypt or basement, under all four arms of the new church, required the removal of much of the pre-Fire cathedral, but small parts of the latter survive outside the Wren footprint, underground. Wren's foundations are described, largely from testpits of 1932. There may have been an emphasis on the east end, with carefully layered foundations, but they were quickly superseded by more practical foundations made largely of stones from the previous building. The construction of the Wren building and its embellishments are then described; this includes brief mention of the carved work above the main windows, recently cleaned, and the panels below the windows by Grinling Gibbons.

Wren's site office, housed in the refurbished octagonal medieval chapterhouse and the southern half of its surrounding square cloister on two floors, can now be reconstructed in outline from 1671 until its demise shortly after 1700. This is from study of the documentary records and pieces of masonry in the ground south of the present nave. Here Wren's Clerk of Works for the majority of the project, Laurence Spencer, worked, and nearby in the crypt of the new south transept, first Spencer's wife and then Spencer himself and his son, also briefly Clerk of Works, were buried. Their graves were excavated and the gravestones moved in 2006.

The second part describes the main works of Surveyors after Wren (Chapters 3–4). Eighteenth-century surveyors were concerned about the settlement of the building and the apparent outwards movement of the south wall of the transept; Robert Mylne inserted metal bracing here in the 1780s. He also made arrangements for the funeral of Admiral Nelson in 1806, which required a hole to be dug in the middle of the dome floor, through Wren's design, so that the coffin could be theatrically lowered into the crypt.

Francis Penrose, Surveyor from 1852 to 1897, brought change to the cathedral and its setting in many ways. His significant work is reviewed here. At the beginning of his surveyorship he oversaw the state funeral of the Duke of Wellington and designed the duke's tomb. He removed the choir screen and divided the organ; moved the choir stalls; cleaned the interior; inserted heating and lighting; radically changed the configuration of the Wren railings by lowering them and removing the section of railings round the west end, replacing them with the present row of bollards; landscaped all the churchyard around the building, by bringing many gravestones from the north-east churchyard into the crypt, afterwards installing a fountain in that part of the churchyard; inserted a new gate to Cheapside; and found and partly exposed fragments of the medieval cathedral and its cloister. Hardly any part of the cathedral or its immediate setting was left untouched by Penrose; only the roofspaces and the western part of the crypt remained in their 18th-century form.

The 20th century also brought changes and conservation projects. In the first three decades the cathedral was reinforced by several campaigns of metal braces and grouting of pillars, notably the restoration and repair of the crossing and dome under Mervyn Macartney in 1925–30. The building was hit by two bombs in World War II, and all its windows blown out. The Wren Chapter House was gutted, and the area around devastated in the Blitz of 1940–1. Plans for the area after the War would have radically changed the setting, but apart from the construction of Paternoster Square immediately to the north, little of the proposals took effect. One road, New Change, was laid out alongside the east end of the cathedral, but other roads remained on their pre-War alignments, some of medieval origin.

During the 1990s and first years of the present century, the west half of the crypt was brought into more and successful use as a public space. The refurbishment of the south-west part of the crypt required the digging of a tunnel through the foundation of the south-west tower, and this produced many architectural fragments reused as rubble, not only from the medieval building but from Inigo Jones's west portico of 1635–42, which had stood nearby after the Fire until it was demolished in 1687–8 to make room for these foundations and to provide some of the rubble for them. The south-west churchyard was landscaped as part of a project to provide better access to the building in 2004–6, and the fragments of medieval cloister found by Penrose briefly re-exposed then backfilled to allow their plan to be reproduced in new stone above them. A simultaneous cleaning of the exterior allowed examination of the carved decoration of the building, including the work of Grinling Gibbons in stone to match his masterpieces in wood inside the building.

Conclusions are presented in Chapter 5. First, many original features of the building remain to be studied, such as the exceptionally large roof structures. Some can only be flagged up here as worthy of study in the future: the dome, the external decorations by Gibbons and others, the choirstalls and several other subjects. Second, from around the time of the burial of Nelson in 1806, the cathedral became even more than before the nation's church and the central church of the British Empire. Third, it is clear that Francis Penrose, in the second half of the 19th century, made the cathedral far more accessible than before, introduced light and heat, and created the public space in the north-east churchyard.

This is followed by archaeological specialist reports (Chapter 6) and a review of the stability and character of the building, by an engineer who knows St Paul's (Chapter 7). The study ends with a gazetteer of the sites in and around the cathedral (Chapter 8) which produced material of the Wren and later periods, and some sites of these centuries which are known only on documentary grounds. The observations and excavations recorded here date from 1831 to 2014.

Wren's St Paul's Cathedral still holds many clues about its own history and about the history of the previous cathedrals on this site in its standing fabric and in the strata of the Churchyard around it. It is the most important historic building in the City of London. This study details some of the major events in the cathedral's life over its first 300 years, and some of the exercises in support of its continued conservation. This is the first monograph concerned solely with the archaeology of a major late 17th-century building in London, and the major changes it has undergone. The monograph hopes to prompt studies of other similar and contemporary buildings. It also stands with the author's previous *St Paul's Cathedral before Wren* (2011), demonstrating how the cathedral and its surroundings form a chain of visible history from AD 604 to the present.

CHAPTER 1

Introduction

Purpose and research setting

This volume is concerned with the construction of St Paul's Cathedral in the City of London under the direction of Sir Christopher Wren in 1675–1711 and the main changes to the fabric thereafter which have left records of some kind. The account is based around archaeological investigations of 1994 to 2014, and it does not claim to deal with all periods of the cathedral's history equally. The history of the building over three centuries is placed in context by a summary of the development of the historic cathedral churchyard, though by 1675 that was almost completely filled with secular buildings. We can assess how St Paul's Cathedral was viewed and incorporated into plans for the development of the area around it, especially after the widespread destruction of the cathedral's surroundings in World War II. When some of these plans were implemented, they had consequences for the survival of archaeological strata and historic buildings. This monograph is a contribution to the history of construction, repair and conservation of the cathedral, so that knowledge of past work can inform decisions about maintenance and care of the building in the future.

There is a small overlap of information with the writer's *St Paul's Cathedral Before Wren* (*SPCBW*) published in 2011, which dealt with the cathedral and its churchyard from Roman times to the Great Fire of 1666 and the first years of the Wren construction, especially in this introductory chapter and in the Gazetteer. The previous volume established the relationship in plan between the medieval and the Wren cathedrals (Fig. 2). The present report also shares the plan of the Wren cathedral produced in 1929 by the Royal Commission on Historic Monuments (England) which serves as a basic map of the building for reference throughout the work (Fig. 3).

This is also a study of how the building responded to different requirements placed upon it by its users, who increasingly came from far beyond London itself. Wren's cathedral inherited from its predecessor a function as the nation's (more specifically, England's) church. Here monarchs came to give thanks, though not to be buried. From the early 19th century, with the burials of Admiral Nelson and the Duke of Wellington, a new purpose as the nation's pantheon of military and occasionally civilian heroes was added. This broadened yet again in the later 19th century as the cathedral was declared to be at the centre of the British Empire, and therefore of a large part of the world. During World War II its miraculous survival in an area devastated by aerial bombardment made it an icon of resistance, propaganda and eventual triumph. All these themes and roles resonate today.

Histories, documentary evidence and main graphic sources

There have been many histories and architectural studies of the Wren cathedral, starting perhaps with the revisions William Dugdale made to his *History of St Paul's Cathedral in London*, which appeared 30 years after his death; Edward Maynard edited it in 1716, as 'the 2nd ed. corrected and enlarged by the author's own hand.' Wren's son Christopher began compiling

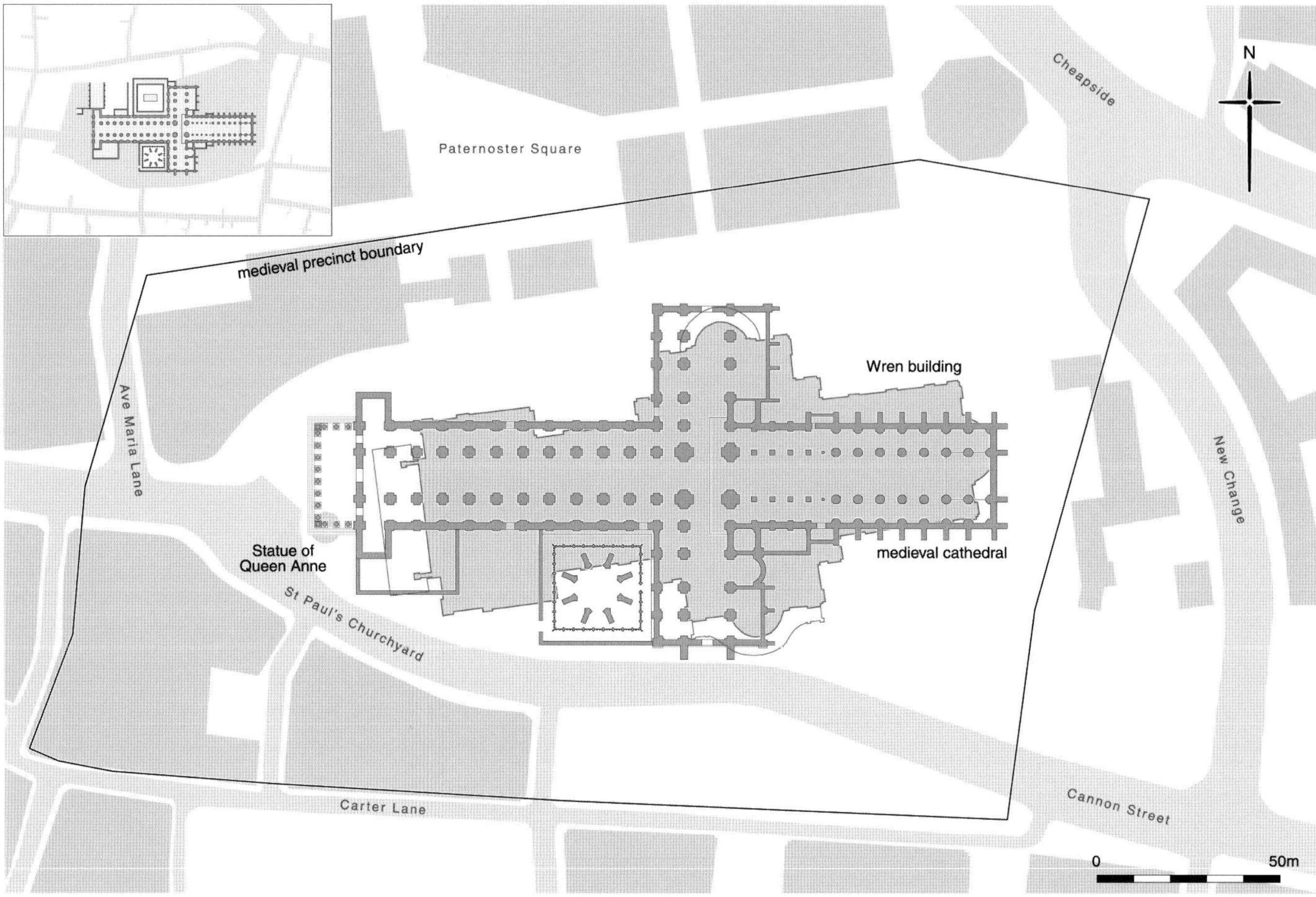

Fig. 2 *St Paul's Cathedral in the City of London today, showing the relationship of the Wren cathedral to its medieval predecessor and the medieval precinct. Inset, the position of the medieval cathedral in its surrounding streets in 1666 (Carlos Lemos, MOLA)*

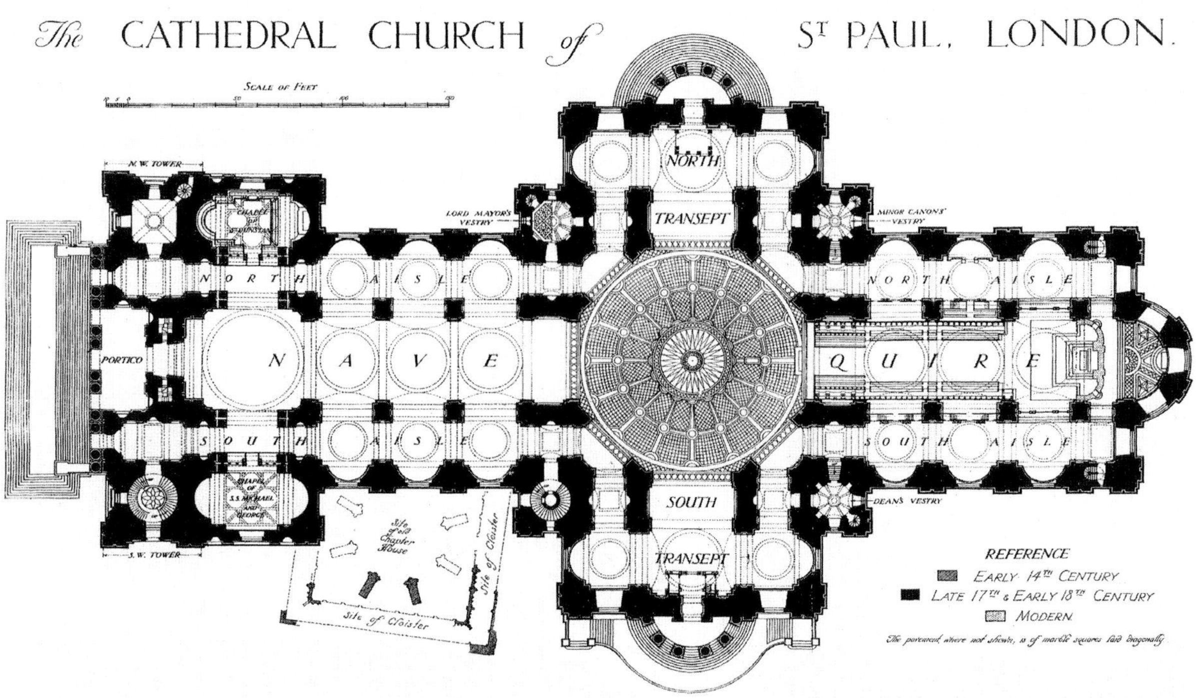

Fig. 3 *Plan of St Paul's Cathedral in 1929 (RCHME 1929, 44)*

a combination of family history and Wren's thoughts on architecture in 1719, and it was published by his own son Stephen under the title *Parentalia* in 1750.[1] Several histories of the cathedral and its personnel were produced at intervals in the 19th and 20th centuries, and culminated in the most recent and most comprehensive in 2004, which includes chapters about the architecture of the building and of its maintenance since completion in 1711.[2] Other shorter accounts of the building, either during its construction period or over its whole history, have also recently appeared.[3] There is a large body of work on Wren's design, especially the drawings produced during planning and construction, a portion of which have survived.[4] Study of the drawings has suggested that the later part of the evolving design was influenced by the building of the domed church of Les Invalides in Paris, engravings of which were available after 1683.[5]

The main documentary sources for the building of the cathedral are the building accounts and related papers, which have survived in quantity. The accounts survive from the earliest clearances in 1668 until the completion in 1711. They were transcribed and partly edited down (payments to individual craftsmen and labourers were given in summary form) in the 1930s by Arthur Bolton and H Duncan Henry and published in four of the 20 volumes of the Wren Society (1924–43), which had been established for the sole purpose of publishing Wren material.[6] In general, the editing is very good; only occasionally might one need to go to the original accounts (Fig. 4), but they are there for checking.[7] In addition, there is some further detailed information still to be gained from inspection of material not transcribed by the Society, such as seven out of the eight surviving Acquittance Books, in which the major craftsmen, Nicholas Hawksmoor and occasionally Wren himself, acknowledged payments made to them for work on the cathedral, the new houses of the Dean and of the canons in Amen Corner, and other contracts outside London.[8] On two occasions Wren authorised his 12-year old daughter Jane to sign for small sums from his due salary (Fig. 5 to Fig. 12).

The cathedral was also the subject of engravings, even before it was finished, and frequently from the early 18th century. These engravings are useful in reconstructing early aspects of the building and its surroundings, but must be used with caution as they can include speculation or omit features.

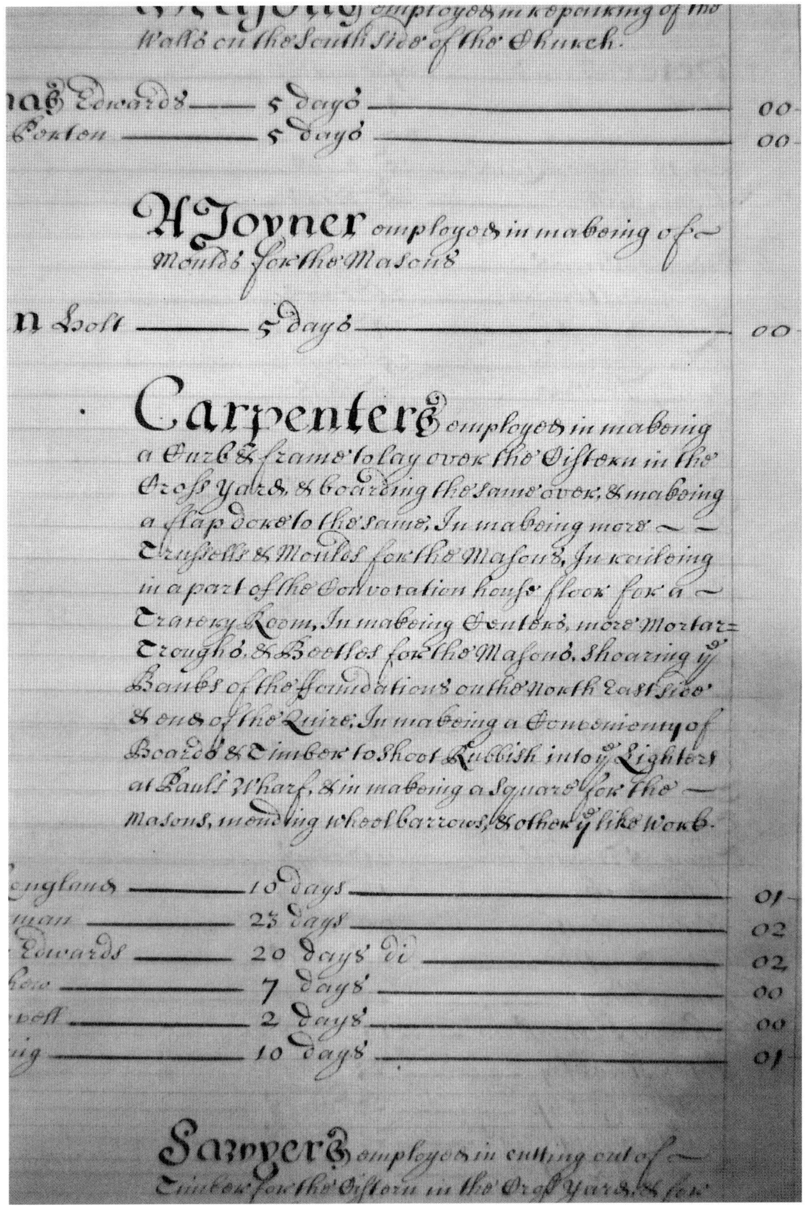

Fig. 4 Detail of a page of the Wren accounts (John Schofield, LMA CLC/313/I/B/001/ MS 25451/16, 1). This section describes work by carpenters in May–September 1674, including 'railing in' part of the floor of the Convocation House (the former medieval chapter house) to make a Tracery Room. The transcription of this page in the Wren Society volume (XVI, 204) reproduces the main paragraph verbatim, but edits the individual payments to workmen

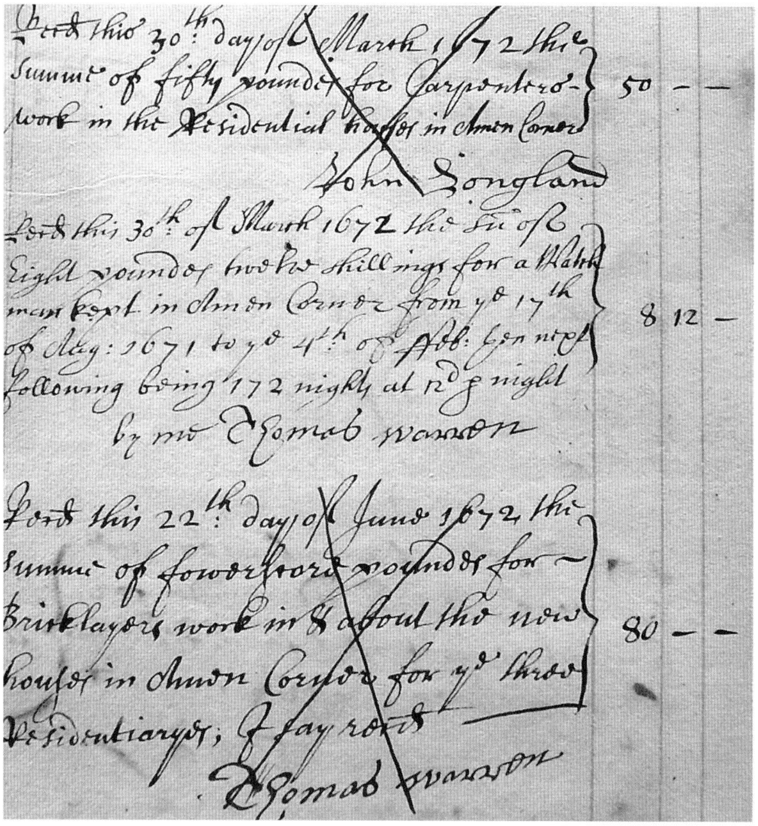
Recd this 30th day of March 1672 the Summe of fifty pounds for Carpenters work in the Residential houses in Amen Corner 50 - -
John Longland

Recd this 30th of March 1672 the Su of Eight pounds twelve shillings for a Watchman kept in Amen Corner from ye 17th of Aug: 1671 to ye 4th of Feb: then next following being 172 nights at 12d p night 8 12 -
by me Thomas Warren

Recd this 22th day of June 1672 the Summe of fowerscore pounds for Bricklayers work in & about the new houses in Amen Corner for ye three Residentiaryes; I say recd 80 - -
Thomas Warren

5

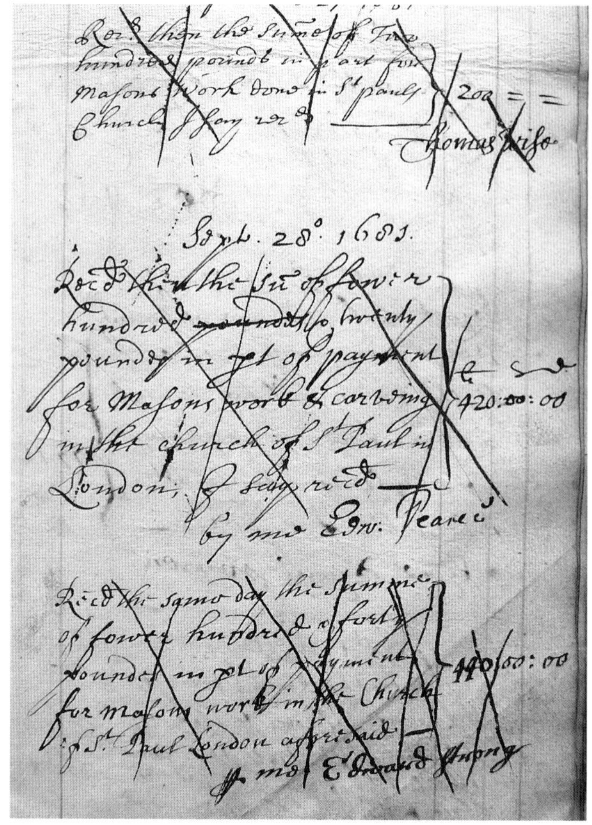
Recd then the Summe of Two hundred pounds in part for Masons Work done in St Pauls Church I say recd 200 = =
Thomas Wise

Sept. 28. 1681.

Recd then the Su of fower hundred & twenty pounds in pt of payment for Masons work & carving in the Church of St Paul in London; I say recd 420:00:00
by me Edw: Pearce

Recd the same day the Summe of fower hundred & forty pounds in pt of payment for Masons work in the Church of St Paul London aforesaid 440:00:00
by me Edward Strong

6

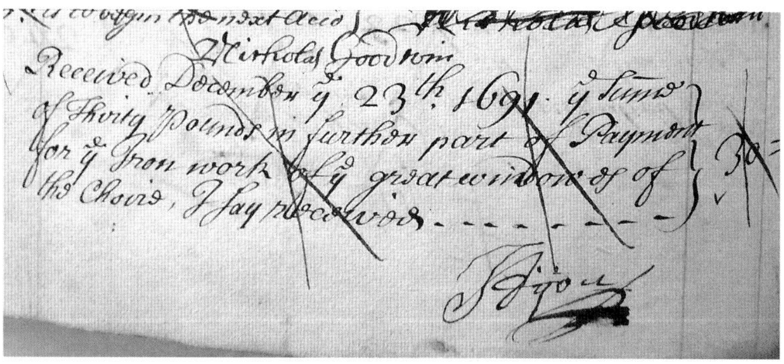
Nicholas Goodwin

Received December ye 23th 1691 ye Summe of Thirty Pounds in further part of Payment for ye Iron work of ye great windows of the Choire, I say received 30
J Tijou

7

Received December ye 24th 1691 ye Summe of Eighteen pounds in full payment for Joyners work done at St Pauls Church to ye last day of November last 18 ==
Charles Hopson

Received December ye 24th 1691 ye Summe of Twenty pounds in part of payment for Bricklayers work done at St Pauls I say received 20 ==
Richard Billinghurst

8

Fig. 5 *This and the following seven figures show signatures from the Acquittance Books, acknowledging payments. Here, carpenter John Longland and bricklayer Thomas Warren for work on the houses in Amen Corner in 1672 (John Schofield, LMA CLC/313/I/B/012/MS 25481/1)*

Fig. 6 *Masons Thomas Wise, Edward Pearce and Edward Strong for masons' work and carving at the cathedral in 1681 (John Schofield , LMA CLC/313/I/B/012/MS 25481/2)*

Fig. 7 *Jan Tijou for the 'ironwork of the great windows of the Choire' in 1691 (John Schofield, LMA CLC/313/I/B/012/MS 25481/4, 14r)*

Fig. 8 *Joiner Charles Hopson and bricklayer Richard Billinghurst for work in 1691 (John Schofield, LMA CLC/313/I/B/012/MS 254814/4, 15v)*

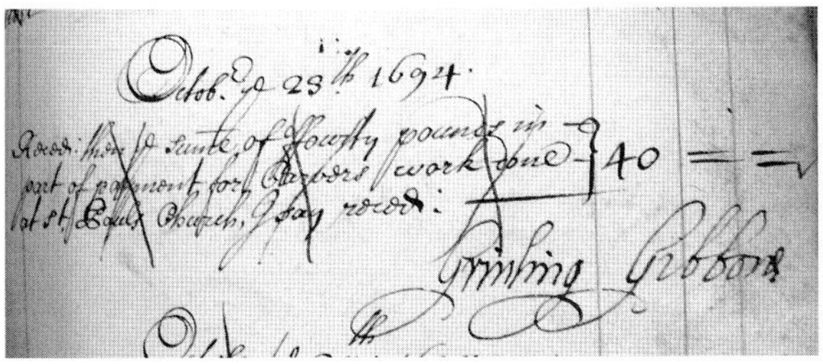
Octob. ye 23th 1694.
Recd then ye sume of fourty pounds in part of payment for Carvers work done at St Pauls Church, I say recd: } 40 = =
Grinling Gibbons

9

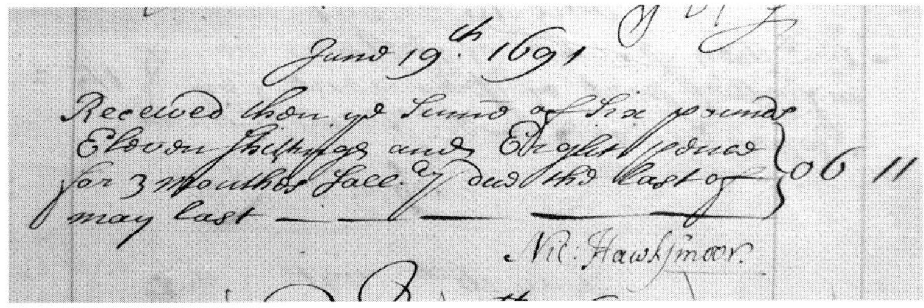
June 19th 1691
Received then ye Summe of Six pounds Eleven shillings and Eight pence for 3 months sallary due the last of may last } 06 11
Nic: Hawksmoor

10

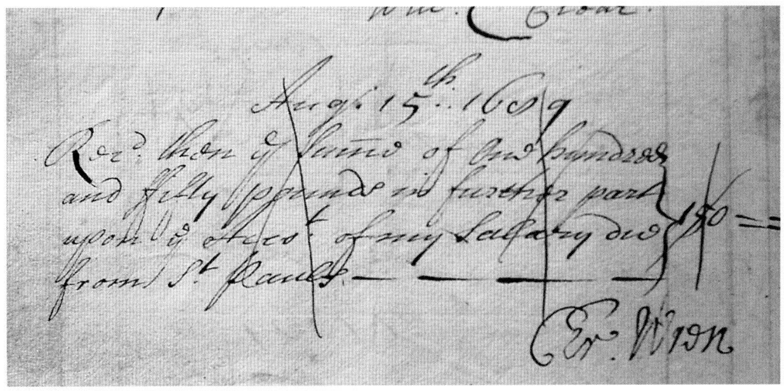
Aug: 15th 1689
Recd then ye sume of One hundred and fifty pounds in further part upon ye arrear of my salary due from St Pauls } 150 = =
Chr: Wren

11

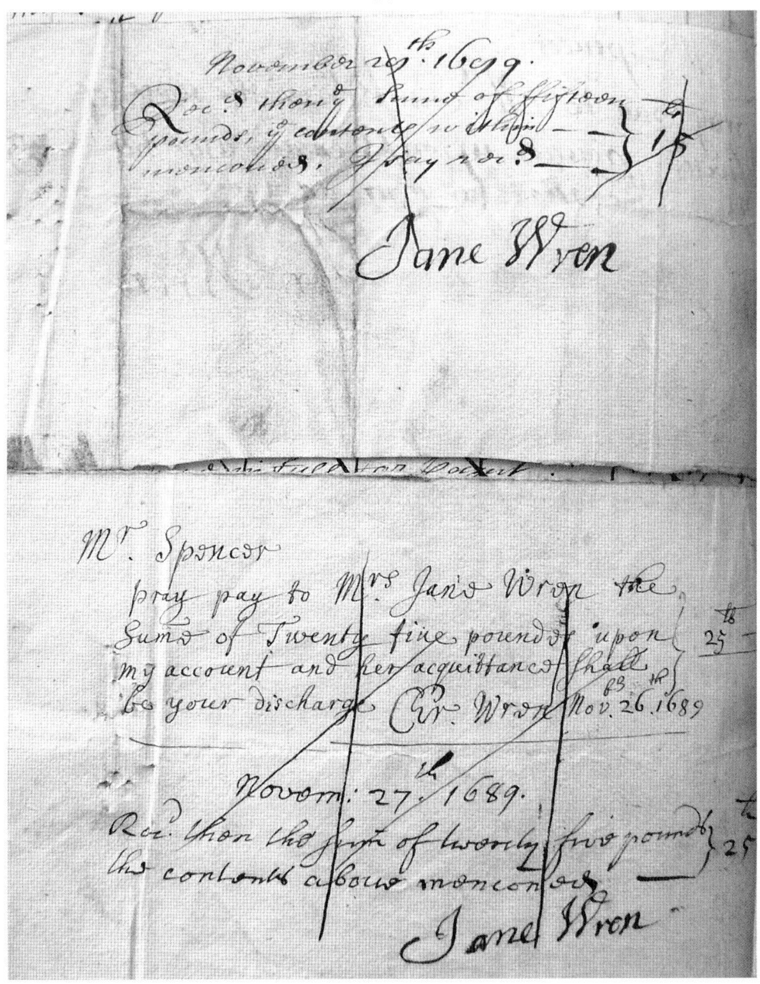
November 20th 1689.
Recd then ye sume of fifteen pounds, ye contents within mentioned. I say recd } 15
Jane Wren

Mr. Spencer
pray pay to Mrs Jane Wren the Sume of Twenty five pounds upon my account and her acquittance shall be your discharge Chr: Wren Nov. 26. 1689 } 25

Novem: 27th 1689.
Recd then the sum of twenty five pounds the contents above mencioned } 25
Jane Wren

12

Fig. 9 *Grinling Gibbons for carver's work in 1694 (John Schofield, LMA CLC/313/I/B/012/MS 25481/4, 61v)*

Fig. 10 *Possibly the earliest appearance in the accounts of Nicholas Hawksmoor, in receipt of three months' salary up to the end of May 1691 (John Schofield, LMA CLC/313/I/B/012/MS 25481/4, 6v)*

Fig. 11 *Christopher Wren, a salary payment in 1689 (John Schofield, LMA CLC/313/I/B/012/MS 25481/3, 69r)*

Fig. 12 *Two notes from Christopher Wren to the Clerk of Works Lawrence Spencer, authorising him to pay Jane Wren £15 and £25 from Wren's salary account, with her signature, now bound in an Acquittance Book (John Schofield, LMA CLC/313/I/B/012/MS 25481/4)*

Archaeological recording of the Wren cathedral and in St Paul's Churchyard

In 1896 G H Birch published a series of photographs of the exterior and interior of St Paul's in his study *City Churches*, but no corpus of measured drawings of the standing building existed. In 1908, when repairs (which included inserting steel rods) clothed the west front in scaffolding, Arthur Poley persuaded the Dean to allow him to record the pediment and its sculpture. As Poley wrote:

> 'a footing thus having been obtained at a time when, owing to the repairs being completed, the scaffolding was about to be removed, an effort was made, as it was gradually being struck, to measure the whole portico from the top downwards.'

Recording of the remainder of the west front followed, and:

> 'the author has grateful memories of the way in which Mr Alfred Dellar, foreman scaffolder on the Cathedral staff, hauled ladders up the various stages of the clock tower, single handed, to enable measurements to be taken'.[9]

Poley's survey then extended to the whole cathedral with the encouragement of the Surveyor, Mervyn Macartney (the survey work would have been assisted by the large amount of scaffolding in the crossing at that time). A volume comprising 32 large pages of measured drawings (an example, part of the west front, Fig. 13) and several smaller details was privately published by Poley in 1927. There are inevitably features of the architecture which Poley did not include; but in general these drawings are still of value today, even when their purpose has been partly overtaken by photogrammetry (as in Fig. 187 below). The Poley drawings are complemented by drawings of 1930 by Cecil Brown which comprised a section through the cathedral at all levels and plans at triforium and roof levels. These are particularly useful for showing the location of the metal ties which had been inserted at the west end and round the dome since 1900.[10]

Shortly after came another set of records which is of great archaeological value: the Gibb-Freeman engineering testpits of 1932 at various points around the perimeter of the building. The 'Gibb-Freeman' book, in the St Paul's Cathedral Architectural Archive (hereafter SPCAA) at the cathedral derives its informal name from the authors, Sir Alexander Gibb and Ralph Freeman.[11] One of the testpit drawings, for testpit 9, bears a note of soil analysis from layers exposed, dated 2 May 1932; the book of drawings was

Fig. 13 *The west front apart from the tops of the towers, by Arthur Poley (1927, pl. xvi)*

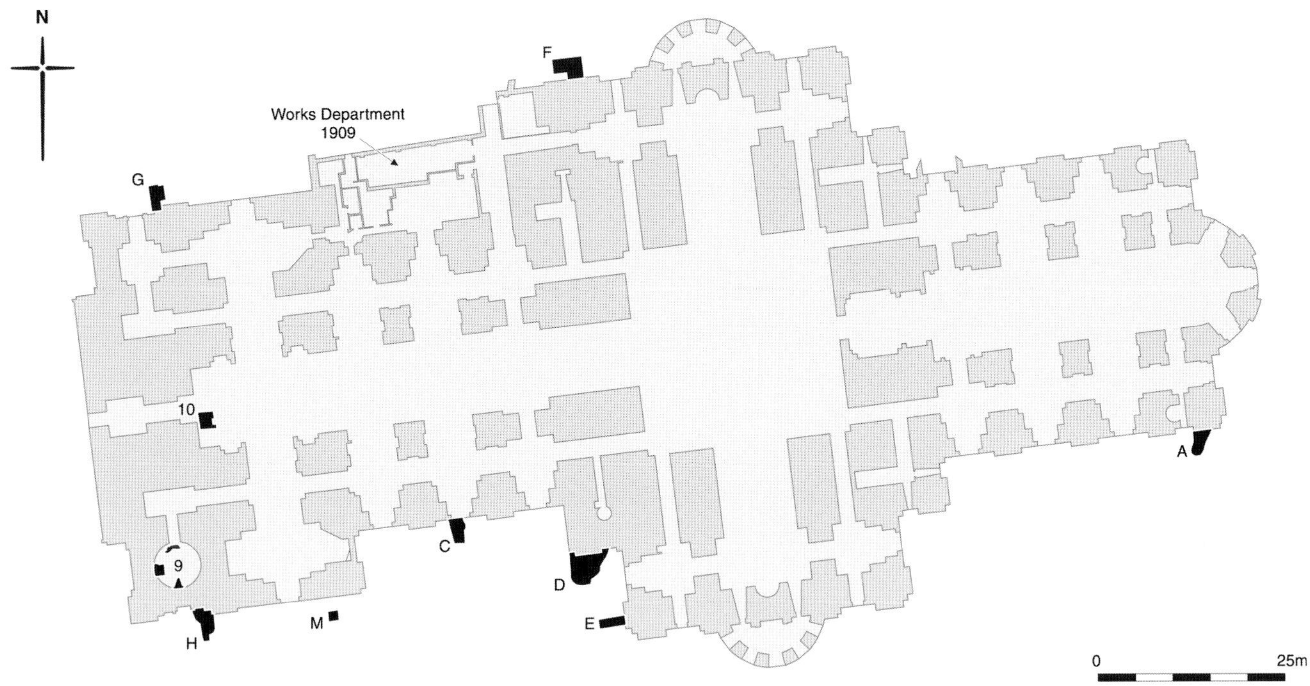

Fig. 14 The sites of the Gibb-Freeman testpits of 1932 used in this study, with their site numbers used in the Gazetteer (plan from SPCBW *fig. 1.9). The crypt is shown before the refurbishments and new passages of the 1990s (Carlos Lemos, MOLA)*

produced in 1933. The testpits are in two series: 11 (numbered 1–11) inside and 12 (lettered A–M except for I) outside. The drawings, in watercolour, show not only the slightly different form of the foundations for the exterior wall of the present cathedral at various points; but also the depth of (Roman and later) strata, and in a small number of cases older foundations from the pre-Fire church. There are also sightings of the walls of St Gregory's church which stood until 1666 at the south-west corner of the cathedral nave, and several points on the Wren drainage system for the cathedral site (both the permanent drainage system and temporary drains). The tops of one group of the testpits, backfilled, were recorded in the excavation beneath the south-west tower in 1996, but not re-excavated (Site 58). The sites of these testpits in relation to the present cathedral (inside which or against the outside of which they were dug) are shown in Figure 14.[12]

Before the beginning of modern archaeological excavation at the cathedral which dates from 1994, only one part of the site had been observed during construction work, on two separate occasions, in 1909 and 1969–70: immediately outside the north side of the cathedral nave, in the space between it and the Wren Chapter House of 1714, in the building of underground facilities for the Works Department of the cathedral (Site A, Table 1). Its chief importance for the present study is the recording in difficult conditions in 1969 of remains of brick houses erected after the Fire in 1666 but demolished in 1710 because they were too close to the new nave. A plan showing the sites of the excavations and observations on the modern map is given as Figure 15.

The sites reported here are either lettered or numbered, continuing the scheme in *SPCBW*. The main or study sites of 1969–2006 are given letters. Sites A–H of 1969–2005 (Fig. 16) in and around the cathedral were reported in *SPCBW*. Sites I–L of 1974–82 were mentioned in *SPCBW*; they were sites outside the precinct on the slope down to the Thames, of relevance to discussion of the cathedral and its setting in the Anglo-Saxon period. The archaeology and history of the Wren and later periods at Sites A to H is described here, continuing their individual accounts; along with the designation of six further sites of 2003–2010, called Sites M–R, which vary in size from individual burials to photographic recording of external carvings round more than half the cathedral. All observations prior to 1969, and some minor ones of 1969–2005, are then placed in a gazetteer which continues that in *SPCBW*. As with the larger excavations, many of these small observations contain information on both the Wren building and its predecessors, or stratigraphy beneath them, so they have already

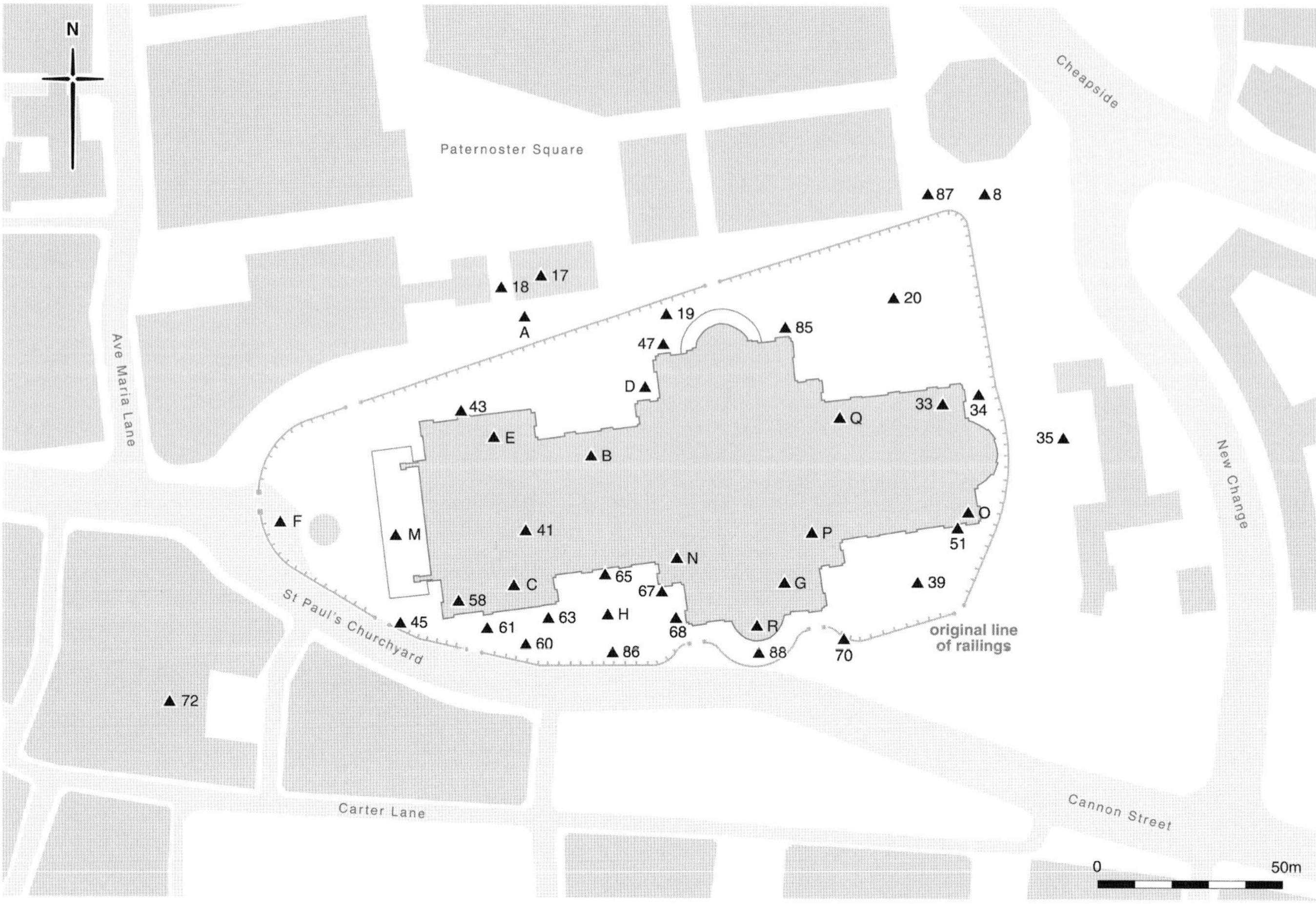

Fig. 15 Site plan showing the sites of archaeological and other observations relevant to the construction of the Wren building in 1675–1711 and features of the churchyard in the period 1700–2006 (Carlos Lemos, MOLA). This uses and extends the numbering sequence for sites used in SPCBW

Site	*Location*
A	St Paul's Churchyard N side (works department), 1909 and 1969
B	N aisle of crypt beneath nave, 1994
C	Crypt, SW and W parts, 1996
D	Corridor from N transept to Works Department, 1997
E	Crypt beneath St Dunstan's Chapel, 1998
F	Drain shaft W of St Paul's Cathedral, 2000
G	Crypt below S transept, 2000
H	S churchyard: medieval chapter house and cloister, S of Wren nave, 2004–6
M	W end, the W steps and the Geometric Stair, 2003–5
N	Main stair and external cleaning, 2006–10
O	SE bay of crypt: creation of Knights Bachelor Chapel, 2007
P	Relaying of ledger of 1883 in centre of crypt, 2008
Q	N aisle of choir crypt, 2007
R	S transept steps, 2007
8	Paternoster Row, E end, 1997
17	St Paul's Chapter House, St Paul's Churchyard
18	St Faith's parish pump, St Paul's Churchyard (now in Paul's Alley)
20	'St Paul's Cross', NE churchyard, *c.* 1910
34	E end of choir crypt, before 1914 (possibly in 1911), Pits A to C
35	St Paul's School, post-Fire (site)
37	The wall around the medieval churchyard: history after 1666
39	St Gregory's burial vault, SE of Wren choir
41	Gibb-Freeman testpit 10, 1932
43	Gibb-Freeman testpit G, 1932
45	Removal of unexploded bomb, S of the W steps, 1940
47	Gibb-Freeman testpit F, 1932
51	Gibb-Freeman testpit A, 1932
58	Gibb-Freeman testpit 9, 1932
60	St Paul's Churchyard (S side), 1980
61	Gibb-Freeman testpit H, 1932
63	Gibb-Freeman testpit M, 1932
65	Gibb-Freeman testpit C, 1932
67	Gibb-Freeman testpit D, 1932
68	Gibb-Freeman testpit E, 1932
70	Wren period Churchyard railings (general note)
85	Gibb-Freeman testpit K, 1932
86	Pavement outside railings, SW churchyard, 2009
87	St Paul's Churchyard [pathway] N of railings near NE gate, 2009
88	Shafts dug around S transept, 1831

Table 1 *The excavations and observations reported here. Sites A–R are excavations and observations of 1969–2010; Sites 8–88 are observations and testpits of 1831 to 2009 and some important buildings in the Churchyard after 1711*

Fig. 16 Sites of excavations A–H of 1969 to 2010 (Carlos Lemos, MOLA). Cleaning of the west end and elsewhere around the exterior is reported as two further projects, Site M (the west end, western steps and Geometric Stair, 2003–5; and Site N (replacement of lift in main stair and external cleaning apart from the west end, 2006–10); see Gazetteer for details

figured in *SPCBW*. A gazetteer number up to and including 84 indicates a site which also appears in *SPCBW*; Sites 85 to 88 are new additions for the present volume. Thus the two volumes can be read together as a two-part gazetteer of discoveries about the cathedral and its site.[13]

Conventions of archaeological recording

The basic unit of cross-reference throughout the archive that supports this text is the context number. This is a unique number given to each archaeological 'event' (such as a layer, wall, grave cut); each site has its own series starting at [1]. Context numbers are shown thus: C[100], which is context [100] from Site C. In the main text of this report context numbers are only used when a specific reference is required. Plans and sections with context numbers are confined to the specialist gazetteer (Chapter 8). The Museum of London site codes and addresses are listed in Table 1.

The documentary evidence and excavations before 1994 are reported with imperial measurements (yards, and feet and inches, the latter abbreviated to ft and in), along with conversions when appropriate (1ft = 0.305m; 12in to 1ft, 3ft to 1 yard). The excavations of 1994 and later are reported with metric measurements (metres). The discussion sections use either system, as appropriate. To understand the 17th-century topography, the character of the foundations in the crypt of the new building and other excavations into the ground, measurements above sea-level or Ordnance Datum (OD) are cited, in the form 15.0m OD, which means 15.0 metres above Ordnance Datum or sea level (at present).

Several of the excavations of 1994–2006 share a method of reporting which assigns the layers to Groups, that is layers which probably are the residue of a single action or related group of actions and so can be reported as one, such as road surfaces, a burial or the floors of a building. These stratigraphic groups are abbreviated Gp and are preceded by their site code; only the groups of the 17th century and later are mentioned.

CHAPTER 2

The construction of the Wren cathedral, 1666–1720

This second chapter presents a detailed account of the planning and construction of the cathedral from 1666 to its official completion in 1711 and some further embellishments up to about 1720; the adaptation of the ruin of the medieval chapter house to form Wren's site office from 1671; the construction of the new Chapter House and the Deanery; and discussion of the main building materials (especially stone and brick).

The general chronology of the construction of the Wren building is both well known and still being debated. After Kerry Downes writing in 1988,[1] the main dates are as follows:

1670	March. First model completed.
1673	Greek Cross design becomes the Great Model; Great Model built by 1674.
1675	14 May. Warrant for Warrant design. 15 July. First foundation contracts confirmed. Foundations of choir and east side of crossing begun. 17 August. Contract confirmed for above-ground masonry.
1676	November. Transept foundations begun.
1678	September. Nave foundations begun.
1685	Choir[2] and transepts finished to top of lower order.
1687–8	Foundations of west end dug; Jones portico taken down.
1694	May. Choir fittings begun.
1697	2 December. First service in the Choir.
1698	Dome reaches Whispering Gallery level.
1699	Cibber's carved phoenix in S transept pediment.
1700	Peristyle floor.
1706	W portico completed.
1708	Outer dome leaded.
1711	St Paul's declared finished.
1714	Chapter House finished.
1717–19	Balustrade on church parapet added.

This has been modified by more recent scholarship. Gordon Higgott argues that there was a major redesign in 1685, after funding had been increased by the new parliament of James II. Wren enlarged the intended dome, added a two-storey western body, and the upper screen walls.[3] An online catalogue of the St Paul's collection of Wren office drawings was published in 2013. Phases of the design and construction are discussed in detail for the first time, including those for the west end, dome, choir, western towers, churchyard and precinct. The western towers are shown to have been designed in five stages between 1685 and 1704, one factor being the decision to incorporate a belfry in the north-west tower in 1700.[4] The division of work between the several master masons, which gives a rough idea of the chronology of construction, is shown by plans in James Campbell's study of 2007.[5]

From the 1690s, artists attempted to show what the building would look like; one view from the north-west, by Robert Trevitt published around 1710, is among the more accurate (Fig. 17). It shows the building without the balustrade which followed, against Wren's wishes and designed by another, in 1717–19, and with more statues on the roofline than were eventually commissioned. Other engravings of the building in the 18th and 19th centuries are used below, with due attention to omission or distortion of individual features.

Fig. 17 The cathedral from the north-west by Robert Trevitt, a view published in c. 1710 (LMA). This shows the intended sculpture (and more of it than finally erected), but not the balustrade (added 1717–19). It also shows a door from the west gallery into the upper portico which was removed in December 1710

Temporary arrangements for worship, demolition of the medieval cathedral and removal of debris, and features of the construction site

This section deals with temporary arrangements for worship (the 'tabernacles') and Wren's first designs, demolition of the pre-Fire cathedral and St Gregory's parish church, and archaeological traces of activities on the building site up to 1711, when the cathedral was declared finished, including disposal of human remains and removal of buildings, including some already built after the Fire. Here also an attempt is made to reconstruct in outline Wren's site office in the Convocation House, the former medieval chapter house.

The temporary tabernacles and Wren's first designs[6]

The medieval cathedral was badly damaged in the Great Fire of September 1666. One fragment survives, though now underground; the south-east corner of St Faith's crypt at the east end of the medieval building, which was found by Penrose in 1878–9 and conserved. It is accessible today from a manhole immediately east of the Wren building. The effect of the Fire is shown on

the stone. In February 1667 Wren submitted a report on the state of the fire-damaged cathedral.[7] He criticised the construction, including that 'it seemed to have been built out of the stone of some other ancient ruins, the walls being of two several sorts of firestone and those small, and the core within was rag-stone cast in rough with mortar and putty'. He thought that the fire of 1561 and the crash of the spire had severely cracked the vault of the nave. The walls had spread out at least ten inches. Jones had made his walls perpendicular outside, but had not cased the walls within. One of the piers, at the south-west end (ie the west end of the south arcade) had fallen since the Fire. He distinguished between the 'old choir' and the 'new choir', which had survived to different degrees through the Fire because of their structural differences; the old choir, nearest the tower, had fared better. The new choir and St Faith's were beyond repair; the undercroft vault of the old choir (presumably with Romanesque origins) was stouter and could be repaired. Although this small space could be reused, he recommended erecting a temporary church in the western part of the nave, by using the two doors in the centres of the north and south sides of the nave. A choir would occupy two bays to the east, an 'auditory' three or four bays to the west, all below a temporary roof.

An order was given early in 1668 to erect this; but it did not proceed very far. In April 1668 the third pier from the west end in the south arcade was recased in stone 'almost up to the Chapitre', but one night during the works, it fell down. Dean Sancroft reported this to Wren in a letter, desiring his presence with all speed and adding 'you will think it fit, I know, to bring with you those excellent draughts and designs you formerly favoured us with'. Wren replied in July with advice that the temporary solution should be abandoned, and it seems that 'the collapse cleared the minds of the authorities'. An order of 1671 to sell some of the building material from the pre-Fire cathedral includes the information that 'there are some parcells of good oaken timber, which were provided for roofing a part of the west end, before the ruines there gave occasion to change that resolution'.[8]

Although that particular solution had been abandoned, the substantial nature of the Fire-damaged structure continued to influence design proposals. In 1668, Wren proposed to build a new cathedral completely within and coterminous with the pre-Fire building;[9] but this idea was shortly laid aside. In 1670, what is traditionally called Wren's first model, which survives incomplete, was discussed.[10] It comprised a new structure to sit on or near the old foundations, the vaults of which would be used for burial; west of it, on the site of the former crossing, would be a domed area square without but octagonal within. The external elevations with their two-storey arcades were perhaps inspired by Palladio's basilica at Vicenza.[11] As Godfrey Allen pointed out, all the site of the medieval nave 'would have formed a great Piazza in front of the New Cathedral.'[12] This plan was superseded by the Great Model scheme by December 1672.[13]

While discussions about the form of the future cathedral continued, people continued to die and require burial. The registers of St Faith's parish show in November 1666 there was a burial 'in St Faith's church, over against the pulpit'. This phrase was repeated in August 1670 and September 1671, and another burial was 'in the demolished church'.[14] Between 1674 and 1676 there were burials 'in the tabernacle', and in February 1677 the burial of Hestar, daughter of Henry Hathy, 'being the first that was buried since the beginning of Pole's [Paul's] church'. This tabernacle had three aisles, since a middle aisle is mentioned. Burials in the tabernacle continued until at least 1679, and in 'St Faith's church' until 1684.[15] But the new cathedral foundations were begun at the south-east corner, within the outline of the former crypt, in 1675; the tabernacle cannot have stood within the outline of the pre-Fire cathedral. The simplest way of explaining these references is to suppose that there was a separate temporary tabernacle erected nearby, in which burials took place, with the exception of the one specially noted as 'in the demolished church'. Given that references to the tabernacle at St Faith's do not start until 1674, it is possible that it was not erected until then, and that sporadic burials had continued in the former crypt between 1666 and 1674. From 1675, the site of the St Faith's crypt was needed for the new foundations. 'Tabernacles' was the term given to temporary parish churches which between 1670 and 1686 were erected in at least thirty parishes. They were built of brick and wood, and paved with tiles; two, at St Thomas Apostle and St Leonard Eastcheap, were afterwards used as schoolrooms. Some tabernacles were on the site of the parish church, reusing the ruined walls, but others were in the churchyard.[16]

Burial had also continued at St Gregory's: one in the register for that parish is dated 16

Fig. 18 The west side of Ludgate, as rebuilt after the Fire, shortly before its demolition in 1760 (artist unknown, LMA). The drawing does not show the gradient of the street, and the shadows come from the north

September 1666, only nine days after the end of the Fire. A marriage took place at the church in March 1675, presumably in the ruin itself; a tabernacle was erected for the parish a year later, in March 1676, and marriages in it continued until 1686.[17] The accounts for 1687 suggest that a tabernacle lay on the north side of the former nave, and it was modified as the new foundations for the north wall were dug there. Part of it was taken down, and the part remaining made into 'Offices'.[18] Perhaps this was the St Gregory parish tabernacle; it is difficult to see how a tabernacle could have been built on the south side of the cathedral, next to the former church.

We can also ask if there were any changes to the levels of the surrounding streets which would have given the new cathedral a different aspect. During the rebuilding of the fire-damaged area, several major streets were straightened or widened, and Thames Street raised through its entire 1-mile (1.61km) length by between 3ft and 8ft (0.92m and 2.4m), to lessen the steep slopes up the lanes which led off from its north side. Similarly, to decrease the incline, Ludgate Hill (street) was heightened with fire rubble, though the heights read strangely: 6ft (2.1m) at Fleet Bridge, 8ft 7in (2.6m) at a distance of 200ft (61m) up the hill, 5ft 2½in (1.6m) at 300ft (91.5m) and nothing where it met the Churchyard.[19] The post-Fire gate (Fig. 18) formed a narrow entrance to the vista of the west end of the cathedral. Robert Bowles suggests that the level of the road where it passed under Ludgate was raised disproportionately after the Fire, to provide a level surface within the gate. The present gradient was formed after the removal of the gate in 1760. St Martin Ludgate church is the only surviving post-Fire building; the pavement outside the church has clearly been lowered, which created the need for extra steps.[20] Thus we can think of the post-Fire approach up Ludgate Hill as steep until the gate was reached, then less of an incline as the cathedral was revealed.

In general, the Churchyard was neither heightened nor lowered after the Fire. It may be that the ground level around the Wren cathedral as it started construction was the same as that of the medieval cathedral in 1666. The only certainly known ground levels around the medieval building are those of the cloister walks on the south side recorded in 2004, at about 15.2m OD (above Ordnance Datum, or sea level); the plinth of the Wren building is at about 16.59m OD. But part of this difference of 1.4m may be accounted for by differences in level between parts of the medieval cathedral. As at other major churches, such as Westminster Abbey, there were almost certainly steps down from the nave of medieval St Paul's into the cloister. It is also unlikely that the notional plinth around the parts of the medieval cathedral was at the same level throughout, due to its long history of building.

Demolition of the medieval cathedral and the significance of the Great Model

Wren was signing the monthly accounts concerned with clearing the old cathedral from October 1668. During 1668 demolition had reached the central tower of the old cathedral, though this large task was carried out in stages and the lowest foundations of the crossing piers were not removed until January 1675. The lead was retrieved where possible. St Faith's crypt was cleared of its piers, and the foundations running between the piers identified by trenching.[21] In March and April 1669 the steps from the crossing into the former choir and the remains of the screen were removed to give access to carts; another cartway was formed down into St Faith's (the crypt beneath the Gothic choir) from the Cross Yard, ie the north-east part of the Churchyard where St Paul's Cross had stood.

In 1670 temporary buildings were constructed

in the Pardon Churchyard: two houses for the almoner and choristers. Around this time, also, a small patch of land belonging to the bishop which came within 6ft (1.8m) of the north end of the Jones portico was purchased to form an access way round the cathedral for general expediting of the works. In the same year rubbish from the site, that is rubble, was taken by cart to Thames Street, presumably to contribute to the raising of that street along its length by several feet which is known from other documentary sources.[22] Thus the carved stones of the medieval cathedral are now spread round the City.

In 1671 some demolition took place of the 'high inside walls' adjacent to the tower. This campaign also included the arches below the steeple on the south and east sides, the west wall of the south transept, and the east gable of the choir. In 1672 a wall was built across the west end of the church, 'a little above the little south and north doors', that is on the east side of the line between the two nave doors.[23] Sometime between April and September 1673 a trench about 10ft (3m) wide was dug along the outside of the north wall of St Faith's, out into Cross Yard. The purpose seems to have been to provide a supply of 'black earth', ie cemetery soil, which was then barrowed down into the space for the future dome. This was probably both to provide a level surface and to dispose of some of the vast amount of cemetery soil being disturbed; beneath much of the Wren crypt today, this layer of soil with bones is found as part of the Wren construction layers. In the summer of 1674 carpenters were paid for 'a large 20ft rod and stakes and for waiting upon the Surveyor for measuring and staking out the east part of the ground of the church according to the new model'.[24] This must refer to the laying out of the design of the new cathedral, which in 1673–4 would be the Great Model (Fig. 19);[25] the latter fits the available site, and scholars and artists have wondered what the cathedral would have looked like if it had been built (Fig. 20). Further, the Great Model may be the explanation of the change of alignment of about 6° between the pre-Fire and Wren buildings. A study by Robert Crayford in 2001 suggested that the design of the Great Model fitted the tight surroundings in only one way, and this required the slight change in alignment; which is the same as the eventual, replacement Wren design.[26] Thus the alignment of the present building is a result of the aborted plans over the Great Model design; the Model had been staked out, and its alignment was kept. Crayford's suggestion is followed here, but with an added observation. The alignment of the present cathedral is also close to that of the major new street which would have connected the new cathedral with other major centres of the city if rebuilt according to Wren's plan. But this is probably coincidence, since Crayford's argument that the Great Model plan only fits in one way, and that this determined the present alignment, is preferred.

Fig. 19 Wren's Great Model, in the Trophy Room of the cathedral (Graham Lacdao, © Chapter of St Paul's Cathedral)

Fig. 20 Great Model: a view if it had been built, by H L G Pilkington (Graham Lacdao, © Chapter of St Paul's Cathedral). The painting is not dated, but the ambiance is of the 1930s. The scale of the building is too large by comparison with the human figures, perhaps an unintended following of the convention of 18th-century views

Fig. 21 View of the dome from within the Great Model (Graham Lacdao, © Chapter of St Paul's Cathedral). This is from the trench or walkway which runs inside the Model

In the 17th and 18th centuries, models were made by architects for the approval of clients, for entering in competitions, and as aids in construction. The Great Model, constructed in 1673–4 by William Cleere, was intended to be a permanent record of the design, in case of accident to the architect. It was designed to be walked through to suggest the experience of the real interior (Fig. 21). The model was originally painted stone colour inside and out; details were gilded. The roofline had 18 statues, since lost. Perhaps the form of any crypt was not yet in Wren's mind; there is an absence of windows below church floor level, as though a colossal podium was intended.[27] Among the many surviving 17th- and 18th-century architectural models of individual buildings from Europe, the St Paul's Great Model is one of the largest. Nor is it the only model from Wren's career to survive. Wooden models were used in the protracted discussions about the royal hospital at Greenwich, and a model of the Hospital by Nicholas Hawksmoor for which he was paid in 1699 is probably that now at the National Maritime Museum; it is also probably the one which Wren took with him to discuss the Hospital with the king at Kensington Palace on 3 April 1701, as recorded by Evelyn.[28] In 1710 Wren had a wooden model made, which survives, of his proposed crossing tower and spire at Westminster Abbey.[29]

On the St Paul's site, demolition continued. The side walls of St Faith's were being removed in May to September 1674. The contracts with masons for the first foundations of the new structure were agreed in July 1675. Later that year the lower parts and foundations of the south-east, north-west and north-east crossing piers of the medieval cathedral were removed. At this point the gable of the north transept was finally scaffolded and taken down. Attention then focussed during 1676 and early 1677 on the west wall of the south transept, the nave walls and the nave arcades.[30]

The cathedral and its surroundings, rebuilt after the Fire, are shown by Ogilby and Morgan in their map of 1676 (Fig. 22); though the plan of the cathedral, understandably for this date, is not the finished one. There is no sign on the map of the old cathedral, but the Jones portico was actually standing for another twelve years after 1676. In fact the cathedral shown by Ogilby and Morgan is a remarkable piece of prediction. It was in June of the same year, 1676, that the contract with Warren to construct the brick vaulting under the choir was signed.[31] At the time of production of the map, only the barest outline of the east end foundations would have been visible. The long process of demolition of the medieval cathedral has already been described in the previous archaeological study.[32]

Archaeology of the construction site, 1667–1711

The features of the construction site recorded archaeologically comprise general layers both inside and outside the footprint of the Wren building, a mortar mixing area and temporary drains at the west end, and a well on the north side, probably a remnant of the pre-Fire buildings; a fragment of an isolated foundation may be the truncated base for a timber shore which would have held up the pre-Fire building during demolition.

One of the first concerns was a water supply. The accounts record an apparent connection with a supply from the New River Company's main on 17 July 1675, but at present we do not know where the Company's network lay near the cathedral. In August of the same year Joshua Marshall contracted to make a cistern, but it is not stated where.[33] In July 1676 payment was made for fencing in the well in the street on the north side of the church. Another well on the north side near Canon Alley was dug out and reused in 1685.[34] Either of these wells could be the well recorded outside the former north transept in 1969 (Site A). There was also digging

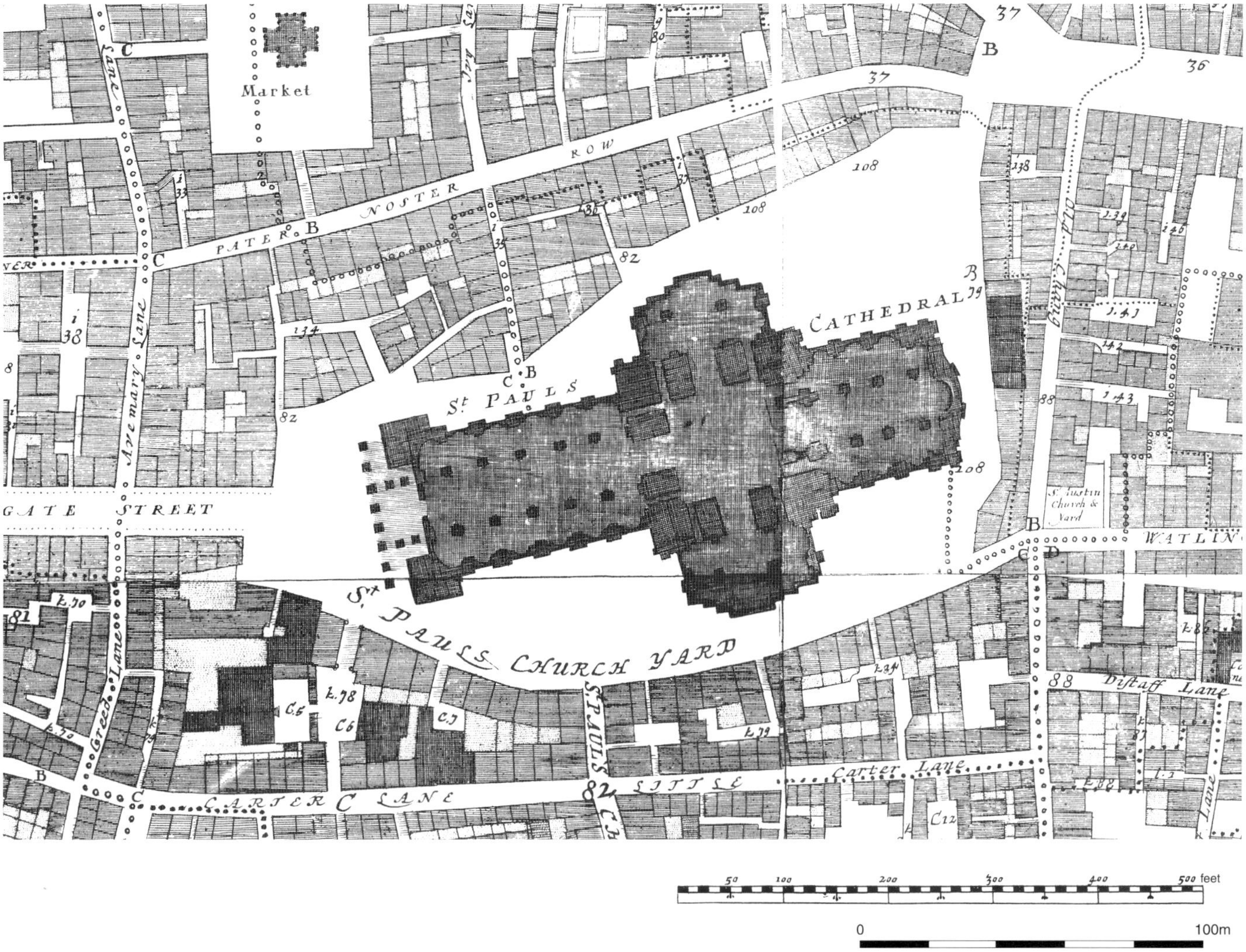

Fig. 22 *The cathedral on Ogilby and Morgan's map of the City of London, 1676 (LMA). The post-Fire Deanery (now the old Deanery) is shown as C5 in the south-west corner; the post-Fire Chapter House of 1714 has yet to be built, partly on the site of the triangular block of houses immediately north of the nave. East of the cathedral, the darkly shaded rectangle is St Paul's School*

in the church of wells for water. In April 1677 a well sunk on the site of the future dome was in use, and another was apparently added nearby in September of that year. A third was added beneath the dome in September 1679.[35] It is not clear why the area marked out for the dome (and where the foundations for the main piers were already in construction) should be singled out for the wells; perhaps it was just because it was a central point. Water was also brought from Cheapside, presumably from the conduit at St Michael le Querne just outside the north-east gate, in a pipe laid in the ground. Temporary cisterns continued to be dug throughout the cathedral's construction; one was as late as 1703, specifically for the construction of the west end.[36] At least one was of stone and paved internally with Portland, so perhaps these cisterns remain in the strata around the building.

A well apparently of medieval date was found on Site A in 1969, immediately outside the north transept of the medieval cathedral (for locations of the sites, see Fig. 16); it was probably adjacent to the stair which led to Sherrington's library of the middle of the 15th century, and may originally have been of the same date. Pottery recovered from it dates to *c.* 1630–80, slightly earlier than some fragments of tobacco pipes in the same group, which date to 1680–1710. A date of 1680–1710 can therefore be suggested for this group. This indicates that this well was reused by Wren's people. It was crossed by the line of the new railings of about 1712, and must have been then put out of use. The well was left undisturbed in 1970, and given a circular cap of concrete, which can still be seen in the north churchyard north-west of the Wren transept.

The sorted rubble to be retained was heaped in various places around the building site, but in 1676 'the great heap in the Cross Yard' is

Fig. 23 The ruin of the medieval cathedral from the west by T Wyck, undated but about 1672 (Bodleian Library, University of Oxford, Gough, XX, 2B). This shows the west end with the Jones portico (and its inscription) and the Jones cupolas, one of which Wren wanted to reuse at the Royal Hospital Chelsea. On the right is the shell of St Gregory's parish church, and right of that the west wall of the medieval cloister, already Wren's site office when the drawing was made

mentioned. The Cross Yard was the former churchyard north of the choir and east of the north transept. There was no doubt a shifting landscape of sheds, stonecutters' workshops and at least one plumbery, for which a furnace was built or rebuilt in 1695.[37] There was much reuse of the lead from the previous building, of which there must have been a large amount. Alabaster, presumably deriving from the medieval monuments, was 'bruised' to make cement for the masons.[38] The surviving Elizabethan effigies escaped this destruction.

St Gregory's churchyard, a walled area adjacent to the parish church at the south-west corner of the medieval cathedral, was used to store stones and a heap of gravel, and as the site of a sawpit. A drystone wall was erected near the pit, probably to ensure safe access to the south door into the former nave. In March 1689 the Commissioners paid £15 to the parishioners of St Gregory's as part of the charge of paving the street by their churchyard, 'in consideration that they have for some time been hindered burying their dead therein, by reason the ground was, and is yet incumbered with stones and other materialls'.[39] It seems likely, from this reference, that the parish attempted to continue burial in its churchyard for some time during the construction period. The date at which St Gregory's churchyard was closed, and landscaped with the site of the parish church (which had already largely disappeared beneath the cathedral's south-west tower), is not established but must have been after 1689, and presumably by about 1711.

From 1667, the site was gradually surrounded by a wall or fence (both terms are used) which was then continually being rebuilt as the new cathedral gradually extended west over the site of the old one. It had gates with bars and spikes on top, to stop people climbing over.[40] The earliest documented piece is a wall '7 feet [high] at West End of Portico' in December 1667, which is shown by Wyck in his drawing of about 1672 (Fig. 23). In March 1668, the front of a house burnt in the Fire (presumably only its ground floor section) was allowed to stand 'until ye pale should be set up in the same place'.[41] The churchyard was still used for all kinds of normal traffic; and in 1673 the fence outside the old south transept had to be taken down and rebuilt to make the street to the south wide enough for the Lord Mayor's procession. The traditional pedestrian route through the south and north doors of the nave of the medieval building was also preserved for the public, at least until 1681; in 1672 a wall was built across the former nave, a short distance east of ('above') the two doorways, evidently to demarcate the pathway from the building works which were all east of it. The 'west gate', presumably of the enclosure, was still standing in January 1702.[42]

Further details of the construction site were forthcoming from excavations of 1994–2006, especially when compared with the relevant engineer's test-pits of 1932. At Site C around the base of the south-west tower, below the floor of the east–west passage to the north of what is now the main room of the Wren Suite (created in 1996 in the crypt below the Chapel of SS Michael and George), a truncated foundation of ragstone and chalk fragments lay roughly north–south at right-angles to the line of the medieval cathedral, not the Wren building, and protruded south into one of the narrow trenches from the north side (Fig. 24). Within it were two parallel slots evidently formerly containing timbers, later covered by crushed chalk presumably when the structure was destroyed. From its alignment perpendicular to the medieval building rather than the Wren building, it is thought to be something to do with the former. It could have been a foundation for the base of a raking shore at the time of dismantling the south side of the nave, which would have been a short distance to the north; or the base of a temporary prop for the nave wall.

Digging into the Roman strata was widespread throughout the cathedral site, as shown by the discovery of Roman pottery kilns and cremations at the time, and as recorded in several of the modern excavations. The gradual clearance of

Fig. 24 Plan of excavations and observations at the west end of the crypt, 1996: with Gibb-Freeman Testpit 10 and the central area of Site C investigated in 1932 (Carlos Lemos, MOLA). A feature interpreted as possibly the base of a temporary shore for the medieval nave is also shown (context [C74]; explained in the Gazetteer entry for Site C)

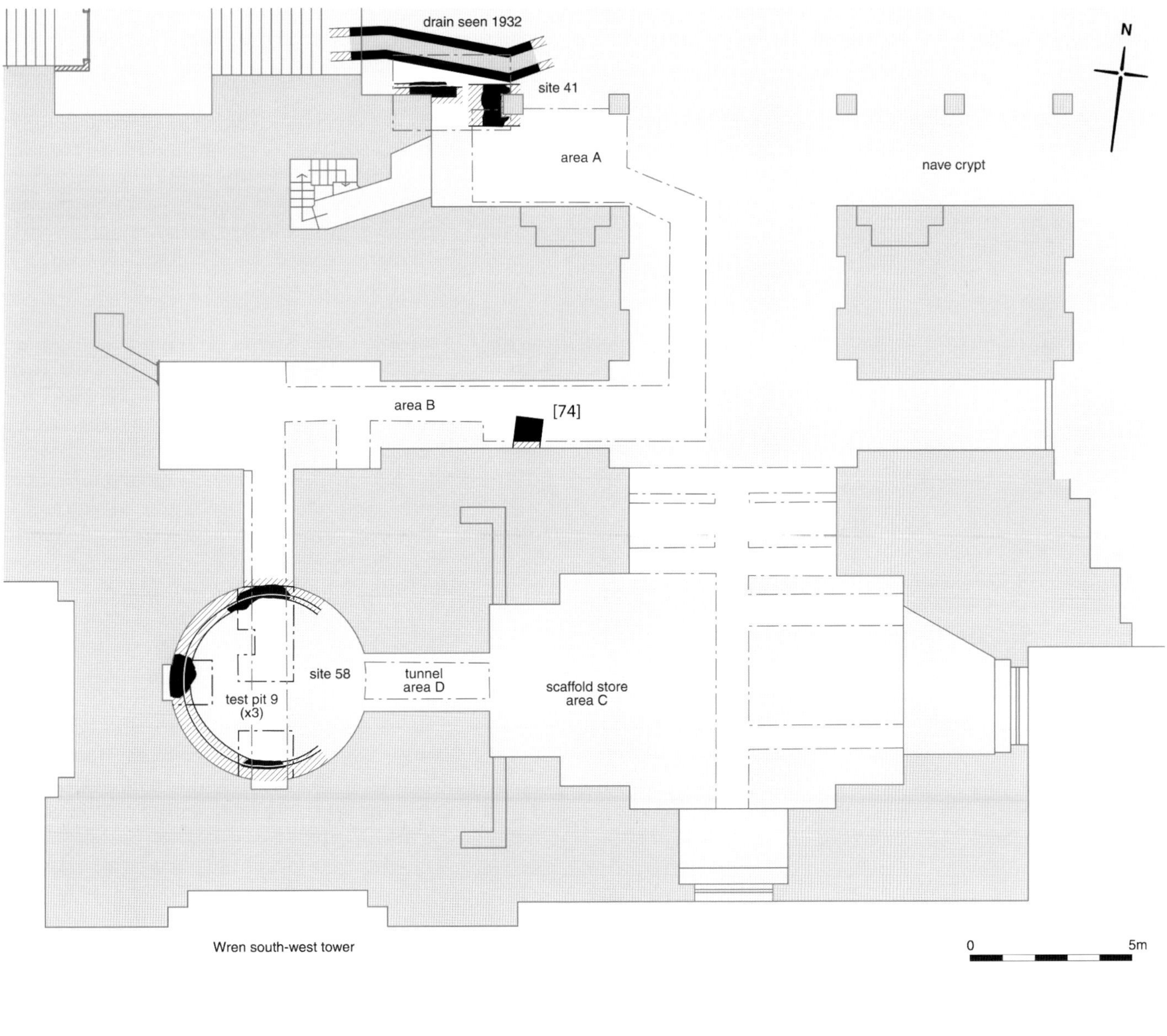

Fig. 25 (left) Site C: the Wren temporary drain, looking east (scale is 2 × 100mm) (Andy Chopping, MOLA)

Fig. 26 (right) Site C: detail of impressions of planks in mortar surface (scale is 2 × 100mm) (Andy Chopping, MOLA)

the site, which included removal of the many crypts and vaults of the former building and old foundations, is described on a monthly basis in the accounts. Two aspects can be illustrated by archaeological study: the general character of the large hole which was being dug, and the provision of temporary drains as the excavation became increasingly filled with water, and the disposal of human remains which would be continually met during the excavations for foundations and the four arms of the new crypt.

Standing water, probably produced by rain rather than by subterranean seepage, was a recurring problem throughout the early years of the new cathedral construction. It would have been exacerbated by the digging of an increasingly large sunken area which was to be the new cathedral crypt. Beneath the floor of the crypt at the west end, traces have been found of two lengths of temporary drain, the second covered by an area which is interpreted as being used for mixing mortar.

First, in Gibb-Freeman testpit 10 (Fig. 24) a length of brick drain was found passing east–west though the westernmost bay of the central vessel of the nave crypt. The drain, which had been backfilled with loose rubble before 1932, had lost its top, even though by comparison with the height of other more complete fragments, it might have been allowed to remain immediately beneath the crypt floor. The sides of brick survived about 0.38m high. A note on the plan says that the bricks were not mortared, and that 'indications of a timber roof were found'; presumably collapsed fragments of timber among the filling rubble.

Second, at Site C, in a small area at the west end of the Wren crypt, excavation ahead of new drains in 1996 went to a depth of about 0.5m below the crypt floor (Fig. 25). This area was immediately to the south of the location of Gibb-Freeman testpit 10, in the next bay (gazetteer Site 41). A drain formed by two walls of soft red brick without mortar surviving five courses high and on a brick base ran east–west for a recorded distance of 1.2m (Fig. 25, Fig. 26). There were traces of timber boarding which originally formed a cover or top to the drain. Some of the bricks had traces of mortar on their broken edges, suggesting they were reused. The drain was later put out of use: pebbles and sand had either fallen or been pushed into the drain, over the board. The board and layers above were perhaps a temporary mixing area for mortar, after the drain had been backfilled.

It seems likely that both the drain seen in Gibb-Freeman testpit 10 and that seen at Site C were temporary drains, running east–west and a few metres apart. In August 1688 payment was made for six wells dug at the west end of the church, to hold river water to make mortar;[43] the recorded

Table 2 Dating evidence: datable features of the construction site for the Wren cathedral, 1667–1711

Site	*Evidence*	*Date*
Construction site and foundation trenches of Wren building		
A	reuse of medieval well outside N transept, ER 1685	1630–80 from pottery; 1680–1710 from tobacco pipes
D	sherd of Chinese porcelain CHPO, 1683–1710, D[340] (Fig. 27)	late 17th century
Construction of foundations of Wren building, nave and south transept		
B	N wall of nave	1680 (WS XIII, 127)
G	backfill of foundation trench for E wall of S transept: portable sundial late 17thc (Fig. 28), clay tobacco pipes 1660–80 in G[21]	1677 (WS XIII, 83–96)
Disposal of human remains		
F	tobacco pipes 1680–1710 from F[5] and F[22]; coffin metalwork of 17th century type	1688 on documentary grounds

drains may be part of those temporary works.

Though the construction of the Wren cathedral is finely dated through the survival of prodigious documentation, the small amount of archaeological evidence may be summarised, as in Table 2.

Two notable artefacts came from the Wren construction layers. Among the pottery fragments was a piece of fashionable Chinese blue and white porcelain, a dish, from Site D (<P34>, Fig. 27; recording is imprecise and this can only be said to be in the Wren-period layer beneath the present floor). Site G produced a fragment of a copper-alloy portable sundial which would have given roughly the hour of day in the late 16th or 17th century (Fig. 28). This very small object, only 35mm across, was found in the backfill of the foundation trench for the east wall of the south transept. When the dial was suspended, correctly orientated, from a thread through the pair of holes at its top in sunny conditions, a ray of sunlight from the slot in the outer ring would be directed, by closing up most of this aperture with the small, missing inner ring, to focus the light at the appropriate point between the paired numerals; here a series of drilled dots marking the hours would direct the user to read what was in theory the correct time (for details see Chapter 6).

Disposal of human remains

In removing the majority of the foundations and vaults of the pre-Fire cathedral, and in digging holes for temporary works such as sawpits and cisterns, Wren's workmen disturbed hundreds of burials, some quite recent since the churchyard had been in use up to 1666 (and in parts still was in use). Sometime between October 1674 and the end of June 1675 a large hole was dug 'in the little yard upon the N. side of the church between the little N. door and the N. Cross Isle [the N transept], to bury the bones'. In November 1676 workmen were further paid for 'digging places to bury the bones digg'd up in severall places', but it is not stated where they buried them.[44] At the west end in 1688, 162 bodies were moved from St Gregory's churchyard to just outside the former west end. This particular burial pit must lie under the present atrium and pavement (since the bollards of 1873 are inside the former line of the Wren churchyard railings at the west end). Whenever old wall foundations were dug up or the churchyard levelled, bones appeared, and their removal to unspecified other places continued as late as 1713, when two large holes 12ft (3.7m) deep and several other smaller holes were dug to dispose of bones.[45]

One example of this disposal has been excavated, at Site F, immediately west of the statue of Queen Anne (Fig. 29). Above the trench dug in 1688 for the drain west of the cathedral, either a special hole was dug for redepositing skeletal remains or the trench itself was backfilled with coffins and skeletons. In the main the burials tended to be in rows and stacked with the skull of the upper body being immediately above the skull of the next body down. Two of the stacks were five skeletons deep. All were still in coffins, laid east–west with the head at the west end and even the semi-articulated bones at the bottom of the

Fig. 27 Chinese blue and white porcelain dish from Site D, <P34> (J Pearce, MOLA)

Fig. 28 Portable sundial from Site G, G<1>: from a construction trench of the Wren cathedral (R Stroud, MoL). Dials of this general type were widely available and this instrument, of late 17th-century date, was probably made in London. Diameter 35mm

Fig. 29 Site F: excavation of burials in progress (Maggie Cox, MOLA)

grave sequence were given this treatment. Some were probably disturbed prior to their reburial during transport. Many possessed coffin fittings of 16th or early 17th century character and earlier burials are not likely to have been transportable as complete units within their original coffins (further details in the Gazetteer entry for Site F). There is little doubt that these burials in the cut for the culvert were repositioned, either from the culvert work or from elsewhere on the site during the rebuilding of the cathedral after the Great Fire. It is possible that the redeposited burials at Site F are the bodies from the nearby St Gregory's churchyard.

Removal of buildings on the north side of the nave

Rebuilding of secular properties close to the future cathedral was immediate. On 9 November 1668 Sir Thomas Davies, alderman, petitioned the Fire Court concerning his house, formerly part of the bishop's palace, and part new erected by the little door of St Paul's, i.e the north nave door. His new foundations were laid out by surveyor Mills on 24 November. A second case on 10 November concerned a property which had been the Beare in 1662, then of three storeys and a garret, next to the property of Davies, since its first-floor chamber and closet lay partly over the latter's shop or warehouse, here called the Bible; it was also within the site of the bishop's palace, and also 'near the little north door of St Paul's'.[46] These would appear to be references to buildings west of Paul's Alley, which formed the east boundary of the bishop's palace.

In 1670, bricklayer Thomas Warren (who was to construct the vaulting of the crypt from 1676) built three houses in the former Pardon Churchyard north of the ruined nave of the medieval cathedral.[47] These belonged to the Cathedral. But the alignment of the new nave in the 1680s came close to them, and a problem ensued. In 1690 the Commissioners heard a complaint from Obadiah Blagrave, bookseller, that his lights in his houses on the north side of the church near Paul's Alley had been much diminished by the wall (ie the north nave wall) of the new cathedral. In 1701 it was decided that one block of houses should be removed, and discussion with the owners began, though negotiations were still in progress in February 1709.[48]

A surviving plan of the west end of the new building and its environs by William Dickinson is dated to a year later, February 1710, though it probably reflects discussions of the previous 2 years (Fig. 30). Higgott suggests that the drawing shows Wren's scheme for wrought iron railings which the Building Committee rejected in 1710 in favour of cast iron.[49] It shows a proposal for the railings coming along the north and south sides, giving way for the north and south doors (now the north door to the crypt and the Dean's Door to the geometric staircase on the south side) and then a tight enclosure round the steps, excluding the proposed statue to Queen Anne (which is not shown in its final or present place; perhaps this was also a suggestion). The north run of railings goes diagonally through the two blocks of houses. In June 1710 Richard Billinghurst was paid for 'pulling down 19 houses on the north side of the church, and cleaning the bricks of the same.' One of the houses was called the Almonry House, and this may refer to a persisting pre-Fire association; but it came down with the others.[50]

On Site A in 1969, Robert Crayford recorded brick buildings (Fig. 31). The walls of soft red brick lay immediately below the modern paving; they survived about 1.5m high. They were divided by the post-Fire Paul's Alley, and called Buildings 18 and 19 in the numbering sequence established for *SPCBW*. Buildings 18 and 19 are not accurately dated by archaeological material, but they can be assigned to the period 1666–76 since they appear on Ogilby and Morgan's map of 1676; they are very likely to be the basements of the houses erected by Thomas Warren in 1670. In 1710, therefore, Billinghurst pulled down the houses to ground level as was required, but left the basements intact.

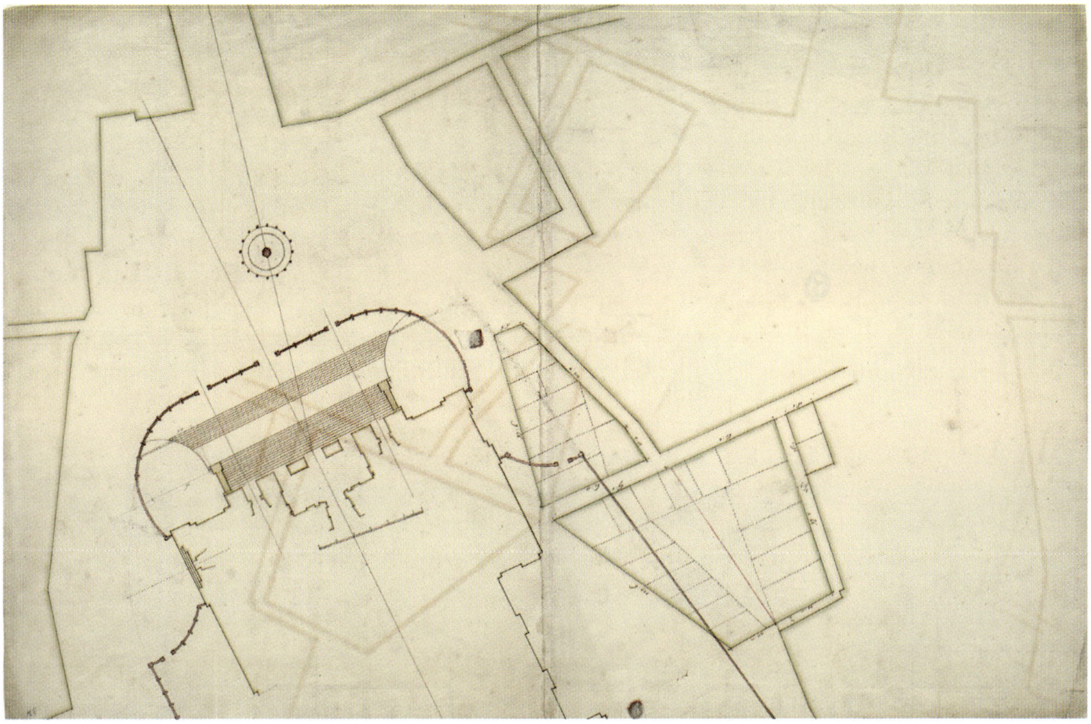

Fig. 30 (left) Plan of the west end of St Paul's by William Dickinson, showing proposed line of railings, dated 24 February 1709/10 on the back (LMA, WRE/7/2/2,© Chapter of St Paul's Cathedral and LMA). This shows the two blocks of houses of post-Fire date which were removed in 1710, on the right-hand side

Fig. 31 (below) Site A: post-Fire Buildings 18 and 19 and the line of the Wren drain on the north side of the cathedral, as suggested in plans at SPCAA and observations on Site A in 1969–70 by Robert Crayford (Carlos Lemos, MOLA)

Adapting the medieval chapter house, 1667–1714 (Wren's site office from 1671)

The octagonal 14th-century chapter house south of the nave largely survived the Fire, and was adapted by Wren and his associates to be the site office for the construction site. There are a number of documentary references about this, and excavation on the site in 2004–7 provided a few details, from which an outline of the office can be produced. Its history can be divided into four short periods: 1667–9, adaptation of the chapter house as temporary offices for the Dean and Chapter; 1671–4, the setting up of Wren's office; 1674–8 adaptations and a major modification when the foundations of the new nave crossed the site and required the removal of three of the bases of buttresses of the chapter house; and 1678–1714, the remainder of the cathedral construction period.[51]

In the immediately post-Fire years the medieval chapter house was still known as the Convocation House, and next to it was Convocation House Yard (though on which side is not known; mostly likely it comprised or included the site of the demolished north cloister). In 1667–9 the Yard was the site of several new rooms, with painted casements and cornices, for the use of the Dean and Chapter; perhaps this was a temporary Chapter House. Bricklayers and carpenters were employed. One new room was to house records. Plastering took place in 'the lowest Room in ye additional Building in ye Convocation House Yard', so presumably this part was of two storeys.[52]

Wren's site office was set up 4 years before the official start of construction. The former chapter house was a natural choice for a temporary site office, as it was one of the very few repairable two-storey stone buildings standing; but it also conveniently stood at the main south entrance into the whole construction site, the former south nave door. In October to December 1671 there are payments for digging foundations for the chimneys 'of a new room [in Convocation House yard] for Mr Surveyor's use' and trenches for foundations for stone pedestals upon which wooden posts would stand to support the new site office. The old and new work was then repaired in brick, 29 window lights were 'coloured', the rooms furnished and the fireplaces given mantlepieces; Wren had 'a large map of London' placed above one of the fireplaces. The new rooms were roofed with lead.[53] In September 1673 John Tillison informed Dean Sancroft that 'Dr Wren & Mr Woodroof [Edward Woodroofe] have been the week last in ye Convocation house, drawing the Lines of ye Designe of the church upon ye Table there, for ye Joyner's Directions for making the new Modell'.[54] This was presumably the Great Model, and what must be some of the drawings have survived.[55] The Model is 6.3m long, and would have easily fitted in the chapter house chamber which had a diameter of about 11m. By the 1690s the Model was a tourist attraction, and a French guidebook to London of 1693 advised the reader to see the rising cathedral and then ask to see the Model.[56]

In the accounts for the period October 1674 to June 1675 are expenses for a large gate for the Yard, with a wicket, which was constructed 'in the Convocation House Yard wall towards St Gregorie's church', that is the west side.[57] There are also detailed carpentry expenses for a stair of '20 large steps. with strings and bridges' and three doorcases, two with lights over them.[58] The location of this stair is not said, but from the context it seems to be an intentionally fine stair to the site office, and one which figures later in the accounts.

In August 1675 payment is recorded for 'railing in part of the Convocation House floor for a tracery room' (see Fig. 4). In the same month Thomas Warren contracted to make four chimneys, lay brickwork and plaster four rooms, two above two, adjoining to the Convocation House wall. Israel Knowles, carpenter, had provided the timber carcase.[59] The rooms built by Warren are said to be 'on the back side of the Office of Works next to the Street'; in the accounts, the term 'Office' may apply to this separate range, but sometimes refers to the chapter house and the range together. It seems reasonable to assume that the Office comprised an amalgamation of the stone chapter house and new rooms of brick, probably on timber frames, to the south. The new rooms may not have fully observed the City regulations about the use of brick in new buildings, perhaps because they were considered temporary. Further references of 1675 mention a door into 'the vault next the Convocation House' and the 'foregate of the Convocation House'. Thirty-six square yards of paving were laid before the 'Office door in St Gregorie Churchyard', which suggests paving in stone (or possibly the large tiles then available) and access through the former parish churchyard on the west side. At the same time, a cistern was dug within Convocation House Yard, 'with broad

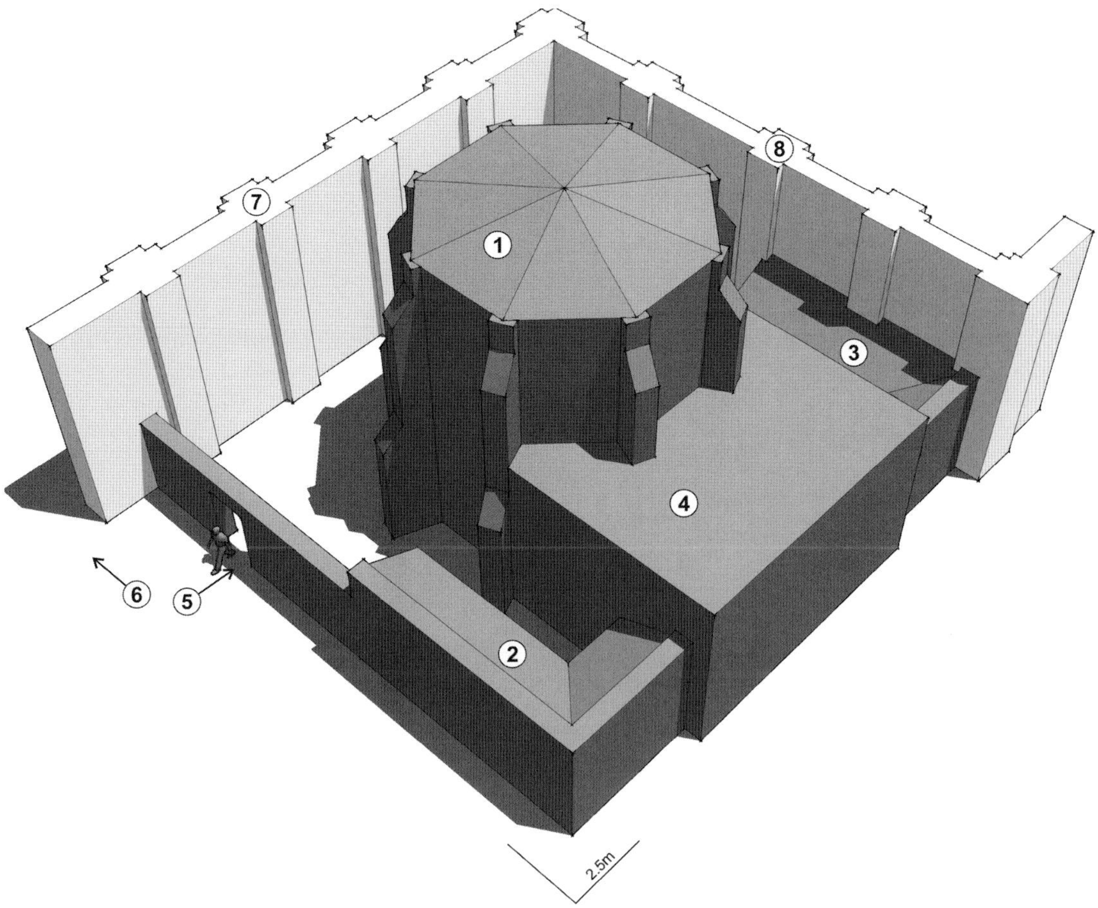

Fig. 32 A sketch reconstruction of Wren's site offices, around 1675 (John Schofield and Carlos Lemos, MOLA). The walls at the rear signify the nave and south transept walls of the medieval building; all the components have been simplified. There would have been several chimneys. Building work in 1690 may have added a further room on the south side. Key: 1, medieval chapter house (roof conjectural); 2, south-west part of cloister; 3, south-east part of cloister; 4, new buildings of 1675; 5, gateway into Convocation House Yard; 6, former south door into cathedral nave, now the entrance to the site within the cathedral walls; 7, south wall of nave of medieval cathedral; 8, west wall of south transept of medieval cathedral

flat stones in Tarris', the special cement which was also used on its walls; and a house of office on the south side of the Yard next to the street 'new walled', which may mean that an existing cesspit was rebuilt.[60] A sketch reconstruction shows the complex at about this time (Fig. 32).

In the next year, 1676, refurbishment continued. An upholsterer supplied 62 sq yards of 'green printed stuff' and 45 yards of gilt leather, with a further 34 yards of gilt leather 'round the top of the roome'; there were seats, 'a large purple chair' and benches, covered and stuffed. The identity of the room is not mentioned, but it was probably the Office in the chapter house. Two months later John Tillison the Clerk of Works was reimbursed for expenditure on 'a dutch ring for a Drawer under the Table in the Office' and 'for greening of 22 yards of Seats in the Office of Works in oyle'. In this or the other rooms there were new window shutters, a press with shelves for books, writings and papers. Payment was also made for taking up a considerable part of walling which was the foundation of the cloister on the east side of Convocation Yard, that is the east walk of the 14th-century cloister. This would have been in preparation for the digging of the foundations of the new south transept as well as for any adjustment to accommodate the new office buildings.[61]

From 1677 at least there was a clock in the office, since a bill for maintaining it from that year up to 1685 was paid in that later year.[62] In 1678 the office and rooms under it had a total of 11 fireplaces, which had been there 2 years. It had a pediment over 'the outer door' which was painted, and a painted sun dial. Within the outer door was a passage.[63] In this year John Oliver, glazier and later to be Wren's assistant, was paid for glazing work and repair of windows both in the Convocation House and in the 'Office', presumably these extra chambers, over the previous 5 years; at this time hearth tax was paid for 'hearths in the Office and Convocation House'.

The Great Model was displayed, though whether in the octagonal former chapter house or in one of the new rooms to the south (both at first-floor level) is not clear. In December 1680 a mason was paid for setting up a chimney and its footpace 'in the new room under the Modell room' in the Convocation House.[64] The only space beneath the main floor of the former chapter house was its open vault. Perhaps there was partial adaptation of it; here a new plumbery had been inserted in 1678, 'for the plumbers to melt their Soder for the leaden pipes'; bricklayers made them a chimney and 'funnell'.[65] Perhaps the stout vault was thought to be suitable fire prevention. Although there are no more details about this plumbery, it may be relevant that three sides of a stone and brick structure were recorded on the flooring which would have been below the vaulting, in a testpit against the south wall of the Wren nave in 1932. This had its north end removed by the new nave foundations, which would have been dug in 1687 (Fig. 33). An alternative is to propose that the room for the Great Model, called the Model room, was in the new range of temporary offices along the south side of the former chapter house.[66] *Parentalia* records that the model 'was for many years kept in the Office of Works at St Paul's, in a shed built for that purpose,'[67] which probably refers to this later period.

Two buttresses on the north side of the chapter house and a third to the north-west were removed for construction of the nave, since their sites underlie the present south nave wall. This is described in the accounts for 1678; the stairs also had to be moved, so they must have been on the north-west side of the medieval chapter house. In February 1679 carpenters had been paid for erecting a 'great partition' to enclose one side of the chapter house where two buttresses had been removed; in April 1682 are payments for removal of probably a third buttress of the Convocation House 'to give room to carry on the new foundations there'. In October 1682 John Grove plasterer was paid for working on a partition where part of the Office had been taken down. Labourers also removed part of the Convocation House wall (ie the outer wall of the cloister), and dug out 'old chalk foundation walls being part of the foundation of the Convocation house and Cloyster'.[68] In 1685 carpenters were paid for cutting out a further part of the chapter house roof so that work on the new nave could proceed. In 1687 there were payments for 'removing the plaster of paris, old alabaster and old marble grave stones out of the Convocation House Yard, to make way for the new foundations' and some of the former outside wall of the cloister on the west side, including an upper part, was removed. Even so the office continued in its place: in 1687 also a version of the Royal Arms on the north side (ie the side facing the building site) was repainted, having been damaged by the fall of a stone, and plastering took place in 'New Rooms adjoyning to ye Office of ye Works', indicating expansion.[69] In 1688–9 the new drain along the south side of the nave would have been dug, and it interfered in some way with the stairs; the line of the drain crosses through the middle of the medieval Chapter House, or rather through the vault beneath it. This was a narrow trench, since in this area the drain excavation left intact a small area of medieval paving beneath the vault, to be recorded in 1932 and 2004 (Fig. 33; Gazetteer, Site 43 and Site H). In 1696 repairs were undertaken to plasterwork on the stairs 'which was broke to make way for the new Draine which runs under the said stairs', which had taken place seven to eight years before.[70] In general, however, the reduction in area of the site office, almost certainly by removing its northern half, is taken as being in the years 1678 to 1689.

In 1690 a new room for the Great Model was framed.[71] There are payments for the construction of a sun dial 'over the Office', probably the setting-

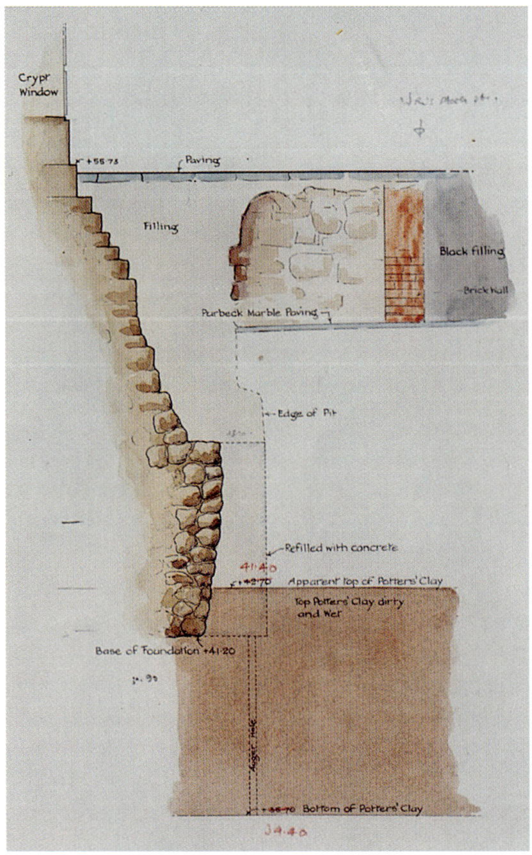

Fig. 33 Extract from records of Gibb-Freeman Testpit C, 1932, showing the foundation of the south wall of the nave, 'Purbeck Marble Paving' (the floor below the vault of the 14th-century chapter house) and a brick structure built on the floor, of unknown but probably Wren-period date (SPCAA D/24/5/4C). The annotations on the levels in pencil are by Robert Crayford, c. 1975. The site of the testpit is shown on Fig. 14 and as Site 43 on Fig. 15

up again of the original which had been on that section of the chapter house and which had to be removed;[72] and Matt Jarman, glazier, fitted and repaired old glass in the 'new Modell Roome'; labourers meanwhile scaffolded and demolished a 'Butterice of the old Convocation house.' This must have been one of those still supporting the building, since those in the way of the new nave had been removed 12 years before. The Model was evidently a showpiece, even though it was not the design being built a few yards away; in the same year a painter was paid for 'Oyle work laid 3 times over on ye pales in ye Yard leading to ye Modell Roome'.[73] In 1691 William Cook, painter, was paid for painting 13 casements 'for rooms under Office'.[74]

The adaptation of the chapter house and the surviving southern half of the cloister can be tentatively reconstructed. One of Wyck's immediately post-Fire drawings shows that the chapter survived well, since it appeared above the ruin of the south side of the nave when viewed from the north-west.[75] We can assume all the new rooms built first in 1668–9 and then in 1674–5 would be on the south side of the chapter house, over the south walk and fronting the public highway to the south, since it would be clear from Wren's plans that the east walk of the cloister would be demolished, in time, for the new south transept. The south walk and the southern half of both east and west ground-floor walks of the cloister were evidently kept in use, since the Purbeck floors of all three were preserved to be recorded in 2006 (the west walk is shown in Fig. 34). They would have formed passageways inside the new buildings. Finally, a plan of the railings around the new building by William Dickinson was drawn in May 1710; this is given in full below at Figure 92. An extract of the area south of the nave is shown here in Fig. 35. The drain crosses the site and is served by smaller drains from the rainwater shafts in the walls. An

Fig. 34 *Site H: the west walk of the 14th-century cloister in 2006, looking east (Andy Chopping, MOLA). This walk must have lain beneath the site office and been used as a corridor to the lower rooms. In the foreground, a jamb of a door for a stair within the west exterior wall of the cloister, which might also have been used as part of the Wren site office*

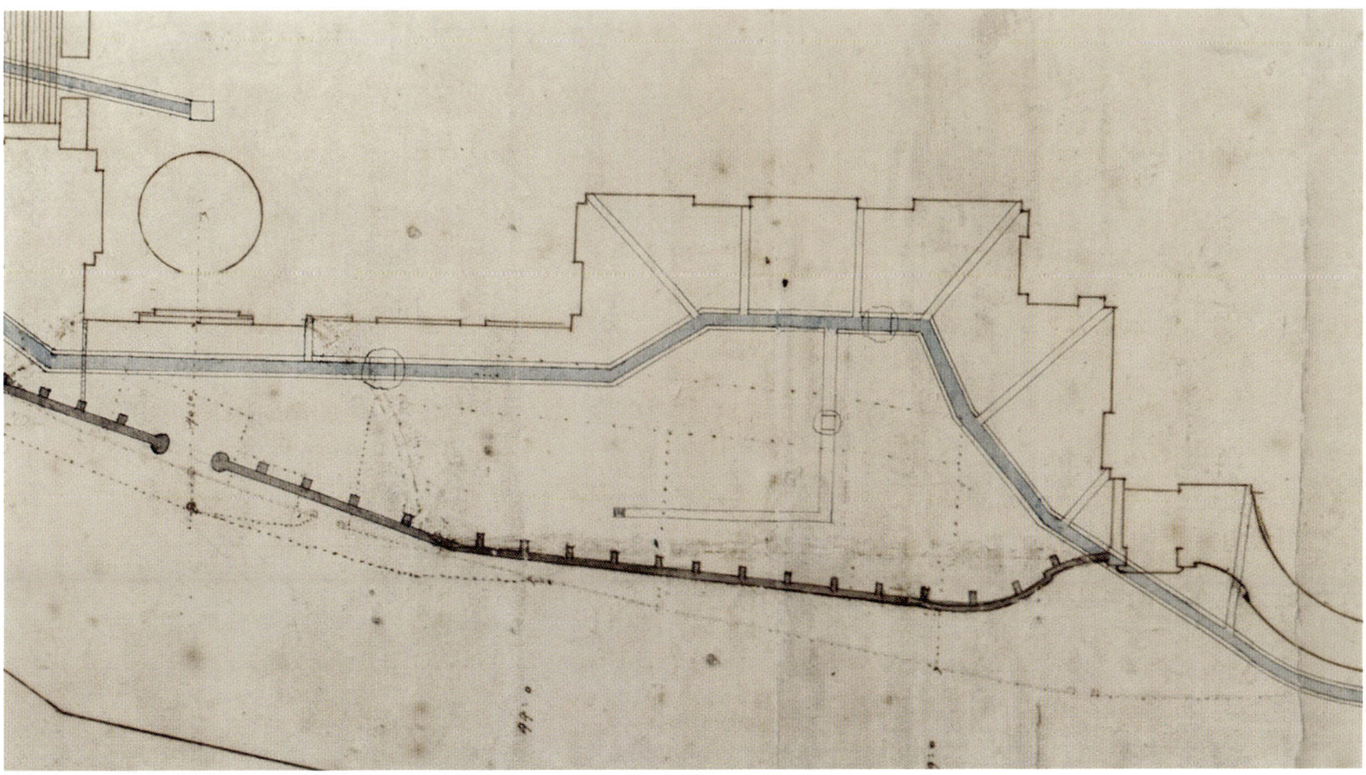

Fig. 35 *Extract from plan of 1710 by Dickinson of the railings around the cathedral, showing the area south of the nave, the line of the drain and in dotted lines the outline of the site offices (LMA, WRE/7/2/3, © Chapter of St Paul's Cathedral and LMA). The stairs of 1674–5 must have been where the drain changes course around the east end of the west block of the building*

Fig. 36 South side of St Paul's from the south-west, showing the finished landscaping of the area of the medieval chapter house and cloister, 2010 (Andy Chopping, MOLA). In the left foreground, a plan of the two cathedrals in inlaid stone by Richard Kindersley, from a plan by John Schofield

L-shaped drain (seen on Site H in 2004, Fig. 199 below) serves buildings to the south, which are outlined in dotted lines; a gateway to the street on the south can be made out towards the west, its site now crossed by the new (or proposed) railings. The dotted lines must represent the site office buildings, and the entrance is that into Convocation Yard, at least in 1710 (it may have changed site several times since 1675).

In 1710 the Clerk of Works Laurence Spencer was reimbursed a quarter's rent for a house on the north side; perhaps a new site office.[76] The line of the Wren railings along the south side were constructed about 4m south of the outer wall of the chapter house cloister, as revealed in a small excavation of 2009 in the pavement (Site 86); this would have been through the rooms added to the south of the medieval remains in the 1670s, that is where the Great Model was probably housed and shown. In February 1711 Wren included taking down the 'old Chapter House' in a list of costed work to be done. In 1714 joiners were paid for taking down old wainscot in the old chapter house (the new one having just been finished, see below) and making moulds for the masons (i.e. the implication is that the wainscot was reused to make the moulds). Since payment followed shortly for Purbeck paving 'all round outside the church', it seems likely that the last pre-Fire walls above ground were removed as part of the final landscaping during 1714 and 1715.[77] By this time the remaining parts of the medieval chapter house and cloister would have been demolished down to the slightly raised new level of the south churchyard, which covered the walls but let them stand about 2ft (0.6m) high, to be discovered by Penrose in 1878.[78]

The present churchyard south of the nave, in 2000 an area of haphazard 20th-century planting, was transformed in 2004–8 as part of a scheme to establish an entrance designed for inclusive accessibility and level access to the church floor and crypt, using the existing door into the building at the junction of the south transept and nave. A gentle ramp was to approach the door from the roadway on the south; this would coincide with the east walk of the medieval cloister. The plan of the cloister and the chapter house (represented only by the feet of its buttresses, on an octagonal layout) was known from the discoveries by Penrose; these parts were now relocated and given protective coverings of sand and geotextile. The plan of the cloister and those buttress bases which lay south of the Wren nave was then laid out in new stone, about 0.6m (2ft) above (Fig. 36). During these works some details of the adaptation of the chapter house and cloister during the period they formed Wren's site office were recorded (in Gazetteer, Site H).

Construction of the cathedral, 1675–1711

There is only one engraving of the Wren cathedral during construction; a view from the north-east by Sutton Nicholls (Fig. 37) dated 1695. It shows the choir and a scaffolded north transept, but seems to omit the nave which was then in

Fig. 37 Wren's cathedral in building: view from the north-east by Sutton Nicholls, 1695 (Society of Antiquaries). On the left hand side, post-Fire buildings in the churchyard with their original windows

construction. In 1695 the north wall of the nave was only at the level of the lower storey, and thus would have been out of view of the artist.[79] In the 1680s and 1690s there were several 'brave guesses', some fantastical, by engravers as to what the cathedral, when finished, might look like in elevation. Official elevations and a plan of the building were produced from 1701–2 (eg Fig. 17), showing the design at that time; the dome had yet to be built and in the event came out differently. Potentially more reliable were those produced after the building was finished, in the 1720s and through to the 1750s, though many continued to contain errors such as supposing the north-west tower had a clock in it to match the clock in the south-west tower.[80]

Little is known about the character and use of the machinery which would be necessary to enable demolition or hoist the materials, at St Paul's as elsewhere on 17th-century building sites. Wren had been very impressed with the site machinery he saw in Paris in 1665. Unfortunately none of the hundreds of construction drawings associated with the cathedral or his other projects show hoists or other site machinery. Rams were used in demolition, and had to be repaired.[81] In January 1677 there are mentions in the accounts of carpenters helping masons to 'sett up Sheares to crane up their stones', and in the next month 'making a Gynn to unload the great Stones, helping to carry out a Crab, & takeing up two great stones which was overturn'd from the Carriage in ye street'.[82] The accounts contain many mentions of gibbets and standards, and occasionally 'engines' used for raising stone. There is little detailed information on what these machines looked like; a 'new Engine that takes Rubble up to the top of the work' in 1692 had barrels hooped with iron.[83] Treadle cranes were known on the 16th-century and 17th-century London waterfront, and larger examples were used in quantity on a large building site such as the Escorial (Spain) in the 1570s;[84] but there is no suggestion yet that they were used in London on building sites. There are a few other references in the accounts to the methods of demolition and erection. The demolition masons cut holes in large stones to insert Lewises, so they they could be lowered to the ground.[85]

The following account, being based on the archaeological work at the cathedral, does not follow the construction in strict chronological order, but describes the major parts individually. Descriptions of the construction level by level, and comprehensively attributing parts to individual masons, is not attempted here, but can be found in other recent studies.[86]

Foundations, walls and vaulting of the crypt

Parentalia records how Wren 'placed Scaffolds high enough to extend his Lines over the Heaps that lay in the Way; and then by Perpendiculars set out the Places below, from the Lines drawn with Care upon the level Plan of the Scaffold'.[87] Before 1675, much of the pre-Fire cathedral had been dug out, down to and below its crypt level, in that part of the ruin east of the wall which had been inserted in 1672 to cross the former nave, east of the opposed nave doors. New digging was required for several sections of the new outer crypt walls for all arms of the new building at foundation level. The external foundations forming the footprint of the Wren building are recorded at several points through the drawings of the Gibb-Freeman testpits (e.g. Fig. 33);[88] but these testpits are only of one side or the other, and nowhere give a full section through the foundation or the crypt wall. A section through the crypt wall was provided in 1994 by excavation through the north nave crypt wall on Site B. The recent excavations have begun to give details of the nature of the crypt wall above the external foundations, the internal foundations, and initial dumping and floor surfaces in the crypt.

The external foundations of the Wren building were dug in foundation trenches with outer sides about 3m deep, from a general level of 15m–16m OD. The new crypt was a sunken area, of an unprecedented size for a City building, and probably roughly coterminous with the building footprint. There are occasional references in the accounts to materials being taken 'down' into the excavated area. General characteristics of the foundations can be gleaned from the 1932 drawings. Though there would have been local variations where deeper backfilling was required, the base of the foundation was kept roughly level for the walls of both the choir and most of nave.[89] The 17th-century ground surface is shown on the south side of the nave in Figure 33.

On the outside, the foundation was battered (sloped down), sometimes to a larger base with perpendicular sides, but this was not consistent.[90] At the north-west corner, as recorded in testpit G (Site 43), the lower part of the Wren foundation was allowed to buckle inwards as it used the probably late Anglo-Saxon foundation which had been encountered. In testpit 2 (not ilustrated; in SPCAA), the foundation beneath the south wall of the nave was seen to be as broad as the combined width of the crypt wall and the deep window embrasures there, and broader still on the inside. Its base extended 3.2m (10ft 6in) from the window embrasure into the crypt, and as it, like all the other foundations, was laid on or slightly within the underlying brickearth, this wide base was 0.8m thick or deep in that part below the crypt floor, which generally lies at about 1.3m (4ft 4in) above the surviving top of the brickearth.

The outside of the foundation was not all built in a consistent character. The Gibb-Freeman drawing of the choir foundation at the south-east corner of the building (testpit A, Site 51) shows the external side of the foundation to be of fine courses of squared ashlar, for the entire depth of the foundation. Sections of the Wren foundations of the north transept, nave and west end however show a foundation with far more irregular courses. This might imply a difference in specification between foundations of the choir and those of the nave; there is no hint of this in the accounts. In that the work started at the east end, the occurrence of the finer ashlar external batter here rather than elsewhere might indicate an initial intention to use the finest stone, but a change soon after to the more economic reuse of the large amount of semi-finished stone available from the previous cathedral.

Elsewhere, the foundation was battered on its internal side, but vertical on the outside. The outsides were of roughly dressed coursed stone, with mixed rubble within.The monitoring of building works in the north aisle of the nave crypt in 1994 at Site B allowed examination of the north crypt wall and its foundation (Fig. 38 shows the coursing in the body of the wall). Here the foundation was much wider than apparently necessary, at 6.3m, and about 1.1m deep, with the nave wall built on its north edge so that at least half the foundation lay within the cathedral body. Study of whether it is typical of the cathedral must wait future work on the nature of the foundations in all parts of the building.

The inner side of the foundation of the eastern wall of the south transept, constructed in 1677, was recorded on Site G in 2000. It was composed of reused masonry from the destroyed cathedral roughly coursed in a hard mortar matrix. Several of the stones were dressed and some examples were

Fig. 38 *Site B: section through north wall of nave at crypt level, looking west (Andy Chopping, MOLA). This shows that lifts in the construction of the wall can be identified. On the right, brickwork probably of the adjacent first Works Department addition of 1909 (scale is 10 × 100mm)*

moulded architectural fragments, including parts of a moulded column and a window mullion. Examples of Kentish Rag, Caen, Reigate stone, Taynton and Portland stones were identified.[91] It is proposed here that the story of Wren digging a shaft 40ft (12.2m) deep and then filling it with a special pier, said by the source in *Parentalia* to refer to the north-east corner of the choir, in fact may refer to the north-east corner of the north transept, since the source speaks of Wren's 'falling upon a pit where all the pot-earth had been robbed by the potters of old time'. This would be an appropriate observation at the north-east corner of the north transept, where John Conyers observed Roman kilns at an exceptionally low depth. Macartney also failed to find evidence of remarkably deep Wren foundations at the north-east corner of the choir.[92]

The four arms of the crypt were vaulted in stages in 1676–88, starting with the choir. On 8 June 1676 the committee in charge of rebuilding the cathedral contracted with Thomas Warren, bricklayer, to construct the vaults under the choir two bricks thick, and to make the groins carefully 'according to the sweepe' (perhaps some kind of simple device to to aid construction of the timber formwork for the arches of the groining; the word *sweep* was used at this time for a large bar of iron which swung down behind a vehicular gate to lock it).[93] Any similar contract for making the crypt vaults apart from those beneath the choir does not seem to have survived, though payments for 'arching the vaults in the middle isle of the church towards the W. end' were made to John Bridges in November and December 1687. Memoranda concerning the foundations of the west end were made with two masons, John Tompson and Samuel Fulkes (they were each to do half) in March 1686, and the building of the crypt vaults reached the west end during 1688.[94]

The crypt floor was evidently left unpaved after the crypt had been vaulted, until the cathedral neared completion twenty years later; in June 1709 Richard Billinghurst was paid for laying 4705 yards of tile paving in the [crypt] vaults and levelling the same.[95] This paving, repaired many times and interspersed with later ledger stones, some of which are over brick vaults, still forms the floor of the crypt (except for most of the west end where it was renewed in 1996–9). The dirt floors of the construction period to 1700, and the tile floor of 1709, were recorded on Sites B and C. At Site B the red tiles were approximately 0.3m × 0.35m by 40–50mm thick.

Fragments of the previous cathedral still in the ground, and the extra excavation at the west end

The Gibb-Freeman testpit drawings of 1932 show small sections of the foundations of the external wall of the medieval south transept and a tiny scrap of what would be the foundation of the south wall of the 14th-century choir.[96] From these small observations we can suggest that Wren's foundations were dug to generally the same level (within about 0.3m or 1ft) as the pre-Fire foundations, at least those of the exterior of the medieval building. Within the latter, other foundations such as those for the 12th- and 13th-century crossing piers, which supported the great tower and the spire, were probably locally deeper. There is no clear evidence that Wren had them specially or completely dug out. But we can say he dug out all the former cathedral over the whole footprint of his intended building, and that the underside of his foundations was roughly at the underside of the pre-Fire foundations.

The Gibb-Freeman drawing of the testpit on the south side of the nave, where the Wren foundation clipped the site of the medieval chapter house (Fig. 33) shows that sometimes the remains of the medieval cathedral were allowed to remain below ground if they did not interfere with the new design. At the east end of the Gothic choir damaged fragments of the late 13th-century east end at crypt level were recorded by Penrose and are now accessible by manholes in the paved area immediately outside the Wren east end.[97] The terminal walls of the medieval transepts, below ground, were perhaps similarly allowed to remain; we do not know. The end of the medieval south transept is below the modern pavement outside and slightly to the west of the present south transept. The terminal wall of the medieval north transept was probably destroyed by the building works of 1969 north of the cathedral, if it had not been destroyed before. Only the chapter house was allowed to stand above ground because it had become Wren's site office.

At the west end the remains of the Jones portico and its foundation were dug out to supply rubble for the new west end, resulting in a larger than usual excavation west of the new building. As shown in the overlay of the Wren and medieval cathedrals in Figure 2, the west end of the medieval building and all the Jones portico lay outside the footprint of the Wren cathedral. In September 1687, the space for the future south-west chapel (now the chapel of St Michael and St George) was being dug out by S Satchell and others; and Satchell was paid 'to take down 714 yds of the old W gable wall from the Stooles [sills] of the Windows to the top of the Capitalls equal with the top of the great dore case'. By December 1687, the west gable and portico had finally been removed; part of the foundation of the Jones portico was later dug out, though it lies well to the west of the Wren building and clear even of the steps.[98] This was partly because trenches had to be dug for the new drains which were connecting to the main drain in Ludgate Hill.[99] In July 1688 bricklayers were paid for turning the vault in the foundation of the present north-west tower, and in August John Thompson was paid for the foundations of the south-west tower. The inclusion of fragments of the portico into the foundations of the tower, as discovered in 1996 at Site C, may therefore be dated to the first half of 1688. In August 1688, carpenters were paid for shoring up the ground where the foundations of the portico had been removed, so the hole was still open.[100]

The foundation of the medieval west end was observed in 1879 by Penrose, in a hole immediately east of the statue of Queen Anne; it seemed that the foundation of the portico had been added to it.[101] So some of the foundation of the portico remains beneath the Penrose paving of the western atrium.

The main stair

The foundations for the south transept terminal wall and the south-west bastion (the term used at St Paul's for the four massive blocks of masonry which support the dome) in which the main or 'great round' stair was to be built date from 1676 to 1678; in preparation for this at least part, presumably the north part, of the 14th-century cloister's east walk was removed. Joshua Marshall was paid for the foundations of the south portico in September 1677. Marshall died in April 1678, and his contract was replaced by new contracts which included Edward Pierce or Pearce [junior] for the south transept.[102]

The 'great round Staires in the South West leg of the Duomo' appear in the accounts in October 1677, when carpenters were putting up centres, presumably for the spiralling vault above the stair. The 'doreway of the great round Staires' is mentioned in March 1678; presumably this was the existing external doorway to the churchyard.[103] 'Kent steps' (ie of Kentish ragstone) appear in the accounts in February 1677. The carpenters were paid several times for 'caseing the steps of the great round staires' but this was probably a temporary measure, as they did this for mouldings, cornices and capitals elsewhere.[104] In September 1678 the executors of Marshall were paid for the section of stairs he had erected, along with surrounding work on the walls. This included the fitting of 61 steps of 'Kentish step'.[105] If we assume this is the first payment for the stair steps, and count from churchyard level, then 61 steps is 40 steps above church floor level. There is no dividing line today perceptible in the fabric to show where Marshall's work stopped. His executors were also paid for Reigate vaulting over the stairs; it seems likely that the vaulting over the stair is Reigate stone, but it is painted and has not been examined.

The construction of the stair and the bastion was taken over by Thomas Wise. In December 1678 an unspecified number of two types of stone were delivered, 'flat Kentish steps' at 14d per foot and 'Neuell do' (i.e. newel steps of the same) at 6d per foot, but not for any specified location. More were delivered in October 1680.[106] What these two types looked like or comprised is suggested in the analysis below.[107]

In January 1681 Wise was paid for setting 45 Kentish steps in the round stairs, i.e. the main stair. Mention in the next section of accounts of the setting of 24 further steps by Wise is probably also to the stair. A further stage with the stair was reached after an interval in the middle of 1684. Then the stair comprised 110 steps, and Wise was paid to add a further ten, though the type of stone is not mentioned.[108] Wise was dead by September 1686, and his place was taken by Thomas Wise junior and Thomas Hill. In December 1687 they were paid for more work on the bastion including 22 steps of Kentish stone. In early 1691 Thomas Wise junior and Thomas Hill were paid for reaching the 183rd step.[109] In September 1696 Wise and Hill were paid for fitting and setting 19 Kentish steps 'from the top of the 204th step'. There are today 234 steps from church floor level to Whispering Gallery level. Wise and Hill went on to build the south-west quarter of the peristyle and dome between 1698 and 1707.[110]

According to John Ward's biography of Wren as a professor of astronomy at Gresham College, published in 1740, Wren intended to mount a very large telescope in the 'hollow in the great staircase on the south side' of St Paul's, but found the height of 96ft 10in (29.52m) less than the 123ft (37.52m) required. This idea was then abandoned.[111] The telescope idea therefore concerned the great stair, as it has always been known, at the junction of the nave and south transept; and not as sometimes thought the Geometric Stair in the south-west tower. The height of 96ft 10in is correct, within a foot or two, for the distance from exterior ground level to the top of the stair.

In 1972, a lift was inserted into the hollow core of the main stair, at the junction between the nave and south transept. In 2006–8 this was replaced with a slightly larger lift car suitable for wheelchairs. Repairs were also undertaken on the lowest section of the stair from church floor level to the existing external doorway to the churchyard, which was to form a more accessible entrance to the cathedral (the external approach being landscaped as part of the south churchyard works). During these works traces of temporary treads within the masonry core were seen. Details are given in the Gazetteer, Site N.

The west end and the west towers

The west end with its towers (Fig. 39) was built between 1688 and 1708.[112] In 1697–9 there was a halt in construction of the west end while Wren diverted shrinking financial resources to the construction of the dome and finishing the choir.[113]

The foundations of the west end had been dug and constructed in 1688. When work here

Fig. 39 The west end of St Paul's, by Thomas Malton, 1801 (WS XVI, pl. xviii). This omits the gates in the railings

Fig. 40 Extract from Poley's elevation of the west end, showing Bird's sculpture in the pediment (Poley 1927, pl. xix). Inspection in 2003 found Bird had signed the work by placing his initials 'FB' on the pyramid towards the left. The shafts of divine light which have unseated Saul/Paul resemble those in Bernini's Ecstasy of St Teresa of 1645–52 in S Maria della Vittoria, Rome. Bird spent some of his early years in Rome

resumed in 1699,[114] the construction of the great west door case was divided between Samuel Fulkes and John Tompson. They each sawed half the marble blocks for it in March 1699. They both set up and polished the marble case of the door in early 1700.[115] Fulkes was paid for much of the work on the west front, including carving 'three whole capitals' at £60 each in June 1704; he was working on the 'great upper portico' in June 1706. William Kempster's first work on the portico seems to date from 1705. Fulkes did the mason's work laying the keystone for the great west window; but Kempster carved a cherub's head with wing on the keystone.[116] Fulkes, who had been employed on the cathedral since 1688, was the third most used master mason on the cathedral, out of the twelve main contractors employed, as measured by his invoices; overall, his work was over three times the value of Kempster's.[117]

In March 1706 Francis Bird was paid for carving the large panel over the west door. This was '16ft broad and 14ft high & the principal figures 18in imbost' and had a large Italian moulding round it. He also carved the smaller panels on the west front. In 1714 Joseph Thomson, painter, was paid for painting the two carved panels at the west end; Thomson's father had been the main painter of the inside of the cathedral with oil.[118]

In December 1706 Bird was paid £650 for 'carving the great pedament of the west portico, in length 64ft and in height 17ft, being the history of St Paul's Conversion, and containing 8 large figures, 6 whereof on horseback, and several of them 2½ft imbost' (shown as drawn by Poley, Fig. 40).[119] In the external cleaning project which reached the west end in 2003–4, the pediment was cleaned but no repairs were necessary.

John Smallwell, joiner, produced a model for one of the towers in the summer of 1700; and it may be this model which a man of his altered in September 1701, 'to show the winding stairs and raising it higher and making the corners square which were hollow before'.[120] The construction of the towers was initially divided, with Fulkes assigned the north-west tower and Kempster the south-west tower (he took over after the death of Tompson in 1700). Fulkes was paid for the masonry of the north-west tower 'from the top of the Upper Capitals to the top of the Upper Entablature' and for vaulting the tower in September 1701. The stage around and above the 'dyalls' may have been later, since Fulkes was only paid for it in June 1707.[121] Kempster had two jobs here, inserting one of the chains and making a model for the finishing of the tower. The roof was being framed in June 1708, when Jean Tijou provided the 'pine' (pinecone, also called a pineapple) to go on top. Fulkes was paid for finishing the tower in December 1708.[122]

The south-west tower was built up to the main cornice by John Tompson until his death in 1700; William Kempster took over and constructed it to the upper composite order in 1701. When construction of the nave roof reached the west end in 1704, a floor was also constructed in what was now known as 'Mr K's tower'.[123] The Dean's door, already in place at the foot of the south-west tower facing south, was cut to allow introduction of the great bell in December 1706. Kempster seems to have finished the tower by June 1707; his bill included 416ft of 'cleansed Rigate ashler' which were evidently used somewhere in the upper part. Payment to carpenters for framing the roof of the tower followed in July, though other bills by them concerned with stairs date from March 1710. Bird himself carved a model of the pineapple.[124] The clock was in place in the south-west tower by 1720. It had three faces.[125]

Cleaning of the west front and all faces of the two west towers in 2003–4 was preceded by a photogrammetric survey of all the exterior faces. This showed all the repairs which might be done, such as stone replacement. In the event the amount of repair work was smaller. The west front was then cleaned and the statues conserved. The west front was then revealed with both upper and lower parts clean, probably for the first time for centuries (Fig. 41).

Fig. 41 The west front after the cleaning of 2003–4 (Graham Lacdao, © Chapter of St Paul's Cathedral)

The Geometric Stair

William Kempster the elder, brother of Christopher Kempster, built the Geometric Stair in the south-west tower. There is payment to him in November 1701 for a model for 'The coveing [here perhaps the underside] of the great stayres at the south-west end of the church', but there is then a gap until the making of another model, perhaps of the whole structure, in February 1704.[126] Kempster's bills for much of the construction work on the stair date from June 1705. It includes payment for 'Cutting Way in the Portland ashler in south-west tower to let in the steps of great stairs' from Sept 1704 to June 1705. The accounts also record a payment of £20 to Kempster 'for Extraordinary Diligence & Care used in the said Carving and his good performance of the same'.[127]

In 1993 Martin Stancliffe reported that there had been movement of the south-west tower over the centuries, and that the large volume containing the Stair was not tied together by any horizontal ties or diaphragms.[128] Penrose had made some repairs with iron brackets (cut into slots which were then obscured by mortar) in 1881, following damage caused by falling clock weights, but further work was considered necessary if the Stair were to be made safe and opened to the public. In 2004, the stair was thoroughly investigated and its chamber (Fig. 42) cleaned. Investigation into the side wall of the stair revealed one of the iron shims which were used to tighten the joint of each tread of the stair within its seating in the wall (Fig. 43). Metallurgical analysis of one removed shim suggested that they had corroded due to their method of production and high slag content. The shims were cut from iron sheet formed by rolling rather than being individually forged, and this had allowed the porous slag to be distributed throughout the metal, thus facilitating corrosion; expansion associated with that corrosion had fractured the treads.[129] The Penrose metal brackets were not removed.

Fig. 42 Geometric Stair, looking upwards from the bottom before cleaning started, 2003 (Andy Chopping, MOLA)

The western steps

The west end of the cathedral and the original form of the western steps, with curving or flared lower sides, are shown by the early engravings and plans, for instance the view by Thomas Malton of 1798 (Fig. 44). An outline of the building history of the west end has been given above.

The vault for the steps began to be constructed in 1708 and continued throughout 1709.[130] The brickwork was laid by Richard Billinghurst; he was paid for the substructure in March 1709. Fulkes and Kempster each laid half of the Irish marble steps above.[131] Kempster was paid in 1711 or 1712 for constructing the two side walls for the steps. Payment had already been made in June 1710 for two sets of railings 'with scroles and spikes and fluted columns' for the western steps.[132] These are presumably the curved railings on the lower steps which are shown in engravings. The completed steps appear on the plan of all the church floor probably by William Dickinson, undated but probably of 1710, and a smaller plan of the west end and its environs which is by Dickinson and dated 24 February 1709/10 (Fig. 88 and Fig. 30, the latter discussed above). The general arrangement of the space outside the west end is shown in paintings and engravings from the middle of the 18th century; one by Canaletto of 1754 has been given here as Figure 1.

Samuel Fulkes made a model for the steps in October 1708 and it is supposed that this model was of the squared form. But then this design was abandoned and a second design actually built, in which the lower flight had flared, curving sides; this dates from 1708–9.[133] In 1872 Penrose rebuilt and relaid the steps, changing the design of the lower flight to the present squared form, which he believed was Wren's original intention. As preparation for this, he made a survey of the steps and the paving inside the lower portico, which was to be relaid (Fig. 45). On this drawing, the floor panels on each side of the central one are plain, not laid with black and white tiles. Since Penrose was always fastidious in his drawing, this may reflect what he saw there in 1872. In any case, after his work the panels are black and white now. This is what is shown on a floor plan of the whole building by William Dickinson of 1709–10, which is discussed below (Fig. 88).

By the 1990s the steps were in need of relaying, and handrails suitable for better access were required. The steps (all but the top step Penrose's work, in Guernsey diorite) were taken

Fig. 43 Detail of the investigation into the side wall of the stair, 2003–4 (Andy Chopping, MOLA). This shows the iron shim which was inserted by Kempster to tighten the joint between the tread and the surrounding outer wall; each tread has its end inserted into the wall. This investigation comprised cutting out of stone above the shim, which was wedged in above the step below it. Scale is 10 × 10mm units

Fig. 44 The west end of St Paul's from the south side, by Thomas Malton, 1798 (WS XVI, pl. xvii). This shows the curved western steps and the cast iron railing (not Wren's original design, but the second imposed by the Commissioners) around the statue of Queen Anne (both railing and statue replaced by Penrose)

Fig. 45 Plan of the interior of the lower west portico and the western steps by Penrose, not dated but probably 1872 (SPCAA D/1/7/5)

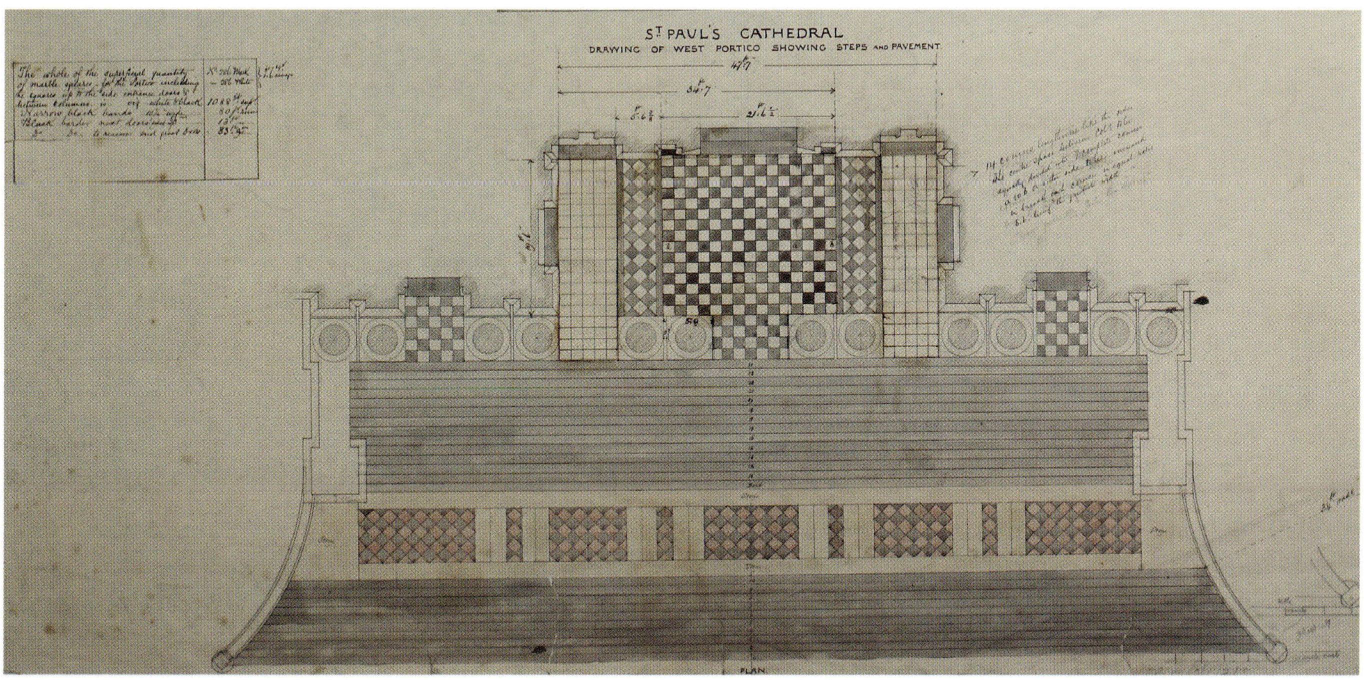

Fig. 46 (left) Original line of lower balustrade of western steps, north side, looking east (Andy Chopping, MOLA) (scale is 5 × 100mm)

Fig. 47 (right) Original line of lower balustrade of western steps, north side, looking west (Andy Chopping, MOLA) (scale is 5 × 100mm)

up and relaid, with occasional repairs. This disclosed the brick vault which formed the main structure beneath the Wren stairs, heavily mortared (Gazetteer, Site M). As no further repairs were intended, this was the limit of the archaeological investigation, though brick samples were taken (various small repairs works at the cathedral, in recent and future years, are providing dated examples of bricks; see specialist report, Chapter 6). At both ends of the western steps, the base of the original flared sides could be seen outside the line of the Penrose rebuilding (the north side shown in Fig. 46 and Fig. 47).

Penrose's rebuilding of the steps in 1872 was perhaps the first part of a grander scheme two years later which went on to include the removal of the railings around the western area or atrium, their replacement with the present Shap bollards, and repaving. This is described below in the section dealing in detail with Penrose's surveyorship (Chapter 3).

The steps of the south portico

In September 1677 Joshua Marshall, mason, was paid for 'rubble work of the foundation of the South Portico from the first bed of loam and all the holes under the same to the imposts of the vaults'. These would be the adjacent crypt vaults. In January 1681, Edward Pearce, who had taken over construction of the south portico after the death of Marshall, was paid for 'setting 135ft of old freestone for steps between the surcases [word not in *OED*: = plinths of the bases?] of the pillers of the portico'.[134] This would have been a temporary measure to aid access and construction. The portico was generally built in 1684–5.[135] It was paved in 1697–8 with 'Red Denmk polished' and 'Swede stone'.[136] C Kempster and E Beauchamp were (apparently together) paid for work on the portico and its steps in April–June 1698. This work included 'halfe ye Irish stepp with half ye Paving & Rubble under same'; paving with the large Sweed tables and Irish Black marble; 627ft of Danish Paving laid upon rubble in Terrace (Tarris); and laying both straight and curved sections of Irish Black Marble step. John Oliver also supplied Irish Black Marble Steps for the north and south porticoes, in the former case in 1696.[137] Tarris was a mortar made with ground tufa from Liège, according to Moxon in 1700.[138] It was durable in water, and thus water-proof. Wren experimented with it, but why he should think it necessary here, in bedding steps on an underlying brick and stone foundation, is not clear.

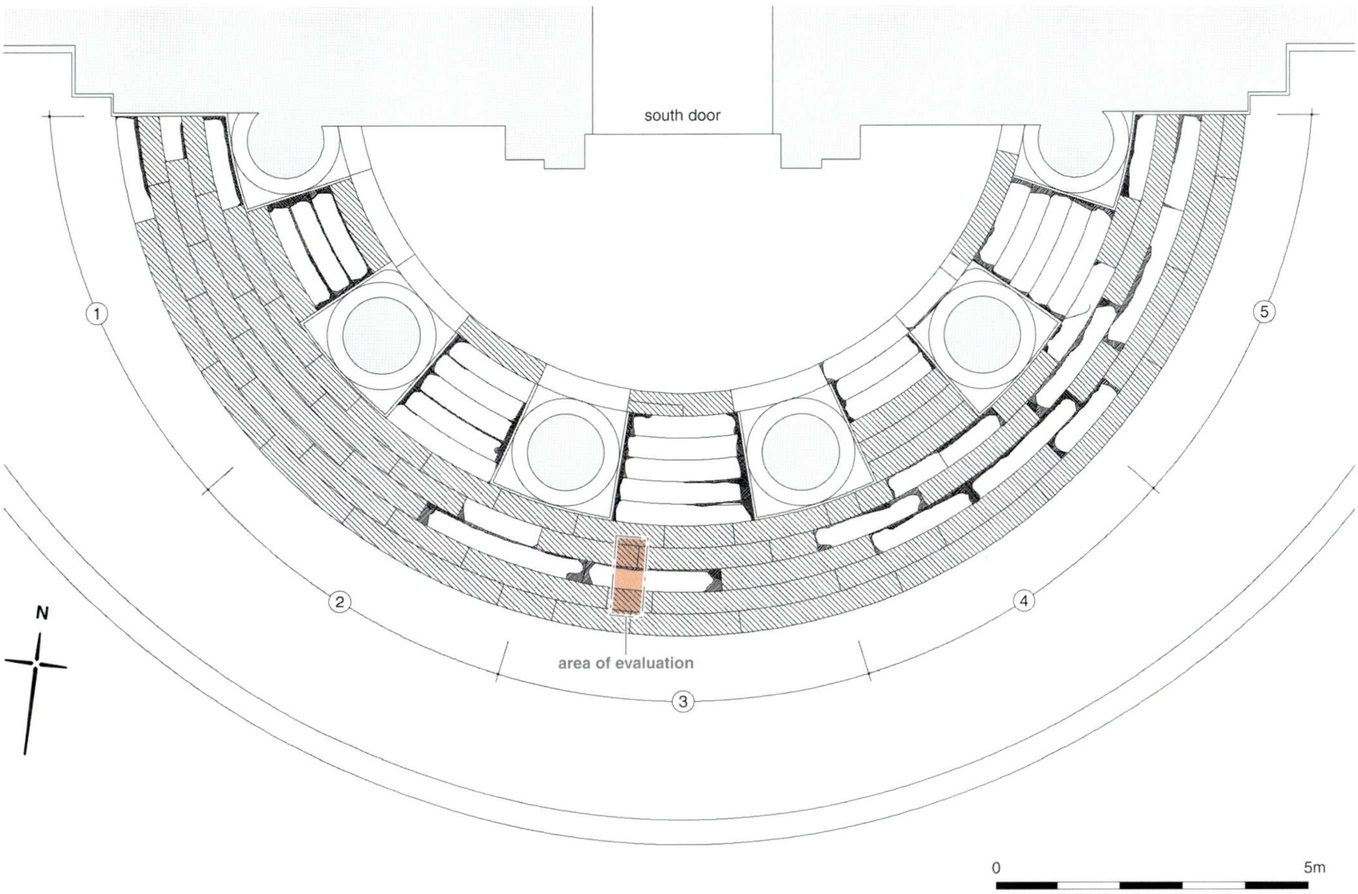

Fig. 48 South portico, 2007: location of the evaluation (Site R) on a plan of the steps as relaid by Penrose in 1877 (Carlos Lemos, MOLA, from a drawing by Martin Stancliffe Architects)

In 1875–6 Penrose replaced the curving steps of both north and south porticoes with black Irish marble, including the best he could retrieve from the original steps of both. At the south portico, all the marble steps were replaced in 2007, and a small archaeological investigation was made of the underlying layers of mortar (Fig. 48; Fig. 234). Three layers were identified as probably being from the Wren construction, and they were sampled by Alan Vince, who specialised in analyses of pottery and other materials as regards the geological origins of inclusions in strata or pottery. In particular, he was asked if the mortar samples provided any evidence of use of volcanic ash, the ingredient of 'tarris' or 'trass' (Gazetteer, Site R).

Three contexts were sampled: from the lowest upwards, first a hard mortar containing fragments of brick, above the mass of mortared brickwork which lay beneath (presumably Marshall's rubble work foundation of 1677); a second or intermediate layer of mortar with fragments of marble in it; and above the insertion cut for the steps, a fairly hard grey fine-grained mortar with pebbles and fragments of brick or tile. The archaeologist was of the opinion that the original portico steps were set into this. The mortar nearest the step was not a lime mortar but a hydraulic cement. The resulting compound will set under water and is resistant to sulphate corrosion. The materials used in this case were volcanic tuff, crushed flint and a small admixture of Thames valley sand. The lack of alteration to the volcanic glass indicates a Tertiary or recent date. These characteristics limit the potential sources in the old world to the Rhineland, Iceland, southern Italy and Greece. A source in the Rhineland is likely. Thus the inclusion of trass in the mortar bedding of the south portico steps can be confirmed.

Vaults and roofs, the dome and the balustrade

The ceiling vaults of the four arms of the cathedral are of brick, arranged in saucer domes. The domes would have been in building throughout the 1690s. A bricklayer's inscribed name and date in the nave roof space provides a date for the whole building, to match the documentary evidence. In

Fig. 49 *Graffito of G Reeve, 1705, on the north side of the roofspace of the nave (Andy Chopping, MOLA)*

one of the connecting links between the central nave space and the passage along the north side of the roof is the name G Reeve and the date May 3 1705, carefully inscribed (Fig. 49). 'Geo. Reeve' (presumably George) was a bricklayer who worked under Billinghurst on the adjacent nave saucer domes, according to the accounts in 1704–5.[139]

The roofs of the cathedral were constructed as the work progressed. In the eastern arm, the roofs over the triforium galleries and main vessel of the choir were roofed in 1689–93, the transepts in stages in 1690–7, the aisles of the nave up to the library and Trophy Room in 1695, the west end, library and Trophy Room in 1701–6 and the nave in 1698–1706.[140] Towards the end of the construction years, the amount of carpentry being undertaken would naturally have increased as the roofs were built: in 1702 there were over 170 carpenters on site.[141]

In both the choir and the nave, the galleries over the aisles were roofed first. The central span required more design and larger timbers. Charles Hopson, joiner, was paid for a model of the roof for the middle aisle of the choir, and a box to put it in, in September 1692. That roof was erected in 1692–3.[142]

For three ceiling bays of the nave out from the dome, the trusses are the same size as those in the choir, just over 43ft 6in (13.27m) long; but the nave widens to accommodate the larger west saucer dome, and here the trusses would have to span an extraordinary 53ft 6in (16.32m). This width was too much for a single beam, so each tiebeam here was produced by scarfing two timbers.

Wren asked John Holles, 3rd Duke of Newcastle, for 50 large trees from his Welbeck estate in Lincolnshire. On 4 April 1695 Wren wrote to the Duke's steward, Richard Neale:

> Sir – Having in my Letter of June 23. 1693, signified to you a particular of all the scantlings of the Timber wee might use in the roofe of St Paules, that His Grace's noble benefaction might be as usefull as may be to the worke, and understanding that what is already designed is none of the Great Beames, wch is what wee are most solicitous for, and being given to understand that wee must expect this season but Ten of the great Trees, I presume once more to acquaint you with the scantlings of the great Beames to prevent mistake. 47 feet long, 13 inches and 14 inches at the small end, growing thicker, this scantling to hold die square as neer as can be without sap. Mr Longland our cheife Carpenter will be sent down this season to take care of this concerne, & the timber brought down to Bawtrey, whom I desire you to converse with in particulars wch at this distance I can hardly determine, and beseech you to present with all advantage our utmost sense of his Grace's Favour, of wch also I am very sensible as becomes.
> Your humble servant Chr. Wren.[143]

A '1st parcell of shorter lengths timber' was sent in 1695. In 1696 ten trees from the estate were brought from Stockwith (presumably West Stockwith, on the banks of the Trent, also called 'Stockworth') to Hull, and with ten more pieces from York were shipped to London. The first ten, presumably some of the 'Great Beames', totalled just over 20 tons in weight, so would have averaged 2 tons each; the ten from York were evidently half the size, as they totalled 10 tons.[144] In 1696 the carpenter John Longland was sent again to supervise the preparation of the timber; in 1698 he was paid for not only for working on the first ten long trees, but for getting them, an exceptionally large load, to the Trent. This involved land carriage requiring a double team of cattle for 20 days to Bawtry, including payment for taking the load through a yard to avoid a corner in the road between Welbeck and Bawtry, and water carriage from Bawtry to Stockwith, presumably on the small river Idle.[145] Other timbers probably came from Kent, since in 1706 Richard Jenings was paid for three journeys into that county over that and the previous year 'to chuse & mark Oak-Timber for the Building'.[146] Since the trusses over the choir also have unscarfed tiebeams which span an identical width as the main section of the nave, 43ft 6in, the timbers for them must have been obtained before Wren had to write to the Duke of Newcastle in 1695; by then the choir trusses had been up for 2 years.

The roofs of aisles and the main vessels are strengthened by screw-threaded iron bolts. 'Screw bolts' for the roof appear in the accounts in March 1690, when the roof over the north choir aisle was being framed, and in August that year, perhaps for the south choir aisle.[147] The first group of bolts weighed 12 lb each. On the nave roof 27 straps and 77 'Bolts with Screws & Nutts' were supplied for the west end by T Robinson, smith, in October 1705; in 1707 he supplied 128 'Bolts with Screws and Nutts' for the dome.[148]

The erection of the trusses over the nave at St Paul's is therefore dated to between 1698 and 1704, when Longland was paid for erecting 11 of them. He fitted three straps to each truss.[149] The final section of roof, from the east side of the 'west dome' (the larger saucer-dome) to the pediment, was erected by Longland and Richard Jennings by May 1706.[150] Richard Jennings was employed as a carpenter at the cathedral from 1696, and from then until 1702 he worked under Longland. From 1703 to 1713 he was almost always paid the same as Longland, and was to share the carpenter's work equally with him from 1704; since Longland had been on the cathedral project since the beginning in 1675, he was presumably quite old in 1704. Jennings thereafter took over the direction of the carpentry; he seems to have played a major part in the design of the timberwork for construction of the dome.[151] One question therefore would be whether the nave roof structure shows any difference in preparation or fitting which would suggest the two parts of the work by the two master carpenters.

Investigation of the nave roof, 2013

A survey of the nave roof structure was undertaken in 2013 by Damian Goodburn and Azizul Karim, with new photography by Andy Chopping. Their main findings are summarised here, and more detailed notes given in Chapter 6 below.

The main nave roof has two sections of slightly different construction, and the roof over the west portico forms a third part or addition. The trusses have been numbered from truss 1 at the east end of the nave by the crossing, thus going westward. The first section is of thirteen trusses, numbered 1–13. For these trusses the tiebeam is a single timber across the nave. Then the roof widens, as the walls on either side are further apart to take account of the larger saucer dome at the west end. This is covered by six trusses, 14–19; here the tiebeam is made of two scarfed timbers, individually shorter than those used to the east which span the nave without scarfing. West of the large saucer dome there are six further trusses of this wider variety, numbers 20 to 25, covering the west end and portico (Fig. 50).

The basic roof truss form comprises a king post (Fig. 51) and two diagonal struts jointed to the principal rafters. The king posts and rafters are also jointed to tiebeams or low collar beams (Fig. 52, Fig. 53). The pitch of the roof is moderate due to the highly waterproof nature of the lead covering. All the lower joints were also reinforced with bolted, wrought iron straps.

Extensive use was made of wrought iron bolted straps. Although the straps were forged to fairly standardised forms the length of the screw threaded bolts used to secure them varied considerably as if they included some originally made for another purpose. To make up the difference in the locations of the threaded sections, pierced iron packing pieces had been used under the heads of many of the nuts. In some cases this amounted to a nut and two packing pieces. The use of screw bolts instead of the earlier wedge locked forelock bolts would have made the adjustment and tightening of the bolts, following the seasoning shrinkage in the timber, much easier.

The straps were broadly similar dimensions at *c.* 20–25mm thick by *c.* 100mm wide and of varying length to suit the locations. Those used at the junction of king posts and tiebeams and those used to joint rafter feet to tiebeam ends had an elongated 'U' shape and either two or three bolt holes. Those used to fasten the western horizontal tiebeam scarfs, and link the ends of the cranked divided tiebeams were flat straps with dovetail ends and six or four bolt holes respectively. A few short straps were noted on the opposing faces of the scarfed beams, such as that linking two bolts (35mm diameter) in Truss 14 (Fig. 54). This truss was of intermediate length between the two groups of trusses to east and west, as the exterior wall began to widen at this point (Fig. 50).

In the second group of trusses to the west (Trusses 14–19) the divided tiebeam was cranked up to a large low collar beam joining the rafters about two-thirds of the way down their length (Fig. 53). The change in roof truss design was essential to allow space for the building of the larger saucer dome beneath; the tiebeams barely graze the top of the saucer dome. The lower ends of the rafters in this form of truss were also expanded in thickness towards the base, as in those of the eastern sector of the roof, but the expansion occurs almost half way up just above

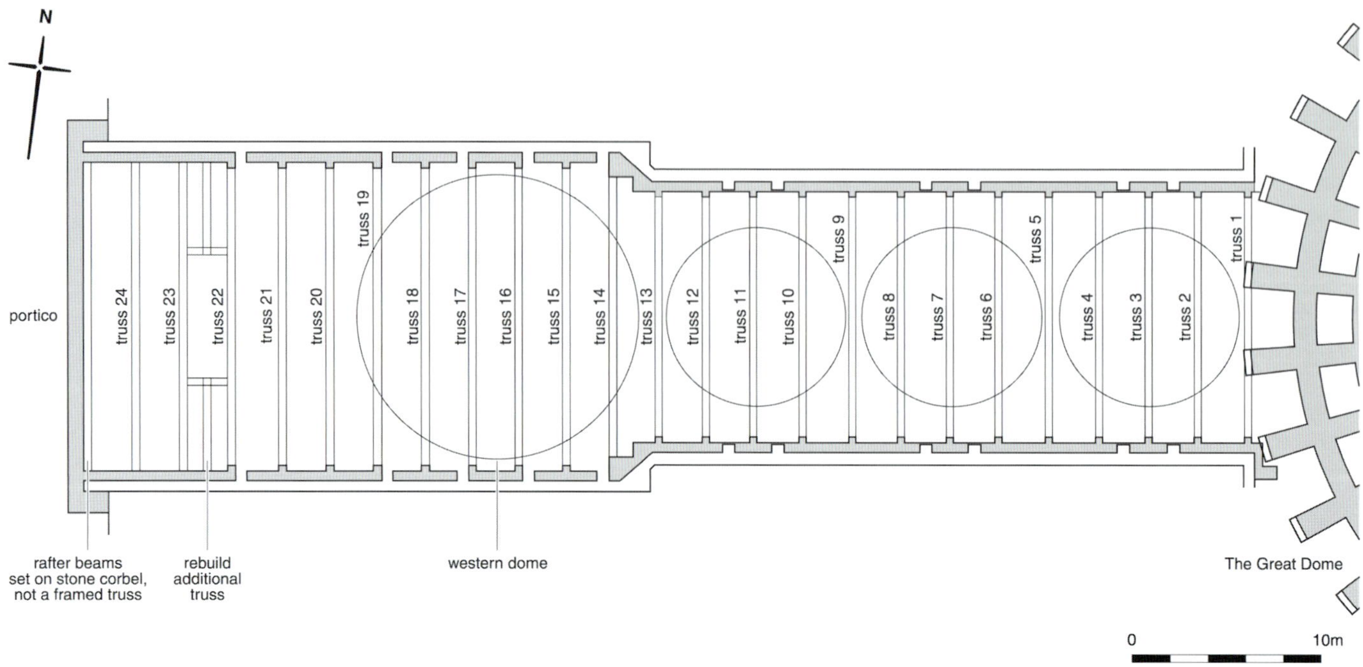

Fig. 50 (above) Poley, plan of nave roof, annotated by Damian Goodburn (Azizul Karim, MOLA, adapted from Poley 1927, pl. xxv)

Fig. 51 (right) Detail of the top of the king post of Truss 15, west face (Andy Chopping, MOLA). The rafter on the right still has some sapwood, shown by the brighter wood on the lower edge

Fig. 52 (below) The east face of Truss 4, with its single-piece tiebeam and carpenter's marks (Azizul Karim, MOLA)

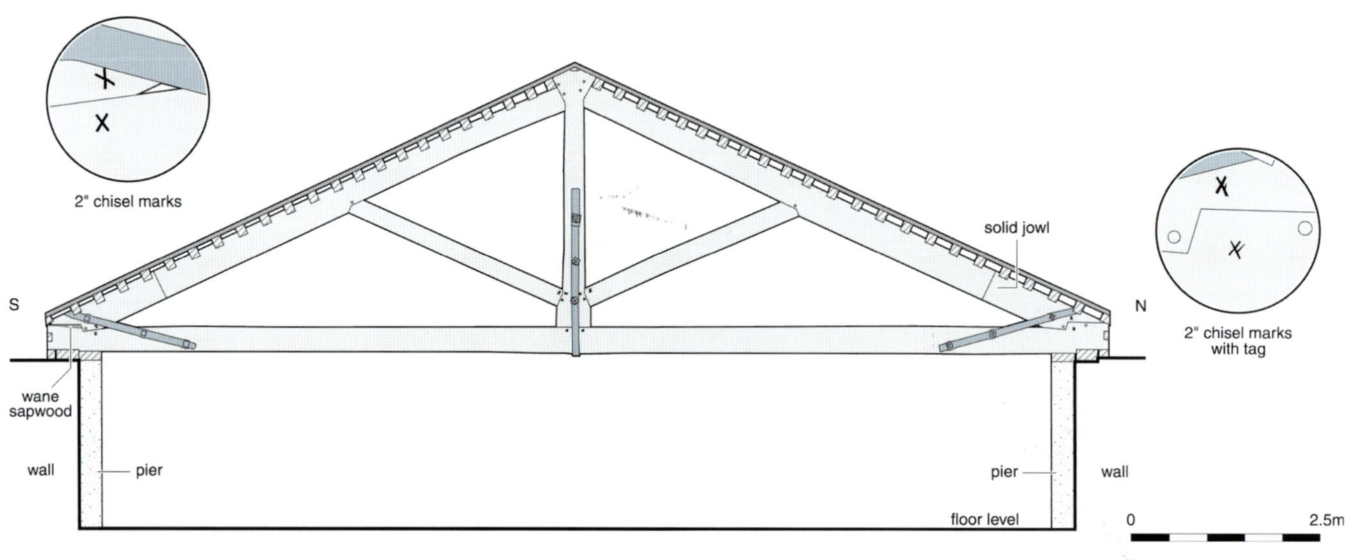

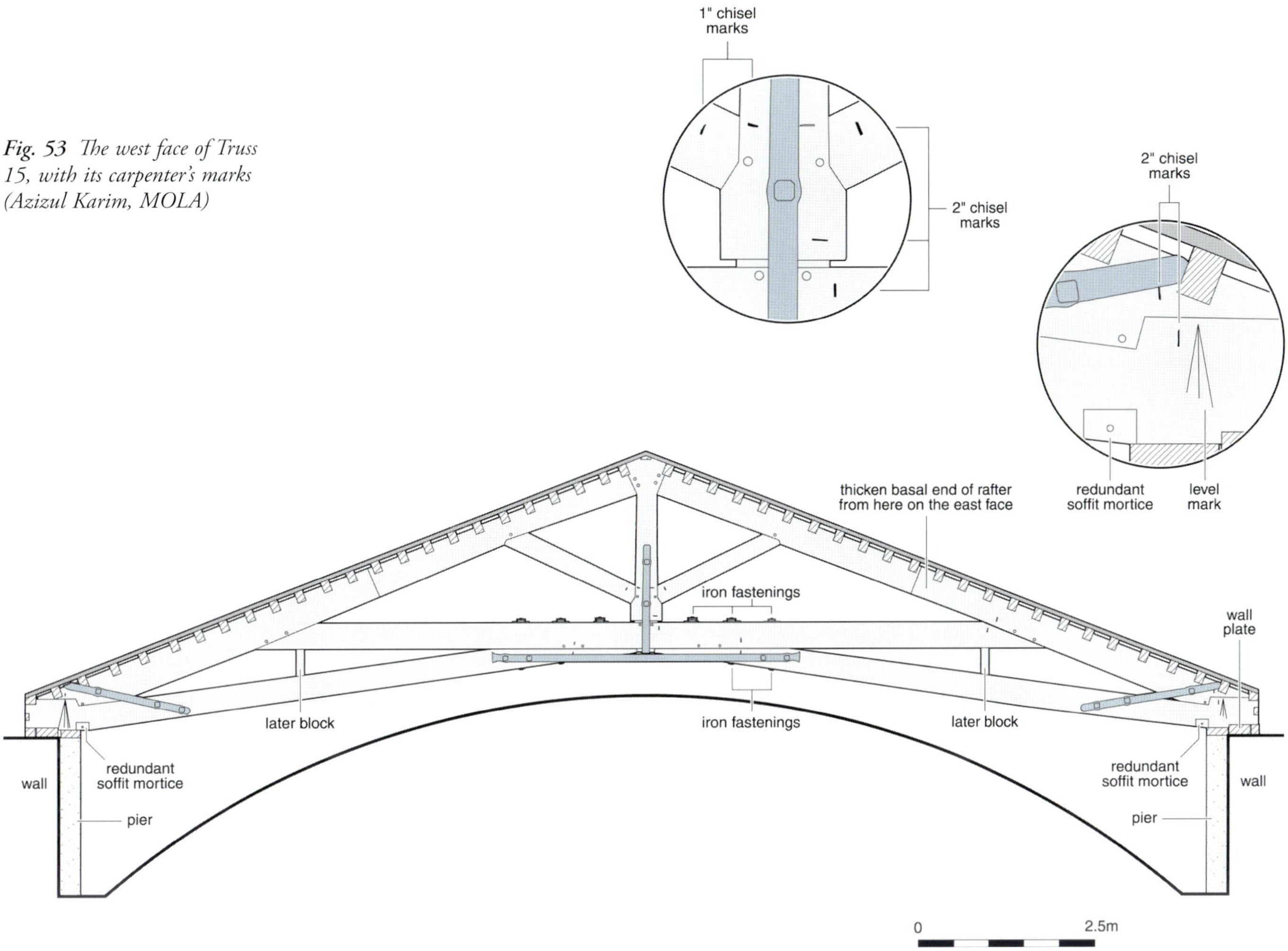

Fig. 53 *The west face of Truss 15, with its carpenter's marks (Azizul Karim, MOLA)*

Clockwise from top left:

Fig. 54 *Nave roof looking east from above the larger western saucer dome (Andy Chopping, MOLA). In the foreground is Truss 14*

Fig. 55 *The soffit (underside) of the tiebeam of Truss 20, showing the end of the scarf joint and the applied iron strap with its dovetail ends (Andy Chopping, MOLA)*

Fig. 56 *The trusses above the western saucer dome, looking south-west (Andy Chopping, MOLA)*

Clockwise from top left:

Fig. 57 *Details of Truss 15, looking east: the form of the truss with its divided, cranked up tiebeams (Andy Chopping, MOLA)*

Fig. 58 *Truss 15: the joint of the diagonal strut and principal rafter (Andy Chopping, MOLA)*

Fig. 59 *Truss 15: the joint of the paired tiebeam and the principal rafter (Andy Chopping, MOLA)*

Fig. 60 *Truss 15: the joint of the principal rafter and the tiebeam (Andy Chopping, MOLA)*

the collars (eg on the east, 'lower' face of Truss 15). The carpenters also fitted a pair of wrought iron straps linking the heads of the paired tiebeams to resist spreading strains. This strap was forged with a dovetail end, four screw bolts and partially inset into the upper faces of the tiebeam ends, presumably with the intention of increasingly holding power (Fig. 55). Although the full span of the western section of the roof is *c.* 17.29m (56ft 7in) the form of truss also allowed the use of much shorter, though still very large timbers (Fig. 56). The longest elements of these trusses are the low collar beams which have a length *c.* 11.3m or about 3m (10ft) shorter than the single-piece tiebeams. From this point westward no single-piece tiebeams were used.

The sample recorded truss of this form was Truss 15 (Fig. 57–Fig. 60). This comprised eight principal timbers all cut from whole logs by pit-sawing. The timbers were fairly neatly converted and fairly straight grained but had some medium sized knots. The paired tiebeams had maximum dimensions of *c.* 450mm (18in) deep by 280–290mm (11¼–11 5/8in) thick, the rafters a maximum of 380mm (15½in) deep by 270mm (10¾in) thick. The post is 300mm (12in) wide by 275mm (11in) thick, the collar 360mm (*c* 14½in) deep by *c.* 290mm (11 5/8in) thick and the struts *c.* 250mm (10in) deep by (8in) 200mm thick. The 'upper face' of the truss, which is now the western face, showed several carpentry marks such as arrow form level marks scribed in the tiebeam ends, and a set of chiselled I combined joint and truss numbers. The 'I' was cut with a smaller chisel on the north side of the truss and with a 2-inch chisel on the south side. Another key feature of note seen on this truss and Trusses 16, 17 and 18 were redundant mortises cut in the soffits of the north and south ends of each tiebeam pair.

The tiebeams in the western part of the central nave roof were very similar to those of the eastern section of roof except that they were a little wider and were made of two timbers scarfed together (Fig. 61). The scarf joint was entirely dependent on the locking effect of the six through bolts used and to some limited extent the clumsily inset dovetail-ended strap on the lower face. As these straps were only a loose fit this effect would have been minimal. It seems that Wren and his master carpenters were unaware of or possibly unwilling to use alternative forms of scarf joint that would have been more secure and would have required much less expensive iron to fasten. By the end of the 17th century shipwrights building very large ships had been using more elaborate, much stronger forms of bolted scarf joints in major cross beams for some years. In these joints ridges of timber were cut so as to interlock, called 'tabeling' by shipwrights and 'counter cogging' in carpentry.

Where the roof widens in span, at the point at which the large western dome appears at Truss 14, it also rises up little (Fig. 62). This change in height is also associated with changing the angles of some of the diagonal struts, even in the horizontal tiebeam trusses. The slight change in external roof line cannot be seen from the ground but is visible on aerial views of the cathedral.

Figure 64, based on the Poley roof plan, shows the numbered roof trusses and the location and style of the combined truss and joint numbers recorded. Various forms of numbering, most commonly in versions of Roman numerals, were used to label particular joints in a timber frame. The key purpose of this was to enable individually cut male and female elements of joints to be refitted on site after the prefabrication of a timber frame. Sometimes in post-medieval London these would be individual numbers for each joint but at other times they would simply be one mark repeated as the components of a frame could only be fitted together one way. In the case of the St Paul's nave roof there were actually four similar elements, the pairs of rafters and the king post struts. The master carpenters distinguished these to avoid attempts at erroneous trial fitting on site in two ways. One involved the use of versions of Roman numerals cut with 2-inch chisels including a small additional cut or 'tag' on one side of the truss (eg Truss 9, Fig. 63). The other involved the use of a 2-inch chisel mark on one side of the truss and a 1in or 1¼in on the other side (eg Truss 15). The marks survived in over 90% of the locations were they would have originally been used, although low angle torch light was needed to reveal the more abraded examples. This patterning in the evidence appears to reflect the supervision of two different master carpenters, and as we know of two named from the documentary sources, Longland and Jennings, it is likely that they were responsible. If we consider that Longland was paid for erecting 11 of the roof trusses of the nave roof in 1704 and that there are 11 trusses marked using the 2-inch chisel and tag system, it seems very likely

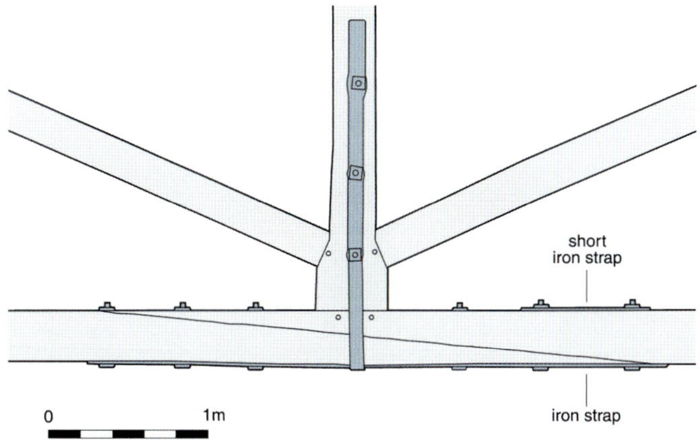

Fig. 61 The scarfed tiebeam used in the wider western trusses (Azizul Karim, MOLA)

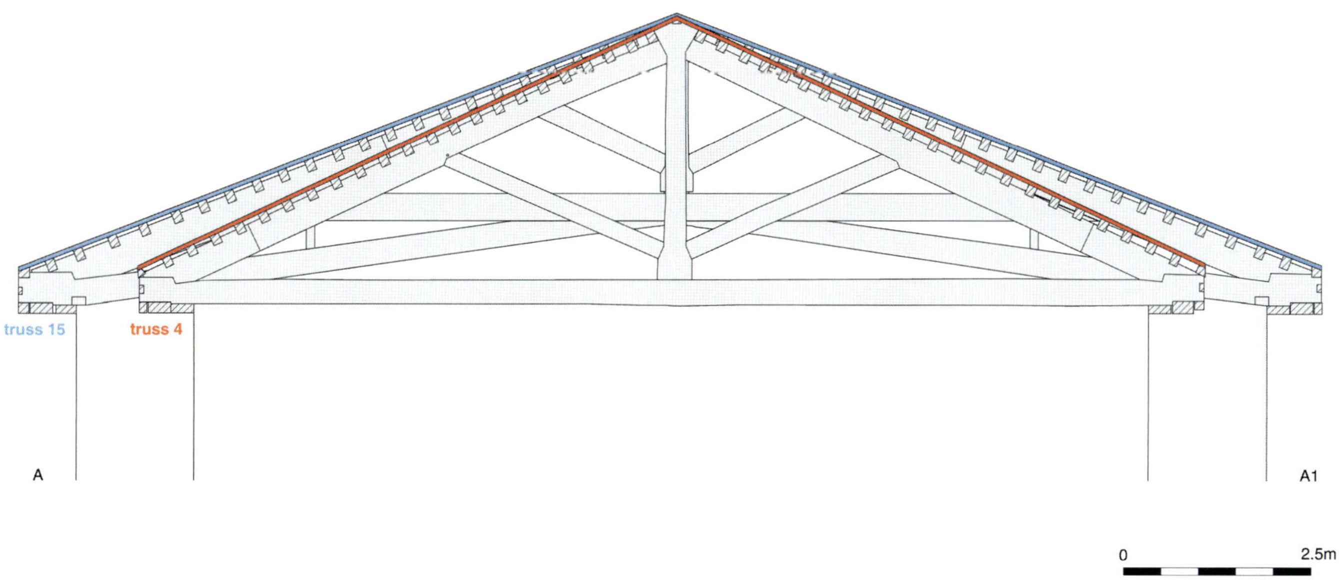

Fig. 62 The roof outlines of the two parts of the nave roof, looking east, as though from the west end (Azizul Karim, MOLA). This shows the wider roof line of the west end (Truss 15) (blue) and the main section at Truss 4 (red). The piers of the wider section are marked A and A1

Fig. 63 *East face of Truss 9, showing a mark comprising a Roman numeral, with a 'tag' on the right-hand stroke (Andy Chopping, MOLA)*

that those were made under his supervision. But they are not in a single group; they are Trusses 1, 2, 4, 5, 7–11, 13 and 18. The other trusses marked using the other system are therefore likely to have been made under the supervision of Jennings (Fig. 64). It is very rare that the work of individual named master carpenters can be associated with the actual frames they supervised the making of rather than just being able to record that a particular carpenter worked on a building or roof.

It might have been expected that the deeper, heavier and stronger ends of the tiebeams from near the butt of the parent tree would have been alternated from side to side along the length of the roof but a plan of how the tiebeams were laid – which side of the nave received the butt end of the timber – in Figure 65 shows that this is not the case. The placing of the butt ends of the tiebeams was apparently arbitrary.

The eastern group of tiebeams of the nave roof appear to be the largest currently known oak timbers recorded in any historic English roof, their lengths varying slightly around 14.08m (46ft 2½in). They are over 1.8m (6ft) longer than the 14th-century Ely Cathedral octagon timbers which previously held this position.[152] Bearing in mind the great length and comparative lack of taper of the longest tiebeams it is surprising that Wren did not chose to use a coniferous wood alternative for these timbers from either northern Europe or North America; coniferous timbers were coming into wider use at this time.[153] But we know that Wren preferred oak for its durability.

Not only were the great timbers required for the St Paul's roof carpentry huge and some very long, but they were also very heavy. The parent logs for the eastern, single-piece tiebeams would have weighed around 2.7 tonnes using a standard average weight for freshly cut 'green' oak of *c.* 1.073 tonnes per cubic metre.[154] This is heavier than water so freshly cut oak will not normally float in fresh water, or often even in salt water, so rafting the timber was not an option. The largest timbers would have been cut to their final dimensions near the felling site. If they were both hewn and sawn out as described below, they would have still weighed *c.* 1.4–1.5 tonnes. Some may have weighed a little more.

Fig. 64 *Plan of the nave roof, based on the plan by Poley (1927), showing the locations and type of the combined truss and joint number marks, which suggests the work of the two main carpenters Longland and Jennings (Azizul Karim, MOLA)*

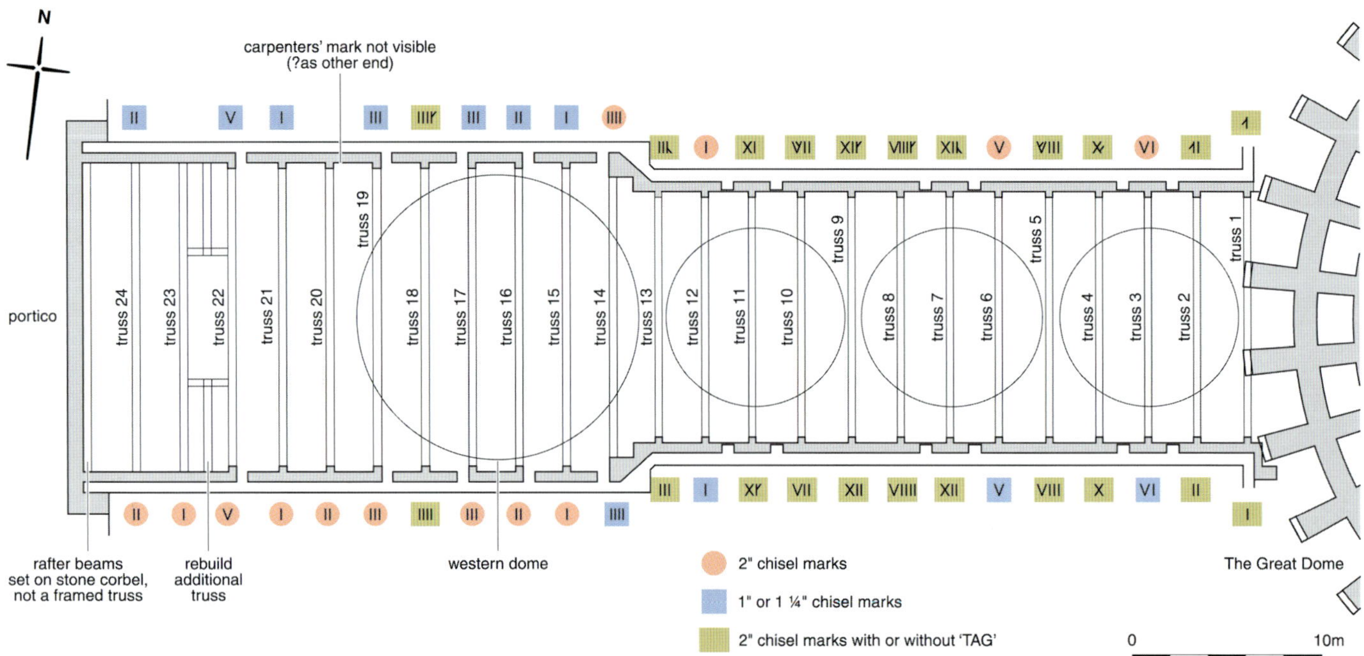

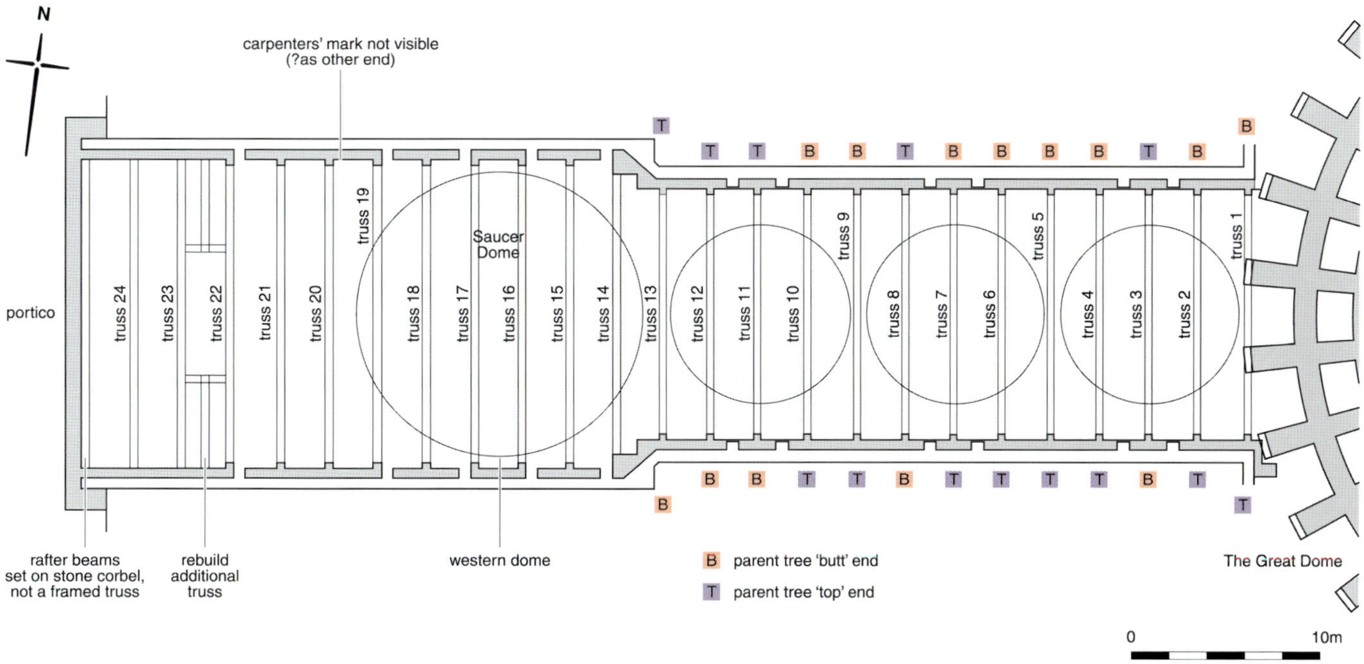

Fig. 65 Plan of the nave roof, showing the orientation of the tiebeams for Trusses 1–13; the location of their top and butt ends (Azizul Karim, MOLA)

This approximate figure happens to be close to the nominal oak timber volume/weight measure used in the timber trades until the 19th century of a 'load', usually given as 1.5 tons or *c.* 30 cu ft. The difference in weight between the parent log and freshly cut beam shows why there was a great incentive to convert the larger timbers before long distance haulage.

During the examination of the roof trusses spanning the high western dome, Trusses 15–18, traces of mysterious empty mortises and staining were found at their extreme north and south ends on the soffits (Fig. 53). These empty mortises were partially blocked by the piers and pads located under their ends which were clearly original historic workmanship. Initially it was thought that these mortises were evidence for the reuse of these timbers but in a short while it became clear from their regular positioning and traces of joint lay out scribing, that they must instead have been evidence for the use of temporary raking posts under the tiebeams (Fig. 66). These posts would have sprung from completed masonry walling lower down and acted as temporary supports for the roof trusses before the side walls of the roof space were eventually built up. Thus it appears that the carpenters were well ahead of the masons and bricklayers and there were actually good practical reasons for this. The raised roof would protect the brick vaulting during their construction allowing time for the slow setting lime mortar to harden. It may also have allowed the bricklayers to work longer hours in the winter and during bad weather. Multiple deep rope wear marks also indicates that the suggested stages of work must have been the case as there would have been no need to hoist anything up if the upper face of the vaulted ceilings had been completed.

Over the portico a pair of relatively recent, rather crudely made, half trusses were seen (Trusses 22a and b). The tool mark evidence and patina of some of the oak timber found in these

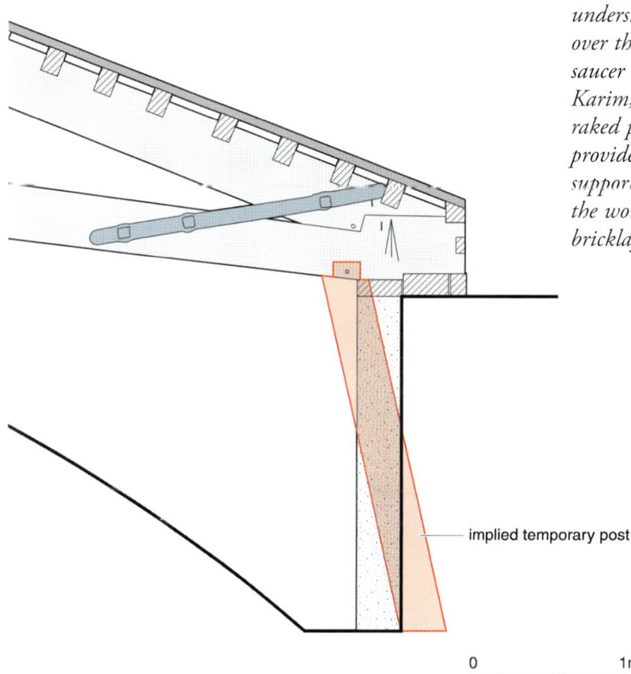

Fig. 66 An interpretation of the probable original function of the partially blocked mortises on the undersides of the tiebeams over the larger western saucer dome (Azizul Karim, MOLA). The raked post would have provided temporary support for the roof until the work of masons and bricklayers could replace it

additions, such as circular saw marks, identified them as modern and possibly from the repairs here in 1903. However, some of the oak timbers had relict joints, traces of pit-sawn conversion and a patina just like that of the timbers of the nave roof. One on the north side (Truss 22b) had simple lap joints and proportions similar to those of the rafters in the nave trusses. It would appear to have been originally a rafter from a common rafter roof in another area of roofing at St Paul's. Low angle torch light revealed a faintly scribed 'daisy wheel' mark (Fig. 67) on this timber, which although cutting through the pit saw marks, appeared to be ancient i.e. dating to the *c.* 1690s to early 1700s. These marks were made with compasses, which were used first to scribe a circle and were then set to the radius of the circle and used to scribe a series of petal-like arcs within it. The daisy wheel marks are often found on historic building timbers and there are two schools of thought as to their meaning and use. One school suggests that they were marks designed to guard against bad hexes from witches; an alternative view sees them as geometrical design aids used to develop accurate angles and shapes by carpenters and masons.[155] There is much variation in the execution of these marks and their location which would suggest that both explanations could apply, depending on the location and execution of the marks. In the case of the daisy wheel on the reused rafter in Truss 22b, its very faint execution might indicate that it was trial work by an apprentice trying to learn the skill of accurate scribing with a compass, on hard oak timbers.

Goodburn's study may be complemented by notes on the national context of the two most important characteristics of the roof design, the king-post truss and the use of screw-threaded bolts. The king-post truss, assisted by metal straps and bolts, was a feature of 16th-century Italian buildings; Wren owned an Italian book in which the truss was described from a mechanical point of view, *In Mechanica Aristotelis Problematica Exercitationes* by Bernadino Baldi (1621). This form of truss was used by Inigo Jones in roofs at the Banqueting House, Whitehall (1619–22), Queen's Chapel, St James's Palace (1623–5), Stoke Bruerne (Northants) (*c.* 1630) and St Paul's Covent Garden (1633–42).[156] Wren used it on buildings from the start of his career, such as at a residential block at Trinity College Oxford, in a drawing of 1665.[157] His intentions for the nave at St Paul's in the same year included straps in the roof trusses. After the Fire the king-post truss was widely used in churches and private houses, in Britain and later throughout the eastern American colonies, though in many domestic cases without straps.[158]

Fig. 67 A reused timber in additional Truss 22b over the portico roof with the faint outline of part of a compass-drawn daisy wheel, cutting through the pit saw marks (Andy Chopping, MOLA)

The king post trusses in Jones's roofs, from engravings, often also used bolts but their nature is unknown. Wren's innovative roof at the Sheldonian in 1664–9, from engravings, used many bolts but again their precise character is unknown as the roof was replaced in 1801.[159] Wren recommended their use in the roof of Salisbury Cathedral in 1668, illustrating his report with a sketch which closely resembles the arrangement of scarfed tiebeams (though with a different scarf joint), bands ('hoops') and bolts, probably screw-threaded; as used in the nave at St Paul's 30 years later.[160] He used screw-threaded bolts in the roofs of Trinity College Library, Cambridge, and St Peter Cornhill in the City of London; both completed in 1680.[161] Screw-threaded bolts did not immediately take over from forelock bolts, but were an alternative. Forelock bolts were used in other roofs over major churches, such as at Winchester in 1699 and at Ely in 1768.[162] They were also the preferred method of bolting timbers together in the roofs at Blenheim Palace in the second decade of the 18th century. Screw-threaded bolts were however used in the high-roof of the choir at Durham Cathedral in a restoration attributed to the architect James Clement who died in 1690, and in large church roofs throughout the 19th century.[163]

There has been little requirement for archaeological recording of the dome in recent years, and only a brief study of its structure and history appeared in the 2004 cathedral history.[164] The development of the design of the dome was assisted by the construction of several scale models from the 1690s.[165] *Parentalia* says that the design was influenced by that of the Pantheon in Rome; the width of the dome space is said to be 112ft

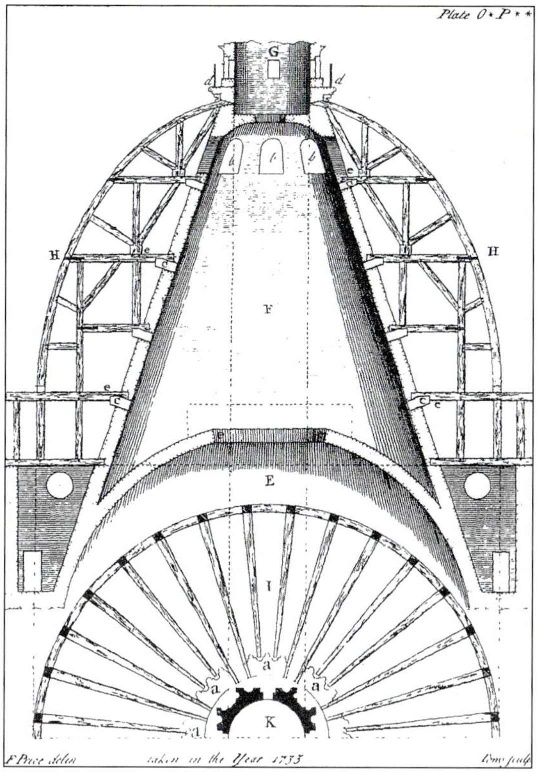

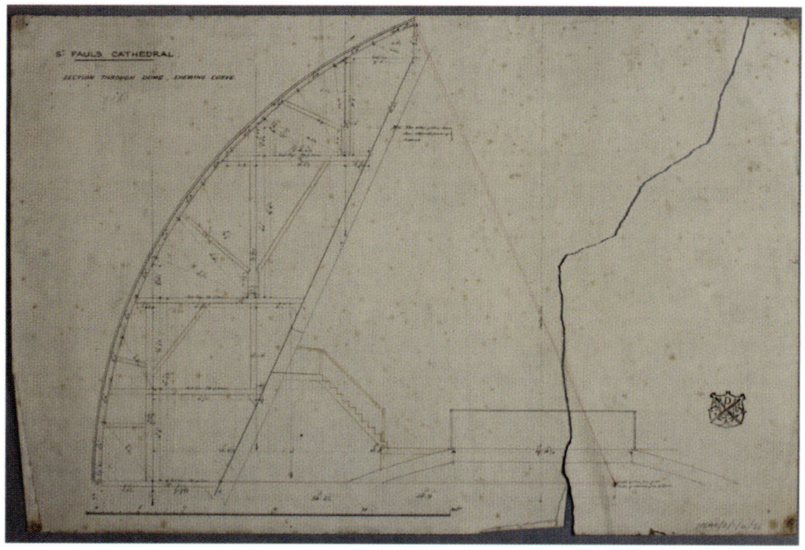

Fig. 68 (left) Timber structure of dome, from F Price, The British Carpenter (1733), pl. O*P**

Fig. 69 (above) Timber structure of dome, by Penrose, not dated (SPCAA D/1/4/26)

(34.2m) in *Parentalia*,[166] but was measured by Poley as 107ft (32.6m), and the diameter of the Pantheon is 142ft 6in (43.5m), exactly a third larger. Construction of the dome followed that of the choir, from 1696 until 1708 when the lantern was finished. Just as the saucer domes of all four arms are of brick, so the structure of the dome incorporates a large number of bricks. In 1699–1700 Richard Billinghurst laid 300,000 bricks 'about the dome.' This must have been around the interior of the base of the drum. Billinghurst was paid specifically for constructing the brick cone in 1707.[167]

The innovatory structure of the dome and its carpentry are shown in two published drawings of the immediate decades which followed. Francis Price included a section drawing in his book on carpentry in 1733 (Fig. 68), though the carpentry structure may be partly speculative. In 1755 John Gwynn published a measured drawing, the main purpose of which was to propose a completion of the decoration begun by Thornhill, in thorough Baroque style. This appears to be based on a survey he made of the dome which was later revised for Robert Mylne around 1789.[168] The dome framework was recorded again by Penrose (Fig. 69), and a fourth drawing is provided by Poley in 1927 (Fig. 70).[169] All the drawings show

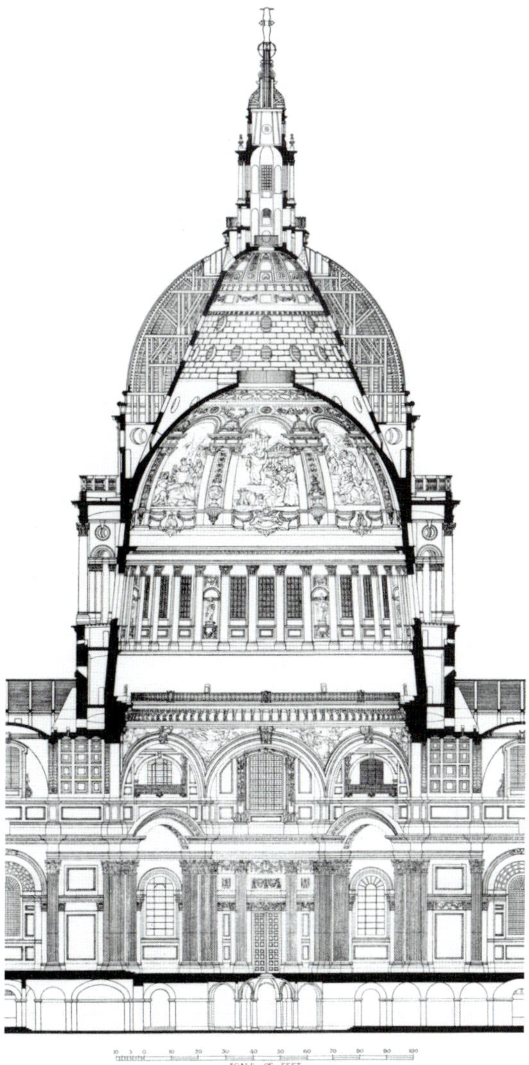

Fig. 70 Extract from the longitudinal section of the cathedral, looking north, by Arthur Poley in 1927 (pl IX), showing the timberwork in the dome

how a major level of the roof structure, about half way up the dome, was composed of trusses which resemble those over the choir and nave.

The balustrade to the main elevation of the body of the cathedral was added, against Wren's wishes, in 1717–19. Richard Jones, the smith who was supplying the churchyard railing, was asked to provide a 'pattern' for a balustrade of iron, under John James's direction, in 1716, but discussion of it was postponed and the Commissioners decided to have it in stone in October 1717.[170] The construction of the balustrade in stone was preceded by the building of a small section in wood by carpenters, as a 'specimen' or trial set up in place. The design of the balustrade was probably by the Assistant Surveyor John James, working with the masons William Kempster (who had been made 'master mason' of works to finish the dome in 1715) and Joshua Fletcher. Then Kempster died, and Fletcher 'not standing to his Proposal, severall other Masons now attended with Proposals for the same, and the Proposal of Mr Christopher Cass being found the most reasonable, It was Ordered That Mr James draw up a Contract for the same according to his said Proposal'.[171] The builder of the balustrade was therefore Cass, who was given an extra gratuity of £25 in February 1720.[172]

External decoration

Construction of the 'great entablature' (the main cornice above the windows, below the upper screen wall) of the choir was in progress in 1686. The work on the choir was shared between three master masons, two of whom had successors on the project. Edward Strong senior built the east end and the first bay and a half of both north and south sides; Jasper Latham (after 1690, Nathaniel Rawlins) built the remainder of the north side and the east half of the north transept; and Edward Pearce (after 1690, Christopher Kempster and Ephraim Beauchamp) built the equivalent stretch of the south side of the choir and east half of the south transept. For the nave, the length from the middle of the north transept west along the nave was built by Edward Strong senior and the equivalent along the south side by Thomas Wise junior and Thomas Hill, with the exception of two bays at the south-west corner of the south transept which were by Edward Pearce until 1690 and by Wise and Hill thereafter.[173] Thus it

Fig. 71 *South elevation of the cathedral in 1927 (Poley 1927, pl. viii)*

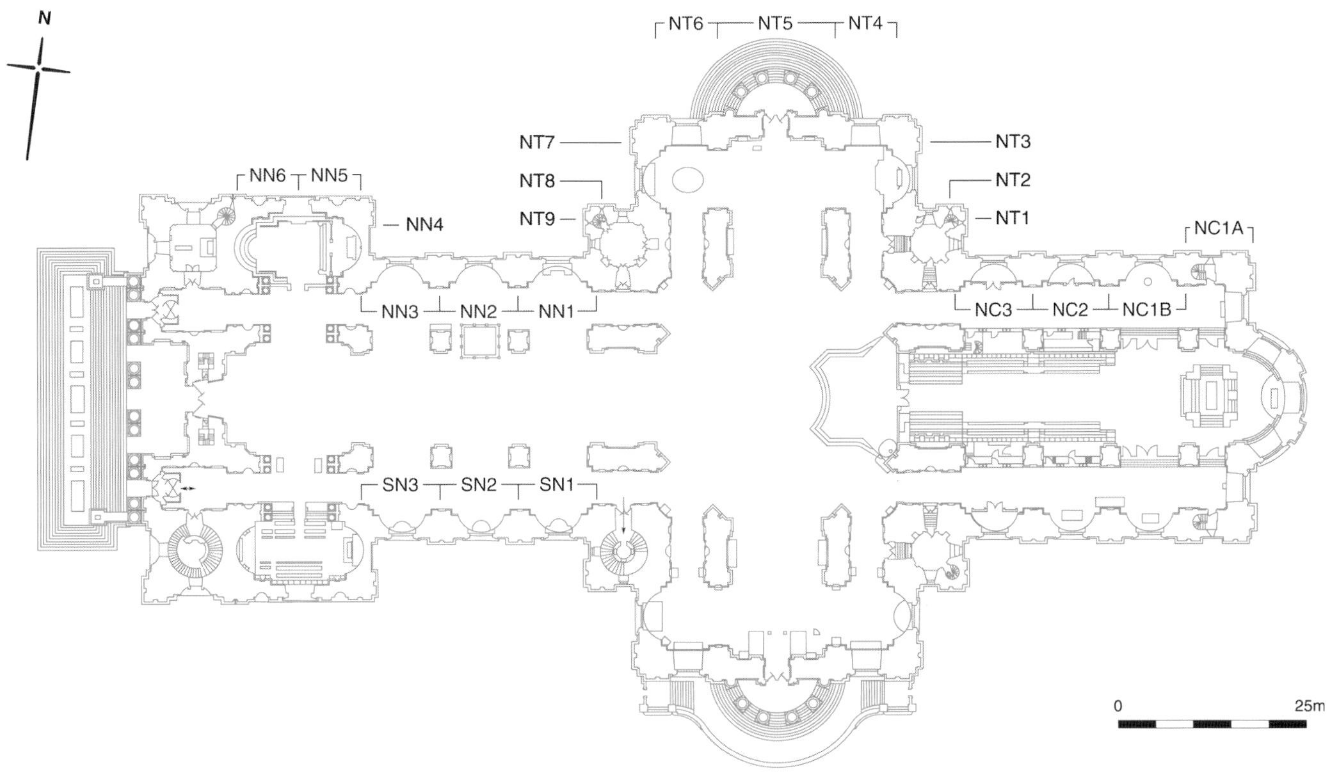

Fig. 72 *Plan of external bays used for recording (Carlos Lemos, MOLA, from a plan by E Hardisty, PMT Architects). Only those bays which were recorded by archaeological photography are numbered*

should be possible to assign any particular piece of external carving to a master mason; but the actual carvers remain anonymous. Much of the carving would have been done in the masons' yard before the blocks were lifted up into position, but the accounts occasionally note carving after the block had been set in position.[174]

The disposition of carvings around the windows and elsewhere on the elevation is shown by Poley's elevation of the south side (Fig. 71). Decoration such as swags, heads of cherubs at the tops of windows and panels below the windows was a feature of the lower, main wall, but less on the upper screen wall. Here, at the upper level, embellishment was used on selected parts only: the terminal wall of the transepts, the adjacent projections containing the stair and vestries and around the east end and the west façade (Fig. 13).

The programme of stonework repair and cleaning of the exterior of the nave took place at the same time as the works in the south churchyard and on the lift in 2006–7 and continued until June 2011 (Gazetteer, Site N). Recording by photography comprised (i) most of the swags and cherubs' heads above the windows, on the south nave and north choir bays, along with one bay of the north transept, before and after cleaning; (ii) most of the Gibbons panels below the windows of the north transept and the north nave, before and after cleaning. For the purposes of management and recording, a scheme of numbering the external bays of the cathedral was devised by Emma Hardisty of PMT Architects (Fig. 72).

Three matters are briefly discussed here: (i) the decoration above the main windows; (ii) the panels below the windows; (iii) the royal arms in the pediment of the north transept.

Decoration above the main (church floor) windows

The swags or festoons, and the cherubs' or cherubim's heads which are at the top of each window, are mentioned under each chief mason's accounts during the 1690s; so one question might be whether there were observable differences in the carvings by the different masons (or their employees). Here the present research can only present the evidence which might be used by future research. The photographic recording at this high level was of the first section, that of Latham and later Rawlins, along the north side of the choir and the east side of the north transept; and to a lesser extent, the south nave façade, the work of Wyse and Hill. The work of Edward Pierce, on the south side of the choir, was not recorded at this time.

On the choir elevation, the accounts mention two potential parts: (1) Edward Strong senior, who built the first bay of the choir from the east (as part of his work on the east end), that is (as named in the plan, Fig. 72) bay NC1A and the east half of bay NC1B; (2) Jasper Latham until 1690, then Nathaniel Rawlins, from the middle of bay NC1B for the remainder of the choir elevation and the first bay of the north transept (bay NT3). Examples of the work of each of the master masons are given here: (a) Edward Strong, bull's eye window in bay NC1A; bay NC1B (Fig. 73–Fig. 77); (b) work either of Jasper Latham or Nathaniel Rawlins, bay NC1B west side (Fig. 78). Any differences between the work of the masons, for instance in the middle of bay NC1B, could not be readily perceived. All the bays which had their decoration photographed, both before and after cleaning, are shown in Fig. 72. No further detailed research has been undertaken, for instance on the styles of the carving or the masons involved, and the wider survey remains in archive for use by others.[175]

One remarkable thing was observed. Several of the cherubs above the main windows have square stone inserts in their heads (Fig. 79; also shown in Fig. 76). This was evident when the sculptures were dirty, but is far less visible now, especially as it is in the top of the head and therefore not visible from ground-level below. The example shown here is from the north side of the choir. The only piece of potentially relevant

Fig. 73 (top left) Bull's eye window and swag in bay NC1A before cleaning (all north nave elevation photographs are looking south) (Andy Chopping, MOLA)

Fig. 74 (top right) Bull's eye window and swag in bay NC1A after cleaning (Andy Chopping, MOLA)

Fig. 75 (middle left) Swag in bay NC1B, east side of window (Andy Chopping, MOLA)

Fig. 76 (middle right) Cherub keystone in bay NC1B; dirty state (Andy Chopping, MOLA)

Fig. 77 (bottom left) Cherub keystone in bay NC1B; clean state (Andy Chopping, MOLA)

Fig. 78 (bottom right) Swag in bay NC1B, west side of window (Andy Chopping, MOLA)

Fig. 79 Detail of cherub over one of the windows on the north side of the choir, before cleaning (John Schofield)

Fig. 80 Cherub's head above window SN1, before cleaning, January 2007 (Maggie Cox, MOLA)

documentary evidence is that in 1710 Strong was paid for a number of repairs and replacements in the existing masonry. These included making good flawed stones inside the building, above the attic and in the great dome arches; but also outside. Here he had to mend the carving of the eight window heads in the 'N & S Cross', that is the transepts.[176] The stone inserts observed in the cherubs on both sides of the choir might be from a similar programme of repair and adjustment within the construction programme.

The walls of the nave reached the level of the main cornice in 1695, about 9 years after the equivalent height was reached around the choir.[177] Photographic recording concentrated on the cherubs' heads and swags (Fig. 80). There are also scattered instances of elements being held in with wires, presumably later repairs (eg Fig. 81). Such repairs started before the building was finished, since in 1709 24½ft of copper wire was bought for Edward Strong's 'use to Fix the Repairs of Capitals & other Carvings'.[178]

Swags ('festoons') are a common decoration of classical Roman architecture, for instance the Ara Pacis, and on ordinary sepulchral monuments.[179] They are not a feature of the earliest Renaissance buildings in the 15th century, but they do appear on prominent, palatial houses in Rome and Paris in the first half of the 16th century, such as the Louvre. Swags on churches, almost all on the west front, are found from the 1560s in Vignola's proposed design for the Gesù in Rome. They are often an accompaniment to Corinthian and Composite capitals or pilasters (as at St Paul's), but there are also less commonly cases of swags with Ionic capitals (as at Jones's Lindsey House in Lincoln's Inn Fields, across the capitals). Swags are generally found on the upper parts of facades, highlighting the importance of upper storeys or the higher parts of religious and secular buildings; but on both upper and lower storeys at St Paul's.[180]

In England swags were authorised by their inclusion between the capitals of the upper storey of Jones's Banqueting House (1622). Swags either carved in relief or as part of internal painted decoration were features of notable religious and secular buildings throughout Britain thereafter until the 1720s. They could also be found on carved furniture such as chairs. Swags are to be seen on Wren's Sheldonian Theatre, Oxford

Fig. 81 An example of a wire ?repair to a leaf fragment, from one of the swags (John Schofield)

(1662–3) and in the pediment of Pembroke College Chapel, Cambridge (1663–5). Bradley and Pevsner suggest that 'the wealth of carving [on the exterior of the cathedral] probably grew from Wren's memory of such Parisian buildings as the Great Court of the Louvre and the Hôtel de Sully'.[181] In the City of London, they would have appeared in 1666 if Wren's pre-Fire proposal for a dome over the old medieval building had been carried out; and they did appear on several public buildings of the post-Fire City, that is on churches and buildings of institutions. Wren employed them as part of the grand temple-front design for the east end of St Lawrence Jewry (1671–80) and on the upper floor of his Custom House. Robert Hooke included them in both storeys of the main range of the College of Physicians in Warwick Lane, near the cathedral (1672–8); they were also on the upper storey of Thomas Cartwright's Moorgate of 1672. Thus the cathedral shared these embellishments with a small number of other major public buildings in the post-Fire city; and as they were carved in the years around 1690, the St Paul's swags were later than all the examples on Wren's and Hooke's post-Fire parish churches.

The human or divine face or head between wings, as with the cherubim at St Paul's, can be seen in diverse places such as over windows at S Susanna in Rome (1603), the courtyard of the Hôtel de Sully (1625), and at several points in the interior at Versailles. It appears on walls and plaster ceilings in British houses, including examples recorded in the London area, from the opening of the 17th century; and over all the windows of the nave and transepts of St Paul's as restored by Jones, so it would have been constantly in Wren's view (Jones may have got the idea from seeing churches in Genoa).[182] The apparent need to reset several of the cherubs over the main windows late in the construction programme noted above may indicate that they were a problem, or that they were incorrectly attached in the first place.

***Fig. 82** (top)* *Bay NT3 (east side of N transept); panel below window after cleaning (Andy Chopping, MOLA)*

***Fig. 83** (middle)* *Bay NT4 (north side of north transept): panel below window after cleaning (Andy Chopping, MOLA)*

***Fig. 84** (bottom)* *Bay NT6 (north side of north transept): panel below window after cleaning (Andy Chopping, MOLA)*

The Gibbons panels below the windows

Grinling Gibbons (1648–1721), reputedly discovered by Wren's friend John Evelyn in 1671, was employed carving in stone both inside and outside the cathedral from 1694; and later, in 1697, beginning his work in wood on the choir stalls.[183]

There are 27 carved stone panels below the windows of the cathedral. Twenty-six, that is all but one, were carved by Gibbons between September 1694 and May 1695.[184] One further panel, that beneath the window of the Consistory Court at the south-west end of the building, was carved by Jonathan Maine in 1701.[185] It contains the bishop's arms, presumably an allusion to the function of the Court. An eloquent account of the panels was provided by David Green in his study of Gibbons in 1964. Even when seen from bus-top level, as Green proposed, they showed much skill and a surprising delicacy beneath the thick coating of grime. Closer up and walking round, one noticed that

> 'these panels, are, with three exceptions [the William and Mary panel outside the apse and the two westernmost panels] in pairs, each panel on the north having an almost identical twin on the south; and that all are brief sermons in stone or at

least reminders of the virtues, the patron saint of the cathedral, the Dean and Bishop and the monarchs who caused or encouraged it to be built... The two panels with bibles kept open by crossed swords (of the spirit) echo the statue of St Paul with sword and book, by Francis Bird... The cardinal virtues are more or less easily recognised by their attributes: the scales and sword of Justice, the mirror of Prudence, the flaming heart of Fortitude. Temperance may be the dove vanquishing the serpent or possibly the two doves perched upon but turning away from cornucopiae. The lesser virtues of Innocence and Purity are hinted at by singing children and by Madonna lillies in a cartouche; while at the east the passer-by is again reminded of self-sacrifice by the pelican in her piety, a device repeated on the outside of the apse and yet again, in wood, within the choir.'[186]

The examples here from the photographs taken in 2008–11 are of the bays around the east and north sides of the north transept and along the north side of the nave, going west, from bay NT3, that is the east face of the transept: bays NT3, NT4 and NT6 (Fig. 82–Fig. 84). The present work does no more than draw attention to their now cleaned state and the existence of a photographic survey which resides in archive, awaiting appropriate scholarship.

The royal arms in the pediment of the north transept
The royal arms of William in the pediment of the north transept were carved by Grinling Gibbons (Fig. 85–Fig. 87; being photographed, Fig. 233 below). In July–September 1698 he was paid £120 for 'carving a bas-relieve on ye N pediment, being 18ft long and 9ft high, with Two Angells, being 8ft figures and 18 inches thick, with a Lyon and Unicorne and the King's Arms and Crowne'.[187] The royal arms are a rare occurrence of the arms of William alone, since Mary had died in 1694. He thereafter used his own arms, which were identical to those of William and Mary except that the escutcheon of Nassau was added in the middle, as here.

Fig. 85 The royal arms in the pediment on the north transept, cleaned (Andy Chopping, MOLA)

Fig. 86 The royal arms in the pediment of the north transept, details of supporters on the left, cleaned (Andy Chopping, MOLA)

Fig. 87 The royal arms, the supporters on the right, cleaned (Andy Chopping, MOLA)

Statuary
In 1711, when estimating the cost of works not yet done or unfinished, Wren mentions that 'statues to the three pedaments' had been proposed.[188] All the original statues on the pediments were by Francis Bird. In 1718–21 statues were added to the elevation of the west front. At the lower corner of the two towers, are the four Evanglists, Matthew (with angel), Mark (with lion), Luke (with ox) and John (with eagle), all shown seated and writing in books. On the pediment are three standing figures, of St Peter on the north, St James on the south and St Paul in the middle. Five statues were added to the north transept in 1720–4; they are of St Barnabas, St Philip, St James the Less, St Jude and St John the Baptist. Five statues were also originally placed on the south transept, but the three central ones are replacements of 1898: St Thomas, St Andrew and St Bartholomew. At the outer corners, two

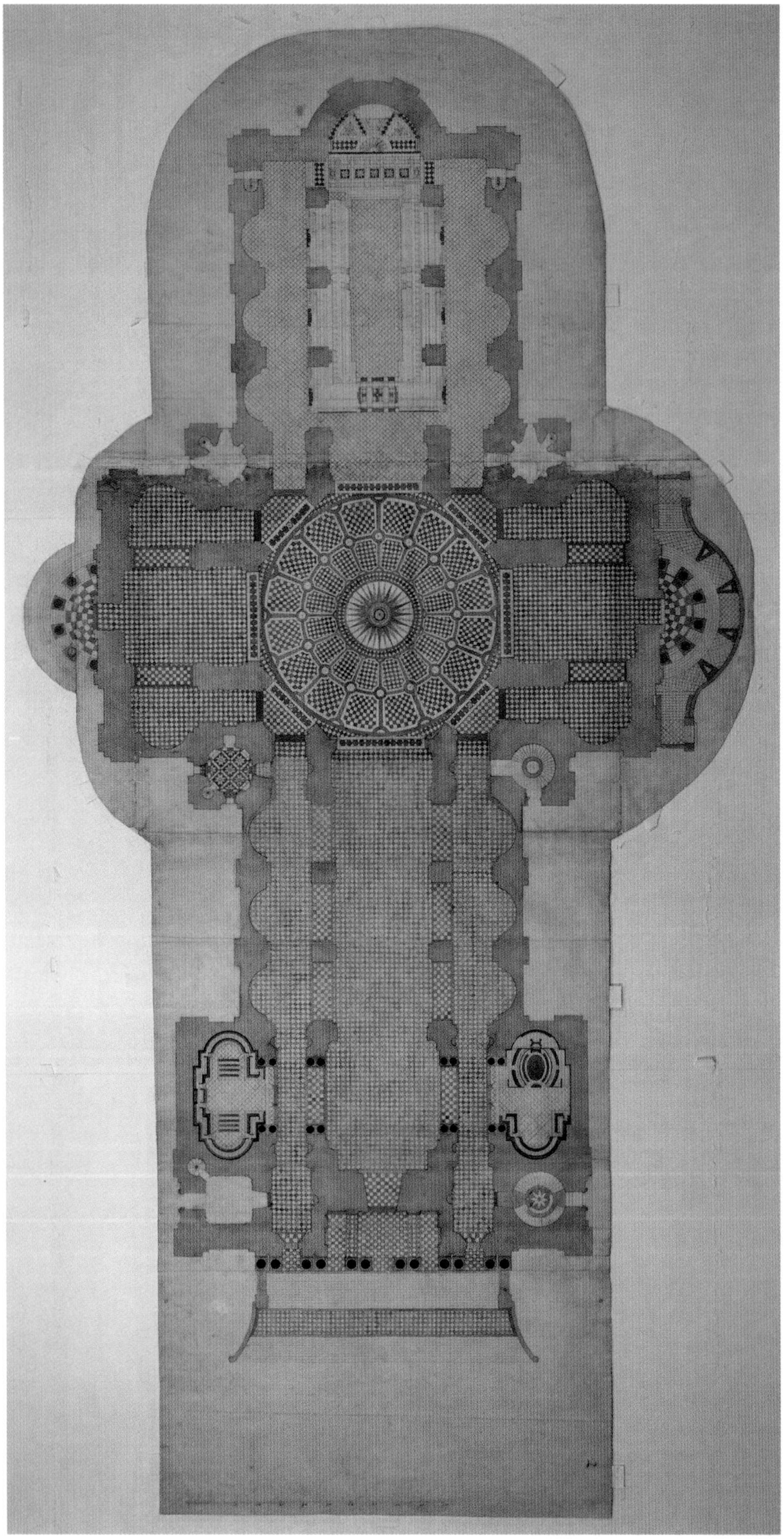

Fig. 88 Floorplan of the cathedral by William Dickinson, 1709–10 (LMA, WRE/7/2/7, © Chapter of St Paul's Cathedral and LMA). This is probably a final stage design rather than a record of what was achieved

of Bird's originals of 1722–4 remain, St Simon and St Matthias.[189]

St Paul's was the only (and therefore, also, the first) building in the immediately post-Fire City of London to have statues along its roofline, though to be more exact they were in three groups, on the west end and the two transepts. Statues at intervals along the balustrade were included in Wren's projects for Hampton Court in 1689 and Whitehall in 1698; there seem to have been statues on the entrance bay of Montagu House in Bloomsbury of 1687 and on the balustrade at Buckingham House in Westminster of 1702–5, the latter by William Winde. The more numerous statues at St Paul's would have stood out on the skyline and would have been another unusual feature of the new building.

Internal decoration and the church floor, 1680–1711

In 1898 Somers Clarke thought that the joints of the internal masonry are larger and coarser than those of the external masonry, indicating that painting of the interior was intended from the start.[190] Little is known about the initial painted decoration of the cathedral interior, and until recently all the paint evidence appeared to have been removed by later restorations and cleanings.[191] Grey or stone-coloured paint, as used by Inigo Jones in the previous cathedral, covered the walls up to the cornice by 1710, and the apse had gold highlights on the mouldings.[192] Here mason Samuel Fulkes had laid 'vained marble block' in the paving under the altar.[193] In 1822 C R Cockerell, the Surveyor, discovered that the pilasters at the east end of the choir, then painted to imitate Sienna marble, had originally been painted blue in imitation of lapiz lazuli; and he insisted that the pilasters be painted blue.[194]

According to John Evelyn the first proper sermon was preached (it would have been in the choir) on 5 June 1698.[195] Engravings of 1703 and 1706 show the choir, dominated by a screen at the west end which had a large organ upon it, obscuring the view of the choir and altar from the nave until it was removed in 1862.[196] The construction of the choir and other furnishings are discussed in the online catalogue of Wren drawings at St Paul's by Higgott, and drawings in the All Souls collection are discussed by Geraghty; there are many drawings of proposed choir fittings by Hawksmoor in collaboration with Gibbons, split between the two collections.[197] But there is as yet no modern study of the carpentry or the extent of repairs over the centuries, which included their removal one bay to the west by Penrose and temporary removal of decorations during World War II. The fitting out of the Morning Prayer Chapel, Consistory Court and Library are also described in the 2004 history.[198]

There is a remarkable floorplan of the completed cathedral by William Dickinson dating to 1709–10 (Fig. 88). This shows two different designs or patterning of the marble paving: for the public areas of the nave and transepts, black and white stones alternated, whereas for reserved areas, that is the choir, morning prayer chapel at the north west and consistory court at the south-west, the flooring was only of white stones. The plan is the only record of the interior of the Consistory Court at the west end before that was dismantled in 1858.[199] It also shows the original arrangement of the choir stalls and choir screen, before the changes of the 1860s by Penrose, and the original design of the circular motif beneath the dome, which was laid by Edward Strong junior in 1709.[200] The plan is not strictly accurate; the tiles or paviours in the nave and aisles are shown by Dickinson laid square, on the axis of the building, whereas they were actually laid in the same year of 1709 turned 45°.

There are differences between some of the patterning of tiles in the apse and the first bay of the choir. In this narrow bay the drawing shows a paving scheme similar to that in a sketch half-plan of the bay and apse by Hawksmoor at All Souls.[201] In the finished work, Wren dispensed with the narrow rectangles at the ends and used six squares containing star motifs. This is shown in Trevitt's view of the service on 31 December 1706 and Lens and Kip's view of the early 18th century. We do not have sufficiently accurate information on the original paving in the apse.[202]

Frequent repairs to small areas of the cathedral floor over three centuries, and substantial interventions such as the raising of the choir floor by Penrose, mean that it may now be impossible to identify areas where the original floor is intact (apart from the special work under the dome). Even when relaid or reused, however, the original black and white stones may retain their original bedding mortar. During small-scale alterations at the south-east end of the choir in 2014 for an incoming artwork by the video artist Bill Viola, a temporarily removed triangular paviour was found to have mortar containing partial and even whole oyster shells (Fig. 89). Though research

Fig. 89 Underside of a marble floor tile or paviour from the south-east corner of the choir, disturbed and relaid in 2014, showing mortar with oyster shells (John Schofield)

would have to be undertaken to confirm this, the character of the mortar suggests it is original. If so, this would have been part of the marble flooring of the east end of the choir, for which Strong was being paid in the first half of 1697.[203]

The ironwork

The many kinds of original ironwork still in the structure of the Wren building are an unresearched topic and only a couple of points will be suggested here. The ironwork of Jean Tijou, added from 1693 to 1708, takes many forms inside and outside the cathedral: window frames, stair rails, the railing at cornice level at the west end, panels in the screens between main vessel and aisles in the choir, the altar rail, choir gates, the balcony to the Whispering Gallery, the copper finial on the north-west tower and the original railing around the statue of Queen Anne, west of the building.[204] Tijou's gates to the choir of 1696, having been removed by Penrose when the choir screen was dismantled, were incorporated into the present screens between the choir and north choir aisle by Bodley and Garner in 1890.[205]

Another piece by Tijou in the public area of the cathedral is the railing at the west end of the nave, above the cornice and for a short distance eastwards along the north and south sides. Tijou was paid in 1707 'for fine ironwork in ye Balcony at W. End, comprising 135ft of panels' interspersed with 15ft of pilasters.[206] As the nave is 48ft (14.6m) wide, as is the east–west diameter of the large western bay, this allows for the west end and 43ft 6in (13.3m) of each of the sides of the bay to be railed. The Tijou railing would therefore stretch up to and stand in front of the two high doorways in the nave walls opening into the triforia behind; as it does today (and in 1896, Fig. 117). This extent of the Tijou railing only along the sides of the large western bay is shown in early views of the nave.[207] The railing

Fig. 90 A wrought-iron casement window in the south triforium, showing the original catch and stay (Graham Lacdao, © Chapter of St Paul's Cathedral)

design incorporates leaves, and panels alternately with a mitre and censer. The mitre is only in the section along the west end gallery, north to south. Thus the railing at the west end of the building, on the entablature, went with the two doorways into the nave space from the triforia, forming a narrow viewing gallery at the west end of the church and along the sides of the large western bay. These higher public viewing places were used on public occasions such as services attended by the monarch.

There are similar Wren-period railings across the openings of the quarter domes around the crossing, showing that these spaces were also seen as potential public viewing spaces. But these are attributed to the other major provider of ironwork, Thomas Robinson, who is less well-known than Tijou. From 1697 to 1715 Robinson supplied ironwork for the cathedral and the new chapter house. The structural items made by him include the railings in the quarter domes, chains for the dome, the railing still present in front of St Dunstan's Chapel, and a number of windows at high level, including a total of 84 'windows' for the dome. It seems that Robinson and another smith, Thomas Coalburne, supplied many of the window frames with their fastenings which survive along the north and south triforia and above the vestries, which would pay further research (Fig. 90).[208]

Repairs during construction; the small piers in the crypt

From September 1707 to July 1708 there are monthly items in the accounts referring to William Kempster, with up to 24 other masons, working 'in the vaults'. In the account for 1708 this work is described as 'masons worke done in repairing severall Flaws in the Vaults, and Cutting way to hang doors'.[209] It seems likely that the vaults of the crypt are meant here, rather than the vaults of the nave or aisle ceilings, for which the world *vaulting* is occasionally but rarely used. This work by Kempster (which may have extended beyond the crypt and continued into 1709) was evidently what modern builders call 'snagging': final touches, mostly of a cosmetic nature, to the structure. The flooring of the crypt with tiles followed in 1709.

Other repairs were clearly after subsidence of parts of the structure. In December 1709 masons were paid for substantial repairs to the higher parts of walls in the central part of the church, 'repairing the Flaws occasioned by the presure, Making good such Stones as could be left remaining with Lead and Plaster, being the 8 Leggs of the Dome, & in the Inside, of the E, W, N & S Walls of ye N. & S. Cross, being above 1,500 foot in Periphery'. Further notices of repairs because of fractures occur in the accounts until June 1711.[210] Despite these repairs, unlevel courses of Portland can be seen in places such as on the west side of the wall running south from the south-west pier, at high level just below the roof, in the present Surveyor's Office above the south transept. Repairs because of subsidence after 1711 are noted in Chapter 3.

As shown by Poley's plan of the crypt (Fig. 91), the two piers at the entrance to the choir crypt (to the east of the Nelson chamber) are different in plan from the other six piers beneath the nave and the transepts. Immediately east of the two piers is a north–south corridor of two rows of slim pillars, forming a kind of vestibule to what is now the OBE Chapel beneath the rest of the choir. There is no clear structural reason for these two rows of piers, but they are positioned directly below the location of the original choir screen. Perhaps they were meant to prop the vault and carry the load of the screen above.[211]

The drainage system for the site, 1687–1710

Twelve years after building started, a comprehensive permanent drainage system was developed and connected to a public sewer which ran down Ludgate Hill on the west. Several branches went round both sides of the cathedral and beneath parts of it. Large parts of the system survive today, the brick and stone channels used for modern pipes, whereas other parts have been blocked

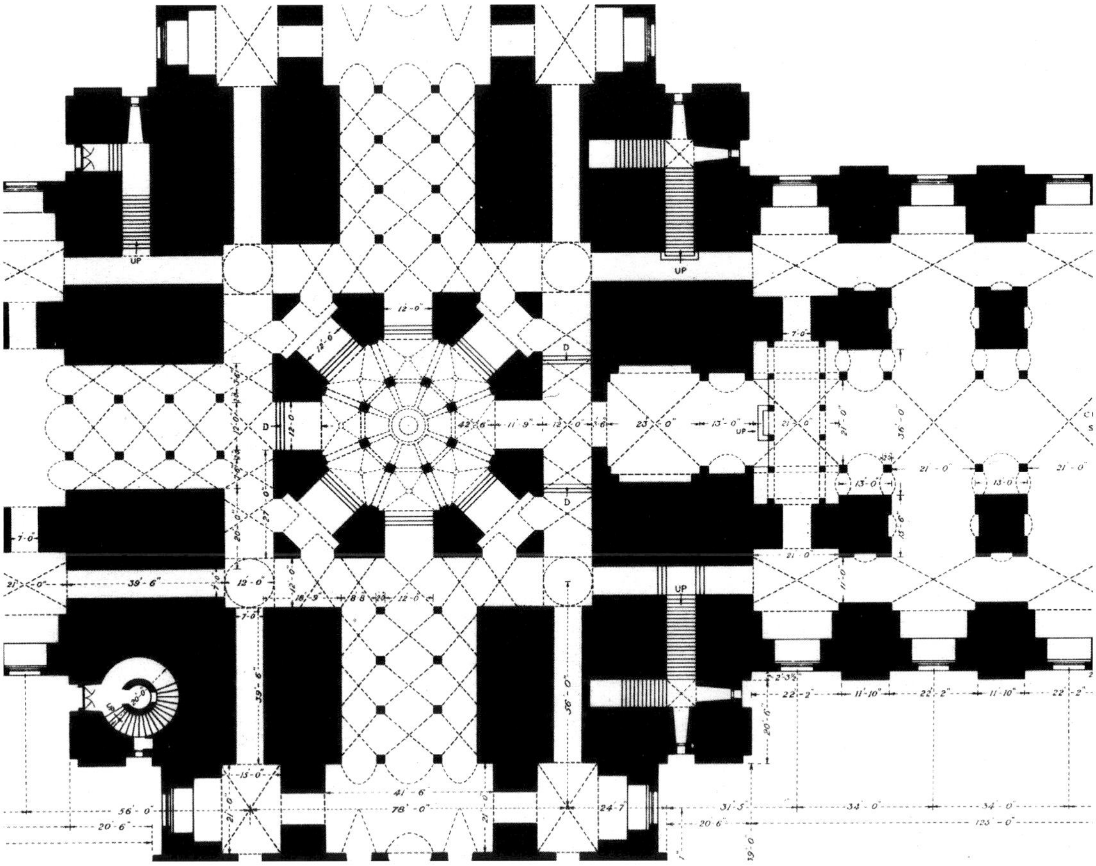

Fig. 91 Extract from the plan of the crypt by Poley (1927, pl. xxii), showing the crypt piers around the Nelson chamber, and the north–south corridor or vestibule for what is now the OBE Chapel (two bays in from the right-hand side). Wellington's tomb is in the chamber west of that, to the left

off and are no longer used. Although parts of the system have been recorded archaeologically or observed, there is no detailed archaeological dating for those parts seen. It is clear that the main drainage system was laid after nearly all the foundations had been dug, and two of its four arms run beneath the building towards the west end. The system was intended to draw water from the roof of the cathedral via vertical shafts ('water holes' in the accounts) in the walls.

A plan of the cathedral with the main drains, drawn by Wren and presumably a plan of the proposal, survives at All Souls College; a date of *c.* 1685–7 has been proposed for it.[212] It differs in detail from the configuration of drains eventually dug. The finished drainage system is shown on a surveyed plan of the completed cathedral of 10 May 1710, with the drains, the original line of the railings, and other contemporary details (Fig. 92, Fig. 93). This plan, which is unpublished, is signed by William Dickinson; there is no documentation in cathedral records to go with it.

In April 1687 is the first payment to bricklayers 'for making the new drain from Ludgate up to the W. end of the old church'. This connected with a drain made by the City 'on the other side Ludgate' which no doubt refers to the city gate; the new length of drain was paved over where it lay beneath the street itself. In August the carpenters were paid for 'covering the drains made on the N. and S. sides of the E. end', so perhaps the main drains there had been dug also, but there is no perceptible payment for the bricklayers for work at the east end. The mason Edward Strong, concerned at the time with the foundations of the north-west chapel, worked and set much Portland ashlar in the sides of the drain and Portland Block along its base, but the construction of the drain was mostly done by bricklayers, who built the sides and the arched roof.[213]

Several branches at the west end of the church are mentioned, and have been labelled A–D here (Fig. 93). A north branch (A) was brought through the new foundation of the west wall in October 1687, and a south branch (C) brought 'into the vaults of the church'.[214] In September 1688, as the west end of the crypt neared completion, the bricklayers were paid for both 'making a drain to carry the water out of the vaults to the common shore [the main drain

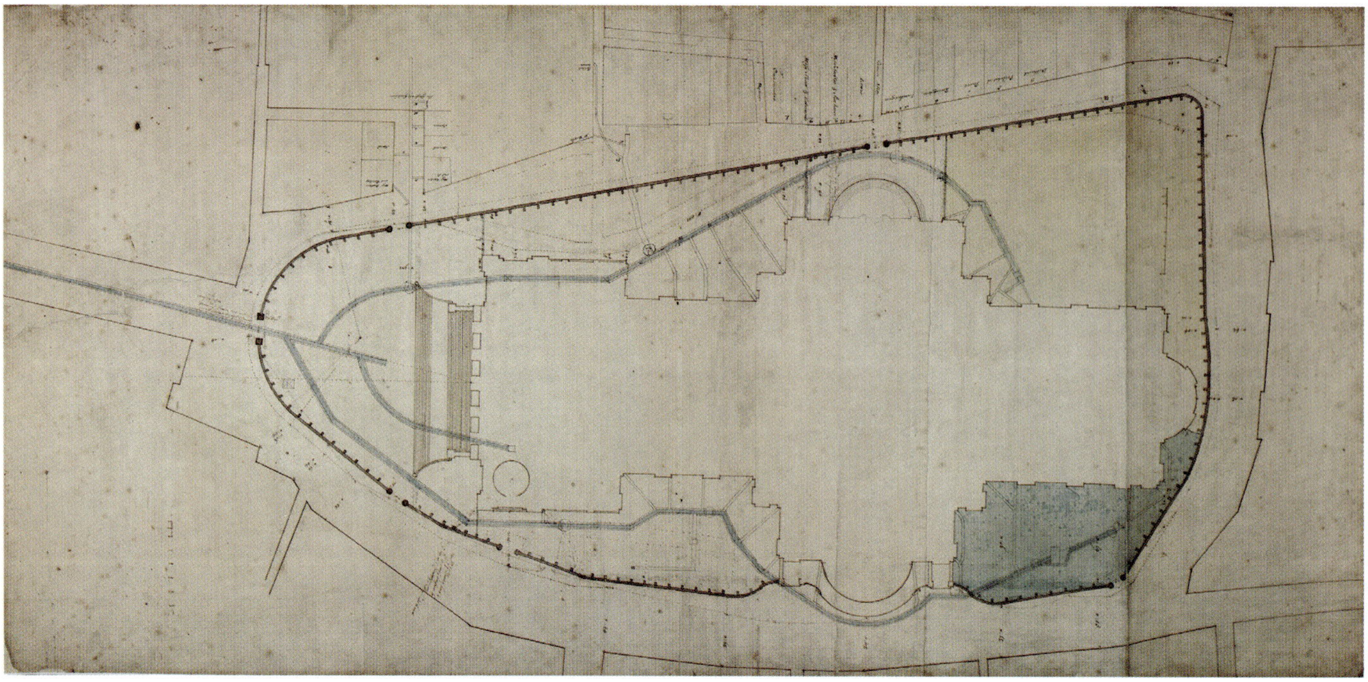

Fig. 92 Plan of 10 May 1710 (LMA, WRE/7/2/3,© Chapter of St Paul's Cathedral and LMA)

Fig. 93 Redrawing of the plan of 10 May 1710 (Carlos Lemos, MOLA, from a tracing in SPCAA). Key: (1) alignment of railings in 1710, with original gates; (2) original position of St Faith's parish pump; (3) drain connected to Chapter House (not seen in any recent investigations, and probably destroyed); (4) drains connected to buildings in London Yard. G1–G8: positions of the original gates. A–D: branches of the drainage system, as described in the present text. The locations of recent archaeological sightings of the drain system have been added; the two points C(1) and C(2) are the two separate sightings on Site C (the first a temporary drain, the second part of the permanent system); points H(1) and H(2) are two separate sightings on Site H

on Ludgate Hill] in the middle of the vaulting', which presumably refers to a drain connecting with the middle of the crypt (presumably branch B, apparently later blocked), and 'bringing on the drain from the W. end to the E. part of the vaulting under the N. Chapell'; in other words, constructing a length of the northern branch from one end of the basement of the north chapel to the other (as found on Site E). In November 1688 labourers had dug a second southern branch (D), this time outside the building as represented by its new foundations.

In January and February 1689 carpenters made 'Hooges' (presumably some kind of centering) for the bricklayers 'to turn over their drain at the W. end and N. portico' as well as shoring the drain by the portico which they had just dug. This indicates that the exterior length of drain, from the east side of the north-west chapel around the north portico (the continuation of A), was dug in a new and particular trench, since by this time the main body of the cathedral was constructed nearly to the eaves. The digging of this length of drain produced 72 skeletons; where they were taken is not recorded, but holes had been dug west of the west end for other human remains. Thereafter smaller drains were dug to connect the various 'waterholes' with the two main external drains. More drain-runs round the building to the north and east of the church, with the smaller drains which connected with the rainwater shafts, were being dug in 1690, 1691, 1695 and 1699.[215] The bricklayer most involved in 'turning over' or vaulting lengths of the drain was Richard Billinghurst. He was paid for the construction of a length of drain from the north portico to the west end in April–June 1699; this part was seen in 1969 and 1994.[216] The main part of the drain around the south side of the church, extending branch D, seems to date from early 1696, 7 years after the one on the north side; this was recorded at Site H in 2006.

Branch A has been seen in three places. At Site A the Wren drain is noted on plans (Fig. 31 above). At Site B this branch of the drain was briefly observed, about 1.6m north of the crypt wall. It was constructed of red brick walls about 0.7m apart and at least 0.95m high, capped here by large flat stone lintels (possibly later, as it contained a ceramic drain pipe, probably inserted by Penrose). At Site E, branch A of the Wren drain crossed the site from east to west. It consisted of a rounded arched culvert, still in use with a modern sewer pipe running its length along the base. Slight differences in construction along the observed section may have been original or may also reflect later repairs. As a length of 20m was recorded, the fall of the drain could also be noted, as about 1 in 40 falling down from east to west.

Branch B, apparently truncated or stopped just before the western steps, has not been recorded in the present group of excavations (investigation of the main branch to the west, going down Ludgate Hill, is recounted below). Branch C was noted at Site C, but only the flagstones of its top observed. This is also dated to 1687, when bricklayers were paid for 'bringing the Draine on the S. side into the Vaults of the Church to carry the water thence.'[217]

The fourth main branch of the system, branch D, lies outside the cathedral on the south side. This was observed in Gibb-Freeman testpits H (Fig. 200, Site 61) and M (not illustrated, see Site 63). The north side of the drain, with part of one of the buttresses for it, was recorded.[218] At this point the top of the drain is only about 1.8m below the present ground surface. It was also briefly recorded during the landscaping works at Site H during 2006. One example of the recording of the drain is given here in the main text (from Site F) and the others are in the gazetteer. The junction between the Wren drain and the Corporation sewer was the scene of the small shaft excavation at Site F in 2000, to improve the connection after the construction of public toilets in the crypt in 1994.

The Wren drain here (Fig. 197, Fig. 198) was very similar to the section of culvert exposed within the crypt of the cathedral in 1998 (Site E). The crypt example was constructed with the same size and type of bricks and the bonding material in both cases was hard, pale grey, chalky mortar. The arched shape was of similar proportions and part of it had a double thickness of bricks laid in the same fashion as the exterior culvert. The differences were due to the fact that the interior crypt culvert ran through stone footings and beneath the crypt floor. Part of it was stone walled and the excavated section, while entirely of brick, was smaller than the exterior culvert because the crypt floor had been lowered above it. The exterior culvert also needed to be larger as it carried the combined drainage from the two main culverts issuing from the cathedral.

Comprehensive drainage schemes had been part of royal and archiepiscopal palaces since the early 16th century, such as at Eltham, and the system at Baynard's Castle in the City south of St Paul's itself, while no doubt including drains into the river, seems to have included a vaulted stone drain on the north side, impinging into the contemporary Thames Street. A system of large brick drains leading to the Thames was also constructed by Archbishop Thomas Parker (1559–75) at Lambeth Palace.[219] It is likely that the technology of drainage schemes, and the increasing use of brick as the main construction material, was developed in the Tudor and Stuart royal palaces. Roger North, writing his notes *Of Building* in 1698, thought it still necessary to argue that covered brick drains were better than open drains, and commended Wren's inclusion of the former at the Royal Military Hospital in Chelsea. Nearly 300ft (97.5m) of brick drains had been installed during Wren's building of the new Privy Gallery at Whitehall Palace in 1686, expressly for the rainwater pipes, as at the cathedral a year later.[220] There may be parallels in construction which could be drawn between the contemporary works at the Palace and the cathedral. Archaeological studies of drainage schemes beneath other large British buildings of the 17th century seem to be lacking.

The railings and gates around the cathedral

This discussion is in two parts. In this first section the initial history, likely appearance and positions of the railings and gates, up to about 1720, is considered. The matter of a fence or wall around the cathedral, with gates, would be one of the last things decided upon, since the building site was restricted in area and its temporary fence was frequently altered and moved. One of the earliest permanent items were gates at the foot of the steps of the south portico. In 1699 Jean Tijou was paid 'for a pair of Great Gates at the W side of the S. Portico with a Wicket, framed of strong Iron, with Ornaments and Points on the top'.[221] The reference to the 'W side' only may be a slip in the accounts, as the two gates are still there, but flank the portico on either side (Fig. 94), between incense pots originally by Gabriel Cibber (those on the east gate are replicas of the 1970s). [222] This embellished double entrance into the cathedral would have stood for at least thirteen years before the gates were joined by the railings to east and west. They are called Gates 5 and 6 in an overall scheme of all the gates to be discussed shortly.

Fig. 94 One of the two iron gates at the south portico by Tijou (John Schofield)

On 28 January 1710 it was resolved by the Commissioners for building St Paul's that 'the fence around the church be of cast and turned iron-work'. The fence was to go round (ie sweep to the west of) the statue of Queen Anne which by now stood west of the cathedral; a separate rail to enclose the statue (no longer surviving, but shown in engravings) would be designed separately. A loose baluster of iron was to be kept at the cathedral as a standard. Richard Jones, the contractor, put up a trial section of fence and a gate which gained approval in February 1711. The fence used 207 tons of iron, and Jones was finally paid in 1717.[223] Wren wanted the fence to be made of wrought ('hammered') iron, not cast iron.[224] He also objected that the design and execution of the railings had been taken from him, and thus he was not responsible for them.[225] The design of the railings is much simpler than that of the wrought iron gates of Tijou, for instance at the south transept, which had preceded them by a number of years. Gervase Jackson-Stops has remarked that the replacement of Tijou (who had left England by 1712) by Robinson, and the dismissal of Wren and Hawksmoor from the Office of Works 'in favour of the incompetent Palladians, William and Benjamin Benson' were connected to the revolution in taste and politics after the death of Queen Anne in 1714; taste had been changing towards the Italian from 1708.[226] The legacy of this change is the difference in appearance between the Tijou gates and the railings. In addition, though the railings may now seem to be almost mundane, they were an innovation, a new item in the street. There

Fig. 95 North front of St Paul's by Thomas Malton, c. 1800 (BM, 1880,1113.3301, © The Trustees of the British Museum)

are no known instances of iron railings on pre-Fire London buildings. The railings at St Paul's were one of the cathedral's new and fashionable features, the nearest comparison being royal palaces and some of the noble houses in the squares west of the City.[227]

The foundation for the wall which was to support the iron fence began to be dug in March 1710. In at least one stretch it incorporated 'bricks from the old houses', but generally it was of rubble. Even so there was at least one batch of 182,500 new place bricks specifically bought for the 'fence wall foundation' in 1711. The accounts suggest that brick arches were only used beneath the fence when thought appropriate, because the bricklayer Billinghurst would be brought in to make them, for instance the section which crossed the site of the old chapter house, 'greatest part being arched', for which he was paid in 1713. During this operation he also pulled down the old wall which surrounded the church, presumably the wall of the building site.[228] The construction of the new railings with their foundation along the south side of the cathedral must also have required the demise of the site office and the old chapter house.

The railings round St Paul's have been called the first recorded cast iron railings in England.[229] It is clear from study of the maps and other plans that the railings which surround most of the cathedral today are almost nowhere on their original alignments, though in places moved only by centimetres. To reconstruct the original alignments of the railings, and the locations of original gates (with what that meant for access to the cathedral and comparatively quiet areas of graveyard), it is necessary to start with the plan of 1710 by Dickinson (Fig. 92), even though this might not be the final scheme, exactly as built. For the original appearance of the railings, the sources are engravings, archaeological sightings, and the present form. Various views of the 18th and early 19th centuries, for instance that of the Wren Chapter House (Fig. 101) and those of the exterior of the cathedral by Malton (Fig. 39; Fig. 95; but he consistently omits the gates), show the general appearance of the railings, but with small differences when compared to the plan of 1710. One view of 1753 or possibly earlier from the north-west shows details not on the other views or plans (Fig. 96).

The railings were originally on a plinth or low wall which was about 2ft (0.6m) higher than that seen today; the wall was lowered by Penrose in

Fig. 96 View of the cathedral from the north-west of 1753 or earlier (this copy of 1794) in John Bowles's catalogue Perspective views in and about London, artist unknown (BM, 1880, 1113.3298, © The Trustees of the British Museum). This view shows lamps on the railings

1879. A higher wall can be seen in paintings of the funerals of Nelson and Wellington, where the top of the wall is at the height of the hips of adjacent soldiers;[230] but in the early engravings and Canaletto's painting, the wall is shown lower. On the inside, the wall had protrusions supporting the bay divisions of the railings, and perhaps occasional lamps hanging above, according to Figure 96 (but not on other engravings). What was very probably the foundation for the wall for the railings was noted as it crossed Site A in 1969 (Fig. 196). The foundation was 4ft 6in (1.37m) wide, and composed of brick arches with an approximate span of 8ft (2.44m). The foundation piers for the arches were of rubble. The foundation of the wall has been seen recently at two sites dug just outside the present railings, for works by Thames Water on water mains (Sites 86 and 87).

The Dickinson plan shows eight gates (numbered G1–8 on Fig. 93 by this study) in the railings. Gates 1–3 formed a trio serving the west end, with Gate 2 being the main gate to the cathedral (it had square posts whereas the other gates had smaller round posts on the plan). This is shown in an engraving by Parr after Schwertfüger, in 1747 (Fig. 97); which also shows a paved walk from the gate to the statue of Queen Anne. But

Fig. 97 The west front and the main gate in the railings (Gate 2) by Schwertfüger, engraved by R. Parr, 1747 (WS XIV, pl. xxxiv)

this was rather idealised, as the gate was a little to the north (as shown on the plan).

There is evidence of a first configuration of the railings at the south end of the steps, later superseded. In the drawings at All Souls is one of the western steps of 1710, with a circular area of railings entered by a gate at the south end (Fig. 98). Why this should be so, apparently just to give access to the door into the vault below the stairs, is not apparent. This could be taken as a proposal, except that Penrose excavated and recorded what must be the foundation for the circular railing wall of 'stone and chalk' but perhaps with some brick buttressing during his changes to the steps in 1873 (Fig. 99). This local feature must have been superseded by the building of the railings after 1710.

Gate 4, at the Dean's Door at the south-west tower, may not be shown correctly by Dickinson in his plan (or Dickinson's plan does not show the final details). As shown in Parr's engraving of the west end of 1747 (Fig. 97) and in many engravings of the south side (for instance Fig. 100), the railings seem rather to have curved inwards from east and west to form an entrance to the Dean's Door. The eastern of these two curvings was already intended on the plan of the west end of February 1710 (Fig. 30), also by Dickinson, which must have been of a previous configuration proposal, where the railings would run tightly round the steps. Sometime during the 18th century the inward-turning sections of railings outside the Dean's Door were removed and the railing became straight.[231] Although it is not shown in several engravings of this section (for instance, a view of 1798 in Fig. 148), a gate may have been retained, since an opening in the railing with a step to the street at this point is shown in the Ordnance Survey map of 1873–4 (Fig. 149).

Gates 5–7, along the south side of the cathedral, are shown in other engravings, for instance that of 1743 by Paul Fourdrinier (Fig. 100). Gates 5 and 6 were at the south portico, and have already been mentioned. Originally they each led only down from the portico to the street, and there was no access from the podium of the portico to the churchyard on either side. This original configuration (to be altered by Penrose in the 19th century) is shown in the cathedral floor plan of 1709–10 (Fig. 88) and several plans of the cathedral in the 18th century.[232]

Gate 7, at the south-east corner of the enclosure of railings, is shown in Dickinson's plan (and in detail below, Fig. 151). It led to the burial vault of St Gregory's parish, south of the choir, and that may have been its original main purpose, to facilitate arrangements after funerals. Gate 8 was outside the north transept, closer to the transept than today. I have not conducted any research into the fabric of the present railings or gates, so the extent of original ironwork (ie the railings which are not replacements) is unknown but is presumably substantial.

In the original arrangement and intention, there was no equivalent of the later and present gate to the churchyard from Cheapside at the

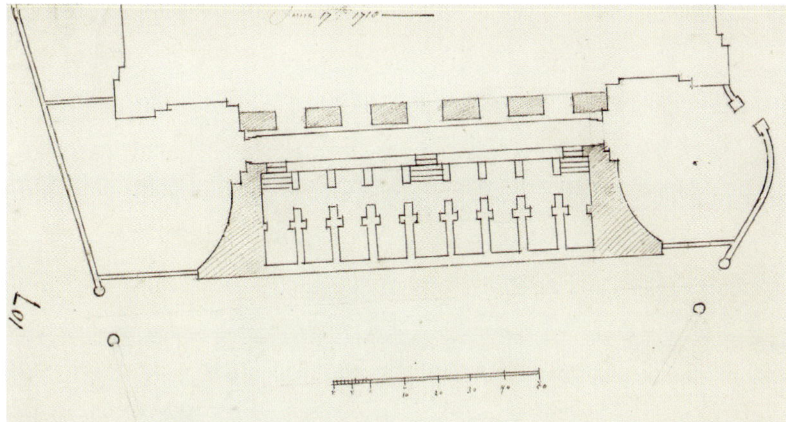

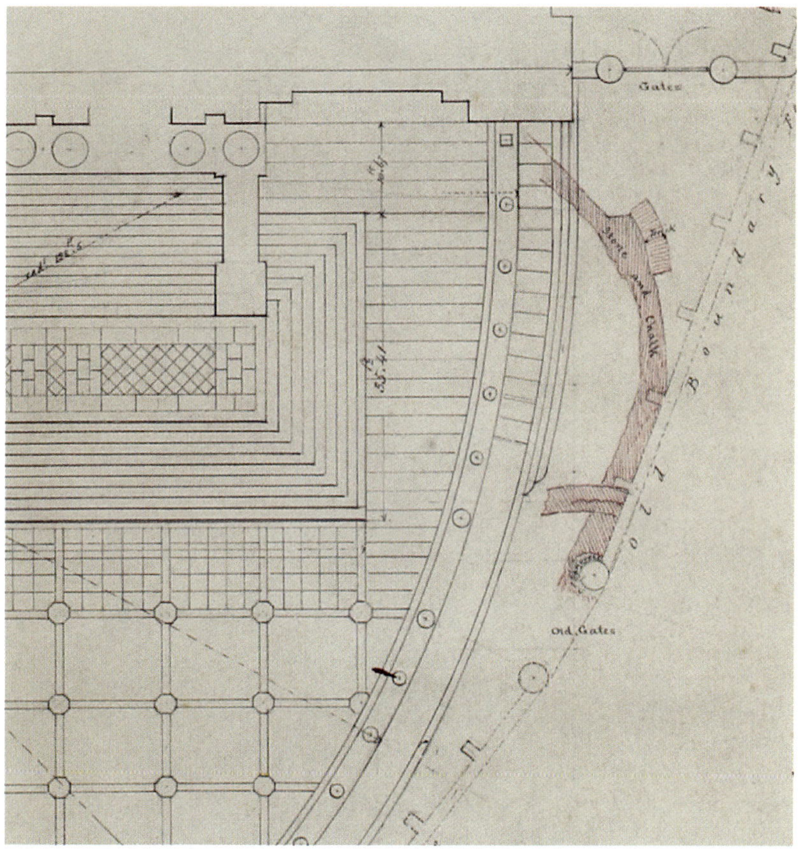

Fig. 98 (top) Plan of the west stairs dated June 17th 1710, drawn by William Dickinson (AS I.107; Geraghty 2007, 84)

Fig. 99 (bottom) Extract from plan by Penrose of 1879, showing a stone and chalk foundation south of the new steps found by him in 1873, clearly that shown by Dickinson in 1710 (SPCAA, D/1/9/6)

Fig. 100 St Paul's from the south-east, by Paul Fourdrinier, 1743 (WS XIV, pl. xliv)

north-east corner. The graveyard of St Faith's parish, north-east of the cathedral, did not merit a gate in the railings until decades after burial had ceased, when Penrose inserted the present north-east gate. The north-east churchyard was a reserved area with no paths through it which became the main graveyard for tombs and ledgers. The railings bordered the east end of the church closely, as there was the street outside to the east, so movement around the east end of the cathedral would have been discouraged. Gate 8 lay outside the north transept, roughly on the site of the gate there today in the post-War alignment of the north railings.

This concludes the description of the Wren cathedral and its churchyard within the railings in the initial period of construction, up to about 1720.

Buildings around the edge of the Churchyard, and the Deanery

The Wren Chapter House

The new Chapter House (Fig. 101), on the site of the cleared group of houses north of the nave, was built in 1712–14, from the contractors' bills in the building accounts.[233]

Fig. 101 (below left) Wren Chapter House (1714): south side, engraved by John Harris (1756–1846); possibly adapting an earlier engraving by Nathaniel Parr. It also shows the original form of the railings around the cathedral, on their buttressed wall (WS XIV, pl. liv)

Fig. 102 (below right) The Wren Chapter House in 1941 (LMA). This shows an attic storey added in 1885 which was removed in the post-War rebuilding

Fig. 103 The Wren Chapter House in 2011 (Andy Chopping, MOLA). This was before the addition of a new attic storey in the refurbishment of 2013–15

Several different types of brick are mentioned: place, stocks (grey) and rubbers. The bricklayer Richard Billinghurst made some vault groins in brick, and these must have been in the basement. The room at the south-west corner of the present basement is vaulted, so a strong room was probably part of the original design. Otherwise the 'naked' flooring above the rest of the basement was originally in oak, with similar flooring in fir on the other two original floors. Edward Strong, mason, fitted stone quoins, chimney-pieces and other details. There were six downpipes, each with the arms of the Dean and Chapter and the date of construction embossed on the hoppers. There are probably blocked features in the main walls which show features of its former internal layout: a plan of 1885 by Penrose in the cathedral archive shows several doorways through the internal walls which are in different places now.[234]

The Chapter House was severely damaged in 1941 (Fig. 102) and rebuilt in 1957 by the Surveyor Godfrey Allen, retaining the external walls (Fig. 103). The external elevation of the foundation of the east end of the building was exposed during the works on Site A in 1969. In 2013–15 the Chapter House was refurbished, with the addition of a new attic floor and insertion of a lift, which produced a small amount of information about the medieval layers beneath, possibly from the hall of the Minor Canons, but no new information on the Wren building.[235]

Other building around the Churchyard, 1668–1700; the Deanery

Ogilby and Morgan's map of 1676 (Fig. 22) shows that the secular surroundings comprising the Churchyard had been almost totally rebuilt by that date, ten years after the Great Fire, and one engraving of the cathedral during construction in 1695 shows the frontage to the Churchyard at the north-east corner (Fig. 37). Further details of the buildings around the cathedral in the years immediately after 1666 can be gleaned from the survey of building sites in the City undertaken by Peter Mills and John Oliver, surveyors to the Corporation. This recorded the staking out of new foundations in the fire-damaged area, comprising much of the intramural City, and the related matter of slips of land taken for road widening.[236] These stakings-out occurred when the owner could arrange it, usually immediately ahead of rebuilding, and thus the redefinition of any particular length of street frontage would proceed sporadically. In this way St Paul's Churchyard was redefined piecemeal between May 1667 and March 1674, with one survey as late as 1677.[237] There is also some evidence of land being laid into the open space of the Churchyard by cutting back

Fig. 104 The post-Fire Deanery, east front (John Schofield)

the frontage; at the south corner of Ludgate Hill with the Churchyard, for instance, the frontage of Ludgate Hill was cut off by between 5ft 6in (1.7m) and 9ft (2.7m).[238] Thus the west end of the new cathedral, whatever form it was to take, was to be made more visible from the west by opening up the approach. By the time of Ogilby and Morgan's map the district included a new butchery market called Newgate Market north of Paternoster Row.

Apart from the Chapter House, the only secular building from this period remaining largely intact today within the boundaries of the pre-Fire Churchyard is the Deanery (Fig. 104), built in 1672–3 by Israel Knowles, carpenter, and the same Thomas Warren, bricklayer, who had built the houses in Amen Court 2 years before (and who was about to build most of the crypt vaulting from 1676). The buildings put up by Knowles and Warren included the main range, a coach house of 2½ storeys, a woodhouse with a gallery over it, a scullery, and the courtyard wall.

Immediately east of the cathedral St Paul's School, re-established by Dean Colet in 1512, was rebuilt after the Fire in 1669–70 on the same site, with slight changes to the extent of the building, to designs of Edward Jerman (shown in 1816 in Fig. 105; its outline is on Ogilby and Morgan's map in 1676 (Fig. 22) and the line of its west façade is on the plan of the cathedral drains of 1710 (Fig. 92). This building was demolished in 1822 and replaced by a Greek Corinthian design of George Smith in 1823–4 (details in the Gazetteer, Site 35). The School moved to Hammersmith in 1884, and its site on the east side of the Churchyard became offices (shown in the background of Birch's view of the south transept published in 1896, Fig. 147).[239]

Thus, in general, it can be said that all the surroundings of the cathedral were built up with new secular buildings by 1675 when the Wren building began. The new Deanery and canons' houses in Amen Court preceded the cathedral; the clergy needed places to live. In large parts of the periphery, the boundaries had been staked out in 1667–71, thus constraining the future building site and Wren's capacity for manoeuvre. In 1676 a street map of the rebuilt city could be bought at Robert Walton's bookshop, advertising itself as being 'just at the west end of St Paul's Church'.[240] This west end would still have been the ruin of the Jones portico and pre-Fire west gable, which would both stand for another 12 years.

Fig. 105 St Paul's School, elevation of west side to Churchyard in 1816 (BM, 1880,1113.3319, © The Trustees of the British Museum)

Use of materials: reused stone, new stone, brick, pantiles and timber

The principal documentary source for the provision and character of building materials for the Wren cathedral is the building accounts of 1668–1714 which have been published by the Wren Society (vols XIII–XVI). The accounts are so voluminous that for the main series which start in 1675, the editors of the Wren Society chose to transcribe the account fully only for one month, the initial month of October 1675, and thereafter to summarise. This means that a large number of names of suppliers of stone and brick, for instance, are omitted from the published accounts, though they could be reconstructed by examination of the original manuscripts in Guildhall Library. The following discussion is based on the published accounts, except where noted.[241]

Reused and new stone

Examination of the interior walls of the Wren crypt shows that there is much reuse of stone from the previous building, mixed with what appears to be new ashlar. But even that distinction cannot be made easily, for two reasons: first, the layers of paint which have been applied to the walls, particularly in the last 150 years as the crypt was brought into more public use, and second, the practice of Wren's workmen of dressing a medieval stone, even with mouldings on it, to present one ashlar face which could then be laid so that the ashlar face was outward, into the crypt. The two medieval mouldings which were cut through by the east end of the tunnel through the west side of the foundation of the south-west tower, to form two linked undercroft rooms, in 1996 were only noticed when cut through, so that their medieval mouldings became evident.[242] Viewed from the front before the cutting of the tunnel, they would be taken as smallish squared ashlars. The foundations of the Wren building have not yet been cut through completely in any part, or their composition of stones comprehensively studied, but at Site G in 2000 a small section of the inner side of the foundation of the east wall of the south transept was exposed, and seen to be largely of reused material, presumably from the medieval building.

The reused stone seems to have been all the geological stone types without distinction, ie Caen, Reigate stone, Kentish ragstone, Taynton, and Portland from Jones's portico.[243] So far no pieces of Purbeck which might be from pre-Fire monuments have been noted in the crypt fabric, but that might be because the area which has been subject to detailed investigation is small. The occurrence of groups of worked medieval stones from the two sites where they have been studied in detail, Sites B and C, suggests that in very broad terms the occurrence of well-defined groups of medieval stones recovered from specific locations in the Wren walls may relate to the demolition of identifable parts of the old building directly before their reuse. Thus the Taynton stones found in the north crypt wall at Site B seem to have come from near the west end of the pre-Fire cathedral; and the stones from Jones's portico were found in the adjacent foundations of the south-west tower at Site C.

By 1675, Portland stone had been the stone of choice for external work on royal or similarly prestigious projects for half a century. Portland had been used by Jones, not only on his extensive refurbishment of the cathedral in 1633–42, but earlier on the Banqueting House in Whitehall. It was also used between 1638 and 1640 on some of the windows on the White Tower (the first of a series of such repairs in Portland which went on into the 19th century), during the Surveyorship of Jones and possibly under his direction.[244] References in the accounts to 'old Portland ashlar' being used especially to line the vertical rainwater shafts (the 'water holes') around the building in 1678 perhaps indicate the reuse of ashlar from Jones's work in these particular but hidden locations.[245] A royal warrant of 1669 regulated the transport of Portland from the quarries in Dorset: in its words, 'in consideration of … the great occasion Wee have of using much of the said Stone both for building and repairing Our Houses and for the repair of St Paul's' all transport was to be authorised by Wren as 'Surveyor of Our Works.'[246] Portland was then supplied, with many transport and other technical problems, until the end of the construction. On two occasions in 1682 some of the blocks are noted as individually weighing six tons;[247] they would then be sawn on site by the masons.

The accounts also demonstrate that stone from the old building was transported off the site for use in other projects, and later rubble was brought in. In 1669, 'rubbish' went out to the Fleet Bridge (perhaps for the quaysides to be erected) and to the new market in Warwick Lane. In 1671, 100 cartloads and two other heaps of ragstone were delivered to the City for use in paving; a further heap went to Scotland Yard for use on royal buildings; much went to the Fleet valley (for general raising of the ground level); and 'freestone' (any fine-grained sandstone or limestone that can be cut or sawn easily) went to parish churches such as St George Botolph Lane and St Michael Wood Street. A load of ragstone from St Faith's church went to help build the Monument. At various points from the middle of the construction period, on the other hand, rubble had to bought in: from Lambeth in 1685, Foster Lane in 1698, from St Mary Aldermary in 1704, and from unknown sites, such as 90 tons in November 1705.[248] In the first case, this was when the dome was in construction; in the second case, the 'rubbish' was brought 'into the vaults', which usually means the crypt; this might have been to help level up the floor of the nave (that of the choir having been finished 10 years before), in anticipation of the final floor of tiles in 1709. This points to the likelihood that scraps of stone and even moulded stones found in layers or walling datable to 1698–1709 may be from other buildings, and therefore nothing to do with the pre-Fire cathedral. Rubble in the wall of the dome may be from other sites in the City, perhaps other churches. Recording and excavation at several post-Fire parish churches has shown that the incorporation of medieval stonework, often carved, as rubble was common.[249]

Several geological types of new stone were employed at St Paul's.[250] Delivery of stone to the wharf in London from October 1675 to August 1710 cost a total of £90,314. Of this, Portland stone accounted for 42%, Burford nearly 24%, 'Headington' 13% and Reigate stone 10%, with the remainder taken up by Kentish ragstone, Beer, Ketton, Caen, Guildford (in that order, by cost) and other stones in smaller quantities.[251] But these sums bear little relation to the amount of each stone used, which has not been quantified in detail; and the Portland was more expensive to freight, as it came by sea (as did the Caen and presumably the Beer stone). On at least one occasion, in 1706, the accounts had to allow for a ship carrying Portland stone, the *Phoenix*, which was taken by a French privateer. The captain, Henry Perry, was taken prisoner but after his return in a group of exchanged prisoners, he went to Rotterdam and bought the ship and its cargo from a merchant to whom it had been sold. The stone was then sold to St Paul's at the cathedral's usual prices.[252] Beer stone from Devon had been specified for use in repairing the medieval cathedral in 1663. New Beer stone must have been used in the foundations, as it arrived on the site in May 1677.[253] Beer cost about one-third the price, per cubic foot, of Portland at least in 1687. A very small amount of stone came from as far away as Tadcaster (Yorks); for a load of 30ft of this stone in 1686, the freight cost as much as the stone.[254] On the other hand, Caen stone, at least in 1687, cost less than Beer stone: 1s 2d per foot as against 1s 6d.[255]

In certain locations the choice of stone was clearly deliberate. Though the majority of the walls and piers were faced with Portland, Beer stone was used for the coffered coved window recesses in the nave aisles.[256] The tawny-coloured pier masses containing tabernacles around the peristyle, which intersperse in every fourth bay with the columns of Portland, are in Ketton stone from near Stamford in Lincolnshire. It is mentioned in the accounts only between 1700 and 1705, when the drum of the dome was in construction.[257] One of Hawksmoor's drawings of 1695 for the details of the peristyle mentions the stone types to be used: not only Ketton and Portland, but Beer and Headington.[258] Other stones were chosen for their soft or hard textures. Easily worked Reigate was used in the constantly curving vault of the stair in the south-west leg of the dome (the main stair to the dome today), and there are several references to the use of Kentish stone (presumably ragstone) for steps and doorways in passages.[259] In the 'circular passage at the E end' the sides of the passage were in Reigate, but the vaulting of it in Portland.[260] The Reigate had to be occasionally protected from the weather in temporary sheds on the ground.[261] The use of other geological types has yet to be researched. A modern geologist has stated that Taynton stone (? the same as the 'Burford' of the accounts), a staple component of the Romanesque building, was used in the interior of the Wren cathedral;[262] this is not yet separately verified, but seems likely. Wren did prefer stone from the quarries round Burford to Reigate for external use,[263] and some of the few unpainted walls in the crypt seem to be faced in Burford or Taynton stone. Several kinds of 'marble' were employed in the flooring from 1694 to 1710.[264] The black marble steps, both inside and outside the building, were either 'Irish' or 'Black Namur' (presumably the quarries of Namur in the French Netherlands, now Belgium); in 1709 the Namur marble was only 60% the cost of the Irish, at 3s per foot against 5s per foot.[265] The geology of original steps (as opposed to replacements in the 19th century, and if they could be identified as originals) has not yet been tested. There is no certain evidence for a tradition in the Isle of Man that Bishop Wilson of that island contributed or arranged for the quarrying of stone in the Poyllvaaish 'Black Marble' quarries there (which were being worked at the period) for the external steps at St Paul's; this story may have originated in the fact that a large area of flagstones from the quarry was provided for St Peter's church in Liverpool in 1701–4.[266]

Some of the stones of the medieval cathedral were pounded into a dust to comprise part of the mortar for the new walls. This was particularly the fate of the fragments of alabaster, that is the medieval sculptures which survived the Reformation and most of the Elizabethan effigies.

There is one intriguing reference in the accounts, for January 1678, to payment to the carpenters who were moving the stairs leading to the site office, for making a penthouse (pentice) over the old pieces of alabaster and marble in the Convocation House Yard 'to keep them from ye Weather, & from breaking'.[267] This suggests more care than would be necessary for piling up fragments for reuse in mortar. Perhaps these 'old pieces' included the fragments of Elizabethan and Jacobean funerary effigies which have survived.

Sometimes the major masons provided stone, or many stone merchants provided only a single type of stone. Between 1688 and 1698 Ephraim Beauchamp, for instance, supplied Kentish stone, Reigate, Caen, Beer, Guildford, Portland, Denmark paving, marble paving, Swedish marble and Purbeck paving. On the other hand in the short period 1680–8 13 suppliers, often with French-sounding names, provided small amounts of Caen stone. The supply of Portland over the whole period 1678–1703 was generally organised by major masons such as Thomas Gilbert, father and son, of Portland, the former in partnership with Thomas Wise.[268]

Brick

The first large task using bricks at St Paul's, the vaulting of the crypt below the choir, dates from 1676; the dome area and transepts followed in 1678, and the nave crypt was constructed by 1688. One other unseen brick construction was briefly glimpsed during investigation of the steps to the south transept in 2007: the large and presumably solid rubble and brick podium for the transept steps and semicircular colonnade there (Fig. 235 below). Bricks have been sampled during several of the excavations reviewed here (report by Terence Smith, Chapter 6 below).

As far as has been observed, no brick was used in the foundations, sleeper walls, or inner (visible) parts of side walls and piers of the crypt, but it was used for vaulting the crypt throughout the cathedral, and would later be used to form the saucer domes over all four arms of the cathedral. The construction of the cathedral would use over 2.6 million bricks in the years 1688–1709,[269] and rather more if the total for the whole construction period could be calculated. In all public or semi-public parts of the building, eg the crypts, the brick would be rendered; but in upper passageways and the roofspace, there is little care over the pointing of bricks, and little rendering.

Bricks first start to appear in quantity in the published building accounts in February 1676, and from June 1676 there are two kinds: place bricks at 13s the 1000 and stock bricks or stocks at 17s the 1000.[270] The stock bricks were better made 'from the stiffest clay', and place bricks were softer. In secular construction of the late 17th and 18th centuries, the cheaper place bricks were used behind facades built in stock brick. Sir Roger Pratt informs us that the two sorts were standard terms and qualities at this time, but nowhere in his published notebooks do we find how they were used in polite buildings.[271]

Since the accounts at this time show deliveries of both stock and place bricks, it is not clear from the accounts alone whether the crypt vault is of stock or place bricks. Samples of fragments taken from the courses of bricks above the vault, below the nave floor, suggest it was probably of stock bricks. The vaults of the choir, nave and the aisles of both, with their saucer-domes, consumed a colossal number of bricks from the late 1680s. A programme of sampling of bricks from many places in the vaulting would be required to establish whether the vaults are predominantly of stock or place bricks. Certainly the accounts indicate that far more stock bricks were bought than place bricks. The latter were arriving in quantity from 1686, when deliveries in two adjacent months totalled 18,000 place bricks.[272] On the other hand, place bricks are rarely mentioned towards the end of the accounts, after 1700. When in November 1704 bricklayers were paid for the 'vaulting over the Middle Isle west of the dome', the same month records purchases of 22,500 stock bricks but no place bricks. One brick taken from a saucer dome near the west end of the north nave aisle in 2003 is a stock brick, with one side axed to make it fit in the vault. Other bricks taken from the lower courses of the original splayed western steps on Site M are also thought to be stock bricks, though of an inferior sort, and they included organic and burned inclusions (called 'Spanish' at the time). It seems likely, from the numbers involved, that the brick saucer-domes of the vaulting are largely made of stocks. Stocks were also used for the cone in the dome, which was largely constructed by 1706;[273] and for paving a small area in the new chapter house (presumably in the cellar) in 1712.[274]

Place bricks, the inferior sort, were certainly used below ground. In 1711, 182,500 place bricks were bought specifically for the foundation of the wall supporting the iron fence around the cathedral, which indicates their inferior status as they would be underground. At the same time 141,500 place bricks were bought for the new chapter house; perhaps they were used in the foundations. There are also references in the accounts to the saving of old bricks, presumably for reuse,[275] though not necessarily for the cathedral building; reused bricks could equally have been used for drains or the many temporary structures such as masons' sheds and cisterns. The known 1680s construction date for the temporary site drain C[109] establishes a *terminus ante quem* for the introduction of the bricks sampled from it, which are in the distinctive orange/red fabric 3047 (see specialist report, Chapter 6). Almost certainly they are not local products and may even be imported from the Netherlands. They are good quality bricks, rather less porous than some other types and therefore suitable for a drain; but thought to be place bricks. Finally, there are references in the accounts of 1707 to 'long bricks' at 1d each, that is about five times the cost of a stock brick. These have so far not been identified. Two quantities are mentioned, of 6396 long bricks in January 1707, and 2984 in October 1707, both batches from the same brickmaker, Thomas Scott. Perhaps these are the bricks each 'two foot' long, which in 1733 Francis Price said were made specially ('on purpose') to build the lower, inner dome (the cone).[276]

After 1666, there must have been a great expansion in the brickmaking industry round London, and the cathedral was only one of many customers. By 1676, as shown in Ogilby and Morgan's map, virtually the entire Fire-damaged area within the City of London had been rebuilt, and largely in brick. This must have required extensive development of existing and new facilities for quarrying brickearth and making bricks. The area north of the City had been the site of quarries and brick kilns or clamps since the late 15th century, and in 1667 tenants with open spaces sought licences from their landlords to quarry the brickearth: for instance in the parish of St Giles in the Fields and along Old Street towards Islington.[277]

The names of several brickmakers, probably the larger suppliers, are mentioned in the published accounts, such as Captain Cudsden who provided 77,500 place bricks in 1676 or T[homas] Browne who provided a batch of 32,000 stocks in 1698, but whether these individuals produced the bricks or were just middlemen is not known. One contract for the provision of 200,000 bricks survives in the cathedral's contract book, that with Captain Nicholas Godwin; dated May 1698, it probably refers to the bricks used in the later part of the vaulting of the domes over the aisles and nave at church level, possibly in addition to some of the drains.[278]

Pantiles

Pantiles are first mentioned in London contexts in the 1630s, and were used as a primary roof covering at Kew Palace, Richmond, in 1631; the majority came from Flanders, both the United Provinces and the Spanish Netherlands.[279] Pantile fragments from the excavations in the south-west part of the crypt (C[11] and [13]) and from the shaft which located the Wren drain outside the west end (F[29]) may have come from temporary sheds or similar buildings set up for the workmen, such as the plumbery which was built on the site in 1689–90 and covered with 1200 pantiles. Later there is mention of a few 'English pantiles' on the site in 1706.[280] In usual building practice, pantiles, as noted by Neve in 1703, were used in covering of sheds, lean-to's, and flat-roofed buildings.[281]

Ceramic floortiles

While the church floor was paved in stages with black and white marble squares, the floor of the crypt was laid in 1709 with red-brown tiles known at St Paul's as 'pammets' (the word should perhaps be 'pamment', the term used in East Anglia). This large area of flooring has been locally repaired many times, and is interspersed with ledgers and vaults from before 1700. In 1993 a local area in the middle of the crypt beneath the nave had stone paving, and this was replaced with new tiles in a compatible fabric. Research to identify original tiles, as opposed to later ones inserted as repairs, would be difficult. A fragment of plain tile incorporated into one of the early burials on Site G below the south transept came from the Greater Netherlands (G[3]). These Flemish tiles are seen in 17th-century Dutch paintings, both outside and inside houses.

Iron and lead

The structure of the cathedral is reinforced with chains of links of wrought iron at many points; some have been removed or altered over the years, and metal reinforcements have been added. The expansion of pieces of iron in the fabric continues to cause cracks and spalling in the stonework. When places in the fabric are opened up, other previously-unknown pieces of ironwork are seen, as for instance a cavity inside the middle cornice of the west front which contains a jack bolt holding up the lintel beneath.[282] Surveyors since the time of Penrose have replaced many iron cramps with bronze or copper, for instance above the south portico or in the main dome above the drum.

Lead has been a different problem. Bernard Feilden (Surveyor 1969–77) found that lead between the base of a fluted column in the western portico and its base had had a mixed effect: 'over two centuries of steady pressure has squeezed out the lead from [the] joint … like cream from a bun. The lead has saved the stone from being split by unequal pressures'.[283]

Timber

The extent and character of reuse of timber from the old building, of which there must have been a great deal despite its burning in the Great Fire, has not been studied. So far all the timber identifiably from the first construction of the Wren building appears to be new. No doubt timbers from the old building were used for making scaffolding, shoring, templates, cabins and other disposable or temporary works. There are occasional references in the accounts to collection of items in the early years, for instance keeping doors.[284] Throughout the construction period for the cathedral, deal planks were obtained from Norwegian and Baltic sources, for instance Christiana (Oslo), 'Dramme' (probably Drammen, Norway) and Danzig (Gdańsk).[285] Oak came from many places, including Lincolnshire and York for the main trusses of the nave roof, as detailed above.

All these materials would have required transport, as did the mountain of rubble from the previous building which was not reused. Principal among the providers of carts was John Slyford (Sleyford), carter and wharfinger, who was another who served the cathedral for a long time, in his case from 1671 to 1714. He took rubble and brought bricks, tiles, sand, gravel, clay, ragstone, chalk and Portland stone; he had wharfside cranes at Redriff and Baynard's Castle, the latter immediately south of the cathedral and next to Paul's Wharf.[286]

CHAPTER 3

The cathedral in the 18th and 19th centuries

The third chapter of this study describes the archaeology of the cathedral in the 18th and 19th centuries, and how it was maintained by Wren's successors as Surveyor to the Fabric, working with the deans and chapters of their day. The building and its surroundings have changed since 1711.

St Paul's quickly became the most talked about and illustrated ecclesiastical building in England in the 18th century.[1] From the moment it was finished, St Paul's also reassumed roles, religious and secular, which had been given in the remote past to its predecessor; and they were extended. Because of its size and centrality, the cathedral was a convenient and suitable place for large gatherings of clergy from all over England. From about 1720, maps were produced which had St Paul's at the centre of London, with circles centred on it to indicate distances on the map. From 1676 to the 1790s St Paul's was taken to mark the meridian of the whole world, until this status was given to Greenwich. In many painted and engraved views of London from 1700 onwards, St Paul's is the centre of the attention or the building which identifies the place. As a landmark in predominantly flat country, St Paul's was one of the highest buildings in London for over two centuries (Fig. 106). The bell of its clock could be heard, on occasion, up to 20 miles away. Notable views of the cathedral, to be protected by law in the first half of the 20th century, were immediately appreciated: in 1766, praising the occasional vertical emphases of the capital's major buildings when seen from afar, John Gwynn said 'let it be supposed that the cupola of St Paul's was taken away, and it would then be found that the loss of that noble ornament would immediately reduce the appearance of the city to a level with that of any other populous city in the kingdom.'[2] In 1848 soldiers constructed a crow's nest of timber on top of the ball and cross on the dome, from which they took bearings in connection with the triangulation of the area for the first Ordnance Survey maps of London.[3]

The cathedral was however tightly surrounded by the buildings of the Churchyard. In 1803, in his appraisal of the cathedral, James Malcolm said

> 'I am sorry the Legislature did not rebuild St Paul's in the centre of some elevated field, where they might have encompassed it with a handsome square of the best houses in London. Many such [fields or squares] might have been found in 1671, which would now be in the centre of town; but by resolving to reoccupy the old site, they were restrained from leaving sufficient room even for seeing the building, without straining the muscles of the neck.'[4]

Others, including champions of the neo-classical improvements which were appearing all over central London, agreed. In 1827 James Elmes wrote that while 'a series of desirable improvements bid fair to render London the Rome of modern history', the hurry of rebuilding the City after the Great Fire had produced an unsightly place, and he hoped that the sooner the corporation could 'emancipate their fine cathedral from this monstrous thraldom, the sooner will their city be enabled to hold its due rank in the splendid metropolis of empire.'[5]

As already noted, the cathedral was a noted

Fig. 106 The City of London from the north in 1730–1, showing St Paul's and many of the Wren parish churches (a view formerly attributed to Bernard Lens III; BM, 1853,0409.43, © The Trustees of the British Museum). The many spires gave the City a Baroque skyline matched by few other cities in Europe

tourist attraction, including for foreign visitors, from the moment of its completion: five parts could be viewed at a charge of 2d per person for each one: the Golden Gallery with its view (quite an experience in the days before aviation), the Whispering Gallery, the Library, the Great Model and the Geometric Stair.[6] Major services were also a spectacle: on 23 April 1789, for instance, an estimated 2000 spectators viewed 6398 boys and girls assembled under the dome.[7] In his account of 1766, John Gwynn went on to criticise the division of the exterior wall into two orders; the turrets (west towers) had too many divisions, the figures on the balustrade were too large, the interior lacked decoration, and perforation of the east end with windows produced a 'prodigious glare of light' which 'totally destroys the grandeur and effect of the church in that part.'[8] Carl Philipp Moritz from Berlin noted in June 1782:

> 'I must own that on my entrance into this massy building, an uncommon vacancy, which seemed to reign in it, rather damped than raised an impression of anything majestic in me. All around me I could see nothing but immense bare walls and pillars.. No altar was to be seen, or any other sign that this was a place where mankind assembled to adore the Almighty ...'

Moritz was given a mechanical account of the building by a cathedral guide, presumably a verger, and then taken to the Whispering Gallery to have its effect demonstrated, which impressed him. Then he went up to the Stone Gallery where he remained for 2 hours, such was the view of the city below and surrounding landscape.[9] Though the cathedral was admired, it had little influence on the architecture of other cities in Britain and Europe except for the dome: in 1776 J-G Soufflot sent a pupil to London to make measured drawings of St Paul's, and the dome of the Panthéon in Paris of 1791 is the result.[10]

Until an internal cleaning of 1802, ragged military flags hung in the nave, relics of victories since 1758.[11] In the last decade of the 18th and especially during the 19th century, St Paul's assumed the further character of an imperial mausoleum or valhalla for Britain and the British Empire. It became the Empire's church. The former Consistory Court at the south-west corner was recast in 1906–13 as a chapel for the Order of St Michael and St George, a chivalric order founded in 1818 for those working in overseas territories and foreign affairs. Nearly opposite it on the north side, in the space beneath the north-west tower, a Chapel of All Souls, also called the Kitchener Memorial Chapel, was redone in 1922 to contain a recumbent effigy of Earl Kitchener (d. 1916). This mingling of patriotism and imperial pride influenced and often inspired the attitudes of those who looked after and recorded the building. In 1927, introducing his book of measured drawings which had taken him 19 years to produce, Alfred Poley wrote

> 'the Cathedral's grip on the Empire's affections is due to a sense of its having been for over two centuries the hallowed recipient of a great nation's emotions, whether of joy for her blessings, or of mourning for her losses.. how vivid are the pictures of an historic past.. not only visions of architectural splendour, or memories of a sentimental nature, but associations of a deep national import are woven around this sacred fabric. Visions of Nelson and Trafalgar; of Wellington and Waterloo! These are the thoughts that thrill. Many are the sailors and soldiers who have made our Empire great, whose names are honoured within these hallowed walls. Here lie the greatest of our painters; and here, too, linger memories of famous poets, musicians and eloquent preachers. A noble record truly; and one which appeals to all who hold history, country and faith in reverent memory.'[12]

The restoration of 1925–30 was largely funded by donations from throughout the British Empire, and the restored cathedral reopened by the king and queen.[13] The campaign initiated by Godfrey Allen in 1936 to preserve the views of St Paul's by controlling the heights of new buildings in its vicinity was grounded in these same feelings: 'for countless citizens of our Empire St Paul's is central in their mental picture of London'.[14]

After Wren, the cathedral has been under the care of a succession of Surveyors who have maintained and repaired the building up to the present.[15] For the 18th century and the first half of the 19th century, only the major restorations are noted here. The long Surveyorship of Francis Penrose (1852–97) was the most important of the 18th and 19th centuries, and some of his projects will be described in their places in the three parts of the chapter: (i) internal works, including the combatting of the settling structure; (ii) external repairs; and (iii) the churchyard, railings, and the wider Churchyard (the streets outside the railings).

The interior and general stability concerns, 1711–1897

This history of the interior of the cathedral from 1711 to 1897 divides the period into two; only the major changes and repair programmes are discussed.

From 1711 to 1852

A recurring theme in the 18th century was concern about settlement. This had required some work even before 1711, as noted above. In October 1719 John James was ordered to 'survey & take care of ye Cracks to ye Stonework on the S. Side of ye Church & fitt in wedges of Stone, To Examine at the end of about Six Months whether the Cracks continue to widen', and then report.[16] From the time of Henry Flitcroft, Surveyor between 1746 and 1756, a plan of the south-east quarter of the crossing and the south aisle of the choir is inscribed 'A the pier which has been Repaired' and endorsed 'Mr Flitcrofts plan of the Peers on the South side of the Church between the middle & side Isles Aug 1752.' This is taken to refer to settling of the rubble core of the east pier of the south transept arch.[17] Robert Mylne became Surveyor in 1766, and in 1781–2 carried out measures to stabilise the dome and south transept, by inserting iron rods or ties at triforium level across the latter, tying the dome piers to the south wall of the transept. Two iron discs or pateras were thereafter visible in the face of the south transept, for instance in the 1890s (Fig. 147), but have since been removed.[18] Mylne also replaced some decaying Burford stone, which may have been on the exterior, with Portland about 1782.[19]

An impression of the interior of the cathedral before the changes of the 19th century can be given by four illustrations from 1736 to 1797 (Fig. 107–Fig. 110). The choir is shown by Jakob van der Schley in 1736 (Fig. 107). The perspective is foreshortened, but it shows how the choir stalls occupied the easternmost two complete bays, that is one bay east from where they are now. They returned along the east side of the choir screen, which was in the third bay (behind the artist). The large organ stood on top of the screen. The pulpit was in the choir, at the east end opposite the bishop's throne, as it had been in the medieval cathedral; there was no pulpit and little religious activity of any kind in the nave or transepts. This concentration of religious celebration in the choir

Fig. 107 *The choir in 1736, by Jakob van der Schley (BM, 1871, 1209.2722, © The Trustees of the British Museum). Two characteristics of people at prayer are shown on the right; several people hold prayerbooks close to their faces and others below are kneeling or standing but facing the wall (in this case the panelling of the stalls)*

Fig. 108 *The choir during the service of thanksgiving for the recovery of George III, 23 April 1789; a print by Robert Pollard after Edward Dayes (BM,1870, 0709.696, © The Trustees of the British Museum)*

Fig. 109 Internal view looking north-west, by Thomas Malton, 1798 (WS XVI, pl. xxii). This shows the paving beneath the dome before Mylne had to dig out the centre to lower the coffin of Nelson in 1806

Fig. 110 The nave in 1797 by Thomas Malton, with figures by William Hamilton (BM, 1868,0328.301, © The Trustees of the British Museum)

is illustrated also by the arrangements which Mylne made for the service in April 1789 which marked the recovery of George III from illness; a contemporary plan in London Metropolitan Archives shows the complicated and no doubt diplomatically fraught arrangements for seating at the service.[20] A view of the choir on this occasion is given in Figure 108. Other drawings show that the nave and aisles were crowded with hundreds of other people, some on temporary wooden raised banks, and the gallery at the west end of the nave was also full of spectators or participants, thus justifying the Tijou railing there.[21]

The crossing is shown, on more normal days, in Figure 109, before the monuments moved in; and the nave in a view by Thomas Malton in 1797 (Fig. 110). In the crossing and transepts the only activity on view is sightseeing or promenading. From 1782 a regular annual event was a service of the London charity schools, held in the dome area, when tiers of timber staging were built to a considerable height.[22]

Mylne suggested that there should be a memorial to Wren on the church floor, in addition to his grave in the crypt where the setting was thought to be dark and unworthy (none of the crypt had any lighting until the 1860s). In 1807 Mylne designed the memorial as an inscription on a block of marble on the choir screen above the gates. This was erected in 1810, but moved

Fig. 111 *Arrangements for the funeral of Lord Nelson, 1806 (MoL). The sole method of lighting was a very large candelabrum with 200 candles. The smaller flags (not the large French flag) were still in place round the dome in 1828*

to the north transept terminal wall when the choir screen was divided around 1860.[23] Its fate in 1941 is noted later.

The cathedral held out against being used as a mausoleum of national heroes for most of the 18th century; this was not one of its original purposes. St Paul's was however sometimes used for state occasions, when the monarch showed himself to the people; a turning-point may have been the service of thanksgiving for the restoration to health of George III in 1789 just mentioned.[24] Shortly after, St Paul's also became the pantheon of national, particularly military, heroes.[25] The introduction of commemorative tablets and effigies onto the church floor began in 1791–5 with the monument to John Howard, prison reformer and philanthropist, and to Samuel Johnson, writer and lexicographer, in 1791–6. The marble monuments which adorn the crossing and the transepts, both groups of statuary and wall panels, were largely introduced in the years that followed. They were mostly of heroes who fell in the war with France from 1793.[26] Thus by the time of Admiral Lord Nelson's burial in 1806, St Paul's was an appropriate place for his burial (Fig. 111, Fig. 112). The state funeral of Nelson was matched by that of the Duke of Wellington almost half a century later in 1852 (noted below under the section dealing with Penrose's surveyorship). They shared several characteristics.[27] Both took place beneath the dome, with an attempt at spectacular funebral lighting; and both services included the slow disappearance of the bier and coffin into the crypt beneath. Mylne cut a hole in the middle of the dome pavement for this purpose for Nelson's funeral.[28]

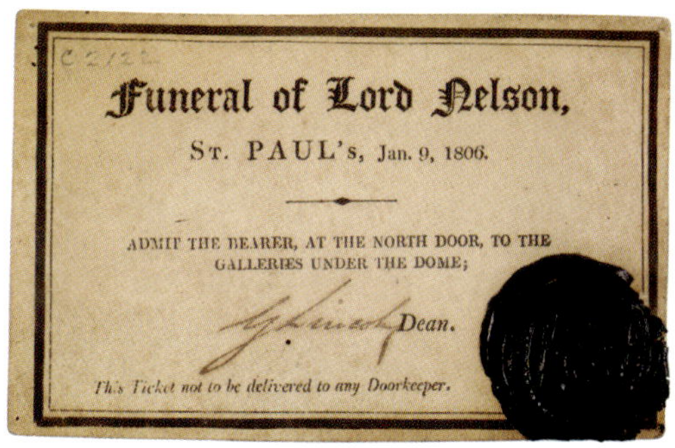

Fig. 112 *Ticket for the funeral of Lord Nelson, 1806 (MoL)*

The state of the building was a matter of concern throughout the 19th century. In 1831, when Sydney Smith became a canon, the transepts and nave (except for the Morning Prayer Chapel and the Consistory Court at the west end) were unused, large vacant areas on which the new monuments now gazed without effect; they were also soon filthy. Many unglazed and unshuttered openings in the fabric allowed dust and soot to permeate the building. Smith introduced mains water into the building and placed portable fire engines at various points in the upper part.[29] In 1822 gas lighting was introduced experimentally into the choir by C R Cockerell (Surveyor 1819–52); pipes were laid from the crypt to 'eight elegant pillars of gilt brass', each furnished with three burners, in the choir, with other clusters attached to the altar rails. Gas was taken on more permanently in 1834.[30]

Early photographs of the monuments around the dome are useful in that they show the extremely dirty nature of the internal walls by the end of the 19th century.[31] The dirt and soot on the fabric, both internal and external, had been a source of comment for decades. One pamphleteer of 1868 spoke of the filth on monuments:

> 'converting classic groups into piebald monstrosities ... black angels are conveying Ethiopian heroes to their long rest. Smutty-faced Britannias vie with much-besoiled Glories and Fames in doing honour to English worthies to whom soap and a scrubbing-brush are a first necessity.'[32]

The monuments themselves, after initial enthusiastic comments, have rarely been praised. To Katharine Esdaile in 1946, they:

> 'were greatly admired at the time, but in them the ravages of Neo-Hellenism are seen at their worst ... Nelson stands on a pedestal adorned by the river-god Nile and two sphinxes, while Britannia points out his figure to the two naval cadets, who are balanced by the worst lion in St Paul's; Flaxman seldom sank to such depths ... General Hay in full uniform falls into the arms of a naked Greek athlete ... the deplorable Captain Cooke (not the explorer) now banished to the crypt ... and so on and so forth'.[33]

One potentially serious matter during the Surveyorship of C R Cockerell was a Corporation of London proposal to dig a sewer in the roadway on the south side of the cathedral in 1831. On 19 August, Cockerell wrote to a Mr Acton in the Corporation's Commission of Sewers asking him to suspend digging operations immediately, or if not Cockerell would apply to the Lord Mayor. Richard Kelsey, Surveyor's Clerk to the Commissioners, whose surviving surveys of the new sewers all over the City in the 1830s and 1840s are today a major source of archaeological information, replied that Acton was out of town, but:

> '... it is certainly singular that, until so late as yesterday morning, you should have remained uninformed of a work which has been in progress for many weeks, especially as a Mr Lingard, who describes himself to be sub-surveyor to St Paul's Cathedral, must have not only known it as a matter of public notoriety in the neighbourhood, but was applied to by Mr Acton, as the only ostensible person he knew in the business, that the bar on the north side of the Cathedral [shown by Horner in 1822, Fig. 157 below] might be opened while the south side of the churchyard was necessarily closed.'

At a meeting of the Commissioners on 24 August it was decided that although they saw no threat of damage to the cathedral by their actions, they would appoint 'Mr Telford and Mr Brunel', with Acton, to 'meet and confer with Mr Rennie and Mr Smirke, together with Mr Cockerell', suspending the works until this group reported. Telford, being busy, was replaced by a Mr Sibley.

The offending works were two shafts or wells, dug on the east and south sides of the south transept, close to the fabric. A third, on the west, was projected but may not have been dug before the work was halted as there is no information about it. The shaft or 'well' on the east of the transept had reached sand at a depth of 33ft 6in (10.2m) and that on the south side a depth of 31ft (9.5m).

The basic account of this incident, in John Hollingshead's *Underground London* of 1862, cites letters between the parties which he transcribed courtesy of Francis Penrose. Trying to take control of the situation, Cockerell claimed that he himself had authorised the three holes to be dug. On 6 September 1831, having received the engineers' report under Smirke's signature, Cockerell wrote again to Acton, asking for the line of the sewer to be moved away from the cathedral. The agreement of the Commissioners of Sewers was communicated to Cockerell on 21 September. The holes were backfilled.[34] Unfortunately no plan of the two certainly dug shafts has been located, and no shaft was revealed on the west side when the landscaping of 2003–6 took place. The two backfilled shafts must remain in the ground. The holes as a group are called Site 88, and their approximate location shown on the map of sites, Figure 15.

The Surveyorship of Francis Penrose, 1852–1897

The Surveyorship of Francis Penrose from 1852 to 1897 is described here from the archaeological and conservation viewpoint as a series of topics rather than a strictly chronological account. It covers (i) the state occasions of the burial of Wellington and the Jubilee celebrations of Queen Victoria, and lesser services of commemoration;

(ii) repairs and cleaning of the internal walls and the dome; (iii) reorganisation of the choir, the new pulpit, the removal of the choir screen and its gates, and works in the dome area; (iv) heating, lighting and other matters of daily management; and (v) monuments. Burials and all external matters, such as the north and south porticos and the west end, are dealt with in other sections.[35]

The funeral of the Duke of Wellington took place in 1852, the first year of Penrose's surveyorship. Outside the west end of the cathedral, a temporary construction with a sloping roof seems to have covered all the western steps, being pierced by an arch in the centre (shown on contemporary illustrations, and on commemorative ceramics, see Fig. 160 below). Illustrations of the event, such as the one adapted for the pot lid shown in Figure 160 shows the enormous funeral carriage bringing the Duke's coffin within the railings which were still outside the west end, having come through a clear and wide gap in the railings;[36] perhaps the western gate and adjacent railings were removed. Inside the cathedral, tiers of temporary wooden galleries contained seats for an estimated 13,000 people (or at least 10,000 by another estimate). Extraordinary temporary constructions of tiered seats or stands occupied the transepts up to the vault.[37] The whole church was lined with heavy black cloth, which had the incidental effect of suppressing the normal 12-second echo so the Dean could be heard. A corona of gas-jets ran round the Whispering Gallery, and a large gas chandelier hovered in the crossing. The corona was retained afterwards for a time, since new burners were fitted to it in 1870.[38] Penrose must have had a major part in devising the machinery which lowered the coffin through the opening in the centre of the dome pavement made by Mylne for Nelson. Here the coffin of Wellington stayed suspended for a period, until Penrose had designed and installed his tomb a short distance to the east.[39] Plans for a separate monument to the Duke were protracted through 'dithering, bureaucratic ineptitude and seemingly endless calls for new competitions to sort the matter out' which may have been partly fuelled by recent arrangements for the tomb of Napoleon beneath the dome of the Invalides in Paris. One startling proposal, not accepted, was to dig out a space under the dome at St Paul's, resembling that in Paris, so the tombs of Nelson and Wellington could lie side by side and be viewed from the church floor above. Luckily, Dean Milman had other ideas for the dome space.[40]

The third occasion of state of the 19th century, after the funerals of Nelson and Wellington,

Fig. 113 The Thanksgiving Service on the Diamond Jubilee of Queen Victoria, 22 June 1897 (LMA)

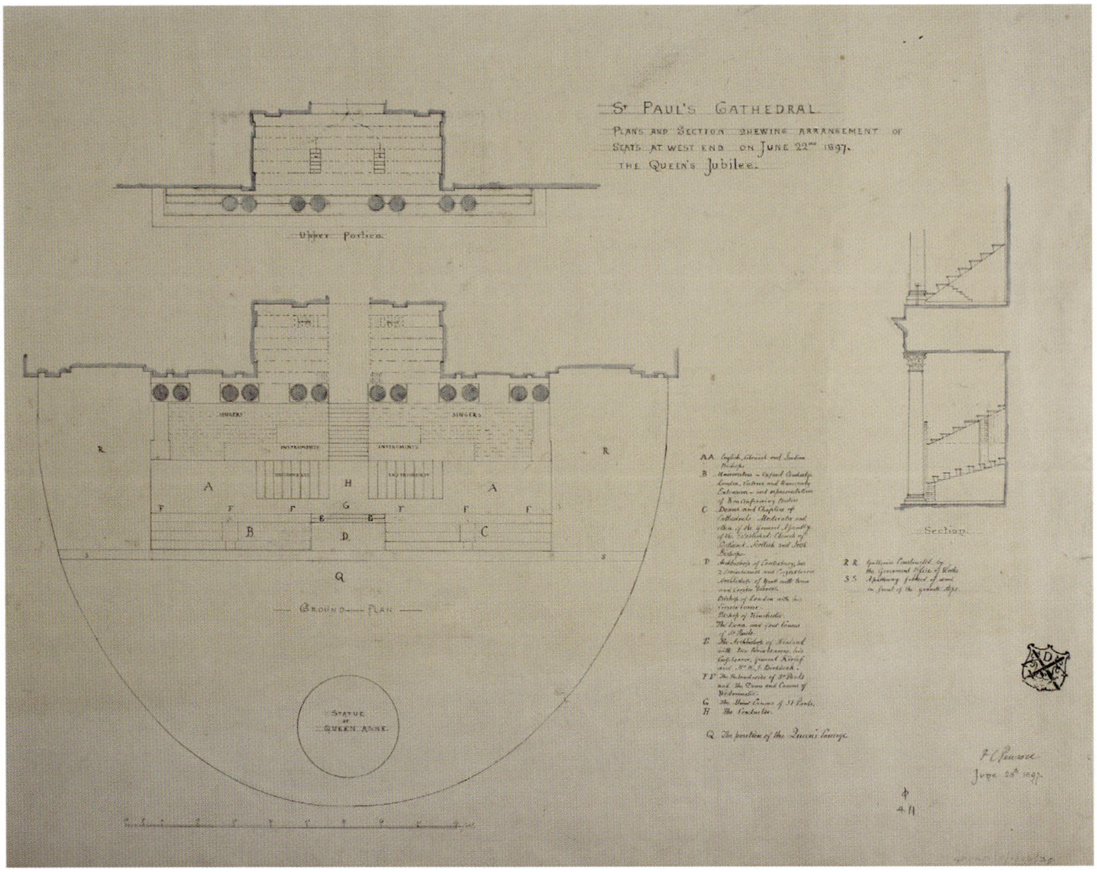

Fig. 114 *Arrangement of the seating, and sections through the temporary banks of seats in the portico, by F C Penrose in 1897 (SPCAA D/1/14/20)*

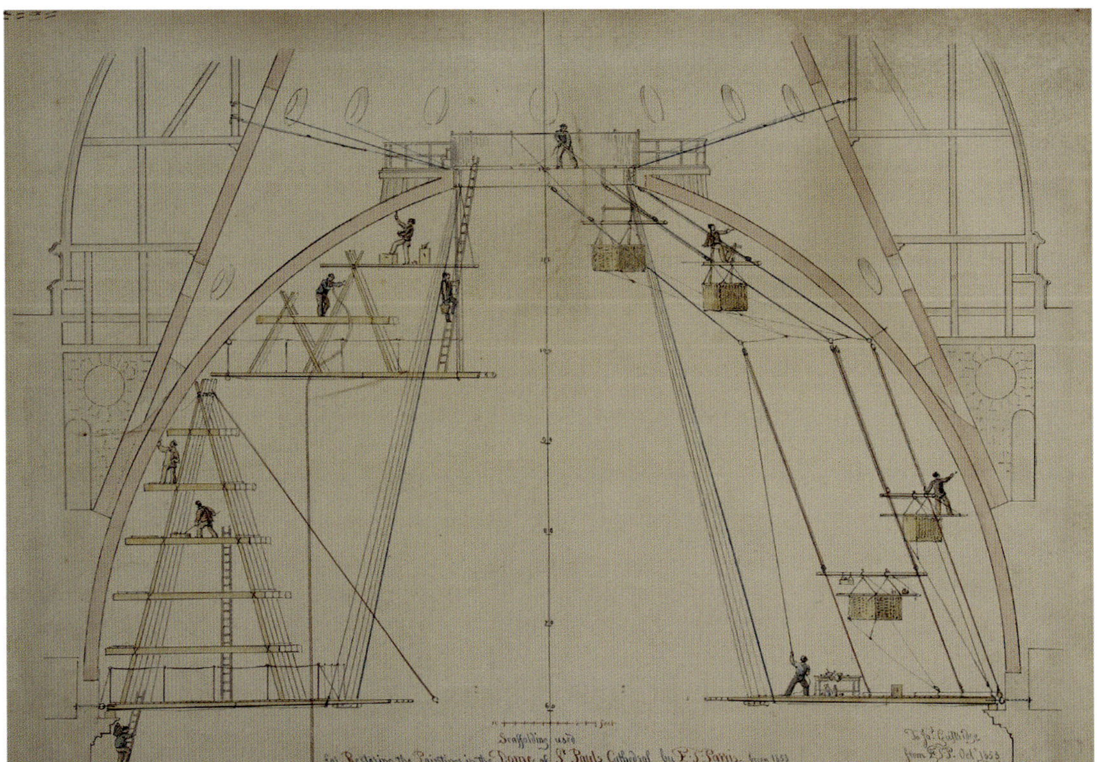

Fig. 115 *Sketch by Penrose of the scaffolding used in cleaning the interior of the dome, 1853 (SPCAA D/1/4/7)*

took place on the western steps outside. In June 1897, Queen Victoria came to the cathedral for a Thanksgiving Service for her Diamond Jubilee, though she stayed in a carriage outside the west end (Fig. 113). Temporary staging for spectators had been arranged on a large scale, including ranked seating in the upper portico designed by Penrose (Fig. 114). The Clerk of Works E J Harding in his scrap book noted 'we had to remove the granite posts (by the entrance to the front) [ie some of the Shap bollards] and the ornamental lamp posts'.[41]

Throughout the 19th century St Paul's continued its role as the nation's church where both the triumphs and setbacks of empire were celebrated on behalf of the nation. There were services in thanksgiving for the suppression of the Indian Mutiny in 1859. In 1861 Prince Albert died, and on the Sunday following there were funeral sermons with the choir 'draped with black with white edging'.[42] Eleven years later in 1872 internal temporary scaffolding was erected for attenders at a thanksgiving service for the recovery of the Prince of Wales from illness.[43] The cathedral's work also reflected traumatic domestic events: in 1866, there was a 'Day of Humiliation for the Cattle-plague.'[44] The increasing use of the dome area and nave for large services in the later 19th century would have required and been made more pleasant by the introduction of heating and the heating grilles in the nave floor, described below.

The history of cleaning the interior and the introduction of the mosaics which presently occupy the spandrels of the dome and the choir during the second half of the 19th century will be noted only in passing here; a detailed study of the internal decoration from 1696 to 1900 appeared in 2004.[45] One of Penrose's early projects was the cleaning of the interior of the dome by E T Parris, begun in 1853, which involved some ingenious scaffolding (Fig. 115). Twenty years later, on 1 December 1873, E J Harding noted in his scrapbook:

> 'this year also saw the beginning of the removal of the paint from the walls of the cathedral, including the nave, the nave aisles, the transepts, and the dome up as far as the quarter galleries. The process of the work was by picking off the paint, and then rubbing the whole of the surfaces with sand and water'.[46]

Two photographs published in 1896 may be compared with the group of internal views of a century or so before: the crossing looking north-east (Fig. 116) and the south aisle of the nave, looking north-west (Fig. 117). The mosaics in the spandrels of the dome were commissioned in 1864–6 but not completed until about 1891; the mosaics in the choir and choir aisles were installed in 1892–1904.[47]

Historians of the architectural setting of Anglican worship have noted that several cathedrals besides St Paul's, such as Ely and Durham, made radical changes to their interiors at this time, probably influenced by the criticisms of the ways cathedrals were arranged by John Jebb, the bishop

Fig. 116 The crossing looking north in the 1890s, showing the mosaics in the dome spandrels (Birch 1896, pl. vi)

Fig. 117 The nave south aisle in the 1890s (Birch 1896, pl. vii). The font was moved to the south transept in 1901, and later to the north transept; it is now at the west end of the nave. This also shows one of the gas standards designed by Penrose in 1876 for heating the nave; and in the aisle, one of the brass coverings for the holes into the crypt to enable circulation of hot air, originally from stoves in the crypt

of Limerick, who wrote two books on the subject in 1841 and 1845.[48] At St Paul's, Dean Milman, appointed in 1849, had ideas about reorganising the cathedral space so that evening services could be held under the dome. He wanted to set St Paul's in order as the great English cathedral.[49] Under Milman and Penrose, the period 1861–86 saw the removal of the choir screen, division into two parts of the organ, the raising of the floor of the choir and the building of a large new reredos. The organ by Smith of 1694–*c.* 1704 was split into two and duplicated, partly in facsimile, with the two parts placed behind the first bay of stalls. According to Penrose, this idea occurred in 1859 when the organ was taken off the screen, and the new unobstructed view down the choir hailed as a great improvement.[50] The choir screen was divided between the north and south transepts and re-erected across the terminal walls (plans of the new arrangement are shown in the plan of 1929, Fig. 3); that on the north suffered damage from the enemy bomb in 1941 and was later removed.

The floor of the central vessel of the choir, but not the aisles, was raised by about 3ft. This higher floor was brought to the west end of the choir so that steps now lay between two of the dome piers. All the Wren-period stalls, which had occupied just over two bays in the choir, were moved one bay to the west, as they now are; they were not raised, but accommodated the raised chancel floor by losing the lowest level of seating which had comprised benches housed under the stalls. The original height of the stalls is now evident in the side aisles, their back view. This movement of the stalls freed a whole bay of space at the east end.[51] The sides of this bay were later to be closed by the present iron screens by Bodley and Garner, which incorporate the original Tijou screens from the gates beneath the organ in the vestibule of the choir screen. In 1886, Penrose also reported that for the foundation of the new reredos of that year by Bodley & Garner 'a strong arch with cast iron voussoirs has been provided underneath the pavements amply sufficient to carry the weight and without interfering with the Crypt.' Presumably this iron structure is still beneath the present floor, since the Victorian reredos was taken down after the War.

Gas lamps had been installed in the choir in 1822. When the Duke of Wellington's coffin was placed in its tomb in the crypt in 1858, gas light was installed there also so that the sarcophagus could be inspected by visitors. Until the funeral of the Duke, the crypt had been shown to visitors by the light of a lantern, and only a portion of the crypt was open, nothing west of Nelson's tomb.[52] The introduction of gas was not without problems: in June 1859 the large gas meter in the crypt exploded.[53] Gas lighting was extended to the nave in 1878. This was presumably the reason for the creation of a circular chamber outside the south side of the nave, in which the 'gas meter' was placed in this or the following year. A curved passage led to this chamber from a small door in the south nave crypt wall (still present, in the cathedral shop but obscured by fittings). The meter chamber was located in the landscaping works of 2004–6, and backfilled (see Site H).

There was no heating at all until the 1850s. 'To go to St Paul's,' wrote Sydney Smith in 1833, 'is certain death. The thermometer is several degrees below zero. My sentences are frozen as they come out of my mouth.' In February 1853, a particularly cold month, Green noted that there was no means of heating the cathedral.[54] Canon William Hale took over Smith's campaigns for improvement. Penrose installed Gurney stoves in the crypt in 1868 (one location at the east end of the north aisle of the choir crypt is shown on a plan of ledger stones he made in 1873), and cut several holes in the crypt vaulting to allow hot air up into the cathedral. At first the gratings were of cast iron, but were replaced by the present ones of brass in 1881.[55] A further practical matter concerned the management of coffins during and after funeral services. In his report for 1886, Penrose noted that he has made a 'new opening in the area of the Dome for lowering coffins into the crypt'.[56] This is apparently the opening in the vault of the crypt now visible from below, though covered above by the present dome dais.

Penrose also gave attention to the monuments. In 1872–4 the division and removal of the organ required some reorganisation of monuments which had been in the way of its new divided position in the north and south choir arcades. Green's diary noted that 'many of the monuments on the church floor were lowered about the same time, and the iron railings around them removed'.[57] Penrose reported that he had lowered the monuments and statues on the church floor by about 18 inches.[58] The present arrangement of the surviving pre-Fire effigies in the crypt is probably also by him; an undated drawing in the cathedral archive shows a proposal for those in the south aisle, and as they are now.[59]

Thus the interior of the cathedral was changed and adapted for both temporary purposes (state funerals, the service of 1789 for George III) and in more permanent ways. For most of the 18th century, the nave seems to have been little used. The 'Peninsular School' of monuments from the 1790s to the second decade of the 19th century moved into a space beneath the dome which had no clear religious purpose, so was perhaps available for monuments to secular heroes. During the second half of the 19th century, in the surveyorship of Francis Penrose, the choir was opened up and its screen removed, the organ divided into its present configuration, and the choir itself reordered. In 1858 Penrose replaced Mylne's pulpit with one of his own design, placed out in the dome area where its post-War successor stands today.[60] Contemporary debates about 'finishing' the decoration of St Paul's concentrated on the area of the dome and the choir, with its aisles, and by 1902, 5 years after Penrose retired, the Byzantine mosaics were in place.

The archaeology of burials, 1680–2000

Wren did not approve of burials in churches, and even suggested after the Fire that churchyards should be placed outside the built-up area.[61] It is no surprise therefore that the crypt of St Paul's originally made no overt provision for burials or monuments (though one large monument found a place in an out-of-the-way corner in 1680, before the rest of the crypt was finished, Fig. 118). There are also no bays of the crypt filled with 18th- or 19th-century coffins, as happened in almost all Georgian London parish churches. But occasional burials were made in the crypt in the 1680s, almost before it was finished; some of these are described here. Edward Hatton noted in 1707 that in the crypt, 'coffins are buried in the ground [ie beneath the floor of the crypt] and lye not on the surface, as in other vaults'; evidently a new or remarkable practice.[62] A meeting of the Commissioners in February 1715/16 ordered that:

> 'the Tyles which have been broken by digging Graves in the Vaults under the Church be repaired and made good, And that for the future, the Relations of such persons, as shall happen to be buryed therein, be obliged to make good the same from time to time'.[63]

Wren himself was buried in 1723 in the crypt, in a side alcove at the south-east corner which in the 19th century had an iron railing with a gate across it. In 1757 the parish of St Faith had burial rights in the north aisle of the choir crypt, reflecting the fact that the aisle lay within the medieval parish.[64] The burial registers of St Paul's do not survive until 1760; the earliest burial in the crypt of which there is documentary record is in 1766.[65] Burials were generally stopped in the City in 1851, though this did not stop occasional burials of both bodies and ashes in the cathedral crypt up to very recent years. The last interment of a body was of Canon Sidney Alexander, Treasurer, in 1948, in the St Faith's aisle.[66]

The inscriptions on monuments in the main church and on the ledgers in the crypt were transcribed and their heraldry drawn in watercolour by Arthur Jewers in 1918–19; at about the same time 16 ledgers prior to 1714 were also recorded by RCHME for its survey published in 1929.[67] The cathedral inventory of 2005, partly based on a survey of 1997, lists 201 ledger stones in the present crypt floor (there are also smaller memorial plaques in the floor, like those on the walls, and burials of ashes beneath small tiles). Some of the burials, no doubt within vaults, are of prominent painters, architects and engineers: for instance Turner, Reynolds, Mylne, George Dance the Younger, C R Cockerell, John Rennie and Holman Hunt. Others are of canons of the cathedral and members of their families. The passage of feet over the most famous graves has required some recutting of inscriptions in recent decades.

Here a study is made of several matters relating to burials at St Paul's, both inside and outside the building in the churchyard, in the period 1680–2000: (i) an overview of the distribution of grave slabs, and how far we can tell if they overlie their original burials or are relaid out of original position; (ii) the varied nature of burials (vaults, coffins, ashes, the interment of a box of bones) as indicated by recording, when required, in the period 1994–2010.

Plans of burials, and whether they lie over original sites

The present configuration of grave slabs throughout the crypt, and the survival of a few box tombs in the north-east churchyard, is the result of several factors over the centuries, which have mixed them and obscured the degree to which they overlie the burials they originally marked. There have been at least two rearrangement of slabs, that is moving some around. First, in 1879 Penrose cleared the

Date	*Person(s)*	*Comment*
1680	John Martin, stationer (b. 1618), and his wife	also wall monument nearby (Fig. 118)
1684	Henry Awson (b. 1633)	
1685	John Tillison (b. 1629)	[called Thomas by Penrose]
1687	Dorothy Spencer	beneath south transept
1692	Thomas Cooke (b. 1625)	on the inscription, 'of Bobbin in the county of Kent'
1693	Oliver Williams	
1694	Elizabeth Wiseman (b. 1642)	wall monument nearby to Sir Edmund Wiseman & Eliza 1704
1696	Edward Roth	Fig. 126
1697	William Holder, and Susanna (Wren) his wife (d. 1688)	wall monument
1702	Jane, daughter of Christopher Wren	wall monument
1706	Thomas Bennet (b. 1664)	also has wall monument nearby
1706	George Dunt and Dunt family	Fig. 127
1707	Martha Shelley	wall monument
1707	Richard Turner and his wife Catherine	
1708	John de la Fontaine (b. 1621)	on the inscription 'of Kerby Bellars in the County of Leicester'
1708	John Howell (b. 1670)	Gentleman of the Chapel Royal (singer)
1711	Thomas Felsted (b. 1657) and his wife Mary (b. 1664, d. 1724)	Prebendary of St Paul's.
1711	Elizabeth Walrond (b. 1682)	wife of Francis Walrond of Ottery St Mary (Devon), merchant
1712	Mary wife of Christopher Wren, with Philip her father (d. 1713), & Constance her mother (d. 1729)	wall monument
1713	Charles Boothe (b 1691)	on inscription, 'of Denham Massey in the county of Cheshire'
1717	William Sibery	
1719	Lawrence Spencer and his son	beneath south transept
1723	Sir Christopher Wren	
1750	Barbara Comyn (b. 1715)	Fig. 128

Table 3 *Ledgers and wall-monuments in the crypt below the choir and transepts from 1680 to 1750*

north-east churchyard of slabs, leaving the box tombs, and laid the slabs in the north-east aisle of the crypt, which is part of St Faith's parish. Second, a group of slabs were moved during the installation of heating pipes in the crypt in 1909–10. Thus plans or other information about the locations of graves up to 1879 may well record the positions of grave slabs over the burials they commemorate; whereas after that date, records will equally possibly show repositioned slabs, often filling in odd spaces and corners. A plan of all the ledger stones and memorials visible in 1873 in the crypt east of Wellington was made by Penrose.[68]

Table 3 addresses the question of the chronology of early burial in the crypt, up to about 1750, beneath the choir and transepts. Some monuments attached to the walls are also noted, as they may imply a burial nearby. A notable early example of a wall monument with an associated nearby ledger stone is that of stationer John Martin (d. 1680) and his wife, in the north aisle of the choir crypt at the east end, attributed to Edward Pearce junior (Fig. 118).[69] This appears to be the earliest datable monument and burial in the crypt. Martin or Martyn, with an associate, had a monopoly on printing the publications of the Royal Society from 1663, so he must have known both Wren and Hooke: he published the latter's *Micrographia* in 1665. Presumably it was these connections which enabled him to be buried here, with a fine monument. It is the largest surviving late 17th-century monument in the City; its survival no doubt largely due to its being hidden away at the end of the crypt, and then in a side alcove.

From Table 3 it may be deduced that at least 19 burials, besides that of Wren himself, took place in the period 1680–1750. Thus Wren not only joined his own family group (and his brother-in-law William Holder), but there was a scattering of others who had preceded him, notably (but not only) his companions on the construction project, the Spencers and John Tillison, Lawrence Spencer's predecessor as Clerk of Works and Paymaster. The large and fine monument to John Martin and his wife, of 1680 or shortly after, is a remarkable survival. It should also be noted that this brief survey is only of the graves beneath the choir and transepts; burials beneath the nave seem to start later, from the 1780s.

A group of notable English and American architects and artists were buried next to Wren in the south-east part of the crypt (Fig. 119). There were already two graves here, of de la Fontaine (1708, no. 13) and Elizabeth Wiseman (1694, no. 14). Between them and the wall recess where Wren and his son lie, the others were interred over a period from 1782 to 1851. Sir Joshua Reynolds seems to have been the earliest artist, but next to Wren was the burial, 10 years before, of Thomas Newton, Bishop of Bristol and Dean of St Paul's, who incidentally had his portrait painted by Benjamin West (also buried here). So

Fig. 118 Wall monument of John Martin (d. 1680) and his wife, in the north aisle of the choir crypt (Conway Library, The Courtauld Institute of Art, London)

Newton started the practice of being buried next to Wren; the burial of J M W Turner was the last of this group, though it could be said that the burials of William Holman-Hunt and Marion Holman-Hunt, beneath a ledger which records their deaths in 1910 and 1931 respectively, seek to be part of it.

Archaeologically recorded burials, 1994–2010

A small number of burials within the Wren crypt and relocated ledger stones were recorded during 1994–2010 as developments of the crypt took place. Four pieces of archaeological recording of burials dating from 1720 (and perhaps 1687) to 1883, are summarised here (Spencers; Channing; Brigdens; Palmer). The relaying of some ledgers (already brought from elsewhere and laid over a trench in the crypt floor for heating pipes in 1909) when a new chapel of the Knights Bachelor was created at the south-east corner of the choir crypt in 2007 is then noted. The sites of these burials in several locations around the crypt are shown in Figure 120, along with the location of the ledgers in the new chapel.

During works in 2000 to refurbish the choir practice facilities in the crypt below the south transept, two graves and their ledgers were removed, the latter being relaid nearby afterwards (Site G; Fig. 121). From their inscriptions, these were the burial places of Lawrence Spencer, Clerk of Works to Wren for most of the period of construction of the cathedral, and his wife Dorathy.[70]

Spencer was a trusted labourer, used as a witness to the payment of all the labourers from the beginning of the detailed accounts in October 1675. In this he assisted the Clerk of Works, John Tillison. After the death of Tillison in 1685, Spencer was Clerk of Works for the cathedral from March 1686 until it was finished.[71] From the inscription on the ledger, he died in 1720. A brief biography of Spencer, from the accounts, is given below in Chapter 6.

One grave contained two skeletons which had been interred together, each in coffin. They were laid supine and extended with the infant coffin beside the shoulder of the adult. The adult was identified by the ledger slab above as Dorathy Spencer née Bradshaw, wife of Lawrence Spencer senior, who died in 1687. There was no mention of the child. A second grave held the skeletons of two adults laid supine and extended and facing

Fig. 119 The burials around Wren: south aisle of the crypt below the choir, looking west (John Schofield). Wren's tomb is on the left, in shadow

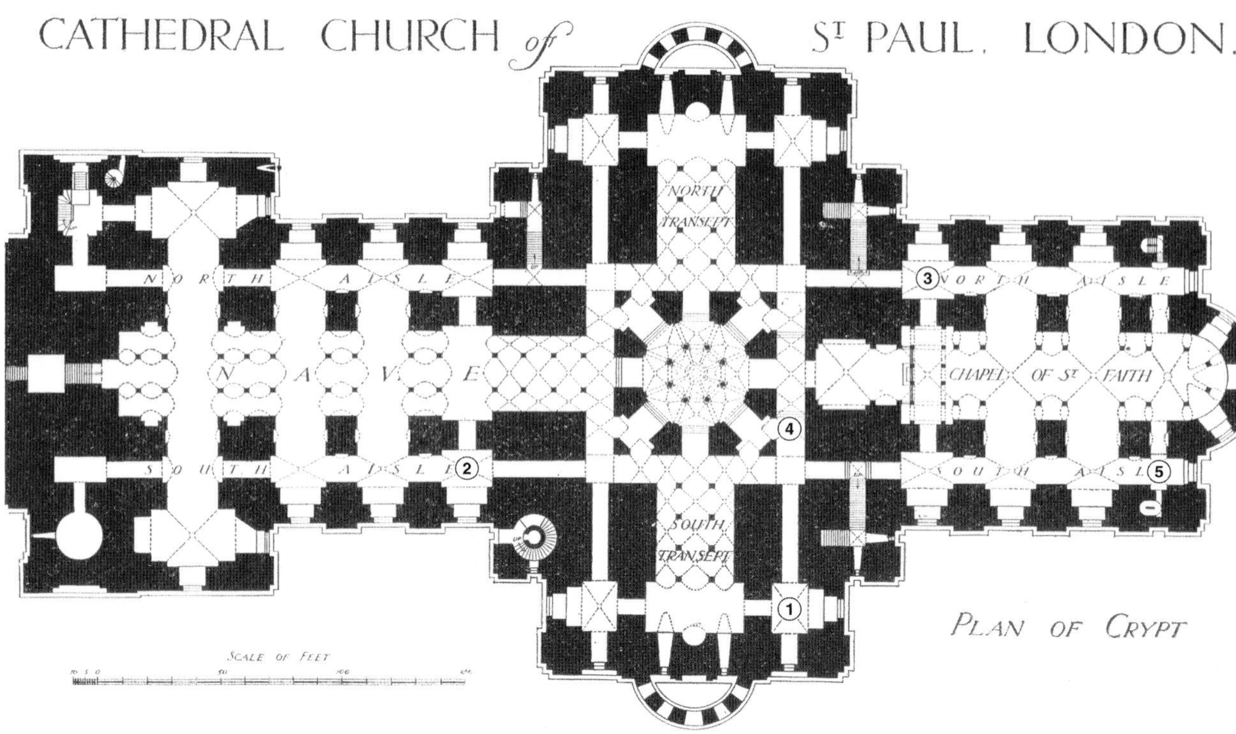

Fig. 120 Location of archaeological recordings of burials and ledgers in the crypt, 1994–2010. Key: 1, Spencers; 2, Channing; 3, Brigdens; 4, Palmer; 5, group of recorded ledgers in the Knights Bachelor Chapel. The plan is of the crypt in 1929 (RCHME 1929, 49), that is before the refurbishments of the 1990s

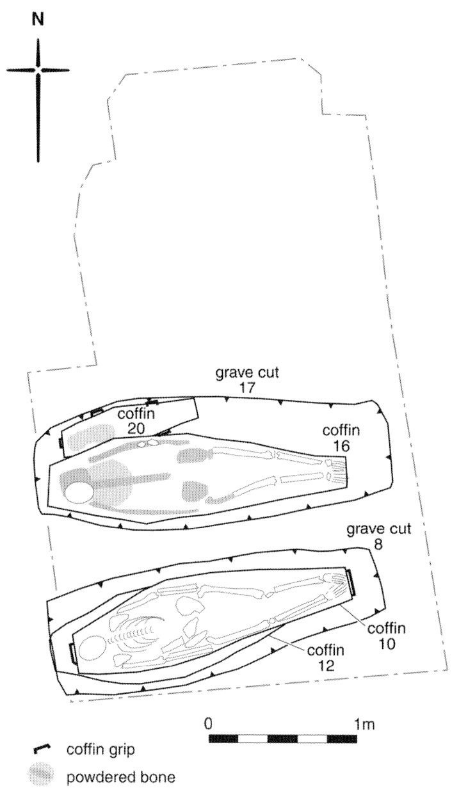

Fig. 121 Site G: post-medieval graves beneath the south transept (Carlos Lemos, MOLA)

east. They were identified as Lawrence Spencer [senior], and his son, also called Lawrence. They died within 5 months of each other in 1719–20 and were buried together, with the elder Lawrence on top. Little survived of their skeletons, but enough to suggest their differences in age at death and therefore their identities.

The skeletons in all four cases were in a very poor state of preservation (details in the specialist report, Chapter 6). Much of the bone had disintegrated into a white powder and the remainder was extremely fragile. The coffins were also badly decayed but the presence of metal coffin furniture showed that they were all decorated to an extent. None of the timber from the coffins survived to any recognisable degree, the shape and dimensions of the coffins being determined purely from the dark brown organic staining around the skeletons. The coffin furniture was made from two types of metal: studs of copper alloy and grips, plates and brackets of iron. The copper alloy studs were in excellent condition, some still retaining their shiny surface, but the iron fittings had corroded. In some cases the shape of the iron objects could be determined but the decorative work was, for the most part, too corroded to record.

The two coffins for the Lawrences were virtually identical and the presence of copper alloy studs were indicative of fairly high-status burials (although not of the same class as lead coffins). Studs, or upholstery pins, were both decorative and functional, used to secure fabric to the outside of the coffin. In both cases the fabric, typically red or black velvet, had decayed away, apart from small traces beneath some of the studs. The use of studs in this fashion dates from the beginning of the 18th century, so these are early examples. The two coffins belonging to Dorathy and the child were too early to possess them. These were instead decorated with iron furniture fairly typical of the period. The grips or coffin handles also indicate a difference in date. In general terms grips from the 17th century were larger, of more solid construction and plainer than those from the 18th century. The grips on Dorathy's coffin were certainly larger and more squarely made than those for the Lawrences. The horizontal parts of the handle were straight in the case of Dorathy's coffin but tapered from a central swelling on the Lawrence Spencers' examples. The latter were a plain right-angled form but, with the tapering, were transitional towards the evolution of the more rounded form of grip, prevalent from the mid 18th century.

The date of 1687 on the ledger of Dorathy Spencer beneath the south transept is notable, since at that date the walls of the transept crypt would just have been built, and perhaps the brick vault of the crypt had been built above the grave. It is one of the earliest securely documented burials in the cathedral crypt, which at the time was a building site.

The Spencers were not in a specially-built brick vault, but such vaults are no doubt widespread beneath the floor of the crypt, and one has recently been seen. In 1994, during relaying of the floor of the nave part of the crypt, a brick-lined vault which belonged to the Channing family was exposed in the south aisle of the crypt (Site B; Fig. 122); it is now (2015) beneath the carpet of the cathedral shop. In the north and south sides of the vault were three vertical rows of putlog holes, approximately 0.35m, 0.82m and 1.34m above the floor of the vault. Some of them still contained traces of decayed wood. They presumably bore timbers on which the coffins were laid, but they had later collapsed. At the top of the vault were three large stone slabs forming the roof of the vault; and on these the ledger was laid. The inscription commemorated six members of the Channing family who died between February 1785 and September 1796:

Fig. 122 Site B: the Channing vault looking west, showing at least two lead coffins (Andy Chopping, MOLA)

Miss Harriott Elizabeth Channing aged 14; Mrs Johanna Channing aged 53; John Channing aged 61; Miss Harriot Eliza Channing aged 3 weeks; and Mrs Charlotte Channing, wife of John, aged 35. The small vault contained at least three large lead-lined timber coffins, with possibly a smaller one against the eastern wall.

The third example of recently-recorded burials has literary connections. Works requiring some disturbance below the crypt floor adjacent to the north wall of the crypt in 2007 came across two superimposed burials, the upper in wooden coffin on top of a lead coffin shell (Gazetteer, Site Q; the burials not illustrated). Both had breast plates. The lead coffin contained Martha Brigden (d. February 1785) and the wooden coffin Edward Brigden (d. July 1787). He was a lace merchant in London in 1774, with an estate in North Carolina; correspondence of his with Benjamin Franklin has survived. Martha, his second wife, was the daughter of the novelist Samuel Richardson who wrote *Pamela or Virtue Rewarded* in 1740. Any stone ledger for this burial had been removed, so the floor had been remade in concrete which covered it by the time of Penrose's survey of 1873, which noted other ledgers in the floor around it but missed this one.

After Nelson and Wellington, occasional

Fig. 123 *Site P: removal and turning of ledger of 1883, 2008: the ledger (above the steps) in its setting before turning, looking south (Andy Chopping, MOLA)*

Fig. 124 *Site P: the grave beneath and the casket, looking west (scale 0.2m) (Andy Chopping, MOLA)*

burial in the crypt of members of the armed forces continued through the second half of the 19th century. One had to be slightly disturbed recently in the passage east of the Nelson chamber in 2008, when the adding of a ramp for disabled access through the crypt required the moving and turning through 90° of a ledger of 1883 (Site P; Fig. 123). This lay over a coffin which contained a casket of bones collected at the site of the deaths of three servicemen in the Sinai the previous year: Professor E H Palmer,[72] Captain William Gill of the Royal Engineers and Lieutenant Harold Charrington of the Royal Navy (Fig. 124). A plaque on the adjacent wall relates how the three were killed by Bedouin Arabs. The inscription on the plaque adds that two others died in the incident, a Syrian and a Hebrew, 'whose remains lie with theirs'; so the casket (which was not opened or disturbed in 2008) may contain the collected bones of up to five men.

A group of ledgers relaid at the east end of the crypt

Examples of the ledgers are given here from a group which had been relaid in a new order over a large heating duct crossing what is now the OBE Chapel, at the east end of the crypt, probably by Macartney in the first decade of the 20th century (Fig. 125–Fig. 129). These were taken up and relaid in a different order as part of the refurbishment of the bay forming the east end of the south aisle of the crypt to become a chapel of the Order of Knights Bachelor in 2007 (for location, see Fig. 120).[73] Correlation with the plan by Penrose of 1873 shows that of the ledgers in this group, those of of Jasper Waters, George Dunt and Barbara Comyn had original sites in the apse of the crypt; that of Edward Roth was in the easternmost bay of the south aisle, so the coffin must have been removed by Macartney in 1909 to make way for the duct. The ledger of Canon Thomas Jackson (d. 1797) is not on Penrose's plan.

Penrose showed the original burial place of George Dunt (who died in 1706) on his plan of 1873, at the east end of what is now the OBE Chapel, that is in the central apse of the crypt, on the south side. The ledger must have covered a vault, since seven people are commemorated on the ledger: George Ludwich Dunt, merchant (d.1706), '& by him 4 of his Children'; his widow Deborah who died in 1748, and a son Thomas, presumably a fifth child, who died in 1752.

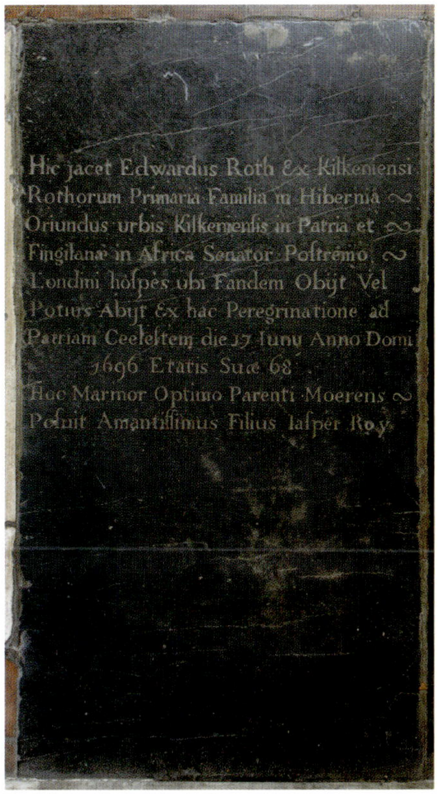

Clockwise from top left:

Fig. 125 *Knights Bachelor Chapel, Site O: this and the four next figures show late 17th- and 18th-century ledgers from the crypt, now in the easternmost bay of the south aisle, where they were relaid in the first decade of the 20th century; here, Jasper Waters (d. 1774) and his wife Deborah (d. 1788) (Andy Chopping, MOLA)*

Fig. 126 *Edward Roth (d. 1696) (Andy Chopping, MOLA)*

Fig. 127 *George Dunt (d. 1706) and members of the Dunt family (d. 1748, 1752) (Andy Chopping, MOLA)*

Fig. 128 *Barbara Comyn (d. 1750) (Andy Chopping, MOLA)*

Fig. 129 *Canon Thomas Jackson (d. 1797) (Andy Chopping, MOLA)*

Conclusions

A conclusion from this preliminary study of the burials at St Paul's is that in addition to the burials of the Wren family, their Clerks of Works and other principals on the project, there were further occasional burials in the crypt, when prominent persons arranged for their burial, sometimes in vaults, before even the crypt was finished, as in the case of John Martin (d. 1680) (though in his case the vaulting over the monument would have been finished, as the latter stands at the east end of the crypt). A grouping of the artistic elite around Wren's grave began in 1792 with the burial of Sir Joshua Reynolds. The last of this group, of Turner in 1851, was shortly before the general stopping of burials at all City churchyards, to be replaced by burial in the new suburban cemeteries. By this time burials had taken place in all parts of the crypt, that is below the choir, transepts and to a lesser extent the nave, though this was not normally open to public view.

One finding of the recent work is that there are also burials of eminent people in the crypt, but their sites were lost and only found by chance, largely because for some reason they do not have ledger stones which were recorded by Penrose or others. One case is the burials of Edward Brigden (d. 1787) and his wife Martha (d. 1785), daughter of the novelist Samuel Richardson. These were found in 2008 in the north aisle of the choir crypt (Gazetteer, Site Q); the site was apparently unknown and the ledger had been removed.

Among the public parts of the cathedral, the crypt is the part which has changed the most since the time of Wren. Use of the crypt for monuments since 1680 has meant that the main church floor is comparatively uncongested in comparison to Westminster Abbey. Today the west end and the nave section of the crypt form an interface with the public, comprising a restaurant and café, a small conference centre, the cathedral shop and toilets. There are only a few ledger stones here. To the east, beyond the Churchill gates (placed there 2004), is the area full of monuments and wall plaques to military heroes mixed with memorials to playwrights, artists, scholars, war correspondents, bishops, politicians and other eminent persons. The creators of the memorials include Rodin (for W E Henley, 1903), Lutyens (Earl Beatty, 1938), Jacob Epstein (Sir Stafford Cripps, 1953) and Richard Kindersley (several, including the Falklands War Memorial, 1985, Fig. 130). The density of burials in the crypt below the choir was evident by the time of Penrose's survey in 1873, before he brought in the ledgers from outside.

Fig. 130 The Falklands War Memorial, 1985, by Richard Kindersley (Simon Carter, © Chapter of St Paul's Cathedral). The name of H Jones VC is marked through many people pointing it out, touching it with their fingers

The outside of the building, 1711–1900

On the exterior, three matters have recently engaged the archaeologist: historic graffiti at the west end and high in the south-west tower; the removal of the railings and rebuilding of the western steps by Penrose; and replacement of the steps at the south portico which allowed investigation of their history since the original construction.

Graffiti within the western portico

Cleaning of the west front took place in 2003–4 (Gazetteer, Site M). A significant part of the recording brief was to record by photography, before cleaning took place, a representative selection of the historic graffiti to be seen around the west doors. Naturally these were at a height where they could have been incised by people either standing or perhaps on small temporary supports such as boxes; they were nowhere higher than 2.3m from the floor. The graffiti were

Fig. 131 (left) Graffito 1 group (Andy Chopping, MOLA). Some areas are covered with indecipherable marks, as here

Fig. 132 (right) Graffito 2 (Andy Chopping, MOLA)

photographed in September 2003 just before the cleaning process reached them. The first five photographs (Graffito groups 1–5) are given here in the main text as examples (Fig. 131–Fig. 135), and others (Graffito groups 6–17 and 20–35) are in the gazetteer entry for Site M below, Figure 202–Figure 229.

The graffiti were inscribed (and some of them must have taken hours) between 1759 (Fig. 226) and the 1790s, from their dates. Besides those shown here, there are many more which are less legible. They were presumably left by visitors to the lower portico around the great west door. None of the legible names has so far been traced in contemporary wills.

The cleaning and repair project of 2003–4 also included inspection of the upper part of the south-west tower, where one capital was to be renewed. This disclosed some more graffiti inside the dome of the tower (Fig. 136). Several initials, names and two dates were inscribed with white paint on the soot-blackened ashlar of the inside of the cupola of the tower (which has been left uncleaned again) (Fig. 137–Fig. 140). The two dates are both 1788, indicating that some kind of inspection or repair was undertaken on the south-west tower in that year, during the surveyorship of Robert Mylne. He and successive Surveyors left this area alone; it is normally inaccessible.

Left to right:

Fig. 133 Graffito 3 group (Andy Chopping, MOLA)

Fig. 134 Graffito 4 group (Andy Chopping, MOLA)

Fig. 135 Graffito 5 group (Andy Chopping, MOLA)

Fig. 136 Elevation and section of the south-west (clock) tower by Poley (1927, pl. xxi); the location of the painted graffiti shown in the following figures is the inside of the upper vault, shown in the section on the right

Clockwise from top left:

Fig. 137 *Graffito 36 group (Andy Chopping, MOLA)*

Fig. 138 *Graffito 37 group (Andy Chopping, MOLA)*

Fig. 139 *Graffito 38 (Andy Chopping, MOLA)*

Fig. 140 *Graffito 39 (Andy Chopping, MOLA)*

The west end changes by Penrose 1872–1874

In the 1870s, Penrose rebuilt or altered all three entrance ways to the cathedral: the steps outside the west end and the north and the south porticoes at the transepts. He also appears to have relaid the paving within the lower portico or narthex at the west end, perhaps with changes.[74]

Various designs for an ambitious scheme for the steps and all the semicircular area around them were discussed from 1870 (for example, Fig. 141); the throwing open of the view of the west end of the cathedral may have been partly prompted by discussions with the Commission of Sewers of the City about giving up the ground occupied by the railings there to widen the roadway (as was eventually done). The final design was that the railings at the west end were to be removed, to be replaced by bollards of Shap granite which were set back behind the former line. Penrose designed the form of the bollards, and a removable fence in sections (Fig. 142), to hang between them. A photograph shows the west end of the cathedral at this time; possibly at the beginning of the project, since objects resembling the new bollards are shown stacked against the north end of the west front (Fig. 143). The railings have not yet been removed.

On 8 January 1874 the iron railings at the west end of the cathedral, including the west gates, were sold by public auction. A portion were sent to Toronto but the ship foundered on the American coast and some railings were recovered from the wreck. One section of railings was bought by J G Harper,[75] a Canadian, and set up in front of the prominent tomb of himself and his wife in High Park, Toronto (his house, now a public park), where it still stands, straightened out. The stairs were rebuilt into their present form, replacing the flared design. The present doors at either side of the steps, into the passage and vaults below the steps, are also by Penrose.[76] He produced a plan of the completed scheme (Fig. 144), and another photograph of about 1900 shows it a few years later (Fig. 145). Penrose also designed the lamp standards which were later replaced with the present ones by Lutyens.[77]

The south portico

In 1875, after dealing with the west front, Penrose turned to the north and south porticoes. He dealt with the north portico first, but information on precisely what he did is lacking. At the south portico, Penrose produced a detailed plan of the flooring and steps of the portico before he started his changes (Fig. 146). He then replaced the steps

Fig. 141 Penrose, 'sketch of a Proposal for laying out the Area in front of St Paul's Cathedral to the West giving free passage for pedestrians between the posts', 1870 (SPCAA D/1/9-9). This incorporates the existing flared design of the western steps and introduces matching drinking fountains at the sides

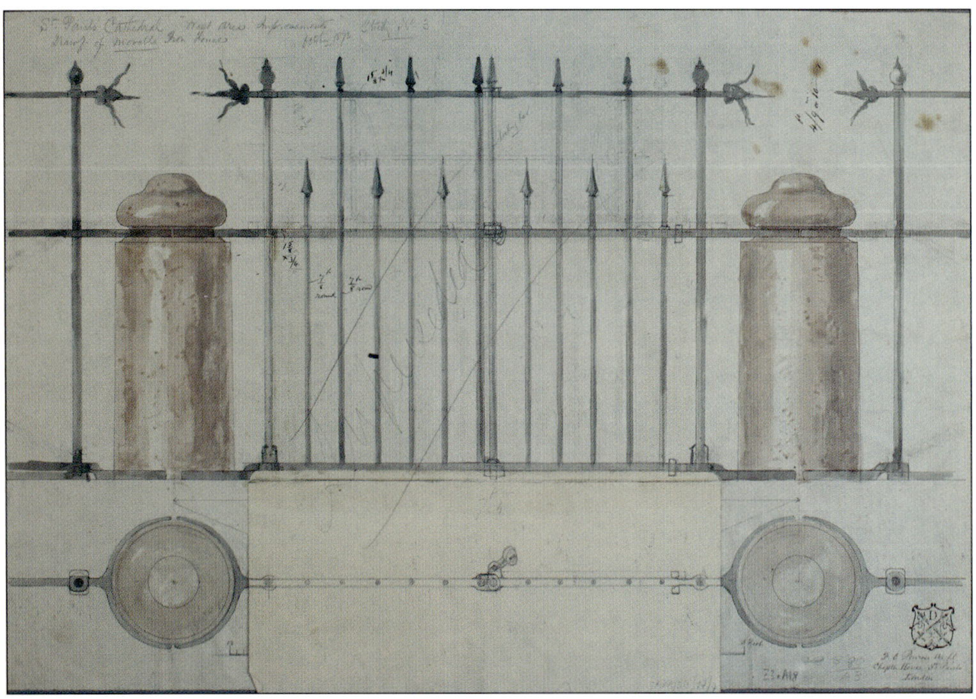

Fig. 142 Penrose, proposed design for the removable fence between the Shap bollards, 1873, showing how the neck of each bollard was designed to form the main support for removable railings (SPCAA D/1/17-4). The final design omitted the upper rail

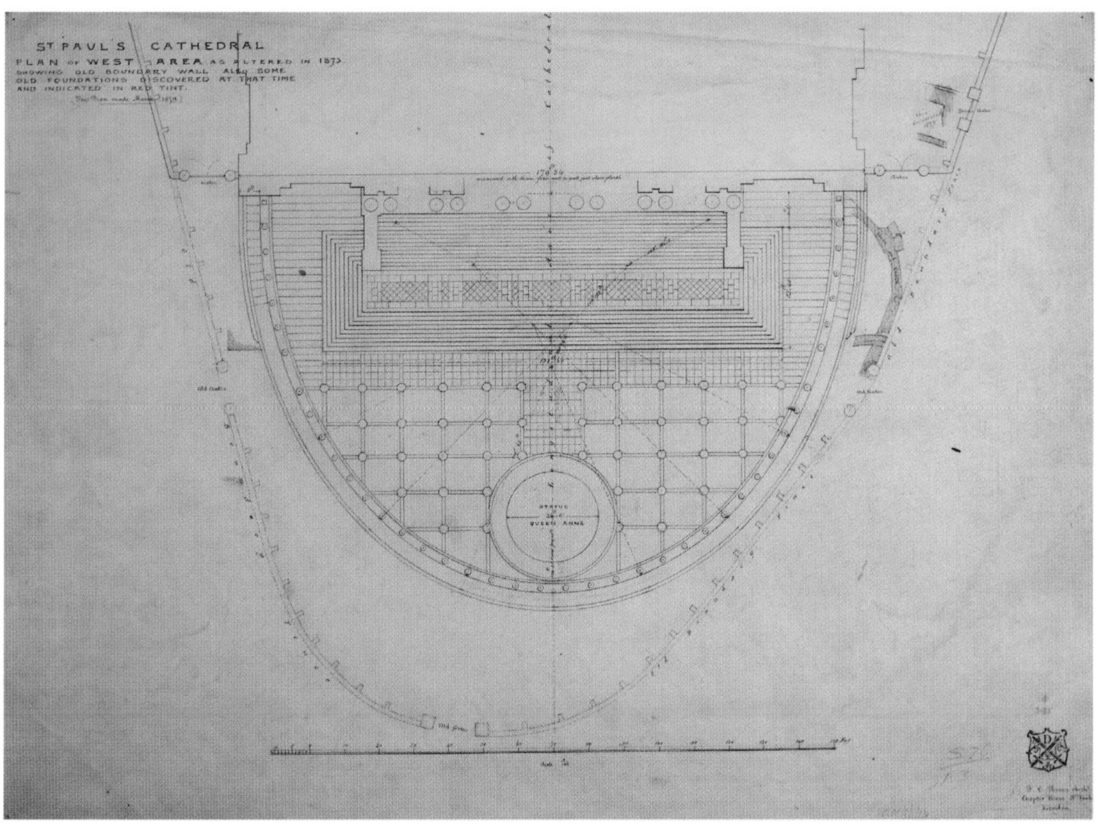

Anti-clockwise from top left:

Fig. 143 *The west end about 1873, before the railings were removed and the western steps altered by Penrose (reproduced by permission of Historic England). What may be the bollards, just arrived, are stacked against the north end of the west front. The difference in cleanliness between the two storeys of the west façade is a demonstration of the effectiveness of Wren's design of the middle cornice, which projects to shield the lower façade from water washing and therefore the effects of acid rain cleaning (comment by Oliver Caroe). Compare Fig. 145 of about 1900 and Fig. 163 of 1924*

Fig. 144 *Penrose, 'Plan of West Area as altered in 1873' (SPCAA D/1/9-6). This also shows the 'old foundations' discovered at the time, shown here in red; and the relationship of the new line of Shap bollards to the line of the original railings*

Fig. 145 *The west end about 1900, showing how Penrose left the western atrium, with the railings now ending at the towers*

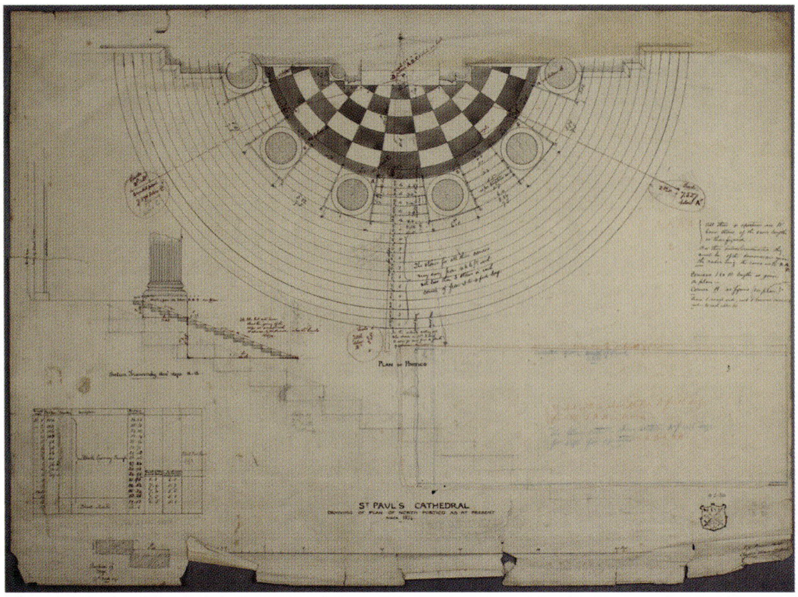

Fig. 146 The south portico in 1874: extract from a plan by Penrose before his changes of 1875 (SPCAA D/1/7/4). In a note on this plan he identifies the stone of the steps as 'Black Guernsey Granite'

Fig. 147 (above right) The outside of the south transept from the south west in the 1890s (Birch 1896, pl. iv). This shows some features no longer present: the original statues on the balustrade and pediment, the inner three of which were replaced in the early 20th century; the paterae from the bracing of Mylne; and an indication of the 19th-century window glazing, blown out in World War II. The steps seen here are those laid here by Penrose in 1875

using 'the best of the old marble collected from the two porticoes'.[78] The floor of the portico within the columns was laid with 'red and white granite'. The portico as repaired by Penrose is seen in another photograph of the 1890s (Fig. 147).

In 2007 the black steps laid here by Penrose were replaced by new steps in a similar Chinese stone. During preparation for this work a small archaeological trench uncovered what are interpreted as the mortar layers in which the original steps were set in the 1680s (see above, Chapter 2).

St Paul's Churchyard inside and outside the railings, 1711–1900

The setting of the cathedral within the Churchyard, and the approaches from several directions, are captured during the 18th century in the paintings of Canaletto and in many engravings, from 1710 (eg of Robert Trevitt, Fig. 17) to 1800 (those of Thomas Malton, Fig. 39, Fig. 44, Fig. 95, Fig. 148). This section deals with (i) the cathedral churchyard within the railings from 1711 to 1900, (ii) the railings and gates in Penrose's time 1852–97 (except for his laying out of the area west of the west front to take its present form which has been dealt with above), (iii) Penrose's archaeological excavations and the laying out of the fragments of the medieval chapter house and cloister in 1879–80, and (iv) a brief survey of buildings which bordered the Churchyard on all four sides, outside the railings, in 1711–1900. As a framework of reference, this section also begins with two maps of the cathedral and its

Fig. 148 (right) Thomas Malton: the south side of the cathedral, 1798 (LMA). This omits the gate in line with the Dean's door. Above, the original form of the clock face before replacement in the late 19th century

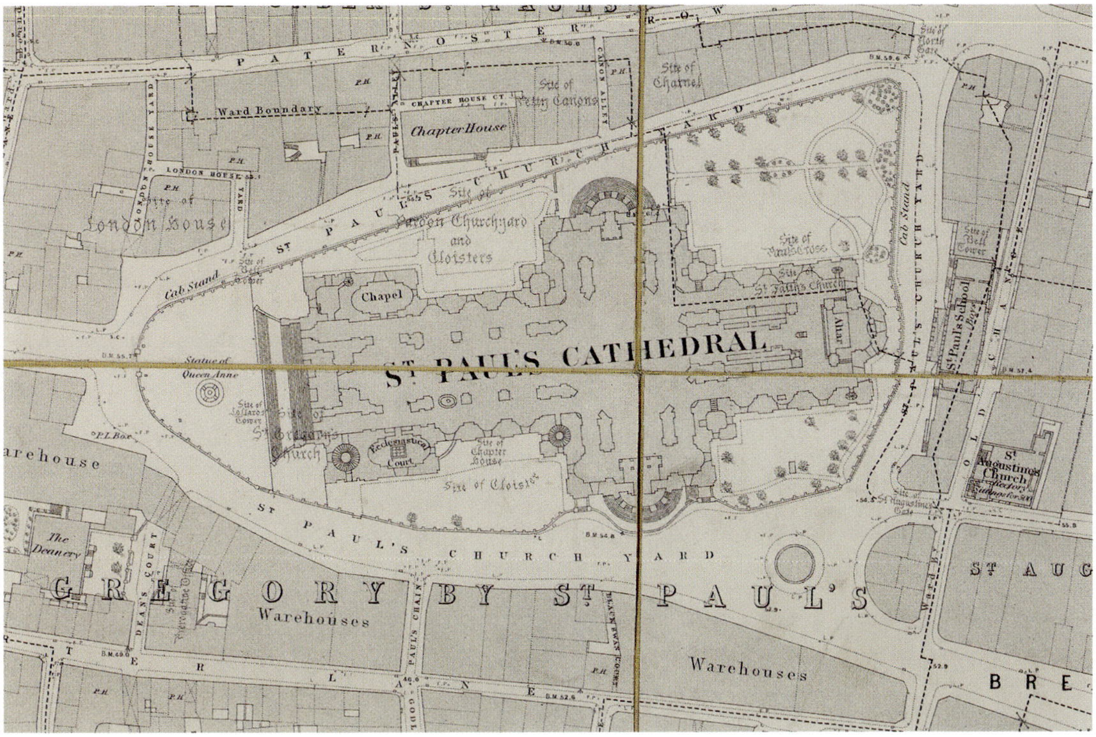

Fig. 149 The cathedral and its surroundings on the first Ordnance Survey map, 1873–4 (LMA)

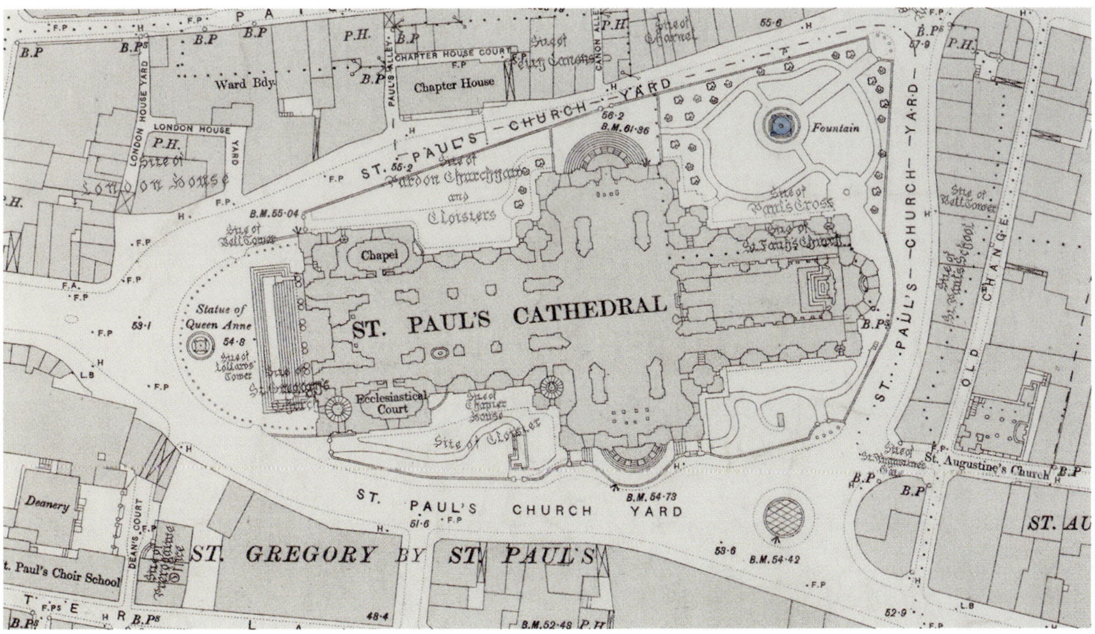

Fig. 150 The cathedral and churchyard on the Ordnance Survey map of 1894–6 (LMA)

surroundings in the late 19th century, which show some of these changes: the first Ordnance Survey map of 1873–4 (Fig. 149) and the Ordnance Survey map of 1894–6 (Fig. 150). These show how the secular City and its infrastructure tightened around the cathedral, which brought concerns. At various times from 1831 to 1910 there were engineering schemes which in the view of the Cathedral endangered the Wren foundations, and they were all defeated and never took place: a major east–west sewer that was to go near the south transept in 1831, underground railway lines proposed in 1870, 1890 and 1901, another sewer in 1907, and a tram subway in 1910 which would have been near the east end, connecting with a proposed bridge across the Thames whose site would have been close to the present Millennium Bridge.[79]

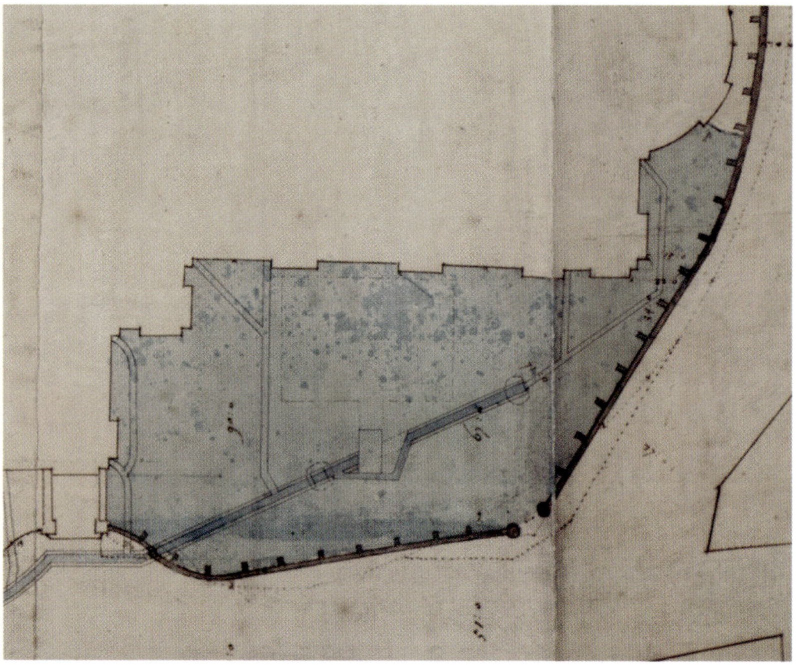

Fig. 151 Plan of the south-east churchyard in 1710 (an extract from Fig. 92) showing an outline of the St Gregory burial vault, its entrance, the drains, and the original form of the south-east gate in the railings

Fig. 152 The entrance to the St Gregory burial vault, looking north-east (John Schofield)

The churchyard within the railings, 1711–1900

The post-Fire parishioners of St Gregory were intent on having a vault for their own parish, at the east end of the parish (ie in the cathedral churchyard), from at least 1685. John Evelyn noted the burial of a former bishop of Norwich in 'St Gregory's churchyard, or vault' in 1698. In August 1707 the Commissioners were unsure where the open air burial grounds of St Gregory's and St Faith's actually lay, and ordered the Dean and Chapter to discuss the matter with both parishes and if possible procure a plan.[80] A vault is shown in dotted outline on Dickinson's plan of the churchyard in 1710 (Fig. 151), with the drains taking account of it, so perhaps an intended construction; the present vault south of the choir was was constructed in the same place in 1715–16 (Gazetteer, Site 39). The vault still stands in the churchyard, now empty (Fig. 152).

There are clearly other smaller presumably private vaults on all sides of the cathedral but the west, and one was located during tree planting south of the nave in 1980 (Gazetteer, Site 60). It is possible that such small brick vaults formerly lay under table tombs of the type still surviving in the north-east churchyard. The post-Fire churchyard was formerly of slightly larger extent, since the railings have been pulled back towards the cathedral in successive reorganisations. In the north-east corner of the churchyard, though now outside the railings (Gazetteer, Site 8), medieval burials were overlaid by a further deposit of cemetery soil, into which three more burials were cut; associated pottery was of the 17th and 18th centuries, so these burials were probably in the post-Fire churchyard. The north-east part of the churchyard was the burial ground for St Faith's parish, in which it lies.

In 1879 the Cathedral agreed with the Corporation of London that the latter should take over management of the churchyard, and this was sanctioned by faculty.[81] Penrose made a plan of the burials in the north-east part of the churchyard, before it was landscaped into a new arrangement. Some of the 18th-century table tombs have been retained up to the present, but the ledgers have been moved. According to Penrose's reports, about 40 were relocated in the north aisle of the choir crypt, which was always part of the parish of St Faith's, as described above in the section on burials.[82] The arrangement of paths in the churchyard before the 1870s is shown in the first Ordnance Survey map of 1873–4 (Fig. 149); that is, before the creation of the gate at the north-east corner by Penrose.

Penrose brought many ledgers inside the crypt, where they pave the aisle on the north side of the choir (now the OBE Chapel). The external area and the north aisle of the crypt below the choir were and are in the parish of St Faith. Mosaic bands were now laid in the crypt to denote the parish boundary; they survive. In the cleared area of churchyard a fountain designed by Penrose and Horace Jones was placed in 1880 (Fig. 153); this was on the site of the present column erected only 30 years later, in 1910.[83] This clearing-up of the north-east churchyard

Fig. 153 The north-east churchyard, looking west, by Philip Norman, drawn between 1880 and 1896 (V&A, D.75-1896, © Victoria and Albert Museum, London). This shows the fountain by Penrose and Horace Jones; and on the right, two of the plane trees which stand today

coincided with the construction of the new gate to Cheapside, as described next, and thus the opening to the secular City and its workers of the recreational space.

The railings and gates, 1852–1897

The Corporation of London bought a strip of land along the south side of the cathedral from the Dean and Chapter in 1873, and the railings were realigned a short distance to the north to provide more space for the roadway; this was presumably the context for a new gate next to the medieval cloister remains exposed by Penrose, described next. At the same time, the railings at the north-east corner were changed and an entrance made. This seems to have been in February 1879, when the diary of Virger Green noted:

> 'The alterations in the Churchyard began; lowering the railings, and widening the south side for a pathway: St Faith's and St Gregory's burying ground (the larger part of the Churchyard ground) to be planted and made ornamental. New entrance at the N.E. corner by Cheapside (very handsomely executed)'.[84]

The new arrangement of paths with the new gate is shown on the Goad Insurance Map of the area in 1886 and the Ordnance Survey map of 1894–6 (Fig. 150). This new gate to Cheapside and new paths to a fountain (later replaced by the column with St Paul) opened up the north-east churchyard as never before. The railings along the west and north sides of the churchyard were rebuilt on new alignments after World War II, so that the present north-east gate is several metres to the east of where Penrose placed it. He also altered the corresponding gate at the south-east corner, which is shown differently on the two Ordnance Survey maps. The new arrangement is seen in the map of 1894–6 (Fig. 150), which also shows that he used four more of the Shap bollards here, in front of the gate. These were still present in 1961 (Fig. 183 below), but have since been removed.[85] The present gate is several metres to the east of the Penrose-period gate and reflects the post-War realignment of a long section of railing which now incorporates St Paul's School and runs along New Change. Back at the south side and further to the west, Penrose also inserted two openings with gates, one on either side of the south portico, in 1881. These led directly down into the churchyard on both sides, behind the railings.

Penrose's excavations, 1879–1880

From his days as a post-graduate student at Cambridge, Penrose studied historic and ancient buildings on the Continent. He studied the Pantheon in Rome in 1843, and the monuments of Athens in 1845–6. He was one of the first to identify the entasis (the deliberate curving of edges to correct optical distortion) of the Parthenon (John Pennethorne had come to much the same conclusion in 1844). Penrose published his findings on this in 1851 (with a revised edition in 1888).

Top to bottom:

Fig. 154 *Site H: remains of one of the piers on the inner side of the 14th-century cloister, exposed and conserved by Penrose, looking north (0.2m scale) (Andy Chopping, MOLA)*

Fig. 155 *Site H: detail of lead bracket for a drain for the monument, with the arms of the Dean and Chapter (Andy Chopping, MOLA)*

Fig. 156 *Site H, 2004: the south-east corner of the medieval cloister, looking north-east (0.5m scale) (Andy Chopping, MOLA). This shows the depth of the medieval fragments in relation to modern ground-level (right); one of the settings for a low rail to contain visitors is shown towards the rear. In the section can be seen the backfilling layer of chalk rubble of 1937*

In 1878, his plans for cleaning up the churchyard around the cathedral would have been advanced, and his habit of fastidious recording of any monuments encountered would have naturally led to investigation of those areas immediately outside the footprint of the Wren building where the medieval structures may have survived. One senses that Penrose was almost as much an archaeologist as an architect. Over the following 2 years he dug small trenches to discover the east end of the medieval cathedral, Paul's Cross, parts of the south cloister and two of the buttress bases of the 14th-century chapter house, and the join between the west end and the Jones portico. These sightings are described in *St Paul's Cathedral before Wren*. The excavations of the cloister and buttress bases illustrate Penrose's efforts at conservation; small lead drains were added to the monument, embossed with the arms of the Dean and Chapter (Fig. 154, Fig. 155).

The fragments found by Penrose, backfilled in 1937 and largely obscured by the 1970s, were re-excavated in 2004–6 in advance of rearrangement of levels in the south-west part of the churchyard. This was part of the scheme to provide disabled access to the door in the corner of the Wren nave and south transept. A gradual ramp of appropriate slope now leads up the line of the east walk of the medieval cloister, which is laid out in new stone a couple of feet above the reburied medieval remains. The investigation of 2004–6 showed how decayed the 14th-century footings had become by 1937, their decay presumably accelerated by exposure to the Victorian and early 20th-century atmosphere in the City (Fig. 156).

Penrose inserted a new gate in the Wren railings, immediately south of the line of the east walk of the medieval cloister. Presumably this dated from after his discovery of the medieval remains, and gave access to them when laid out as a display. The gate is shown on the Goad insurance map of 1886 and the Ordnance Survey map of 1894–6 (Fig. 150).

Penrose also excavated immediately outside the east end of the Wren building, finding the east end of the medieval cathedral, in several damaged parts, in 1879.[86] These were afterwards made accessible from manholes, which they are today. Apparently he laid out the form of the medieval east end in gravestones, as reported by Somers Clarke in 1904, when the stones were in need of treatment,[87] but any such outline is not visible today in the paving. Perhaps it was removed in new paving which came with the commemoration of St Paul's Cross by laying out the extent of the Cross in the paving immediately to the north in 1904.

Outside the railings and the outer edge of the churchyard, 1711–1900

In the 18th and first half of the 19th centuries, the cathedral was surrounded on all four sides by Georgian buildings which had some of the character of a London square, though many had ground-floor shops facing into the Churchyard (shown in the background of Fig. 96, which also shows the entrance to Dean's Court and the Deanery on the right-hand side, in 1753); thus completely different in character from the squares of the West End. Ludgate Hill and the Churchyard became a fashionable shopping area, as the development of gas lighting and plate glass windows made shops extremely attractive. Cheapside was a major shopping street as it had been in the medieval city. At this time, however, there was no access to the churchyard from the corner of Cheapside with what was then Old Change (rerouted after World War II a short distance to the east to form the present New Change). The main entry points into the cathedral were the transepts or the west end.

Some details of individual buildings in the Churchyard are available from the early decades of the 19th century. Thomas Horner shows a view along the north side of the Churchyard in 1822, though with modifications (Fig. 157). On the extreme left is the entry to London House Yard. Beyond is the Wren Chapter House, though the western of the two doorways is obscured by the building in front, and the eastern doorway is shown. In front of this door the barrier of posts and a bar is a 'turnpike' placed there in 1701, renewed in 1714, to stop coaches passing along the north side of the cathedral and in front of the Chapter House.[88] Two painted lead name plates, referring to the 'west' and 'east' parts of the Churchyard, were recovered from Site A in 1969–70 (finds report, Chapter 6; not illustrated). They are without further documentation, but it seems probable that they were on the wooden barrier which stood here until 1970.

Another artefact of this period is an intact jar which once contained anchovy paste for sandwiches, made at the shop of J Wingrave and Company at 80 St Paul's Churchyard,

Fig. 157 *Looking east along the north side of the Churchyard in 1822, by Thomas Horner (LMA). The north portico of the cathedral is shown in section*

Fig. 158 Top of anchovy paste jar, found on Site A in 1969 (Andy Chopping, MOLA)

found unstratified on Site A in 1969 (Fig. 158); the company took advantage of their location to link the cathedral's most famous aspect with their produce. As shown on Tallis's view of all buildings in the Churchyard in 1838–40,[89] no. 80 was a thin building over the west entrance to London House Yard in the north-west corner of the Churchyard.

This introduces another strand in the history of pictures of St Paul's and therefore its influence, in this case on material culture of City workers and visitors. From the 19th century are examples of transfer prints showing the cathedral which are placed on various forms of ceramics. Two further examples from the Ceramic Collection of the Museum of London are given here: a strainer of 1823–42 which shows the form of the western steps before Penrose's changes of the 1870s (Fig. 159), and a plate with a design commemorating the funeral of the Duke of Wellington in 1852 (Fig. 160), which shows the temporary arch erected at the foot of the western steps. Perhaps a sign of the times, two of these three examples of pottery cashing in on the aura of St Paul's probably contained the filling for city workers' sandwiches.

The buildings which bordered the Churchyard on all four sides, apart from St Paul's School on the east side, were standard three- to five-storey post-Fire buildings, most of them with the ground floor given over to a shop. The stationery and bookselling trade was still a strong feature of the area, and continued so in part until 1941.[90] In Tallis's drawings of 1838–40 the shops included those specialising in playing cards, fancy goods and haberdashery, millinery, glass and china, books, straw manufacture (two establishments), medicine, brushes and combs, sheet music, and cheese; the buildings also contained the offices of a surgeon, an optician, two tailors, two chemists and a 'working cutler'. The premises shown by Tallis survived, in some few cases, to the end of the 19th century, mixed with newer buildings (Fig. 161); but most of the Churchyard was rebuilt in the second half of the 19th century, with the result that it resembled other major streets in the City (Fig. 162). One five-storey office building at the north-west corner of the Churchyard, on the site of the medieval bishop's palace, was notable for its interior steel frame which allowed the architect, Sir Banister Fletcher, considerable panache in the design of its front elevation (76–78 St Paul's Churchyard, 1898; Fig. 163).[91] A large intrusion was Cook's wholesale drapery warehouse of 1852 in the south-east corner of the churchyard; this overbearing building (Fig. 164) 'kept the sunlight off Wren's masterpiece for three generations',[92] only being removed after World War II. The nature of properties forming

Fig. 159 (left) A ceramic strainer with a north-west view of St Paul's, including the original flared lower western steps (ie before the 1870s) (MoL, Ceramic Collection A28173). It was made in Staffordshire by Thomas and John Carey, whose factory flourished from 1823 to 1842. This piece was one of a series which included views of two other cathedrals and York Minster

Fig. 160 (right) A pot lid commemorating the funeral of the Duke of Wellington in 1852 (MoL, Ceramic Collection A28202). The pot may have held potted meat

Fig. 161 The south-west corner of St Paul's Churchyard photographed about 1895 by Henry Dixon (LMA). The range on the left, on the south side of the Churchyard, dates from before 1840 since it is shown by Tallis. Note the cast-iron hoist on the fourth floor of the Dakin building. In rebuilding on the site about 1900, the corner shown here was smoothed out and the present alignment established

Fig. 162 The buildings at the junction of the Churchyard with Ludgate Hill around 1900, looking west (LMA). The buildings on the right (north) were replaced by banks before the World War II, and in turn replaced first by Juxon House in 1961, then the present Paternoster Square in 1997

Fig. 163 The north-west corner of the Churchyard, looking north-east, 20 January 1924 (reproduced by permission of Historic England). 76–78 St Paul's Churchyard is on the left. This also shows the taxi stand which was already well-established by the 1870s. For the differential darkening of the stonework on the two storeys of the west façade, see caption to Fig. 143 above

Fig. 164 Cook's warehouse, St Paul's Churchyard (built 1852); it survived until after World War II (BM, 1880, 1113.3314; © The Trustees of the British Museum). In the bottom right, what is probably meant to be the gate at the south-east corner of the churchyard railings, before being altered by Penrose

the historic churchyard and in the streets around St Paul's is shown in the first Ordnance Survey map of the City, surveyed in 1873–4 (Fig. 149).[93]

One feature of the post-Fire churchyard has survived, though moved and in a later form. In his drainage plan of 1710, Dickinson shows the site of the St Faith's parish pump as a simple square (Fig. 92, upper right); that this square is the pump is seemingly confirmed by the view of the cathedral from the north-west of about 1800 by Thomas Malton, though the pump may have been moved a little in the drawing (Fig. 95). The pump was apparently replaced by one which bears a date of 1819; this remarkably survived into the 20th century (it is shown by the letter 'P' on the Ordnance Survey map of 1873, Fig. 149) and having survived the Blitz was moved in 1973 to Paul's Alley, on the west side of the Chapter House, where it now stands.

Conclusions: the transformation of the cathedral by Penrose

Though the work of several of the Surveyors who succeeded Wren, particularly Robert Mylne, was important for keeping the cathedral standing and in good condition, the work of Francis Penrose from 1852 to 1897 was one of transformation for the cathedral. In partnership with Dean Milman, Penrose cleaned the interior and removed the choir screen and organ, opening up the whole interior for the first time, and as it now appears. The internal changes were driven by religious initiatives. Outside, perhaps the motives were different. When he started in the 1850s, the cathedral was surrounded by a high fence on all sides, with no gate to Cheapside, and the only use of the space within the railings was for burials, which were stopped in 1861. By the end of his time in 1897, the west front had been made far more accessible by removal of the railings there; the access to north and south porticoes had been improved by repairs; a gate inserted at the corner with Cheapside; and most importantly, the north-east churchyard turned into a public space with a fountain jointly designed with the City Architect, Horace Jones (whose other work included Tower Bridge and the three markets of the City at Smithfield, Billingsgate and Leadenhall). All the churchyard spaces around the building were landscaped by Penrose. Both outside and inside, therefore, Penrose and opened up the cathedral so it could play more of a part in secular life at the local and national level. This opening up of the cathedral complemented the wholesale rebuilding of the secular frontages to the Churchyard, with more businesses and larger shops which brought more people to the area.

Use of stone and other building materials, 1711–1900

Archaeological research into the stone used both in the original Wren building and in its later repairs under subsequent Surveyors has not yet been undertaken. Here are some initial remarks on the geology and weathering, since 1711, of the Portland stone, and observations on the use of other stones.

As early as 1728, a French visitor noted that the Portland stone 'would retain its whiteness and its polish were it not for this accursed smoke which is so corrosive that it eats away other kinds of stone and blackens this kind almost all over.'[94] In contrast to the interior, records seem to be lacking about any efforts to clean the exterior of the building before the 20th century.

In 1923 J V Elsden and J A Howe published a survey of the use of building stone in London, *The Stones of London*, from which the following is reproduced. Portland stone is a shallow water limestone foundation. At the Isle of Portland, the main source, the chief beds of the stone, in descending order from the surface, are the Roach, the Whit bed, and the Base bed. Each is an oolite of fine to medium grain, but each possesses characters that fit it for certain restricted uses. The Roach is a buff-tinted strong stone often with hollow spaces due to the solution and disappearance of fossil shells; its rough appearance makes it suitable for docks and engineering works.[95] The Whit bed (also called the Brown bed by quarrymen) is the harder of the two 'freestone' layers, but it has layers of broken shells in places. It is found on buildings in London, and is suitable for gate posts or outdoor statuary, such as the figures round the Victoria Memorial opposite Buckingham Palace. The Base bed (also the Best bed, Lower tier, Bottom bed and White bed) is paler, softer, and therefore less durable than the Whit bed. It has been much used for interiors and finer carvings. Narrow veins of calcite sometimes cross the stone, and these resist weathering better than the rest of the stone, standing up as whitish streaks.

Elsden and Howe also looked at the appearance of the cathedral in their own day:

> 'Although much blackened by smoke, St Paul's is in fairly good condition, especially on the north and east fronts. The carvings of flowers, fruit, and other decorations are nearly as perfect as when freshly executed. There is more sign of deterioration on the south and west fronts, which suffer the direct attack of the prevalent winds, and owing to the wind and rain the stone is washed clean and exhibits a whitened and weather-beaten aspect. Where the stone is protected by its position or by its form from this direct attack, it is completely blackened with a deposit of soot, and under some of the cornices and similar projections thick accumulations of stalaglitic gypsum mixed with soot bear testimony to the decomposition of the stone. There is also some visible disintegration in the drum of the dome and in the cupola above it, very possibly due to a slight inferiority in the quality of the stone.'[96]

The coming of railways after the 1840s meant that a larger variety of stones could be obtained from greater distances, including from abroad. In 1861 Penrose used Cork Red carboniferous limestone for columns of his new pulpit (now in store in the north triforium of the nave), along with dark purplish columns of stone from Angelsey, grey columns from Plymouth, and marbles from Siena and the Greek island of Tenos. The landing of the western steps includes the fine-grained hematite-stained calcite marble from Laconia in the Peloponnese (where the ancient quarries were reopened in the 19th century) and dark grey stone from Porto Venere near Spezia (Liguria, Italy). His bollards of Shap (Cumberland) granite,[97] introduced in 1874, stand in a semicircle outside the west end of the cathedral, and others, transposed, are outside the north transept. Thus a considerable variety of exotic types of stone at St Paul's, both inside and outside, may be a result of the coming of the railway age in London.

CHAPTER 4

St Paul's 1897–2013: protection and conservation

This chapter presents a summary of the history of the cathedral in the 20th century and the opening of the 21st century, to 2013. It is a brief account of the ways in which the cathedral and its surroundings were perceived, especially by modern planners and the local authority, the City of London. Here we describe how the cathedral and its churchyard are seen (in several senses) and conserved today.

The first decades of the 20th century, the works of 1925–1935, and the creation of St Paul's Heights and St Paul's Depths

Somers Clarke, Surveyor 1897–1906, reported in 1902 that movement had been observed in the west portico, and he then tied the front back with metal rods; he had already inserted rods above the window in the south transept.[1] He also replaced three of the statues on the south transept (the inner three; the outer two are the originals). He wrote that they were 'made not of three or four very large stones as should have been the case, but of many small ones, tied and cramped together in all directions with iron which, having rusted, has now broken the stones.'[2] Somers Clarke introduced electric light to the interior in 1899; and extended (to a different design) the railings along the nave entablature and across the terminal walls of the transepts at entablature level in 1898 (the previous vertiginous and unprotected path of boards on joists around the entablature of the north transept can be seen in one of Birch's photographs in the 1890s).[3]

Mervyn Macartney, Surveyor 1906–31, directed several important repairs and improvements. The greatest problem, settlement, is described below. In 1909–10 he inserted the present hot-water heating system, the pipes of which run in large channels beneath the crypt floor and along the walls of the triforia.[4] Presumably he then removed the stoves put in the crypt by Penrose. Macartney also placed fire-resistant partitions in the dome in 1912.[5] During his time, there were two significant excavations on the north side of the building. First, in 1909, Macartney created the first part of the subterranean Works Department, alongside the north side of the nave, roughly coterminous with the area now contained by the post-War alignment of the Wren railings (Gazetteer, Site A). He recorded medieval graves of several periods, including stone-lined coffins, and parts of the 14th- or 15th-century Pardon Cloister.[6]

Second, in 1912 he erected the monument today called St Paul's Cross, the pillar in the north-east churchyard, designed by Reginald Blomfield, which replaced the fountain (only of 1880) by Penrose and Jones on the same site. Macartney drew the sides of the excavation required for this large monument, recording burials and probably the surviving top of Roman strata beneath.[7]

During World War I, searchlights were placed around the cathedral, and in 1915 young soldiers practised signalling from the Golden Gallery. The cathedral was not hit by enemy action, though on 30 September 1917 it was struck 'by one of our own shells, which landed on the cornice of the south-east corner of the Cathedral'.[8]

Macartney, who had been instrumental in establishing the first St Paul's Watch of firewatchers in 1915, had inserted water tanks in the upper part of the building before the War, and an undated plan at triforium level, later annotated but apparently of about 1916, details hoses and tanks in the triforium.[9] There is also one large tank surviving, in the 'Plumber's Aisle' (the north choir triforium), where there has been no development since that time (Fig. 165). This is shown on the plan in outline, and therefore must date from just before or during World War I. Victory in the War brought new furnishings, though temporary. Celebrations at the end of the war included several services attended by King George V; at one, for the Royal Regiment of Artillery, an 18-pounder gun was placed in the choir (Fig. 166).

The years of World War I or immediately after must have been the time of compilation of the account of the cathedral and its pre-1714 furnishings and monuments which was published by the Royal Commission on Historic Monuments (England) in 1929;[10] the plan from that survey, perhaps drawn in the early 1920s or even a few years earlier, is Figure 3 here.

A conservation matter of the greatest importance had been the subject of debate since the opening of the century: the stability of the building. In 1901 the dome had been plumbed by Somers Clarke and found to be 4 3/8 inches (111mm) out of the perpendicular in a south-westerly direction. When measured again in 1913, it was found that the divergence had increased to 5¾ inches (146mm).[11] Sir Francis Fox, who had just stabilised Winchester Cathedral, and other eminent engineers discussed what to do. Fox thought the depth of foundations were generally too slight and the piers, particularly those round the dome, were unsound, being built of skins of Portland with inherently unstable rubble behind. A report of 1907 showed that the eight piers around the dome had settled to different degrees. The piers were badly cracked, and of the 32 buttresses which were meant to distribute the weight of the dome onto the piers and walls, 23 were badly fissured and in some cases practically sheared. In previous years cracked stones had been removed and replaced, but the new stones in some cases had been crushed. On one visit Fox found a separated piece from a pier which had flaked off 30ft above the floor, but fortunately had lodged in one of the ornaments. It was 24in (600mm) long and 20in (250mm) wide. He also criticised, as contributing to the increasing weakness of the structure, the redecoration of the cathedral a few years previously, when large panels, some inches in depth, had been cut in the great arches carrying the dome 'to give more shadow' (this cannot be correct, and perhaps refers to the cutting out necessary for the mosaics). Fox, another engineer and Macartney advised the Dean and Chapter in 1913 that there should be immediate strengthening of the supports of the dome, the grouting up of piers and masonry generally, the insertion of bonding stones and the removal of iron cramps.[12]

Some work on these lines followed during the War years, but did not settle the matter. It came to a head around Christmas 1924. The District Surveyor of the City of London served

Fig. 165 *Water tank in north choir triforium, probably inserted in the early 20th century (John Schofield)*

Fig. 166 *An 18-pounder gun in the choir for a memorial service, 1918 (Topical Press Agency/Hulton Archive/Getty Images). Behind is the Victorian reredos*

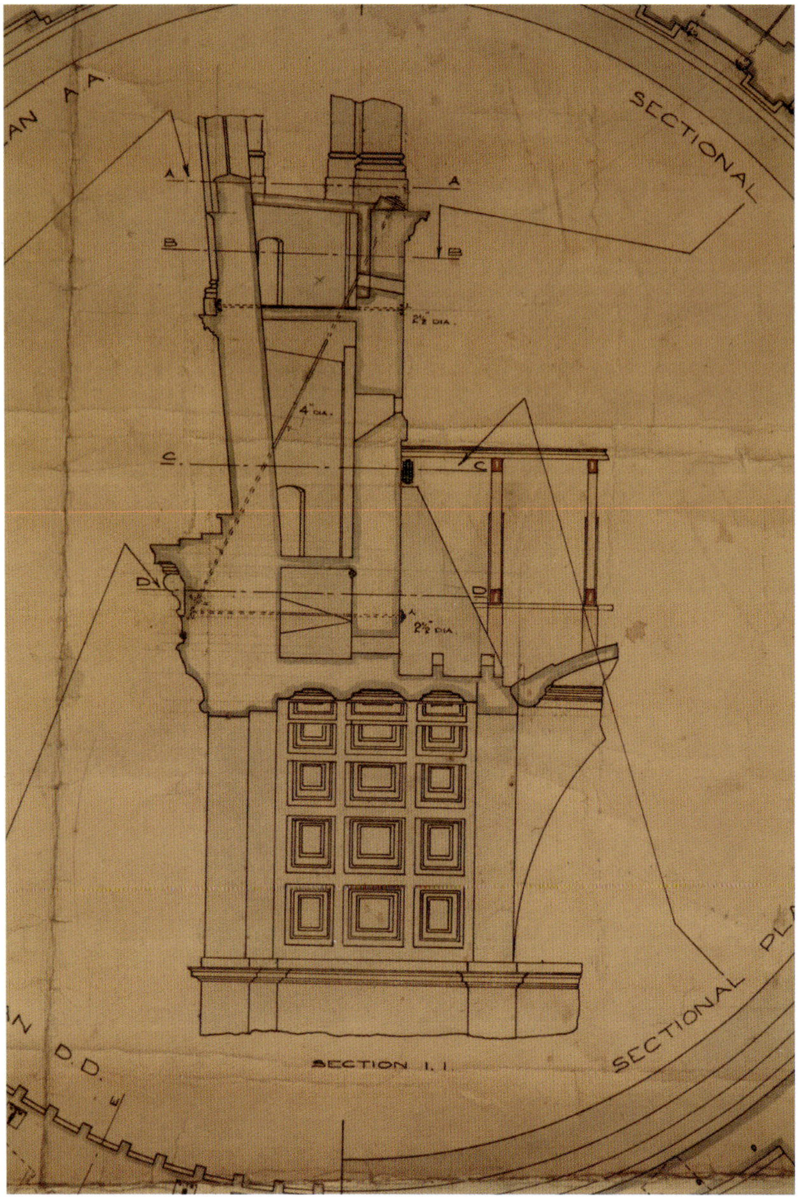

Fig. 167 Detail of the steel rods inserted by Macartney into the peristyle behind the Whispering Gallery; drawing of 13 February 1928 (SPCAA D/14/11/2). The seats of the Whispering Gallery are shown on the left-hand side above the diagonal line of one of the braces. The first two trusses of the choir roof are shown on the right-hand side

a Dangerous Structures Notice on the Dean and Chapter concerning the dome, but accounts differ as to when this was done: either Christmas Eve 1924 or 7 January 1925. This instigated a 5-year programme of repair which included grouting (an estimated 90 tons of concrete was injected into the dome piers), removal of many corroded iron cramps in the stonework, insertion of two new girdles of stainless steel around the dome, together with a radial array of steel tie-rods at the base of the dome (Fig. 167). These replaced some previous wrought iron tiebars by Mylne.[13] These and other repairs are reviewed by Robert Bowles in Chapter 7 below.

A second group of horizontal tie-rods were introduced into the triforium spaces. They tie the main dome piers back to the bastions, and replaced iron ties which were part of the original construction but now fractured. Some of these horizontal rods are still visible, but others have been covered over. In 1927 Macartney raised the floor of the south nave triforium, east of the library, by two steps so its east end would go over one of the horizontal rods at the dome (Fig. 168). Thus there are now six steps down from the triforium to the library. The historic collection of architectural fragments from the pre-Fire cathedral was by then already in place on the inner wall; its date of initial arrangement has not yet been established with certainty. Now it functioned with the new floor. Tie-rods in the north-west part of the central area were only floored over for the new Reserve Collection Store installed above the north transept in 2009, and others in the adjacent and untouched north choir triforium (the 'Plumbers' Aisle') and elsewhere around the upper space are still visible (Fig. 169).

The stability of the cathedral was now assured, but opinions continue to differ about what the Great Restoration achieved. When assessing the structural character of the south transept in 2003, Martin Stancliffe wrote:

> '[In 1938] Both the Surveyor [Godfrey Allen] and the engineers Sir Alexander Gibb and Ralph Freeman were of the opinion that stability of the dome structure had now been achieved, and that ground settlement beneath the cathedral had ceased. Some commentators have over the years misinterpreted this statement as thinking it means the major restoration of the dome support structure stopped the movements. In reality, their measurements and studies gave them the objective evidence to prove that the movements had effectively ceased sometime previously, as those closest to the facts had believed for some years.'[14]

At this time, in the 1930s, another problem arose and was addressed: the height of new office buildings around the cathedral, especially on its south, riverwards side. Faraday House, on the north side of Queen Victoria Street south of the cathedral, was built in 1932–3 and 'denounced immediately it went up for the damage its nine storeys and square-towered skyline inflicted on St Paul's; protective measures swiftly followed.'[15] Godfrey Allen (Surveyor 1931–56) proposed an area of control where building heights would be limited to protect and restore important views of the cathedral.[16] The proposals were put to and accepted by the City and from 1938 the St Paul's Heights Controls were implemented as a gentlemen's agreement between the City and developers. It was incorporated into statutory building policy in the City from 1992. The height controls are operated to protect viewpoints from the Thames bridges and south bank between Hungerford Bridge and London Bridge (see Fig. 170) and a number of views from streets to the west, north and east. They protect views of the dome, western towers and main entablature from the south, to provide a sense of the length of the cathedral. Many of the views are from surrounding boroughs and are operated by the relevant local authorities. Some local views from Ludgate Hill, Watling Street and Cannon Street, and within St Paul's Churchyard are protected by setback limitations on certain building frontages. Some buildings which exceeded the Heights limitations, either before or after 1938, have been redeveloped to conform with the controls. Examples include Vintry House, Upper Thames Street, (built 1930 and demolished in the 1980s), Sudbury House, immediately north-west of the cathedral (built 1964 and demolished in 2003) and Winchester House (built 1962–8 and demolished in 1997). There is a similar safeguard on depths which can be excavated around the cathedral in the City of London (St Paul's Cathedral Preservation Act) 1935. This was the result of a five-year campaign by Canon Sidney Alexander, Cathedral Treasurer from 1909 to 1945.[17]

Fig. 168 (above) View east along the south triforium of the nave, early 20th century before 1928, showing the floor before it was raised by Macartney (SPCAA D/7/22/1)

Fig. 169 (left) One of the steel ties of 1929 in the north triforium of the choir (John Schofield)

Fig. 170 (below) The cathedral from the south, across the river; Faraday House is still obtrusive, June 2015 (John Schofield)

Damage in World War II

In the years immediately before and during World War II, various preparations were made against damage expected from aerial bombardment. Tijou's grilles in the choir aisles, the Great Model, some of the Gibbons carving from the choir and part of Mayne's woodwork from the library, along with other fittings, were removed, either to the crypt or distant country houses; the tomb of Nelson, Wren's grave and Wellington's monument were encased in brick. A strong room for the archives and pictures was constructed in the crypt, and an air-raid shelter, but no evidence of these has survived. Marion Gibbs noted in her introduction that the final checking of her manuscript of the early charters of St Paul's in proof was rendered impossible because 'threatening "political tension" necessitated the removal of the muniments of St Paul's from the cathedral for an indefinite period'.[18]

In 1940–1, large areas of the City north and east of the cathedral were destroyed by aerial bombing (for the bombs near the cathedral, see Fig. 171). On one night people in an air-raid shelter in nearby Friday Street found themselves surrounded by fire, and a group of 40 or 50 men, women and children fled to the north-west crypt door of the cathedral, where they demanded (and were given) refuge inside.[19] During this period of months several large bombs fell nearby, including one immediately outside the south-west tower which, although unexploded, is recorded as a site in the present gazetteer because it had to be dug out of the ground (Site 45; Fig. 172). Two bombs hit the roof of the cathedral and caused serious damage. The first (Fig. 173), on 10 October 1940, hit the choir roof and exploded against the top of the choir vault. It unsettled the entire choir roof structure and showered masonry down on to the altar and its reredos; the lead covering of the roof 'billowed like the waves of the sea.'[20] The second (Fig. 174), on 17 April 1941, hit the north transept roof, went through and exploded; falling masonry dug a large hole in the floor of the transept, including the crypt vault beneath.[21] It destroyed the inner porch of the north transept, and Mylne's inscription commemorating Wren.[22] The east clerestory wall of the transept was blown up to 8in (203mm) out of the vertical, and some of the external ashlar dislodged. Scrutiny of the south transept by the cathedral engineer in 2003 suggests that

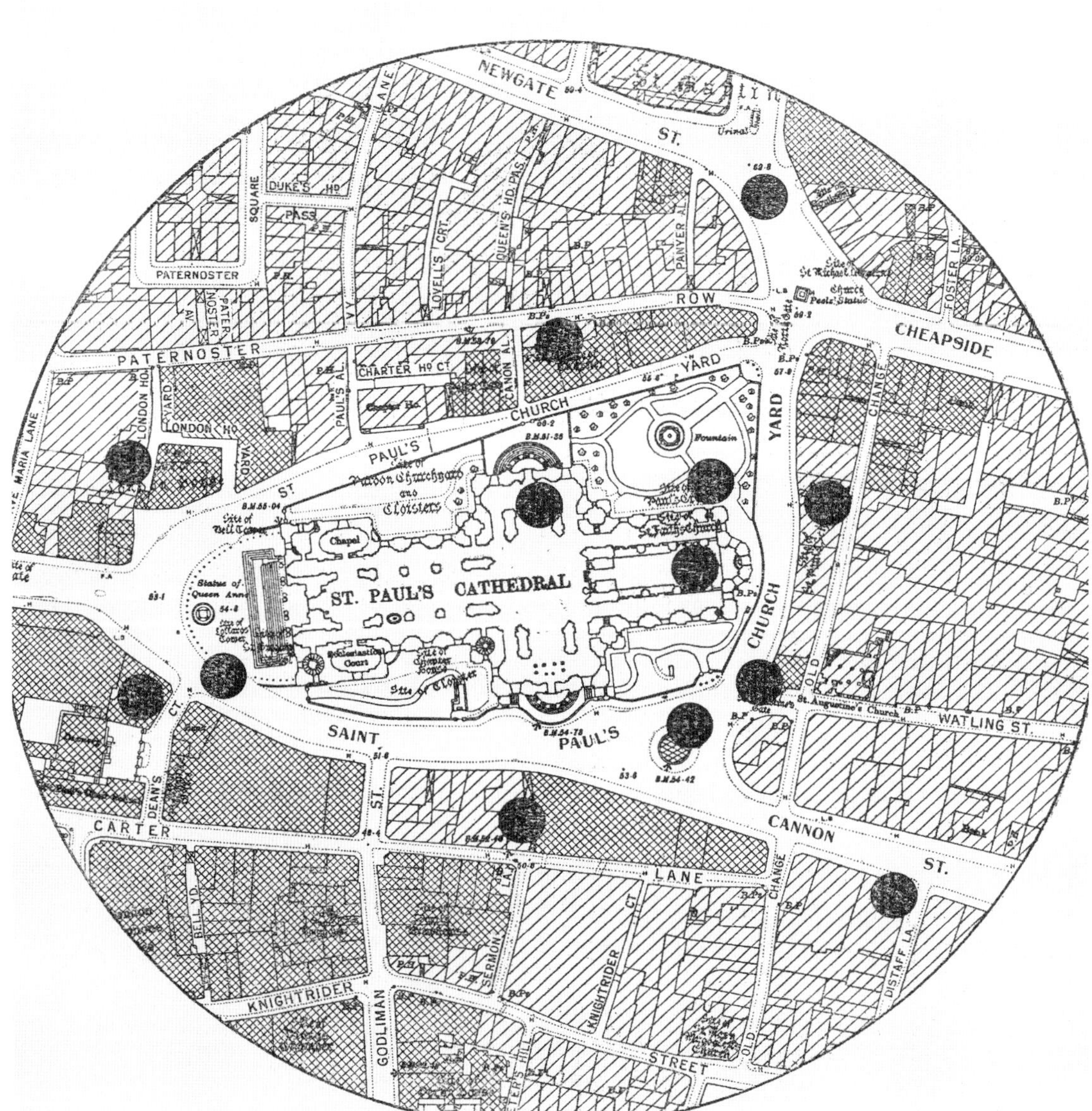

Fig. 171 Bomb damage at St Paul's and in the immediate area around during World War II. The black circles represent where high explosive bombs fell on or near the building (that south-west of the cathedral is shown in Fig. 172); the light shading indicates buildings destroyed by fire or bomb damage, mostly in 1940 and 1941 (Matthews 1946, 39)

the explosion caused up to 12mm of movement in parts of the masonry of the south transept.[23] In his account of 1946 of the wartime period Dean Matthews, in a text no doubt authorised by Godfrey Allen, thought that 'there was little doubt that the wonderful resistance of the Dome and its supports to the effect of the blast could not have happened but for the work of repair and consolidation which had so recently been carried out.'[24] Apart from these two bombs, the cathedral survived the War with only scratches from shrapnel (from bombs near the cathedral; still evident on the apse and vestigially on the south transept) and having the majority of its windows blown out, mostly by the explosion of 1941. A significant number of incendiary bombs landed on or immediately around the cathedral, but they were dealt with by members of the St Paul's Watch. It is the incendiaries which caused the fire storm which destroyed the area around the cathedral, and without the action of the Watch the cathedral would also undoubtedly have caught fire.[25]

Fig. 172 (left) Site 45: excavation for a high explosive bomb which penetrated the pavement south-west of the cathedral, 1940 (LMA)

Fig. 173 (right) Bomb damage to the choir roof, 1940: debris around the reredos, which was largely unscathed (MoL)

Much of the area around the Churchyard was bombed and buildings gutted, right up to the walls of the cathedral (Fig. 175). Afterwards cleared spaces were used for water tanks or propaganda purposes (Fig. 176 of 1943; clearly the intended juxtaposition for fund-raising purposes was between the (assembled) Stirling bomber and the cathedral behind). The flying bombs of 1944 passed by (Fig. 177). The area destroyed by enemy action in 1940–1 was large and lay mostly to the north, east and south-east; St Paul's looked 'strangely shrunken amidst horizontal wastes of streets lined with empty basements and dotted with burned husks of Wren churches'.[26]

The cathedral's survival was largely due to the vigilance of the St Paul's Watch and its steel reinforcement. After the War it began to figure in films, mostly because of its location in the

Fig. 174 Bomb damage to the north transept, 1941 (LMA)

Fig. 175 *(top left) Firefighters tackle the blaze in St Paul's Churchyard at the east end of the cathedral, 1941 (LMA). On the right-hand side, the chancel window has buckled outwards from one of the internal bomb blasts*

Fig. 176 *(top right) A Stirling bomber assembled on the bombed area west of Friday Street in 1943, with the shrapnel-marked cathedral behind (Davis/Hulton Archive/Getty Images)*

Fig. 177 *(bottom left) A V-1 flying bomb passes over or near St Paul's, 1944 (MoL)*

Fig. 178 *(bottom right) The cathedral from the north-west, 1949 (Kurt Hutton/Picture Post/Getty Images)*

bomb-damaged landscape, but occasionally additionally for itself.[27] St Paul's had become a symbol of national survival through the War, to add to its already considerable stock of symbolic roles. Meanwhile in the streets around, life picked up and some of the bomb sites were reclaimed for recreational use (Fig. 178).

Post-War planning and archaeological work to 2014

In the immediate post-War years people looked ahead, not back. The buildings destroyed in the area east of St Paul's were almost all less than 100 years old, and in some quarters the Blitz was regarded, like the Great Fire had been in the 1670s, as a cleansing mechanism which would enable up-to-date office accommodation to be constructed in quantity.[28] This brief section describes the post-War period not in terms of the various urban plans for regeneration, discussion of which can be found elsewhere,[29] but from the cathedral's point of view.

During and after the War there were several schemes for rebuilding the City of London after war damage, of which the most important was that by the Corporation of the City itself; the period of planning from 1947 was summarised in 1951. The view now opened out from the south-east by the Blitz, it was suggested, should be preserved 'as a thank-offering for the almost miraculous preservation of the Cathedral'. A new pedestrian approach to the cathedral from the south crosses the Thames via the Millennium Bridge today.[30] Discussion and practicalities altered many of the planning proposals, but as a further example we may cite a more specific report called *The Precincts of St Paul's*, by William Holford, presented to the Corporation of London in March 1956. The main objective was to improve the setting of the cathedral, ensure its practical future and contribute to an improved flow of traffic. The cathedral then lay in an area of bomb damage (Fig. 179). In terms of results on the ground, the scheme came to fruition with the Paternoster Development on the north side and the concomitant movement of the south end of Ave Maria Lane to join Ludgate Hill a little to the east of its medieval junction. Similar new buildings, a new alignment for Creed Lane and a south-east garden including a large jet of water (Fig. 180) were proposed; every stretch of the original line of Wren railings would have been removed (the section at the north-east is by Penrose). Holford proposed that Temple Bar was to be brought back and rebuilt, not in Fleet Street where it had been historically, but adjacent to the

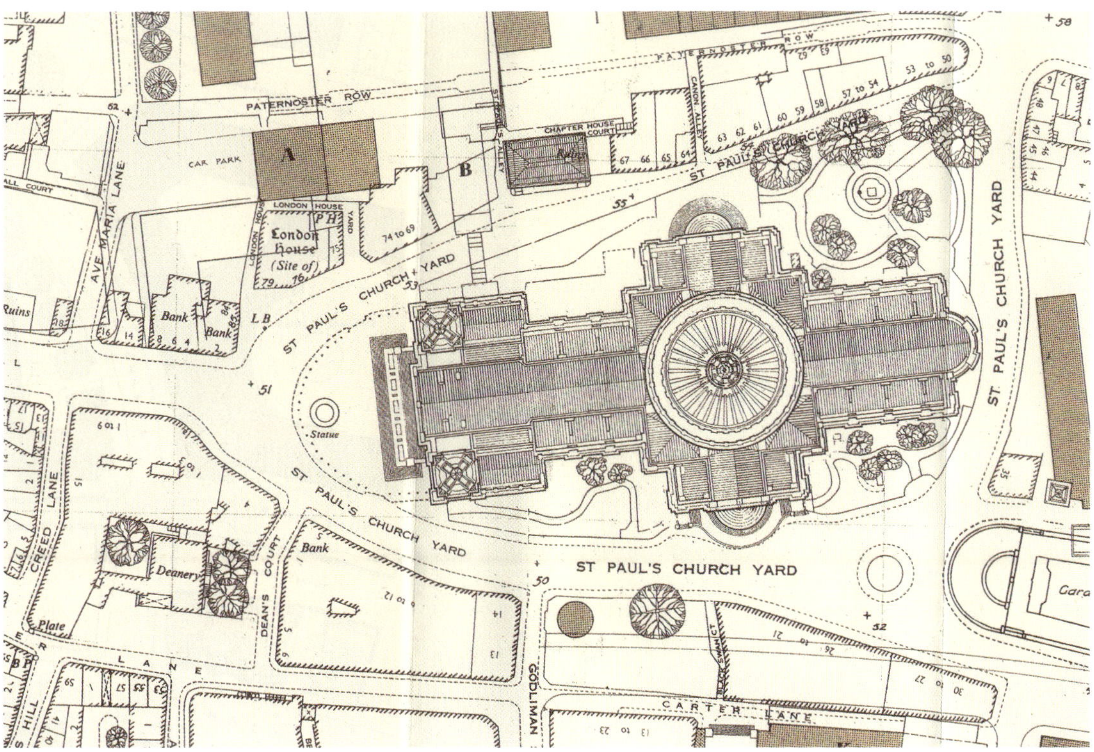

Fig. 179 William Holford: Stage I proposal, 1956 (Holford 1956). This shows the churchyard in its immediately post-War state, with many of the bombed building sites, and the proposed realignment of the south end of Ave Maria Lane on the west side

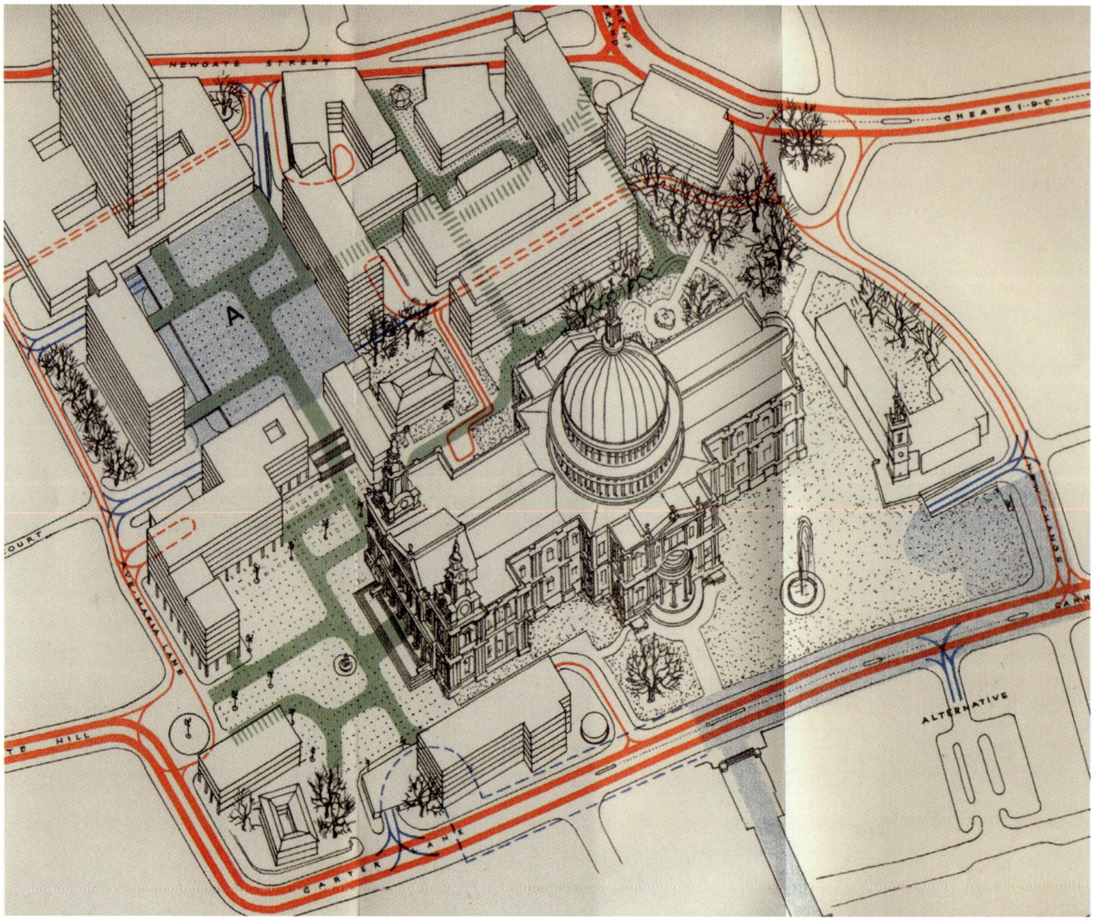

Fig. 180 William Holford: Stage III proposal, 1956 (Holford 1956). The Deanery is marooned south of a new building; the south churchyard is an open space, and traffic diverted along a widened Carter Lane. The circle south-east of the cathedral was to be a large water jet*

Fig. 181 A sketch of the 'forecourt' of St Paul's as proposed by William Holford in 1956, with Temple Bar rebuilt on the north side of the cathedral (Holford 1956). By 2002 the building in the foreground, Juxon House (1961), had been built and gone; in 2004 Temple Bar came back to a site very near the one shown here, but at right-angles to it*

Fig. 182 Temple Bar in its present situation between the cathedral and the rebuilt Paternoster Square to the north (Andy Chopping, MOLA). This shows the present north side, which was originally the east or internal side with the City arms and the statues of James I and Anne of Denmark. The other side, originally the west side, has the royal arms and statues of Charles I and Charles II*

north side of the cathedral (Fig. 181).[31] Holford's scheme, presented in 1956, was given its final form in 1961. This is the date of construction of the Paternoster Square development, which Pevsner hailed as an 'outstandingly well conceived precinct, the architecture of the buildings ... sensible and unobtrusive, ie not competing with the cathedral'.[32] Although the Paternoster development has now been demolished, Temple Bar was erected on the west side of the Chapter House in 2004 (Fig. 182). This is perhaps the only relic of Holford's scheme, which had more freedom in its planning than Wren had after the Great Fire; indeed, one has to go back to the expansion of the precinct under Bishop de Belmeis in the early 12th century to find a parallel in magnitude of scope.

One feature of the post-War exuberance which has survived is the Festival Garden south-east of the cathedral, laid out in 1951 by Sir Albert Richardson as part of the City's contribution to the Festival of Britain. As Simon Bradley notes, 'its formal plan, classical stone parapets and fountain are hardly what one associates with the event.'[33] A paved section through the middle of the garden represents the line of the late Saxon and medieval Old Change, which formerly went past the west end of St Augustine Watling Street (marked now by its tower) up to Cheapside. The Garden was restored by the City of London in 2012, and the adjacent coach park closed to be landscaped.

In 1961, the roadway of St Paul's Churchyard still ran round the east end of the cathedral (Fig. 183). The subsequent moving of the street away from the east end of the building established the present east boundary of the churchyard and incidentally freed up the space where Penrose had left manholes over fragments of the medieval east end. The railings were extended first to the tower of St Augustine's church, then on a totally new alignment a considerable distance to the east, following the curve of the west side of New Change to meet the north-east corner, as they now are. It follows that the flower garden now in the south-east corner of the churchyard within the railings lies over 19th-century and perhaps earlier buildings between the former streets of St Paul's Churchyard and Old Change; these buildings were outside the railings and the Wren-period churchyard.

The gradual repair of the cathedral after the War, by Surveyors Godfrey Allen (to 1956), Lord Mottistone (1956–63) and Paul Paget (1963–9), is not dealt with in detail here.[34] The cathedral extended Macartney's Works Department to the north, as far as the façade of the Wren Chapter House, by digging a large hole several metres deep and into the natural brickearth, in 1969–70. An immeasurable amount of information about the Anglo-Saxon and medieval cathedral, and the famous Pardon Cloister, was lost.[35] The railings were realigned along the north side as a consequence of the adjacent Paternoster Square redevelopment. The upper part of the exterior was cleaned, leading to the complaint of Ian Nairn in 1966, that 'because soot and Portland stone work such a funny magic on each other, St Paul's should never have been cleaned. The scrubbed parts show a small gain in clarity of detail and an immense loss in personality'.[36]

Fig. 183 The east end of the cathedral viewed from the south in 1961, showing the former line of Old Change and the basements of buildings formerly on the east side of the Churchyard, including the building of the 1880s on the site of St Paul's School, destroyed in the War (LMA)

Sir Bernard Feilden (Surveyor 1969–77) organised much repair externally at high levels, core-sampled the walls, and inserted the present lift within the hollow tube of the inner side of the main stair at the junction of the nave and south transept. Initially this lift, of great value today (and rebuilt to take wheelchairs more easily in 2006), was inserted partly to get firefighters to the roof in an emergency; a second lift to get higher, to the base of the dome, was started but abandoned because of technical issues.[37] He was concerned in particular about two other threats, as he saw them, to the building: air pollution and traffic vibration. His study of the external stonework, including the roofline statues, found that erosion over 260 years had removed up to 2in (51mm) of the depth of some stones. In his opinion:

Left to right:

Fig. 184 *The roof pocket on the south side of the choir, looking west, in the early 20th century, published 1929 (RCHM 1929, pl. 94, by permission of Historic England)*

Fig. 185 *The upper, inner east wall of the south transept, 2015 (John Schofield)*

Fig. 186 *Site H, 2006: one of the buttress bases originally beneath the 14th-century chapter house is re-examined before being buried in sterile sand below paving (Andy Chopping, MOLA). Copnall's statue of Becket, falling back, was placed on a new plinth of stone on the medieval work in 1973; it was moved to a new site further east in 2006*

'Bankside Power Station, built shortly after World War II, has undoubtedly caused damage to St Paul's Cathedral and should never have been sited so close to a national monument … As the generating station is now [1982] obsolescent, it is to be hoped that it will be demolished'.[38]

Now, the power station is Tate Modern. In 1980, under Surveyor Robert Potter (1977–84), a series of micro-erosion meter (MEM) sites was set up on the Portland balustrade, and measurements taken on six occasions up to 2010. The project was designed to examine whether acid rain, particularly from Bankside power station, was affecting the erosion of the stonework. By 2010, the study concluded, rates of erosion had much reduced from their levels in the 1980s, and now resemble the natural rates of stone decay.[39] The roof pocket areas behind the upper screen wall have not been cleaned during the 20th century, and are now intentionally left alone, so they still bear the grime of many decades, perhaps several centuries (Fig. 184, Fig. 185).

The 1970s saw the creation of the underground Works Department north of the nave, with unfortunate archaeological consequences (see Gazetteer, Site A) and various cleaning and other works which are not treated here, except to note one addition to the south-west churchyard. In 1973 a bronzed resin statue by Bainbridge Copnall of Thomas Becket, shown falling to the ground during his murder, was added to one of the barely-protruding 14th-century chapter house buttress bases (Fig. 186). This was moved to a site south-east of the cathedral in 2006, as part of the landscaping works of the south-west churchyard.

No major works were undertaken at the cathedral in the 1980s, though the metalwork of the railings along the border of the south-west churchyard with the highway were removed to be placed in store, from which they were retrieved three decades later.[40] In 1990 Martin Stancliffe was appointed Surveyor, and in 1993 he produced a Quinquennial Report which proposed several immediate and long-term programmes of repair, maintenance and improvement.[41] Most of the major projects of the next two decades were either proposed or hinted at in this Report: stonework repair and cleaning of the exterior (as an example, analysis of the south transept is shown in a project drawing of 2003, Fig. 187), a cleaning of the entire interior (using carefully researched cleaning methods to replace the damaging or ineffective methods previously employed at various points in the cathedral's history), the removal of the *ad hoc* cathedral shop from the west end of the nave, the liturgical reordering and relighting of the interior, and a staged bringing of the entire crypt into public use together with extensive facilities for staff, choir and educational purposes. He also recommended that a proper inventory of all historic material and artefacts stored at the cathedral should be made, noting that this was a requirement under the recent Care of Cathedrals Measure (1990); the compiling of the inventory, along with the creation of two full-time archive

Fig. 187 *Marked-up photogrammetric survey of the south wall of the south transept, ahead of repairs, 2003 (Purcell Miller Tritton Architects). This is an archaeological record, by the Surveyor Martin Stancliffe, of what the south transept has endured during almost 300 years since 1711: cracks in the stonework, missing elements of carving, erosion, exfoliation, repairs, bomb damage (more evident further east, but here only in the bottom left corner), and scarring from carborundum cleaning of the 1960s. The cathedral now has such photogrammetric records for the entire exterior of the building*

manager posts to deal with the collections and documentary archives of the cathedral, is one of Stancliffe's many achievements. He also adapted extensive parts of the triforium to house the newly created Fabric Archive and its staff. The present author was appointed Cathedral Archaeologist in 1990; projects which resulted in recording are noted at the front of this report (Table 1) and summarised in the Gazetteer. Martin Stancliffe retired from the Surveyorship at the end of 2011, having completed the majority of his larger projects.

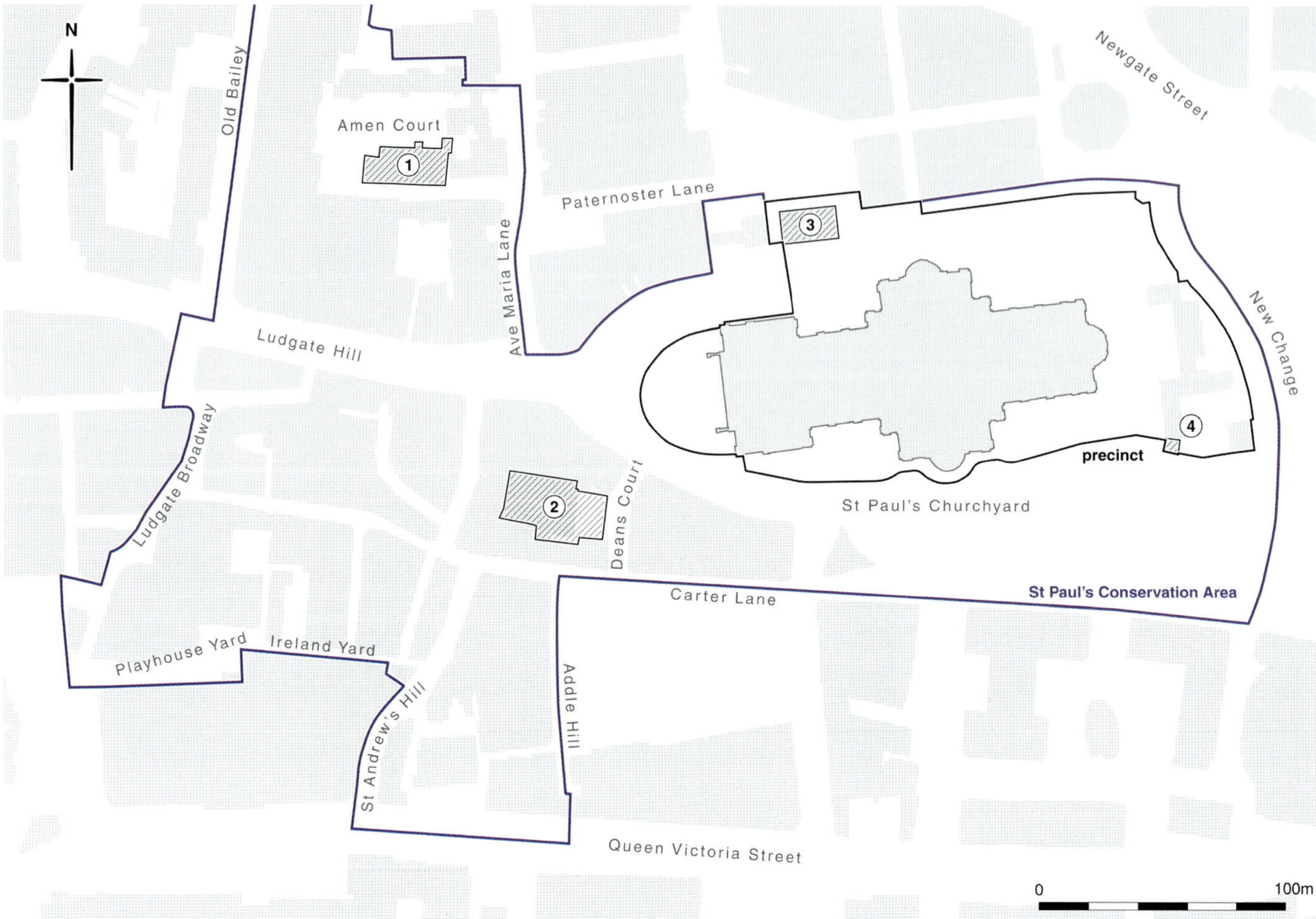

Fig. 188 The St Paul's Cathedral Conservation Area, as defined in 2007 (City of London), with added locations of the surviving Listed Buildings of relevance to the Cathedral within it and the boundary of the cathedral precinct as defined by CFCE in 1994. The buildings are 1, Canons' houses in Amen Court; 2, The Old Deanery; 3, Wren Chapter House; 4, tower of St Augustine Watling Street

- An area of international significance, a focal point of the City of London, part of a major processional route and a focus of national celebration;
- The setting of St Paul's Cathedral, a building of international architectural and cultural significance and one of England's most important classical buildings and a seminal building in the history of English architecture;
- an area of great historic significance which has been a centre of Christian worship for 1400 years, and encompasses streets, buildings and spaces spanning a period of 1400 years;
- an area of great architectural significance, including one of the largest concentrations in the City of London of Grade I, Grade II* and Grade II listed buildings, as well as numerous non-designated buildings of high architectural quality from different periods;
- an area of internationally important archaeology relating to the adoption of Christianity in Britain, and including the City's largest intact extent of area and depth of archaeological deposits remaining of the medieval and Roman city;
- an area where the urban grain varies from tightly knit historic streets and alleys to open spaces around St Paul's Cathedral and churchyard;
- an area of predominantly masonry buildings with traditional proportions and materials;
- a visual character and groundscape that is enriched by a wealth of materials, features, monuments, public sculpture, signs, plaques, statuary, and other structures;
- an area characterised by the restrained presence of modern signage and advertising;
- an area of ecological value, rich in open spaces, trees and greenery which provide an important aspect of the Cathedral's setting;
- an area which attracts community events and public gatherings, particularly at the Cathedral and its churchyard;
- an area associated with nationally significant cultural and historic events and notable people, including the burial places of numerous historic figures.

Table 4 Summary of character of the St Paul's Cathedral Conservation Area, from the policy document of March 2013 (City of London Corporation 2013, 10)

The City of London now seeks to develop itself as a world city of culture as well as an international centre of business. There is now a perception that this means conservation of all kinds of historic monuments and the archaeological strata they are based on, to make the City an attractive place in which to live and work. It is therefore appropriate to end this short survey of the setting of St Paul's since 1945 with a City document of 2013. The St Paul's Cathedral Conservation Area was designated in 2007, incorporating the former Ludgate Hill Conservation Area. In March 2013 the City adopted a Special Planning Document (SPD) concerning the character of the Conservation Area and a management plan as part of a series of such documents for the Conservation Areas in the City of London.[42] This reviewed the City's policies in maintaining the character of land uses, building and materials types, open spaces and trees, the use of the area for local and national cultural and political events, ecology and archaeology. The document summarised 'the characteristics which contribute to the special interest of St Paul's Cathedral Conservation Area' as a series of 12 points about the area, from its international significance to its value as an open space with trees and greenery (Table 4). Fig. 188 shows the extent of the Conservation

Fig. 189 The north transept from the alley to the north, 2014 (Andy Chopping, MOLA)

Fig. 190 (left) The south transept, from the approach to the Millennium Bridge, 2014 (Andy Chopping, MOLA)

Fig. 191 (right) A fragment of post-Fire St Peter's Hill, in its pre-War form, now preserved along the east side of the College of Arms in Queen Victoria Street, looking north, 2015 (John Schofield)

Area, the historic buildings of relevance to the Cathedral within it, together with the outline of the cathedral precinct as defined legally by the Cathedrals Fabric Commission for England (CFCE) in 1994. This is therefore the current protective framework provided by legislation.

These characteristics of the cathedral's setting can be appreciated in a final tour of the churchyard, viewing the building from various points. The west end of the cathedral, the landscaped south-west churchyard and the recently-arrived Temple Bar have already figured in the text (Fig. 36, Fig. 182). To these we add some views of the cathedral and of features in the south churchyard, from the north and south (Fig. 189–Fig. 191). The reinstatement of the view in Fig. 189 and other views of the cathedral are the achievement of Sir William Whitfield (Surveyor 1985–90), during his master minding of the Paternoster scheme north of the cathedral.

From the west, north and east, St Paul's is attractively hemmed in by buildings, providing gradually unfolding and interesting views. This is also a feature of the view from the Millennium Bridge on the south, that is when one stands on the bridge itself or the immediate avenue to the north. The Bridge in fact is not aligned perpendicular to the axis of the cathedral, but crosses the river at a slight angle to the river so that it is at right-angles with the south bank and with Tate Modern, the former Bankside power station. Thus St Paul's and the other 'cathedral', of modern art, are not quite in parallel alignment, but few people notice that.

The south part of the churchyard, including the public highway which crosses it (an important bus-route), is without any prominent feature apart from the south side of the cathedral itself, and especially the south transept, and is less successful. It is a mixture of displaced architectural features from elsewhere, recent and new monuments and works of sculpture, and the new City of London Information Centre. Since everything in this area dates from after World War II, there has been no imperative to retain any large landscape item from the past. With the closing of the coach park, it is now a landscaped open space incorporating the Festival Garden.

Along the north side of the churchyard today are three large plane trees. There was originally a fourth, but it became unsafe because it was too close to the railings, and was removed after a storm in October 1987. The three remaining planes, and a walnut tree, were granted Tree Preservation Orders by the City of London in 1991. The Superintendent of Parks and Gardens to the Planning Committee reported that the plane trees 'are probably in excess of two hundred and fifty years old … it is in my opinion essential that no engineering works whatsoever should take place again within twenty feet of the base of these trees.'[43] If this opinion about the age of the trees is correct, they were planted around 1740 or even before.

CHAPTER 5

Conclusions

Towards an archaeology of Christopher Wren within the history of the cathedral

This has been a study of many aspects of a Wren building throughout its life up to the present; a partial archaeological biography of St Paul's Cathedral in its first 300 years. These conclusions briefly review some overall points: the present state of archaeological study of Wren buildings, and of Baroque buildings in general; questions about the cathedral which are amenable to further study; the place of Francis Penrose in the history of conservation and development of the cathedral and its setting; and the several important functions of the cathedral within the City of London and the nation today.

Monographs on Wren and his buildings written by architectural historians are numerous; but archaeological investigations of prominent buildings of the late 17th and early 18th century in Britain, whether by Wren or others, are as yet few in number. There have been three recent comparable studies of major buildings in London which have combined historical analysis and archaeological recording of their late 17th and 18th-century phases. At Guildhall and at the White Tower within the Tower of London Wren was involved, though more so at Guildhall, where his contribution to the rebuilding of the hall and porch in 1671–2 has been analysed.[1] His work at Whitehall Palace in 1685–95, illustrated by excavations of 1937–9, has also been elucidated.[2] These are, including St Paul's, four of the most important historic buildings in 17th-century London. Less is known about the archaeology of the post-Fire City parish churches of Wren and Hooke. There have been many excavations or salvage observations at parish church sites in the City, which include recording of details of the post-Fire church which lay above its medieval predecessor; these have usually been on the sites of churches destroyed either in the 19th century or in World War II, but have included observations during remedial work to surviving Wren buildings.[3] But there has not yet been a synthesis of the archaeological information to compare with the good surviving building accounts for many of those churches in the post-Fire decades.

There is much still to find out, by archaeological methods, about the construction of Wren's St Paul's from 1675 and the use and management of the cathedral and churchyard thereafter. The documentary record is voluminous, but it has deficiencies which archaeological work may be able to remedy. The small amount of excavation reported here (the Gazetteer of sites in this volume is only one-third the length of that in the report dealing with the site up to 1666, *St Paul's Cathedral before Wren*) has demonstrated that much fresh knowledge can be gained concerning the construction of the foundations of the Wren building and the crypt; of temporary works and features of the building-site; and of burials in the crypt. A study of the roof structure over the nave has been presented; what may be the largest surviving roof of its time in Britain still holds many secrets about how it was put up. The present study has agreed with Robert Crayford's suggestion that the difference in alignment between the Wren and medieval buildings is most likely to be a consequence of marking out on the ground the outline of his Great Model design; and has proposed where the would-be telescope was meant to be placed, within the core of the main or great stairs. An outline of Wren's office in the former chapter house has been constructed, and the history and extent of the Wren drainage system partly reconstructed. Since the burial registers at St Paul's only survive from 1760, the early history of post-Fire burial in the churchyard is unknown, and will have to come from archaeological work. All the major changes in the layout and boundaries of the churchyard through the period can be traced in the ground. Wren's cathedral remains on an island or pillar of intact strata going back to the Roman period about 6m below, and potentially very informative for the centuries after 1675.

It is clear that much evidence for the construction of the Wren building still resides in its structure or in the ground around it. Cumulatively, also, as every future intervention in the ground is recorded, we will have a better idea of the state of survival below ground of the pre-Fire cathedral. The accounts suggest that Wren's workmen dug out the greater part of it, and on several occasions dug large holes for various purposes outside the footprint of the future building. But archaeological investigation is suggesting that the medieval cathedral was too large, and sometimes too deep, for the robbing to be complete and utterly destructive. Combined with the fact, now amply demonstrated, that much of the fabric of the pre-Fire cathedral lies in jumbled form in the crypt walls of the Wren building, this promises that the destruction of the old building and the construction of the new will be informed by any future intervention in the ground beneath or around the cathedral, and any new piercing of the Wren walls, primarily at crypt level but also possibly higher up. Study of the provision of the various types of new stone, not only Portland, has begun.[4]

Studies of other building materials of the cathedral are possible but not yet advanced. St Paul's does not figure in the published histories of English brickwork, perhaps because the bricks are nearly all hidden behind plaster. Several hundred thousand bricks were used in the construction of the crypt vaulting and the ceiling of the church in its saucer domes, a new form in England of all four arms of the church so vaulted. The weight of the lantern on the dome is carried by the brick cone laid by Richard Billinghurst. Fragments of the fairly new pantiles were found in the backfill of Wren's drains. The Wren building offers great potential for the student of building materials in the second half of the 17th century, in the context of the rebuilding of the City after the Great Fire.

Several subjects have been lightly dealt with here because they were summarised throroughly in the cathedral history of 2004: for instance, fittings and liturgy, decoration such as the mosaics, the monuments, extended treatment of national occasions at the cathedral, the precinct and the book trade, the setting of the cathedral in the last two centuries and the reputation or perceptions of St Paul's.[5] To complement these, some conclusions about the archaeology of the cathedral and its churchyard from the middle of the 17th century to the present and suggestions for future work are made. First, some comparisons between the present cathedral and its predecessor are appropriate. The Wren building was largely complete in 1711, 36 years after construction started. The building it replaced probably contained portions of standing fabric more than 600 years old when it burned in 1666. Thus the construction period of the entire post-Fire building was shorter than many of the building periods of parts of the medieval cathedral. This comparative speed of building (though some contemporaries thought it was slow) was in keeping with the rest of the fire-damaged central part of the City, which had been virtually all rebuilt by 1676. The new cathedral was smaller in extent and volume than its predecessor; it had a single architectural style (with variations) where the pre-Fire building would have had many from the 10th century to the 17th; the Wren building in its original form of 1711 had a far more limited range of colours and textures in its appearance.

The construction of the cathedral in 1675–1711 can be followed minutely in the building accounts and through the large collection of surviving architectural drawings, which cover every phase of the building work, but the present study is one of only a few which attempt to match the accounts and the workmen portrayed there with the actual fabric. St Paul's may be well known, but for that very reason further research can be detailed. Two of the initial characteristics of St Paul's have been mentioned here, but there seem to be few if any studied analogies for them: having an undercroft or crypt below all four arms of a church, and inserting drains over much of a large site in an organised manner to take away rain water from a great building. These may seem mundane, but both ideas must have been new in the 1670s. We could profitably explore or suggest where Wren got them from, and whether their existence at St Paul's had any effect on other building projects in London and Britain.

Further, an archaeology of Christopher Wren is needed. Just as there is no large body of archaeological research at present on the post-Fire parish churches in the City of London by Wren, Hooke and others, so there are few archaeological studies at those large complexes in Britain to which Wren made a significant contribution.[6]

Since 1711 there has not been any substantial addition to the cathedral or subtraction from it at the level of the whole building. There has been a process largely of opening up the space within at church floor level and below in the crypt, which began in the 1860s; and both levels are now filling with monuments. For the first century, little happened, until the Peninsular School of monuments began to appear in the dome area and transepts. Penrose relaid the steps at all three major entrances, and removed the railings at the west end. He replaced the clock, cleaned the interior, drastically altered the choir, and inserted gas lighting. Subsequent surveyors pulled the structure together with steel rods at the west end and round the dome, so the cathedral now wears a hidden 20th-century metal corset in addition to the chains and a very large number of ties (usually only 230mm or 9in long) between individual blocks of stone inserted during construction. Recent work has brought more parts of the building into public use and improved access. The conservation of the building and its surroundings take account of the needs of many different groups: not only worshippers, but city workers, tourists, organisers of state occasions, television crews, and researchers into its archives. By understanding the history of the building, we can both appreciate and manage it.

This monograph is a contribution to the understanding of St Paul's. Beyond the practical matters of conservation, this study has hopefully addressed two further themes in the history of the cathedral. First, its increasing and now major symbolic role as the nation's church, as a place to which the whole country looks for guidance in times of crisis or national events, and formerly as the religious centre of the British Empire, has moulded the building, particularly the space outside the west end and the interior. Second, which is less known, of all the eminent Surveyors who succeeded Wren, we can single out Francis Penrose, who between 1852 and 1897 brought the cathedral into a closer relationship with the surrounding City of London, so that the cathedral and its remaining churchyard are now enjoyed by those who work and live in the City. Since at least 1500 St Paul's Churchyard has not been a quiet enclave within its town, unlike cathedral closes elsewhere in Britain; but now it has the chance, within the modern townscape, to regain some of the qualities of such special places.

This monograph, finally, follows the work on its predecessor *St Paul's Cathedral before Wren* which was published in 2011. The present cathedral by Sir Christopher Wren is 300 years old, but beneath it are a few fragments of previous cathedrals which together formed a chain of buildings over the 1000 years before 1666. Their archaeology and history from AD 604 is a seamless story. St Paul's must be a remarkable site within Britain and rare within Europe, a place where successive buildings have served the same purpose for over 1400 years.

CHAPTER 6

Specialist reports

Pottery and clay tobacco pipes

Lyn Blackmore and Jacqueline Pearce

The small amount of post-medieval pottery from the excavations of 1969–2006 has already been reported in *SPCBW*, 248–9. Because some of the 17th-century deposits may be from before or after the Great Fire of 1666, the sherds are described here again. Selected sherds were given numbers, as P<1>, for illustration purposes. The selected sherds which are mentioned here were numbered P<35> to <40>, and illustrated in *SPCBW*, figs 5.43 and 8.1. The Museum of London codes for the types of pottery represented here are explained in Table 5.

Site A: Most of the post-medieval pottery, amounting to 48 sherds (24 ENV, 6.7kg), was recovered by Crayford and was boxed together with the Roman and medieval sherds. Two sherds of English porcelain were from 'the car park base C3, pit in potter's clay' (ie excavation for the new underground car park on the north-east side of Site A), and three other sherds from the same cup must derive from this feature. The remainder must now be considered unstratified. A smaller group of seven sherds (125g) was found in the lower fill of the well excavated by Peter Marsden as [ER1685].[1] There were also two Frechen jugs (FREC, <P39> and <P40>).

Sites C and D: the post-medieval pottery from these excavations amounts to 32 sherds from a minimum of 23 vessels (881g) found in four contexts (C[55], [151]; D[339], [340]); in addition there is one unstratified sherd.[2] None

Table 5 *Fabric codes for post-medieval pottery used in this publication, with their date ranges*

Code	*Expansion*	*Date*
BORD	Surrey–Hampshire border ware	1550–1700
BORDG	Green-glazed Surrey–Hampshire border ware	1550–1700
BORDY	Yellow-glazed Surrey–Hampshire border ware	1550–1700
FREC	Frechen stoneware	1550–1700
MERC	Spanish mercury jar	1500–1800
MPUR	Midlands purple ware	1480–1750
PEAR	Pearlware	1770–1840
PMBL	Post-medieval black-glazed ware	1580–1700
PMBR	London-area post-medieval bichrome glazed redware	1480–1600
PMFR	Post-medieval fine redware	1580–1650
PMR	Post-medieval redware	1580–1900
PMSRG	London-area post-medieval slipped red ware with green glaze	1480–1650
PMSRY	London-area post-medieval slipped redware with clear yellow glaze	1480–1660
RBOR	Surrey–Hampshire border redware	1550–1900
TGW	English tin-glazed ware	1600–1800
TGW C	Tin-glazed ware with plain white glaze (Orton type C)	1630–1846
TGW D	Tin-glazed ware with blue/polychrome decoration (Orton type D)	1630–80
TPW1	Refined white ware with underglaze blue transfer-printed Chinese-style line-engraved decoration	1780–1810

of the sherds shows any sign of heavy burning, which would be expected in debris resulting from the Great Fire. The earliest pottery dates to the 16th century (fabric PMBR), while the latest comprises part of a late 18th-century transfer-printed ware saucer (TPW1, intrusive in D[339]). The bulk of the finds, however, date to the mid to late 17th or early 18th-century century (fabrics BORD/G/Y, MPUR, PMBL, PMFR, PMR, RBOR, TGW, TGW C, TGW D), with few imports (FREC, MERC). A range of domestic forms is represented, including kitchen wares used in cooking and food preparation (tripod pipkin, dripping dish, bowls), tablewares (dishes, saucer), storage (jars) and hygiene (chamber pots).

Site F: Seven sherds of post-medieval pottery (312g) were found in contexts [1], [5], [22] and [34], comprising fabrics BORDG, BORDY, PEAR, PMFR, PMSRG and FREC.

Site G: Three sherds of post-medieval pottery (267g) dating from the late 16th–18th century were recovered from context [21].[3] Two are in post-medieval redware (PMR), while the third is a sherd of Frechen stoneware, from the Rhineland (FREC). Clay pipe stems found in contexts [5] and [7] can only be dated to 1580–1910, but a pipe bowl from [21] dates to 1660–80. Context [5] also contained single fragments of green bottle glass and window glass.

London and Essex Redwares

The most complete form is a chamber pot from Site A in slipped post-medieval redware (PMSRY) with flat base and one loop handle and everted lid-seated rim (<P35>). Also present is part of a large flaring dish with external sooting in post-medieval redware (PMR; diameter 350mm). The finds from a well [ER1685] include the base of a pipkin in post-medieval fine redware from Essex (PMFR).

Taken together, coarse redwares from London (PMR) and Essex redwares comprise the most common group on Sites C and D (36% of the total sherds, *c.* 57% by weight). The former include a jug handle and a horizontal handle from a bowl or jar in post-medieval redware (PMR, both from C[55]), part of a dripping dish (PMR, C[339]) and the rim of a cauldron in post-medieval bichrome glazed ware (PMBR, C[339]). Rim and base sherds from a large pipkin or cauldron in PMR were also found on Site G ([226]).

The Essex wares include part of a sooted jar or pipkin in fine post-medieval redware (PMFR, C[151]) and the rim of a chamber pot in post-medieval black-glazed ware (PMBL, C[55]). In addition, part of a bowl with horizontal handle in PMFR was found on Site F ([34]).

Surrey–Hampshire border wares

Of note is a complete Surrey–Hampshire border ware lid (<P36>) from Site A with patch of clear glaze inside and a patch of green glaze on the outer wall, which has a kiln scar. Another complete, but fragmented find from this site is a deep bowl with flaring profile (<P37>).[4] Other sherds from this site include the complete externally lid-seated rim from a small type 4 tripod pipkin[5] and sherds from three chamber pots; one is of type 2, with flanged rim[6] and dated to after 1650. Finds of Surrey-Hampshire border redware comprise a dish and part of a pipkin, the latter found in the well outside the north transept [ER1685].

Surrey–Hampshire border wares (both red and white fabrics), are the second most common group on sites C/D (16% of the total sherds). They comprise sherds from drinking jugs, a tripod pipkin and a deep bowl.

Tin-glazed wares

Sherds from two 17th-century English copies of dishes with Wan Li borders and 'daisy' motifs at the centre decoration were found on Site A, one of which is burnt on the underside. The design is typical of the Pickleherring factory in Southwark and these examples probably date to *c.* 1640–50.[7] A third rim is from a dish of similar date, while one sherd is from a jar; also present is a complete ointment pot with plain white glaze (<P38>). The five sherds recovered from the fill of the well [ER1685] derive from two blue and white plates and one that was probably plain white, a plain white carinated porringer, and a jar/albarello with decoration in blue and purple. Part of a large polychrome dish or charger was found on Site C, together with the handle of a chamber pot (both C[55]).

Other English wares

Only one sherd from a Midlands Purple ware butter pot found on Site D (C[339]) is earlier than the 19th century.

Imports

The imports mainly comprise Frechen stoneware, with two substantially complete Bartmann jugs from Site A (<P39, P40>) and the bases of three others. Sherds of Frechen stoneware, all probably from Bartmann jugs, were also found on Sites D (C[339]), F ([1] and [5], a rim/neck fragment), and G ([21]); the latter is a mortar-encrusted body sherd. Other imports from Site D, also from C[339], include the base of a small, unglazed baluster-shaped Spanish/Mediterranean 'mercury' jar[8] in a calcareous redware fabric (MERC). Finds from London include a complete example from Guy's Hospital.[9] Also present is the base of a triangular crucible of Hessian type (acc no. <19>).[10]

A piece of Chinese porcelain from Site D

Of particular interest is a piece of Chinese blue and white porcelain, found, without any other associated pottery, in context D[340] (so recorded, but this number was also given to an Anglo-Saxon skeleton also excavated, so there is an error). The complete base of a small dish, comprising three joining sherds, was recovered, measuring 60mm across the footring (Fig. 27). The central design is a fairly common one and consists of a boy with long sleeves dancing or leaping and waving his arms, and a woman seated on a 'perforated' rock, holding a small branch, or possibly a musical instrument. A tree branch overhead is represented by curvilinear brush strokes and dots. The base alone survives, so the border, probably variation on floral and diaper panels, is missing. The painting is clean and competent, although not of the highest quality. The so-called 'Long Eliza' and 'jumping boy' pattern had a long history as a motif on Chinese export wares, and variations of the theme were in use in the 16th century and also after the Kangxi period. This particular version, however, appears only in the middle Kangxi period (late 17th–early 18th century).[11] Figure designs are particularly common on Kangxi period export porcelains, much more so than they are a generation later; for example in the cargo of the *Geldermalsen*, which was wrecked in the South China seas in 1752. It seems that by the middle of the 18th century, blue and white was used more for landscapes, riverscapes and flower designs, while painting in enamels was favoured for 'imaged' wares, as they were called in contemporary shipping and sale lists.[12] The piece was most likely made in Jingdezhen, in the inland province of Jiangxi, where the vast majority of ceramic wares for both home and export markets was made. Numerous small manufactories operated here, as well as at the Imperial kilns, probably producing as much as 90% of the exported blue and white wares.[13]

Many museums have examples of the 'jumping boy' pattern in their collections, although these are illustrated in very few catalogues; published parallels are therefore hard to find. The vessels are often marked, and recorded examples include Kangxi reign marks, commendation marks and apocryphal reign marks, falsely indicating manufacture during a particularly prestigious, earlier reign. The St Paul's dish falls into the last category. Instead of the usual four clearly separated characters arranged centrally underneath the base in a square, the mark in this case appears as a close-knit web of characters that cannot be easily disentangled, but which reads 'Chenghua' (1466–87). This was a very common mark in the Kangxi period, when it was generally imperial pieces that used the imperial mark.[14]

The reign of Kangxi (1662–1722) is conveniently divided by modern ceramic historians into three distinct periods. The 'middle period', from which the St Paul's dish dates, starts in 1683 and ends *c.* 1710.[15] First period Kangxi is essentially a continuation of the Transitional period, and marks the restoration of stability after the civil war that brought the Ming dynasty to an end, with the establishment of Qing rule. After a period of considerable turmoil in which production at the imperial porcelain factories was interrupted, the middle years of the reign of Kangxi saw the resumption of imperial control and the manufacture of much fine quality porcelain.

In 1915, R L Hobson wrote that 'western collectors have agreed to give the place of honour to K'ang Hsi blue and white.'[16] This is a reflection of the regard in which Kangxi porcelain was held by connoisseurs in the late 19th and early 20th centuries and although the position has now altered somewhat, these wares are still highly collectable and known for their quality. They are justly famous for their pure, sapphire blue decoration, with delicately graded washes of colour, clearly visible on the St Paul's dish. Great care was taken in the preparation of the cobalt, and blue and white was considered to be the ideal medium for decorating porcelain throughout at least the first two periods of Kangxi's reign.[17] The demand for blue and white increased to such an extent during the middle Kangxi period that mass production was widely introduced, particularly important in the manufacture of porcelain for export to the West.

It is not so easy to view these Kangxi porcelains through early 18th-century eyes, although the Kangxi 'jumping boy' design was closely copied by English porcelain makers in the middle of the 18th century, a time when the influence of Chinese blue and white export porcelain was particularly strong and widespread. Examples are known in the early Liverpool porcelain of Richard Chaffers and Co, offering a reasonably faithful version of the Chinese pattern, as on a small plate formerly in the Watney Collection, dated to *c.* 1758–60.[18] While the Chinese 'jumping boy' prototypes appear not have been made to go with teabowls or cups of any form, Chaffers versions are often associated with cups, showing that the dishes or plates could be used to serve more than one function. Other forms made by Chaffers with the 'jumping boy' design include octagonal teapots, tea canisters and related teawares, often with pseudo-Chinese reign marks under the base. The pattern was also made at Samuel Gilbody's Liverpool porcelain works, which operated from 1754/5 to 1761, and was the most common type recovered on the factory site.[19]

The only other English factory known to have used the 'jumping boy' design is Bow, again appearing very close to the original as can be seen from a comparison of the two designs.[20] The pattern was made on underglaze blue wares at Bow in the so-called 'Middle period', 1755–63, at a time of expansion in the factory's operations. When Bow was set up in the 1740s, the proprietors, Alderman Arnold and Co traded on the popularity of imported Chinese porcelain and called their London works 'New Canton'. They made porcelain in imitation of Chinese wares and, unlike Chelsea, concentrated from the beginning on production of 'the more ordinary sorts of ware for common uses'. These were aimed largely at the middle-class market, with utility foremost, and it has been estimated that between the 1740s and mid 1770s probably over 90% of their range used oriental designs, some of them with imitation Chinese marks underneath.[21] The 'jumping boy' is typical of these 'cheap blue and white oriental useful wares',[22] and would have been made alongside more sophisticated ornamental china based on European designs.

By 1700, the English, French and Dutch East India Companies were importing very large quantities, and rich merchants and other men of influence were amassing enviable collections. It is likely that the vessel belonged to a household or individual of relatively comfortable means, and that it was part of a set of similar dishes. Most of the imported porcelains of the first quarter of the 18th century were tea- and tablewares, and they were auctioned by the East India Company not as complete services but as groups of the different components, such as cups and saucers, teapots and so on.[23] It is worth noting that saucers did not necessarily come with cups or teabowls at this time, and so dishes, such as the St Paul's example, could have been purchased as a set on their own and used with drinking vessels of different design, as well as other vessels in completely different materials, such as a silver teapot and tea canister. The St Paul's dish is therefore a good example of the kind of fashionable ceramics favoured by those who could afford to acquire what to much of the population was still something of a luxury.

Clay tobacco pipes

Fragments of clay tobacco pipe stems and bowls were recovered from Sites A, C, D, F and G; they date from the 1660s to the 1820s.

Non-ceramic artefacts

A ring or 'pole' dial

(H. Forsyth)

Site G: G<1>, Context [21] (Fig. 28)

A portable sundial in the form of a brass ring (oval 35mm × 31mm); with a calendar scale on the outside and a time scale on the inside. The dial was originally suspended from a pendant loop (now missing – there are two surviving holes for the rivet plate) and in use, was held in the vertical position to admit the sun's rays through a pin-hole located in a revolving band retained within a central groove (also missing). The calendar scale, indicated on a non-concentric arc, is divided into two parallel bands with punched month initials: January to June (I F M A M I) on one side, and July to December (I A S O N D) on the other. The month scale divisions are further sub-divided into quarters, the graduations slightly narrower for the first half of the year (January to June). There is a small dash between the September and October scale divisions which could indicate the position of the equinox, with possibly a corresponding mark between the months initials for March and April for the Spring equinox, now obscured by corrosion. The inner face has paired Arabic numerals with hour-marks for all seasons, indicated by individual dots: the hours 4–12 and 1–8, corresponding to the hours of daylight (sunrise to sunset) for European latitudes from about 42–54° north.

This dial is a rather unsophisticated version of the type, with crudely delineated scale divisions, punched letters and numbers. The letter 'F' for February is barely recognisable and the letter 'D' for December has been double-struck; presumably correcting an initial misorientation. The numbers 10, 11 and 12 are also shown upside-down relative to the other numerals.

Dials of this general type, known colloquially as 'poke 'dials (an archaic term for pocket) were in general use from the late 16th to 18th centuries. The style of the numerals on this dial suggests that it was probably made in London in the late 17th century.

Other artefacts (not illustrated)

(Jackie Keily)

Glass

<G> Wine glass
A<9>, A[+]
Incomplete; length 43mm, maximum diameter 28mm, minimum diameter 15mm. Tapering pedestal stem fragment, quatrefoil in section with remains of ring knops at each end; 18th century.

<G> Bottle
A<10>, A[+]
Near complete; height 88mm, base diameter 26mm, rim diameter 35mm). Mould-blown in natural green glass with raised lettering on both faces, reading: 'True cephalick snuff' and 'By the Kings patent'. 19th century.

Iron

The iron from the main area of Site A mainly comprises nails and spikes of assorted sizes (not accessioned), the largest *c.* 180mm in length; all have shanks that are rectangular in section.

Lead

<M> Mount/plaque
A<14>, A[+]
Near complete, rather bent; extant length 213mm, width *c.* 40–41mm. The front reads 'St.Pauls.Churchyard.East.' and has traces of red paint. Left end missing, right side irregular and apparently repaired with new piece of lead that is folded back on itself a projecting tongue on the underside; the sides of the latter are bent up to form a channel of semi-circular section, presumably to house a nail. On the front is an applied raised pad, presumably to strengthen the repair the attachment. 19th-century.

<M> Mount/plaque
A<15>, A[+]
Near complete, rather bent; length 208mm, width 34–35mm. The front reads 'St.Pauls. Churchyard.West' and has traces of red paint. Left end missing, right side folded back on itself, with a straight edge; the centre of the underside appears be perforated and so may originally have been an eye for attaching the plate to a larger object. The upper face is raised by a neatly applied pad of lead, possibly to strengthen this junction. 19th-century; both plates must have been fixed to gates or signposts.

Bricks

Terence Paul Smith

Bricks were retrieved from several places during the work on the west front (Site M); not only from the original substructure of the western steps, but from the vault over the west end of the north nave aisle, where modification was being made to enlarge a hole for hanging one of the chandeliers. Two complete bricks from context M[1], the substructure of the original western steps, two half-bricks from context M[2], layers of bricks over the vault over the crypt, and one almost complete cut brick from context M[4], the vault over the north aisle, have been examined. The top of the crypt vault (context M[2]) was laid *c.* 1688. The western steps (context M[1]) date from 1708. The vault over the north aisle (context [4]) dates from the first decade of the 18th century.

The standard MoL descriptions of the fabrics in this report are as follows:

3032 Red or purplish red, often with yellow surface tinge; hard texture with yellow or white carbonate specks and often with dark organic inclusions or voids where these have burned out during firing
3033 Orange or red; soft, sandy with moderate quartz and black iron oxides

3034 As 3032 but with white or yellowish streaky inclusions

3047 Orange; fine sandy with common quartz and dark red iron oxides and with distinctive fine moulding sand on surfaces.

The bricks sampled from or found as fragments at some of the sites (Table 6) are of types familiar within London. In some cases they are in firmly dated contexts, a fact which is of particular value in connection with the fabric 3047 bricks. Some shed light on use of the material in building work under Wren's direction, albeit sometimes in minor applications.

Context	*Brick fabric*	*Type*	*Date and comments*
M[1]	3032	stock	Western steps: lowest course at SW corner
M[2]	3032	stock	crypt vaulting & bricks above
M[4]	3032	stock	saucer dome over N aisle, near W end
F[38]	3033	stock	Wren drain outside W end, 1688
C[10]	3033	stock	Wren construction surface, 1680s
C[13]	3033	stock	Dump within Wren construction sequence, 1680s
C[109]	3047	place	Temporary drain at Site C, 1680s; possibly Dutch imports

Table 6 Details of sampled or recorded bricks

Bricks in fabric 3032

The two bricks from context M[1] are in MoL fabric 3032, although one of them has fewer organic/burned inclusions and rather more calcium carbonate than usual. Dimensions are given in Table 7. Both bricks have blackish surfaces, probably the result of slight overfiring. In that respect, they may be regarded as 'seconds'. But they were used in a utilitarian structure within the cathedral, the substructure of the western steps: for such an application they were entirely serviceable products.

The organic/burned inclusions – known as 'Spanish' at the time – are the result of adding ash and cinder, derived from domestic fireplaces, to the raw material. According to a document of 13 May 1714, the advantages of this were discovered accidentally, in Moorfields, 'about forty years since'; that is, in the 1670s.[24] Thereafter, bricks of this sort rapidly superseded earlier types throughout the London area. The advantages included a saving on fuel, given extra point by the imposition of the Coal Tax to pay for the reconstruction of public buildings after the Fire. Like the redder bricks already discussed, though unlike most fabric 3033 bricks, these too were made as stock rather than as place bricks. Aesthetically, the newer bricks were valued for their dark red, almost plum, colour, which acted as an effective foil to the brighter red-brick dressings to doorways, windows, and other features, as on Deanery in Dean's Court (1672), which must represent one of the earliest uses, and the chapter house (1712–14). The brighter bricks, which could be easily cut and rubbed, were brought in from elsewhere, principally from the Weald of Kent. The same building method was employed for some of the City churches, whether by Wren himself or by Robert Hooke, for example at St Benet Paul's Wharf (1678–84 and 1692–3[25]). The particular value of these bricks, as of others from various works at St Paul's, is that they can be closely dated from the documentary records of the building programme.

The bricks sampled here are stock bricks. Those from contexts M[2] and M[4] are in a fine version of MoL fabric 3033, close to fabric 3047; that from context M[4] is similar but with a few small silty inclusions. Dimensions are not given as the samples were fragments. All are hand-moulded products with sharp arrises and quite smooth faces. They are of high quality, superior to the general run of fabric 3033 bricks. Occasional strike marks are visible on the upper bedfaces. One from context M[2] has particularly smooth faces, and one header and one stretcher face are very slightly vitrified, the result of slight overfiring in the clamp or kiln. That from context M[4] has been cut, most probably with a brick-axe, removing most of one bedface and rather more than half of a stretcher face. This gives a broad sloping face so that the brick could serve as a springer in an arch or for some similar purpose; or it may be that the brick was cut simply to enable it to fit in an awkward space within the vault ceiling. The bricks do not have sunken margins, and indeed their smooth faces and sharp arrises almost certainly indicate that they were made as stock bricks rather than as place bricks. Stock-moulded bricks were formed with the mould placed over a small wooden board (the stock) and were demoulded at the moulder's

Table 7 Dimensions of brick samples in fabric 3032 (mm)

Context	*L*	*B*	*T*	*Comments*
M[1]	218	103	61	Blackish surfaces
M[1]	222	108	66	Blackish surfaces; fewer inclusions than usual

bench and carried in batches, the individual bricks separated by small wooden pallets, to the drying ground, where they were set on edge for drying. The latter procedure would also account for the absence of squodge marks along the arrises of the lower bedfaces, for these are not formed on stock-moulded bricks.[26]

Bricks in fabric 3033

Bricks in the sandy orange/red fabric 3033 were sampled from three contexts: F[38] the Wren drain outside the west end; and two found in the Wren construction levels, C[10] and C[13]. These are local products. Bricks in fabric 3033 and its variants were used in London from the late Middle Ages down to *c.* 1700. The drain F[38] is dated by documentary evidence to the 1680s, and the bricks are consistent with this. They range in length from 217mm to 221mm, in breadth from 96mm to 100mm, and in thickness 60–68mm (median values: 220mm, 99mm, and 60mm respectively). Some show a degree of overfiring.

Fragments of bricks in fabric 3033 (one containing a little crushed shell) were also recovered from C[10] and [13], dating from the Wren construction period in the 1680s. They have been somewhat overfired and this gives them a slight and misleading resemblance to the later London brick types. No full dimensions are preserved but in thickness they range from 55mm to 65mm. The thinner bricks are unusual for the late 17th century, and the fact that they have mortar on their broken edges suggests that they may be pre-Fire products salvaged and reused as rubble.

It was very soon after the Great Fire that new types of bricks (they are MoL fabrics 3032 and 3034) began to be manufactured in London, darker in colour, harder and more brittle, and incorporating domestic ash known at the time as 'Spanish', a practice apparently discovered accidentally in 'fields contiguous to the city' in the mid-1670s.[27] But the older types continued for a while, probably down to *c.* 1700. The writer has examined the surfaces of bricks comprising the saucer-domes of the nave and paving at triforium level in the south transept, all completed before 1700. These appear to be of the older type – that is, to be in fabric 3033 or one of its variants. Wren opposed the adding of Spanish, for in the letter already quoted he claims that 'Brick-makers spoil the Earth by mixing and hasty burning'; and it was, he considered, worth paying for the unadulterated products: 'good Bricks are not to be now had, without greater Prices than formerly, and indeed, if rightly made, will deserve them'.[28]

Bricks in fabric 3047

Four bricks sampled from drain C[109], a temporary drain of the 1680s construction period, are in the fine sandy orange/red fabric 3047, although two have been a little overfired and are somewhat darker red and slightly distorted. The firmly dated context is important in providing a *terminus ante quem* for the introduction of these bricks: hitherto their start date has often been taken as *c.* 1700. The samples range in length from 220mm to 226mm, in breadth from 104mm to 110mm, and in thickness from 45mm to 50mm (median values: 225mm, 107mm, and 48.5mm respectively). Such thinness is unusual in English bricks of the late 17th century but is typical of bricks in this particular fabric. It is possible that they were imported from the Netherlands, where post-medieval bricks generally remained thinner than their English equivalents. Dutch bricks were imported into London, for example in March 1669, when 20,000 'bricks' and 7,000 'brickstones' (probably dense yellow bricks of small format used mostly for paving) were brought in.[29]

The fabric 3047 bricks from St Paul's show small raised 'lips' along their edges and one shows a narrow sunken margin: these do not occur with stock bricks but only with place bricks, which were made without a stock and were carried individually by a woman or boy and still in the mould to the drying ground or 'place', where they were demoulded. The 'lips' were formed when the mould was pulled upwards, and the sunken margins were formed as an incidental effect if the 'lips' were pushed down, as was often but not invariably done, using the bottom of the mould itself. The absence of any grass or straw marks and the fine finish of both bedfaces indicate that the 'place' was carefully prepared as a level area strewn with sand. For initial drying the bricks lay flat and one from St Paul's shows the paw print from where a dog walked over it whilst it was still soft. This brick must have been turned over completely during drying since the small 'lips' are on one bedface, which must therefore have been uppermost when the brick was first laid out, but the paw print is on the opposite bedface, which must have been facing upwards when the animal walked over it. Possibly all the bricks were treated this way in order to speed the drying process. Later, when the bricks were sufficiently firm, they were 'skintled' (turned on edge and stacked in a honeycomb arrangement) for further drying; three of the examples show slight pressure marks from where they were stacked whilst a little too soft. It is clear that they were stacked diagonally, a common 17th-century practice both in Britain and in the Netherlands.

They are rather well-finished products with quite sharp arrises and it may seem odd that they should be used in so quotidian a setting as a drain. But they are somewhat less porous than the fabric 3033 and variant bricks and would therefore have been particularly suitable for such a use. In fact, it is likely, irrespective of whether they are English or Dutch, that they were specialist products, used principally for the construction of firebacks or for paving; indeed, large (10in) paving tiles (pammets or pamments) were produced in the same fabric.

In summary, therefore, the sampled bricks from both temporary and permanent brick constructions around the west end during the period *c.* 1680–1705 can all be classed as stock bricks; and those in the temporary drain on Site C, in the 1680s, may have been imports from the Netherlands, whereas the others were probably made in the London region.

Detailed notes on the investigation of the nave roof, 2013

Damian Goodburn and Azizul Karim

The timbers of the roof

The roof is of a common purlin type in which multiple, light, longitudinal timbers (purlins) are supported by 24 roof trusses. From Truss 14 westward the roof span widens and two modified forms of truss were used which are described below. The use of multiple light purlins set on widely spaced heavy trusses is typical of roof framing in historic buildings on the east side of the North Sea and in parts of the north-eastern USA, but relatively uncommon in England. The system has some practical advantages with a roof of this huge scale, particularly as it was erected in stages. The simply joined purlins were lap jointed into the faces of the rafters, presumably after facing pairs of trusses were erected. They did not need to be fully framed early in the prefabrication of the complete roof frame as would have been the more commonly found butt or clasped purlins. The fitting of the relatively light purlins also allowed for slight adjustments to take account of irregularities in some of the very large oak timbers used. Once this had been done in situ a flush, regular, outer surface was made for the nailing on of the pit-sawn oak sarking planks that the lead outer cover was then laid on. No windbrace timbers were used but the combination of a modest pitch, robust trusses with closely set purlins, sarking planks and a heavy sheet lead covering is clearly quite strong enough to resist racking strains imposed by several 100-year storms.

The roof trusses were evenly spaced about 7ft (2.2m) apart. The light multiple purlins and ridge piece beams were of pit-sawn oak and varied slightly in cross section ('scantling') but centred on *c.* 130mm (*c.* 5½in) deep and 110mm (*c.* 4½in) wide. When noting dimensions recorded now we must realise that the 'nominal' dimensions the green timber was marked out in would have been larger allowing for shrinkage. The purlins were simply notched and housed in the top edges of the rafters: 23 on each side of the roof in the eastern half of the nave central roof and 24 each side in the slightly, larger western trusses.[30]

The roof framing and even much of the plank covering laid over the purlins is nearly all original, a testament to the strength of the workmanship and the weather tightness of the lead sheet roof covering. It is also clear that the stone supporting walls are also in a robust condition having experienced little movement except for a small drift westward in part of the northern wall which has broken the scarf joint in the wall plate at one point.

The dimensions of several of the long and relatively straight tiebeams were found to vary a little but were generally *c.* 430mm–450mm (16½in–18in) deep at their largest end tapering down to *c.* 370mm–350mm (14¾in–14in) deep at the other end, cut from higher up in the parent oak. They were also a little less deep over the middle section that is each end thickened a little to allow for the jointing in of the rafter feet. The beams varied a little in thickness but were *c.* 280mm–300mm (*c.* 11¼in–12in) wide east–west) and *c.* 14.08m (46ft 2½in) long. The length fits the building accounts evidence where a length of '47ft' is specified by Wren for the very long oak beams sourced from the Duke of Newcastle's estate. The missing 9½in (241mm) could be easily explained by a little shrinkage and the recutting

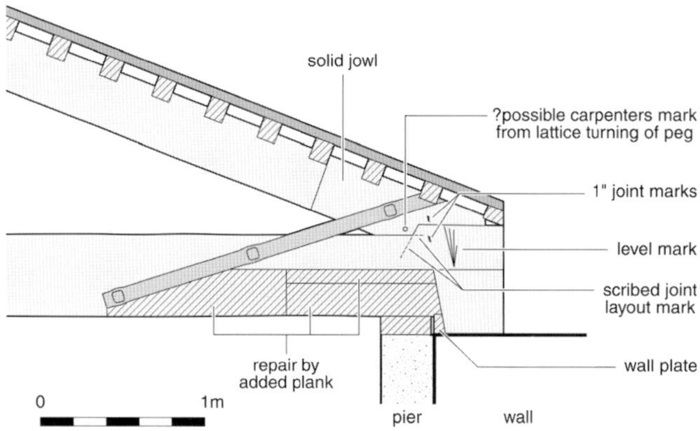

Fig. 192 Carpentry details surviving on the east face of Truss 1 at its north end: arrow-shaped level marks, scribed joint layout marks, chiselled combined truss and joint numbers marks and pit-saw marks (Azizul Karim, MOLA)

of the beams to remove the extreme ends which might have been slightly split by drying. The scantling or cross sectional dimensions, described in the Wren letter as '13 inches and 14 inches at the small end, growing thicker' are also close to those found in the surviving tiebeam smaller ends, allowing for a little shrinkage.

The types of joints used in all the roof trusses could not be examined in detail in the central nave roof as all the carpentry seen was still fully assembled. However, the location of the oak locking pegs (26mm–28mm in diameter), some surviving joint layout marks and the presence of small gaps that could be looked into with torches. The rafter feet joined the tiebeam ends with an unusual form of shallow bridle joint (Fig. 59) rather than the common place chase mortise and tenon. It seems likely that this adaptation was made to allow easier assembly of the very large, heavy timbers and because the joint was always to be reinforced with a large, bolted, iron strap. A fairly standardised double-pegged mortise and tenon was used for the foot of the king posts and a single pegged mortise and tenon for each end of the king post to rafter struts. Unfortunately we could not closely access the joints of the rafter heads with the top of the king posts. The joints used were secured with two oak pegs each and are most likely a form of standard mortise and tenon, but we could not totally rule out the use of some form of bridle joint.

Truss 4 is the illustrated sample truss of the eastern group, and was a fairly typical example, although the tiebeam was one of the straightest. It must also have been cut from a slightly larger tree than most as it had pit-sawn faces extending from one end to the other and only a little sapwood on its outer corners at the south end which would have been uppermost in the parent tree (Fig. 52). However, the tops of rafters were both cut out to follow a slight curve in the parent log and the common purlin joints adjusted accordingly to maintain a flush upper surface for the roof. The rafter feet had solid sawn 'jowls' on the eastern, upper face and added planks nailed on to thicken the western faces. Combined truss and joint numbers cut with a 2in chisel were found on the eastern face in the form of an 'X' with an extra 'tag' added on the north end. This was one of two forms of combined truss and joint numbers found in the central nave roof and different to those found on Truss 15. One feature only recognised on the north end of this tiebeam east face was a strange obliquely augured hole of no obvious function, though its use as an attachment hole for a bar used in the hauling of the large beam or partly worked parent log might be a possible explanation. Oblique holes have been found in broadly similar large oak baulks of Roman date excavated from London at the Regis House waterfront site, and it was clearly the case that they were used for hauling out the timber there.[31]

The wall plates into which the ends of the tiebeams of each truss were jointed were of quite modest proportions, presumably because the beams were well supported by a robust masonry wall, at least when the roof was completed. The north and south wall plates were made of pit-sawn beams *c.* 300mm wide and 150mm deep (12in × 6in). They appeared to have been cut out of roughly half a medium sized log i.e. 'box halved'. The beams making up the long plate were joined with a form of bridled scarf in which the tongue of the bridle is secured with in the joint and secured with two pegs. The form of the joint used where the ends of the tiebeam engaged with the wall plate was hidden from the investigating team but we can say that it must have been a shallow lap joint of some form as the tiebeam soffits (lower faces) are recessed by *c.* 20–25mm (1in). The loading at the point where the rafters joined the wall plates was spread by using small oak plank pads on masonry piers projecting inwards from the main wall line and a second oak longitudinal beam, or pseudo wall plate, level with the outer end of the tiebeams (Fig. 52). The wall plate and pier support system was the same in both the eastern and wider western parts of the roof.

Carpenters also had to use many fine and often hard to recognise reference marks which have only been identified over the last few years. These were normally scratched or scribed. The carpenters would have made the roof trusses laid out horizontally on trestles or beams. To ensure the joints and timbers were aligned accurately even if the timbers were a little uneven, they had to be set up nominally level. Later the horizontal plane would of course become precisely vertical for the roof trusses. When they were set up the level marks would have been accurately checked for verticality. To set up a plumb level the surface of the timber had to be flat and fairly smooth so unevenness was sometimes trimmed off in the area used as the reference for levelling. Many of the tiebeam ends in the nave roof had surviving level marks in the form of faint scribed arrows, which were orientated up or down in the finished truss. The example presented here is that recorded at the north end of Truss 1 on its east face (Fig. 192). In this case the pit-sawn surface was clearly planed level and smooth before the arrow level mark was made.

Another essential feature of the methodology of timber framing is fine scribed lines used to mark the timbers for joint cutting. These types of marks survived in many places on the roof truss timbers but were very faint. Some of the clearest and most accessible were recorded around the redundant mortises on the soffits of the tiebeams of Trusses 15–18.

Types of trees used

By noting the size and shape of timbers and the section of the tree they represent with details of the grain and outer sapwood present it is possible to reconstruct the size and type of tree from which they were cut.[32] By preparing this graphically and using a knowledge of the grain patterns and requirements of different conversion methods, ideally combined with information gained from tree ring studies, an even more accurate picture of the historic parent tree can be derived.[33] Large knots on the faces of boxed heart timbers, cut from whole logs, like those of the central nave roof trusses, represent branches in the parent trees existing when it was felled. We note that there are two closely related native oaks in Britain and they hybridize so we can only loosely talk of 'English oak'. All the original St Paul's nave timbers had the clear, visually diagnostic features typical of our native oaks such as boldly marked rays and cream coloured outer sapwood.

A detailed measured sketch was made of the west face of the tiebeam of Truss 1 with the sapwood and large knots indicated. Using this information, graphically represented, an outline reconstruction of the great parent oak can be made allowing, a little height for felling and extra girth for the bark and sapwood largely removed (Fig. 193). It appears that the Truss 1 tiebeam parent tree was actually slightly smaller and a little less straight than some of the trees used for the other eastern tiebeams, such as that in Truss 4, though it was still huge. To appreciate just how large and tall this parent oak was, a typical, large managed woodland, or rather tall hedgerow standard oak, such as was used for more common place timber frame construction at the end of the 17th century, is shown alongside that derived from the Truss 1 tiebeam. Not only where the parent trees for the largest tiebeams of fairly large girth with diameters of 0.65m–0.75m at breast height, but they were also unusually tall, straight

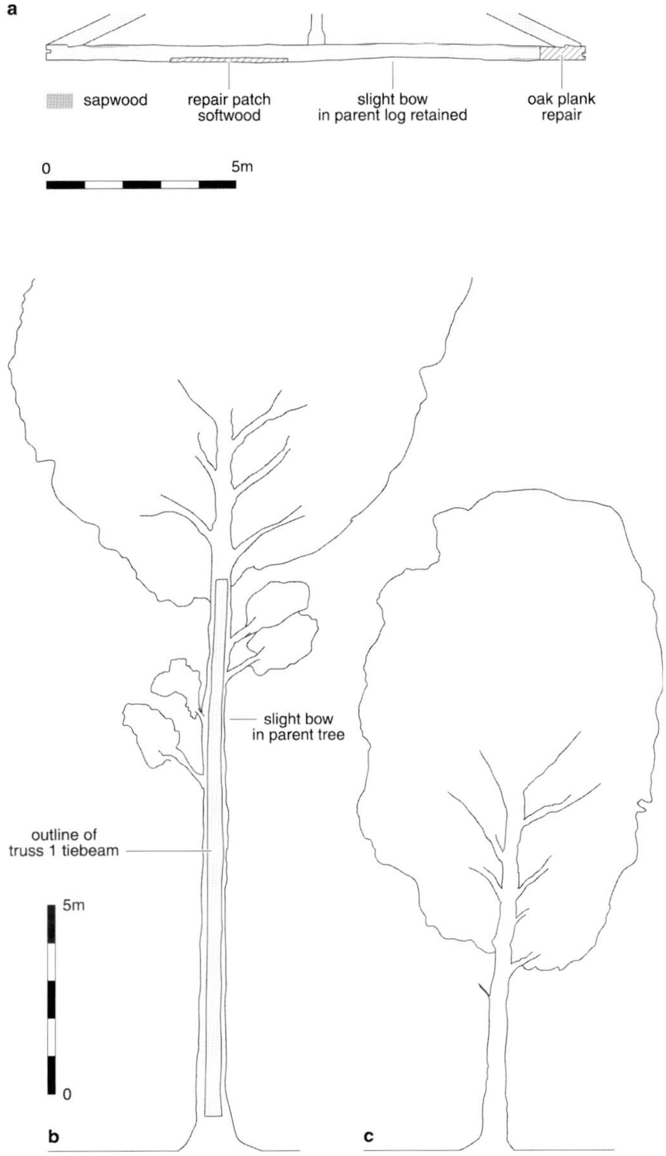

Fig. 193 The size and form of the oak trees used for the eastern trusses: (a) the western face of Truss 1 tiebeam, showing its slightly curved shape, zones of sapwood and more recent repairs; (b) an outline of the tree from which it was cut; (c) an outline of a more typical large oak used in English buildings of the period (Azizul Karim, MOLA)

and had little taper compared to typical English managed woodland oaks then and as found in ancient woodland today. The parent tree for the Truss 1 tiebeam would have been around 0.45m in diameter at over 15m from the ground.

The form of great parent oak reconstructed can now occasionally be found either in very old high forest plantations or clumps of large parkland trees where those near the middle of a planted clump tend to grow straight with few low branches. Up until about 1250 remnant areas of natural, high, dark, and wildwood-type woodland have been shown to have existed in some parts of England. This type of tree land could produce, huge straight oaks sometimes even knot free for over 8m.[34] These conditions produced narrow annual rings, straight grain and a slow taper in most trees. By the 17th century very little of this type of woodland still existed anywhere in western Europe but substantial areas still survived in what is now eastern Poland and southern Lithuania and the fine quality slow-grown oak there was much exported. The same situation pertained in parts of the north-eastern United States and oak similar to the English material was also exported from there. Only intensive tree-ring sampling could rule out the use of imported oak in the Wren period cathedral, although their sheer size and the documentary record makes it unlikely for the largest structural elements. On balance we might suggest that the straight and tall oaks felled for the largest St Paul's roof timbers probably derived from clumps of large timber trees grown in some form of parkland setting. Such timber would have been much prized for naval use at this time and the St Paul's roof project made exceptional and ultimately successful efforts to obtain them.

Preparation of the timbers by sawyers and carpenters; evidence of lifting materials

Apart from sawing a much older technique of conversion also left traces on many of the longer St Paul's nave roof timbers, that of squaring up with axes or 'hewing.' This general method of timber conversion died out very early in England though it is even now in use in some remote parts of continental Europe. However, experimenters in historic woodworking and some timber frame carpenters have rediscovered the craft of hewing large oak beams in the last few years and so the quality of the workmanship evidenced in the St Paul's timbers can be more practically assessed. It is quite clear from the irregular scalloped surfaces of the smaller ends of many of the longer nave roof timbers that 'hewing' was the technique used to remove sapwood, bark and waste heartwood where the parent logs were only just big enough. Several metres of the smaller ends of many of the single piece eastern tiebeams had moderately roughhewn faces with some sapwood left on the corners. A clear example of such axe hewn surfaces surviving on the south end of the tiebeam of Truss 9 is shown in Figure 194. The hewing was only moderately regular, not finished by smooth broad axe work as it normally was in medieval London carpentry. Detailed recording of post-medieval carpentry work in southern England has shown that by the 17th century hewn surfaces were typically not expected to be very smoothly, broad axe finished but a moderately flat, regular surface was generally adequate.[35] No evidence for the shipwright's practice of surface smoothing with an adze was found on any of the St Paul's timbers.

Work by present-day English timber framers has shown that following marking out a log, firmly held in place, was then scored at intervals with a heavy, felling-type axe. This was followed by using the same tool to split off large amounts of waste, close to the full depth of the scores. The rather rough, uneven surface that generally then resulted was then hewn back with axe blows at a shallower angle, using a plumb bob occasionally to check the face being hewn was fairly plumb. These general hewing stages were the same as used in later medieval times, but usually this was where the carpenters hewing stopped in the 17th century. Often traces of the scoring grooves from the first cutting stage and facets from the next stage were left rough on hewn surfaces at this time as is shown in the hewn surfaces of the central nave roof timbers. On the soffit of the Truss 9 tiebeam at the south end, and in several other examples, the remains of scores slightly overcut and very clear, rough, relatively narrow axe facets can be seen. A very smooth regular finish was not deemed necessary. In most cases the hewn surfaces

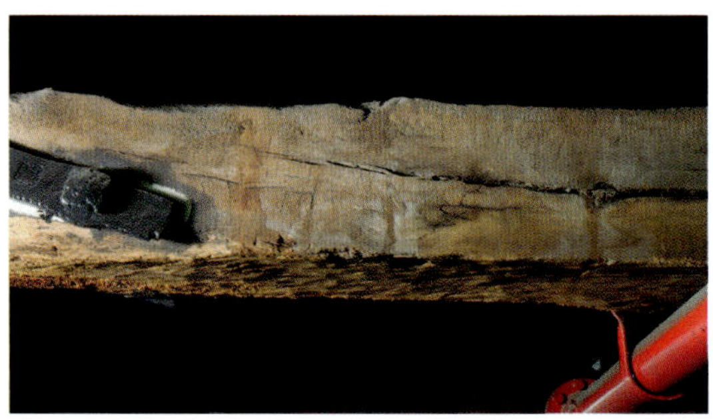

Fig. 194 The south end of Truss 9 tiebeam, west side: the side is sawn, the underside axe hewn (Andy Chopping, MOLA)

only survived at the smaller ends of the timbers with either all or about 75% of the length of the beams having sawn finishes. This demonstrates an economically minded combination of sawing and hewing except for the largest and straightest of the logs where the faces were all sawn, such as in Truss 4.

Most of the surfaces of the roof timbers in the central nave roof still show clear manual sawing marks from accurate pit-sawing, the most common technique of conversion by saws in London carpentry from the early 15th century. With pit-sawing the sawyers did their long wise cutting of minimally trimmed logs or axe hewn baulks, from one end of the timber to the other, leaving a small right angle triangle of split surface at one end. This distinctive signature of the pit-sawing technique is clear on several of the roof timbers, with a particularly clear example visible on the south end of the Truss 24 tiebeam in the portico section of the roof. Although we would expect pit-sawing to be the dominant technique used at the end of the 17th century, evidence of another technique of sawing was also found on two tiebeams of the eastern half of the nave roof: distinctive traces of sawing on two high trestles or possibly some form of raised gantry. Figure 195 shows this evidence on the north end of the Truss 9 tiebeam. With this method of sawing the sawing was carried out from both ends resulting in the cuts or 'kerfs' meeting on the sawn faces usually leaving a small unsawn ridge where the last section split off. Experimental sawing shows that wedges driven into the saw kerfs to keep the timber from binding on the blade often cause the last section to split. As we know from the surviving building accounts that the timbers were derived from at least two sources, then the use of slightly different conversion methods for identical roof elements may indicate be a mark of separate origins. The widespread and distinctive use of thickened ends (rather like jowls on main post heads) in the rafters and king posts made special demands on the sawyers' and or master carpenters' marking out skills as two sawn surfaces for each face had to be accurately created, except where a spiked on thickening plank was used instead. It is likely that even where sawing was the predominant method used, at least two faces would have been roughly hewn first.

Multiple grooves were noted on the top corners of most of the tiebeams of the roof trusses in the central nave roof; it became clear that they had been made by the frequent passage of ropes under load. The deepest were measured at *c.* 18mm–20mm wide and up to 30mm deep. On the top corners of the tiebeam for Truss 1 over 20 such rope wear grooves were found. The tiebeams had clearly been used as purchase points to haul up materials, in small parcels, for the bricklayers and masons creating the vaulting for the nave ceiling. This vaulting now acts as the floor of the roof space so it is easy for us to forget that it had to be built from temporary staging once the walls of the nave had been erected. With the roof up, even if not permanently covered, the masons and bricklayers could have worked undercover allowing the slow setting lime mortar to go off without being damaged by weather. The relatively low clearance between the top of the vaulting and the bottom of the roof trusses would have made it difficult to rig pulley blocks with hooks below the beams.

Fig. 195 *Truss 9 looking west; this shows a ridge left where sawing out the face from both ends converged but did not quite meet, probably indicative of sawing on two high trestles (Andy Chopping, MOLA). This also shows a combined joint and truss number ('XII') cut with a 2in chisel and given a 'tag', the small mark on the right-hand*

Human bone

Bill White

On Site G (below the south transept), parts of four human skeletons were recovered. The bones were in a very poor state of preservation. None of the skeletons was complete, therefore the information available from analysis was limited and variable.

The grave of Lawrence Spencer yielded two individuals, in accordance with the inscription on the ledger stone. Buried individual G[11] comprised bones representing *c.* 30% of the skeleton chiefly from the lower half but there were also fragments of both arms, the right hand, a few teeth and part of the skull vault. This individual was an adult but the areas of the skull and pelvis that are most reliable for the assessment of sex were lacking. However, joint size strongly suggested that the deceased was male. He was fully adult but the condition of the skeleton does not permit closer ageing. The few remaining teeth are from the front of the jaw and show no wear, suggesting that the deceased was not elderly. The only vertebrae to survive, the lumbar vertebrae, show osteophytic lipping which could be a sign of advancing age but equally could reflect the performance of heavy manual labour in early adulthood. The tibiae (shin bones) show a 'fore-and-aft' type of flattening known as platycnemia. The significance of this is not known for certain but it may represent a mechanical modification of the bone to cope with occupational stress and strain. Following the disintegration of the two wooden coffins, skeleton G[l1] had been directly overlain by skeleton G[9]. This was an adult skeleton about 80% complete. This person had a female type of pelvis with a very wide greater sciatic notch but unfortunately the pubic bones had not survived to confirm identity as a female. The skull was limited to the mandible and the rear of the cranium, considered insufficient for sex diagnosis. However, the large joint size (based on measurements of the head of the right humerus and of both femora) was strongly suggestive of the male sex. This person had lost all the rear teeth during life and was in the course of losing the anterior teeth. This suggests that he died at a great age. Measurement of the left femur showed that he had originally stood about 174.6cm (5ft 7¾in) tall but he would have been a little shorter in the latter part of his life (had this individual been female, calculation would suggest stature 170.2cm or 5ft 7in, not impossible but rather tall for the period). Osteoarthritis affected the cervical and thoracic vertebrae but not the lumbar region.

With merely the legs and lower spines of the two occupants of the Lawrence Spencer grave exposed, it was difficult to separate the two in terms of age. The visible presence of osteoarthritis suggested that G[11] was the older of the two, almost by default. Had the upper spine of G[9] been available for close inspection at that time the presence of osteoarthritis here would have made identification equivocal. Only the exposure of the mandible of G[9] would have permitted a separation of the two on the grounds of age, for this is consistent with the jaw of a man of Lawrence Spencer senior's age at death (even if the state of the pelvis has raised some uncertainty over the identification). The identification of the lower skeleton as that of Lawrence Spencer junior would have been aided by the presence of a few back teeth or the clavicles (breast bones), which ought to have permitted confirmation of his youth. The evidence of lumbar osteoathritis and platycnemia (present in the son and not in the father) suggests that the younger man had been obliged to indulge in heavy labour from his late teens.

Skeleton G[15], from the grave of Dorathy Spencer, was about 25% complete. Only parts of the lower half, the left arm and portions of the skull vault were present. It was evident that this was an adult person but the extent of the remains permitted neither more precise ageing nor establishment of the sex. A second skeleton G[19] from the grave of Dorathy Spencer now consisted merely of a few fragments of the skull vault. The cross-section of the bone, with the lack of separation of the inner and outer tables, revealed that this was a young infant, rather than a child some years of age. Whether the deceased was stillborn or lived several weeks of life could not be stated with certainty. The death of both of them in childbirth cannot be ruled out.

Coffins and coffin furniture

Adrian Miles and Robin Wroe-Brown

Coffins were recorded, in fragmentary state, on Site G (below the south transept) in 2000. The furniture from four coffins was examined. The coffins were excavated from the two named graves of Dorathy Spencer (d. 1687) and an unnamed child, and of Lawrence Spencer and his son Lawrence (d. 1720 and 1719 respectively).

None of the timber from the coffins survived to any recognisable degree, the shape and dimensions of the coffins being determined purely from the dark brown organic staining around the skeletons (for their outline, see Fig. 121). The coffin furniture was made from two types of metal: studs of copper alloy and grips, plates and brackets of iron. The copper alloy studs were in excellent condition, some still retaining their shiny surface, but the iron fittings had corroded. In some cases the shape of the iron objects could be determined but the decorative work was, for the most part, too corroded to record.

Coffin G[10] (Lawrence Spencer senior)

Decayed kite-shaped wooden coffin, 1.82m long × 0.54m at the shoulders, nailed together with iron nails. Coffin furniture included lines of copper alloy studs, six square iron grips with the remains of ornate grip plates, a breastplate which was severely decayed and illegible and a single copper alloy shroud pin. Since this coffin had collapsed into the one beneath, G[12], the furniture of both had become intermingled to an extent and the pattern of the studs was not determined.

Coffin G[12] (Lawrence Spencer junior)

Decayed kite-shaped wooden coffin, 1.82m long × 0.60m at the shoulders, nailed together with iron nails. As with coffm G[10] lines of copper alloy studs and six right-angled iron grips with the remains of ornate grip plates were present. No breastplate was found but it may have been destroyed by the collapse of the coffin above, G[10]. For this reason the pattern of the studs was not determined but they were found in double vertical lines on one side.

Coffin G[16] (Dorathy Spencer)

Decayed kite-shaped wooden coffin, 1.80m long × 0.57m at the shoulders, nailed together with iron nails. A name plate was present over the head and neck area, but it proved to be illegible. There were eight right-angled iron grips with fairly well-preserved decorative grip plates which had been nailed to the side and end panels of the coffin with six iron nails each. There were also several smaller iron decorative plates but these were badly decayed. At least four were diamond-shaped, and they had been arranged in a pattern, but had fallen or collapsed with the coffin. No studs were found.

Coffin G[20] (unnamed child)

Decayed kite-shaped wooden coffin, 0.88m long × 0.26m at the shoulders, held together with decoratively shaped angle-brackets known as 'hinges' in the undertaking trade.[36] The lid was nailed on. There were six small right-angled iron grips on shaped, but apparently unadorned, grip plates. No other decorative features were found. The two coffins for the Lawrences were virtually identical and the presence of copper alloy studs were indicative of fairly high-status burials (although not of the same class as lead coffins). Studs, or upholstery pins, were both decorative and functional, used to secure fabric to the outside of the coffin. In both cases the fabric, typically red or black velvet, had decayed away, apart from small traces beneath some of the studs. The use of studs in this fashion dates from the beginning of the 18th century, so these are early examples. The two coffins belonging to Dorathy and the child were too early to possess them. These were instead decorated with iron furniture as described above, again fairly typical of the period. The grips or coffin handles also indicate a difference in date. In general terms grips from the 17th century were larger, of more solid construction and plainer than those from the 18th century. The grips on Dorathy's coffin were certainly larger and more squarely made than those for the father and son Lawrences. The horizontal parts of the handle were straight in the case of Dorathy's coffin but tapered from a central swelling on the coffins of the two male Spencers. The latter were a plain right-angled form but, with the tapering, were transitional towards the evolution of the more rounded form of grip prevalent from the mid-18th century.

Lawrence Spencer, Clerk of Works, and his family

John Schofield

Christopher Wren achieved a rare distinction of building a complete cathedral within a single lifetime. But there were others who worked with him for nearly all the construction period. The mason Edward Strong (1652–1724) worked at the cathedral from 1681 to 1714, that is for 33 years; before that, he was probably in his older brother Thomas Strong's team before taking over as master mason following Thomas's death in 1681.[37] There is a third person who actually worked on the entire project of 36 years from 1675 to 1711. This was Lawrence Spencer, Clerk of Works (1648–1720).

Spencer first appears in the accounts in September 1675, 3 months after work began on the foundations, as a labourer at the higher daily rate of 2s when the other labourers were paid several rates between 12d and 16d. The labourers were removing rubble, digging new foundations, a reservoir for New River water and temporary drains.[38] Though the term is not used, he was probably a foreman. In 1675 he was one of two witnesses to the monthly payments to labourers. He was still receiving this rate for the same job in 1685.[39] In this year the Clerk of Works John Tillison died, and Spencer was appointed in his place on 29 April 1686. He was assigned the same salary as his predecessor, £8 6d 8d a month, and the lodgings 'adjoining to the Office of ye Workes' which came with the post. He had been dealing with office expenses since Tillison's death the previous December.[40]

As Clerk of Works he had many duties, including preparing and witnessing contracts in 1678–1711, going to Portland to review problems in the provision of stone, arranging for the printing of the approved engravings of the finished cathedral, and managing the workmen. He was requested to ask the Archbishop of Canterbury to call a meeting of the Commissioners in 1711, at the time of spirited discussion about the railings (and Wren's absence from their meetings).[41] After the Convocation House had to be demolished around 1712, he must have been given lodgings in the new Chapter House, since a meeting of the Commissioners in the Chapter House on 25 October 1715 ordered that 'the Staires at entrance into Mr Spencer's Lodgings in the Chapter House be altered (they being very inconvenient) and that Mr James [the new Surveyor] do give directions therein.' At this time Spencer was clearly a trusted official, since at the next meeting of November 1715 it was ordered that:

> '£33,000 of the Church money, now in Mr Spencer's hands, be deposited in an Iron Chest in the Chapter House, screwed to the floor with two iron screws with 3 locks & Keys to it, one whereof to be kept by the Lord Bishop of London, or his deputy, the second by the Dean, or Residentiary of St Paul's in waiting, or his Deputy, and the third by Mr Spencer, Paymaster of the Works.'[42]

In 1718, three on the project were given gratuities for their work over the previous few years. John James, Assistant Surveyor, was given £375 to cover the years 1715 to 1717; James Lucas, who had followed in the steps of Spencer in his career and was now assisting James, received £66 10s for the same period; and Spencer received £300 for the period from Christmas 1711 to Christmas 1717.[43]

From the details on his tombstone, Spencer was born in 1648. In March 1718 he resigned in favour of his son, also called Lawrence, who is mentioned as a labourer in 1714–15. But in February 1719 it was reported that Lawrence Junior had died (the date on his tombstone is 20 October 1719, which must be an error for 1718). He was 24. Spencer senior was 'ordered and hereby chosen' to be the Clerk of Works and Paymaster as formerly. In February 1720, he asked again to resign by reason of his age and ill health, and this time the Commissioners appointed James Lucas in his place. His death on 31 March 1720 is not noted in the accounts.[44]

The double burial of the Spencers is the only occurrence of burial beneath the transepts, as opposed to beneath the choir and nave. It may be more than a poignant coincidence that this location is near the site (the precise position of which is unknown) of the lodgings of the Clerk of Works which were part of the site office, and which Spencer senior occupied during his tenure from 1685 to 1712. As a self-made and prosperous manager of the large building site, responsible for five-figure budgets, Spencer presumably also had a house elsewhere in London.

Dorathy Spencer is described on her tombstone as 'daughter of John Bradshaw late of Bradshaw Hall in the county of Lancaster', and she died on 19 February 1687 at the age of 35. She was therefore 4 years younger than Spencer senior. Bradshaw Hall survives as part of the Bolton Museums Service.

CHAPTER 7

The engineer's view of St Paul's

Robert Bowles

Introduction

The structural stability of St Paul's Cathedral has been the subject of much discussion over the years, starting while it was still under construction. Sometimes there has been great concern about it and at other times there has been little concern. Regular measured monitoring of settlements took place between 1930 and 1990. During the programme of internal and external cleaning during the last 20 years, access has been available to all parts of the building for the first time in 100 years. At the start of the 21st century there exists for the first time sufficient knowledge of the structure and its behaviour over time for a considered engineer's view to be formed. The conclusion is that the building is in a stable structural state, with no major structural issues to be addressed. There are some issues over corroding embedded ironwork and weathering of masonry, but these are common to most buildings constructed of loadbearing stone masonry during the late 17th and 18th centuries, and there are established procedures for mitigating these so that the life of the structure can be extended indefinitely.

By any standards the cathedral is a most impressive structure, whether viewed from the inside or the outside. Wren devised a design which was innovative in terms of its layout, and ingenious in its details. However, even by the standards of the time it was not a daring piece of engineering as were some of the medieval Gothic structures. A characteristic of Wren's design is that it is extremely simple in concept and repetitive in detail. Where potentially challenging situations might have arisen, these were anticipated by Wren and he devised ways of avoiding them, rather than addressing them head-on.

Description of the structure

The materials used in the structure of St Paul's are stone, brick, timber and iron.[1] The predominant material is stone, which was used for all the vertical structure up to whispering gallery level and for the principal arches in the main vaults. Most of the visible stone originates from Portland in Dorset. These stones were dressed on five sides, with the sixth side left rough, and this forms an encasement to the masonry cores of main piers and walls. The core material is also stone, but of random sizes, selected and laid in mortar to form something akin to a mass lime concrete. Generally referred to as 'rubble' this stone was retrieved from the old cathedral as the ruins were demolished. Many of the stones were carved and some were painted.

Brick vaults support the cathedral floor and saucer domes of brickwork, rendered and painted, lie between the stone arches in the main roof vaults. Above the Whispering Gallery, the inner drum and the cone and inner dome are brick. There is nothing particularly special about the bricks, though they were clearly selected and are of generally good quality.

The roofs and the outer dome are oak. Wren was doubtful about the life expectancy of softwood, and conscious of the risk that the structure might get neglected once complete. He insisted on oak being used, even where, as in the tiebeams of the roof trusses, timber of adequate section and length was hard to come by. His concern about possible neglect influenced the way he detailed the ends of the main roof trusses behind the parapets. Box gutters in this location are notorious for leaking and allowing the ends of the trusses to get wet and rot. Wren designed-out this risk by bearing the trusses above the level of the gutters. He went further in his precautions, and paved the passages under the gutters with stone laid to a slope with drain holes lower in the external walls to shed any water that gets in if a leak in a gutter goes unnoticed.

Iron was used for bolts and screws and for cramps used to connect individual stones. It was also used for various chains that run around the drum and cone, and in an ingenious arrangement for levelling up the architrave stones of the peristyle. The ironwork was carefully detailed to avoid the need for forge-welding. Lead was not used in the structure but plays an important role as the water proofing material for the roofs, gutters and downpipes and the iron cramps and chains.

The overall structural form of the cathedral is best considered by breaking it down into components. The principal components are the dome and its supporting structure; the nave, chancel (quire) and transepts; and the west front.

The dome is surmounted by a golden ball and cross. These are clad in copper sheet fixed to a wrought iron framework down below the bottom of the ball and is anchored in the masonry of the stone lantern. The Golden Gallery at the base of the lantern is at the level of the top of the lead-covered outer dome, and appears to be supported by it. That is not the case. The lantern is carried on a cone which, in structural but not architectural terms extends right down to the Whispering Gallery. The angle of the cone becomes steeper at the level of the stone gallery and it is pierced by large windows. Architectural descriptions miss this relationship and treat the lower cone as a separate component, the inner of two concentric masonry drums. However, as will be seen elsewhere, the structural arrangements do not always follow the architecture.

The upper cone contains various circumferential chains, and there is a much larger chain at stone gallery level provided to constrain the outwards thrusts which would otherwise be generated where the angle of the cone changes. On the outside the cone is hidden by the lead-covered outer dome. The lead is supported on timber boards spanning between radial oak frames comprising posts and beams and bearing on the brickwork of the cone. On the underside it is hidden by the inner dome, which is built of brickwork two bricks thick and supports only its own weight. The top of the upper cone is visible through the oculus of the inner dome from the church floor immediately beneath it.

Outside the lower cone is a circular colonnade, the peristyle, which sits on a vertical stone cylinder, the outer drum. There is a circumferential iron chain in the top of the peristyle whose purpose is primarily to constrain and stabilise the capitals of the columns and provide tensile capacity so that seasonal movements due to changes in temperature and moisture content are fully reversible. A second role for the peristyle is to provide a large downwards force to base of the lower cone, and make the reaction on the eight piers supporting the dome more vertical. This role is akin to that of the pinnacles on flying buttresses in Gothic buildings.

At the bottom of the drum and lower cone there is a transfer structure which concentrates the uniformly distributed loads into eight point loads which are carried on the eight piers. Once again the structural and architectural roles are different. Architecturally the eye is encouraged to think that the piers go not higher than the capitals which are just below the level of the triforium, and that the dome is supported on eight vast arches. In structural terms these capitals are only half way up the structural piers, which continue past the quarter-dome galleries disguised as wing walls and terminate in a corbelled structure behind the spandrel panels containing mosaics of the prophets and evangelists. This robust support arrangement is buttresses by the four bastions. The eight major piers sit on eight even larger piers in the crypt, and the whole structure is founded in brickearth (potter's clay) about 1.2m below the crypt floor level.

The nave and chancel are each three bays long and the transepts one bay. In cross section there is a high central space flanked by lower aisles. In other respects they are structurally similar. The timber roof trusses are of a simple robust design and they are all the same. Below the roofs are masonry vaults, mostly of brick but with some stone. Flying buttresses provide lateral support to the tops of the clerestory walls of the nave and chancel and help resist the thrusts from the vaulting and generally stabilise the long straight walls. The transepts are much shorter and flying buttresses are not required. These flying buttresses are concealed from view (except from above) by the screen walls running round the perimeter of the building.

The west front comprises, from a structural point of view, the west steps, the west towers, the portico, St Dunstan's Chapel, the Chapel of the Order of St Michael and St George, the Library, the Trophy Room and the domed vestibule between the chapels. These structures are almost all made up of components which can be found elsewhere in the building, except for the long low vault spanning between the towers at level of the tympanum, the scissors roof trusses over the vestibule saucer dome, the geometric stair and the cantilevered oak gallery in the library.

Concerns over the stability of the structure

The original building accounts record that the masonry was being repaired even before the building was completed. However the accounts do not shed a lot of light on exactly what the repairs comprised, but the payments were to masons and it is most likely that they involved cutting out cracked stones and inserting new stones.

Robert Mylne certainly undertook repairs of that sort at the end of the 18th century, and we know that these involved replacing cracked stones in the south transept. He also inserted iron ties with plates (paterae) at the level of the triforium cornices to tie in the end walls of the transepts. There is much reference to the use of iron wedges and pins. Mylne's written notes suggest that he was not convinced that the transept walls were still moving outwards, but he could see that they had in the past and inserted the ties as a precaution.

The next significant incident related to structure occurred in 1831. No damage was caused to the cathedral, but the incident underlines the general concern about the stability of the south transept. The Commissioners of Sewers were improving the sewer system and were constructing a deep sewer some 30ft (9m) below road level and running parallel to the river on the south side of the cathedral. The intended route was along the south side of St Paul's Churchyard, passing quite close to the south transept. Because of the depth of the sewer and to reduce disruption it was proposed to build the sewer in a heading (tunnel). Shafts were dug near the south transept to the relevant depth, where the ground encountered was sand and gravel (Gazetteer, Site 88). The cathedral authorities objected to the sewer on the grounds that its construction could destabilise the foundations of the south transept. Various experts, including Telford and Brunel, advised the Commissioners that it would not, and work on the sewer was suspended until the issue could be resolved. After a month's delay agreement had not been reached, not least because of the difficulties in getting all the relevant parties to meet. The Commissioners took a pragmatic approach because their contract was in delay. The sewer was diverted down Old Change and Carter Lane. They took the view that if they built the sewer as originally intended, they would be blamed for any future movement of the Cathedral, regardless of the opinions of experts.[2]

For most of the rest of the 19th century the focus was on cleaning, heating, decorating and re-ordering the interior and removing the organ screen. However, in 1881 Francis Penrose turned his attention to the geometric stair. Many of the treads were cracked, and Penrose devised a repair system using iron brackets. Slots were cut into the soffits of the stone treads and into the supporting wall and the brackets were inserted from below and grouted up. They were clearly intended to act as individual cantilevers for individual stones.

Not long after this work was complete the stair was damaged again in the 'incident of the clock weights'. The clock is located immediately above the geometric stair, and when the wires supporting the clock weights broke, the weights crashed down onto the stair, smashing about half of the top stone landing and damaging many of the treads below. Concern remained over the structural stability of the stair until a full study of its construction and structural action in 2004 revealed that the cracks had not been caused by normal loads but by the corrosion and expansion of hidden iron wedges which had been inserted at the time of construction of the stair as a means of fixing the treads in position.

Penrose retired in 1897 to be succeeded by Somers Clarke, and with that appointment attention returned to the structure. In his report to the Dean and Chapter in October 1902 Somers Clarke identified the west portico as 'the most pressing matter'. He devised and implemented a scheme for improving the tie between the portico and the rest of the building, concealing iron plates amongst the carving of the tympanum and tying them back to large blocks of brickwork built within the roof space to act as anchorages.

Somers Clarke's concerns led the Dean and Chapter to appoint a Commission of Architects to report on the structure of the cathedral, the likelihood of it being affected by changes in the ground conditions, and what should be done to reduce the risk of future problems. This commission took the view that the basic structure was stable, that the foundations did not require underpinning, that the cracked superstructure should be repaired and that monitoring of the structure and of the ground water levels should be undertaken.

These recommendations were implemented by Somers Clarke's successor Mervyn Macartney, who was appointed Surveyor in 1907 and was also a member of the commission. However, there continued to be a debate in the press and there were those who were convinced that there were more serious problems than the commission had acknowledged. In 1912 Sir Francis Fox, a civil engineer, was asked for his opinion, and in his report he took a much more grave view of its condition. This prompted the appointment of a second commission comprising three engineers and two architects. That commission failed to agree. The engineers produced one report and the architects another, and many of the points in the engineers' more pessimistic report were contradicted by the architects. The architects were asked to make a further examination, when they took a more serious view of things, and certain works of repair were carried out, but there was no consensus. A third commission, again comprising two architects and three engineers was appointed in 1921. They initiated a detailed measured survey of the dome and its supports, and an engineering report (described as a Memorandum) was prepared early in 1922 by a Mr R A Piercy.

Piercy's conclusions were, in broad terms, that the building was stable, but that there was insufficient evidence to show conclusively whether it was still settling. He thought it was not. He then identified something which had gone unnoticed in all the previous debates, which was that the drums beneath the dome appeared to gradually increasing in diameter due to seasonal variations in temperature and humidity. Wren had not provided chains or radial ties at this level, and engineering calculations based on loads and stresses do not show the need for them. They are, however, and effective mitigation measure to provide the tensile capacity necessary to counter the tendency to spread due to thermal movements.

Piercy devised a system of chains and ties which the commission endorsed, along with various other ties. Steel reinforcement was to be introduced into the piers, and a programme was set up to measure and monitor for on-going settlement. No work on the foundations as to be undertaken until on-going settlement had been proved to exist.

These proposals were developed during 1922, 1923 and 1924, and work to repair the fabric continued in a low key manner. However, events took a dramatic turn just before Christmas 1924, when John Todd, the Surveyor in the City Corporation responsible for issuing Dangerous Structures notices, served one on the Dean and Chapter. This brought matters to a head, and precipitated a further round of public debate, much of it based on minimal information about what the real issues were. Todd was firmly of the opinion that nothing less than the complete reconstruction of the eight piers supporting the dome would secure the cathedral in the long term.

Such an extreme position did not attract a lot of support, but opinion was divided. The outcome was a decision by the Dean and Chapter, agreed with the Senior Officers of the Corporation, that the course which the commission had recommended was the right one. It would however be implemented more quickly than planned. A screen was erected on the west side of the dome and everywhere to the east became a building site.[3] Public worship continued in the nave.

There was one thing about which all parties to the debate were in agreement. There would be serious structural problems if the foundations were to move, and that action was necessary to make sure the ground conditions and in particular the ground water regime was not altered. Sir Alexander Gibb and Ralph Freeman, Civil Engineers were appointed to investigate and report on the foundations and the subsoil and in their report of November 1933 they reiterated concerns about the undesirable weakness of the sand and ballast, and the risks of altering the ground water regime. This led to a call for construction activity in the vicinity of the Cathedral and which might trigger such changes to be controlled. This control took the form of an Act of Parliament, the St Paul's Cathedral (Preservation) Act 1935, which defined zones around the cathedral within which all proposals to excavate or extract water below prescribed depths would be submitted to the Corporation for approval. This period of intensive work on the structure supporting the dome was successfully completed in 1930.

Four years later World War II broke out and the structure of the cathedral was subjected to loads which nobody who had taken part in the debates in the 1920s had considered. The cathedral became a symbol of hope as photographs published around the world showing it standing intact amidst the ruins of the City of London following the air raids of 1940 and 1941. Most of the destruction was caused by incendiary bombs, and some buildings which had concrete roofs survived. The Cathedral roofs are all timber with no inherent resistance to incendiary bombs. It was saved by the St Paul's Watch, a brave band of volunteers who went out on the roofs during the air raids and extinguished the devices which landed before they had time to burn through the roof boarding and set light to the roof structure.

There were however two direct hits from high explosive bombs which both detonated (Chapter 4). One landed at the east end over the high altar and the other on the north transept. They were estimated to have been of about the same size (approximately 500lbs) but the scale of the devastation inside the building was quite different. The difference is accounted for by the structural form of the masonry vaults. These are made up of stone arches of immense strength and brick vaults that are less robust.

The bomb at the east end fell on a stone arch which broke its fall and caused it to explode in the roof space (Fig. 173). Much of the energy from the explosion vented upwards into the air, and the arch was able to resist most of the downwards forces, so that the amount of masonry which fell onto the high altar was quite limited, and nothing penetrated the cathedral floor.

The north transept bomb landed on an area of brick vaulting, punching its way through before exploding inside the building (Fig. 174). The hole formed by the bomb as it entered the building was probably no larger than the diameter of the bomb itself, and quite insufficient for any effective venting to take place. The brick vault was momentarily subjected to huge upwards forces which were far greater the force of gravity acting downwards. This disrupted the geometry of the vault to the extent that it became unstable and large amounts of brickwork fell onto the cathedral floor, causing it to collapse. Those who were in the building at the time described it as feeling as if there was an earthquake. From an engineering point of view one can be fairly certain that the damage from the north transept bomb would have been far more severe if the masonry of the dome piers had not been repaired and the stainless steel reinforcement had not been inserted in the 1920s.

After the war the east end and the north transept were screened off and the first priority was to repair the roofs and get glass back into all the windows. The east end came back into use on 7 May 1958, and the north transept in June 1962. By the time the war damage had been prepared the Clean Air Act was in force and absence of black smoke caused many building owners to clean their buildings in the expectation that they would not immediately get dirty again. The west portico was cleaned in 1957 and the result was so impressive that the whole of the exterior was cleaned in the 1960s; very little repointing or other conservation work was undertaken. During the 1970s the main focus was on building the 'undercroft' (the present Works Department) below ground between the Chapter House and the north nave, but a fireman's lift was inserted into the shaft in the centre of the Whispering Gallery stair. At this time also concern about the stability of the south transept when the Surveyor, Sir Bernard Feilden observed cracks and open joints. The cracks were not particularly large, no more than a millimetre or two. The concern arose because they were new. The concern grew because nobody knew when the cracks had appeared. They had clearly not been there in 1930, when a complete crack schedule was drawn up, and no movements had been observed in those cracks. Feilden's successor Robert Potter undertook monitoring of these cracks over a period of a year using what was, at the time, quite advanced electronic equipment. This showed that the cracks were opening and closing much more than might have been anticipated, but that over a year the total movement was negligible. This provided some assurance that the south transept was not currently moving, but the absence of an explanation for the movement between 1930 and 1970 was of concern since no one could tell whether the circumstances conducive to movement would recur.

The mystery was not solved until the whole of the exterior of the cathedral was cleaned and conserved under the direction of Martin Stancliffe between 2000 and 2010. A thorough and wide ranging engineering investigation and appraisal of the south transept structure was undertaken by Alan Baxter, the Dean and Chapter's Consulting Structural Engineer, assisted by Robert Bowles, whose memories of the cathedral stretched back to 1958 when he became a chorister in the cathedral choir. The appraisal included a comparison with the north transept, whose north wall was out of plumb in a similar manner but to a lesser extent than the south. The appraisal demonstrated that the out-of-plumb of the walls was directly proportionate to the amount of settlement that had occurred in the nearest dome pier, but these were known to have not settled since 1930, so that particular mechanism could not have caused the mystery movements.

Although the new movements were small, the volume of masonry which had moved was large, and in the absence of foundation movement, a very large amount of energy amount of energy must have been required to cause the movement. The damage caused in World War II had long since been generally forgotten, but Robert Bowles recalled the scale of it having observed the final stages of the repairs as a chorister. He had also been invited to tea with Dean Matthews in 1963. The conversation had turned to what things had been like during the war. Matthews had recounted how he was in the crypt when the north transept bomb landed, and had thought momentarily the whole building might collapse because it felt like an earthquake. The mystery of the movements was solved. The explanation was that the shudder caused by the bomb had been sufficient to generate the small amount of movement that had occurred, and unless some similar event took place, further movement was unlikely.

Conservators regularly reported finding cracks in the plaster of the Thornhill paintings in the dome, but none was of structural concern since they had traces of paint in them from previous paint conservation work. They were old cracks. Then came reports of extensive 'new' cracks, with no paint in them, running horizontally around the entire circumference of the dome. An engineering appraisal was commissioned to determine their cause and significance. Cracks in masonry are caused by tension or shearing forces, neither of which should occur under normal circumstances at the location of the cracks. The position of the cracks was drawn on a cross section through the whole structure and this showed that the cracks were just above the point where the inner dome and cone become one structure. The north transept bomb was the most likely cause, since it would have delivered a significant upwards force which was thankfully insufficient to cause the inner dome to disintegrate like the north transept vault, but enough to crack the plaster.

The material in the core of the masonry

This comprises lumps of stone of various sizes recycled from the medieval building and laid in sand and lime mortar. This form of construction is quicker and cheaper than making the core of brick or coarsed, dressed masonry, especially when a source of rubble was readily available, as it was the 1670s at St Paul's. 'Rubble' is now often taken to refer to poor quality mixtures of materials arising from a demolition site, but in a masonry context it simply refers to stones of varying sizes which have which have not been dressed to a regular shape. When carefully selected and bedded in mortar to fill all the voids a rubble core can produce a very strong structure. We now know that is what is in the cores of the walls of St Paul's. However, that has not always been the case elsewhere, and in the 19th century there were several dramatic collapses where the lack of quality in the cores was a contributing factor.

Nothing has ever collapsed at St Paul's because of problems with the material in the core, but nevertheless over the years it became accepted that the cores were suspect, full of voids, and liable to simple pour out of the enclosing Portland stone like sand in an hour glass if given the opportunity. It has now been established that the traditional view was unduly pessimistic. Projects undertaken at the Cathedral over the last 20 years have provided several opportunities to appraise the material in the core of the masonry walls and piers. In the south transept, 75mm-diameter cylindrical holes were drilled. The surrounding material was found to be free of voids and completely stable. Intervention on a larger scale was undertaken under the south-west tower and under the south-west bastion. This involved excavating large amounts of masonry to create passages wide enough and high enough for two people to pass each other.

The design for the first of these for the present Wren Suite, a short tunnel through the east foundation of the south-west tower (part of Site C in 1996, see Gazetteer), assumed that the traditional view of the core was correct, and that it would be necessary to advance slowly and carefully, installing and grouting up precast concrete liners to form a stable passage. In the event progress was slow, but that was because the material was dense and solid like mass concrete. It had to be drilled out, not spooned out. Nothing fell from the crown of the tunnel and it was clear that the proposed concrete liners were quite unnecessary, so they were omitted. The same was found in the second and larger excavation, taking the lift shaft down to crypt level a few years later (Site N).

Conclusion

The structure has been monitored by measuring levels over a long enough period for us to be sure that it is not moving or unstable, which is what most surveyors in the past thought but could not prove. The scientific basis for modern geotechnical engineering which has developed since World War II has allowed a reassessment of the issues surrounding brickearth, sand and clay. There are records properly stored and indexed recording what happened, when and why, over its 300-year life.

There is no reason to think that its life cannot be extended indefinitely by the right regime of visual monitoring, maintenance and local repair. There are some ongoing issues, such as the corrosion of ironwork in the masonry, but even for that there is a strategy based on intervening when problems arise. After 300 years the cathedral is in better condition than it has ever been, and its structure is better understood.

CHAPTER 8

Gazetteer of sites

This Gazetteer of sites describes findings on many of the same sites as those which make up the gazetteer in the previous volume which was concerned with the cathedral and its setting from Roman times to 1666 (*SPCBW*, 299–347). There is some duplication of text between the two gazetteers for Sites A–H. Four sites on the slope down to the Thames, south of the cathedral, were given letters I–L in the previous publication. They are relevant only to the setting of the cathedral in the Anglo-Saxon period, and are not included here; this Gazetteer concentrates on strata and remains of the period from about 1666 to the present. It comprises summaries of 14 principal sites (A–H and M–R) recorded in the period 1969–2013; then those other sites of previous years which already have numbers because they appear in the earlier gazetteer; and finally new site numbers which form an extension of the series. The locations of the sites in the Gazetteer are shown in Figure 15 and the sites are listed in Table 1. Archaeological work on all Sites B–H was funded by the Dean and Chapter. For Sites B–F, the detailed location of trenches within (for B–E) and outside (for F) the building will be found on plans already published in *SPCBW*.

Site A

St Paul's Churchyard N side (Works Department), 1909 and 1969

In 1909–10 the first stage, S part of the cathedral's modern works department facilities were constructed immediately N of the nave. Observations of medieval foundations and stone coffins were made by Macartney (reported 1913–14), but no records of anything of the Wren period made. In 1969 the works department was greatly extended, also underground, further to the N; a large excavation was made between the Macartney extension and the Wren Chapter House. There was no provision for archaeological recording. Robert Crayford, then attached to the project, was able to make notes, take some photographs (now in SPCAA) and retrieve a small number of finds (now in MoL, Site GM307, except for a small number of architectural fragments). Observations were also made by Ian Bristow (drawings in SPCAA) and Peter Marsden of Guildhall Museum (including obtaining one finds group, also MoL GM307; for the pottery see Chapter 6). No detailed plan of the extent of the excavation is available, but it has been indicated on Figure 16.

Crayford recorded brick buildings of post-Fire date (they appear on Ogilby and Morgan's map of 1676, Fig. 31). The walls were built of soft red brick, and they lay immediately below the modern paving; they survived about 1.5m high. They were divided by the post-Fire Paul's Alley; this section of the alley was removed with the buildings in 1710. They are called Buildings 18 and 19 here. They are not dated by archaeological material, but can be assigned to the brief period 1666–76 since they appear on Ogilby and Morgan's map of 1676.

On the E side of the site a stone well at least 30ft (9.15m) deep was uncovered in 1969. Crayford noted that (in 1969) the well had a brick cap, presumably from 1715, since the Wren railings foundation crossed it. Pottery and tobacco pipes datable to 1680–1710 were recovered from the silt in its base by Peter Marsden for Guildhall Museum (MoL site code GM307, context ER1685; Schofield with Maloney 1998, 121); they are reported in Chapter 6. The well was allowed to survive the building works of 1969–70, since it lay immediately E of and outside the excavation required for the construction of the subterranean works department; it is also immediately S of the underground garage dug at this time. The well was then given a circular cap in concrete, and can now be seen just inside the present railings N of the N transept. It is likely that this is a well mentioned in 1598, and reused by the Wren building site (*SPCBW*, 302–3).

Crayford also noted the foundation for the wall of the Wren railings as it crossed the site. This was 4ft 6in (1.37m) wide, and composed of brick arches with an approximate span of 8ft (2.44m) (Fig. 196). The foundation piers for the arches were of rubble. Crayford also recorded the N branch of the Wren drain (photographs in SPCAA).

Fig. 196 *Site A: railings foundation (Robert Crayford, SPCAA). This view is looking north, and shows a brick arch at the back of the trench. This is likely to be one of the arches supporting the Wren-period railings along the north side of the cathedral*

Site B

Crypt beneath nave, 1994

A watching brief on several simultaneous pieces of refurbishment was undertaken by T Thomas of MoLAS. In the N crypt aisle, a series of linear trenches was excavated by contractors to a depth of 0.9m in two bays; the N wall of the crypt was pierced for a passageway. The relaying of parts of the crypt floor and adjustment of several ledger stones, involving disturbance of about 0.2m deep, was also monitored (Thomas 1995; *SPCBW*, 304–6 with plan of trenches, fig. G5; site code SPL94).

The Wren nave crypt wall was cut through in the first bay W of the Lord Mayor's Vestry (ie the first true bay of the nave) (Fig. 38), producing 195 moulded stones from various periods of the medieval cathedral, from Norman to post-medieval, reused as rubble in the wall. The foundations of the Wren nave wall were not revealed in this exercise, but one of the Gibb-Freeman testpits, no. 1, of 1932 (not illustrated; in SPCAA), had been dug in the bay immediately to the W. This recorded the foundation, extending up to 13ft 6in (4.1m) into the interior of the building. In a separate part of the refurbishment works, relaying of the original floor (of 1709 where not repaired) and adjustment of some ledger stones in the S aisle of the crypt (now the cathedral shop) allowed brief examination of the brick burial vault of the Channing family (Fig. 122; its location shown on Fig. 120). The vault was 2.19m by 0.92m by 1.75m deep, its walls of hard pinky-yellow unfrogged bricks. In the two long sides were vertical lines of putlog holes. Some retained traces of decayed wood. These were apparently bearers for the stack of coffins, but when they decayed, three lead-lined coffins had collapsed on top of each other. The ledger recorded four family members in the vault: Harriot Elizabeth Channing (d. 1785); Johanna Channing (d. 1789); John Channing (d. 1792), Harriot Eliza Channing (d. 1792, 3 weeks old), Charlotte Channing (wife of John, d. 1796). Perhaps the new-born child was in the same coffin as John Channing; but the lead coffins were very crushed so perhaps the child's coffin was not visible. The vault had been sealed by three large stone slabs, on which the ledger was laid. The vault had been used over a period of eleven years. Presumably John Channing, who died in 1792, was head of this family, and the vault had been used for burial of family members since 1785.

Site C

Crypt, SW and W parts, 1996

Excavation here was carried out ahead of refurbishment of the crypt chambers at the SW part of the cathedral to form a conference centre (now the Wren Suite), which included the digging of a tunnel from the main chamber below the chapel of St Michael and St George, W through the E wall of the SW tower at crypt level; and digging or monitoring of trenches for drains and other duct work both for the centre and for a restaurant to be placed in the main nave crypt at the W end (Fig. 24). The archaeological work was by John Schofield and T Thomas of MoLAS (*SPCBW*, 306–7; MoL site code SPU96; Schofield 2014). Excavation nowhere exceeded 1.2m in depth. Only features from the 1670s onwards were observed; but this included the reuse in Wren's foundations of stones from Jones's portico of 1635–42.

Beneath the floor in the bay at the W end of the central aisle of the nave, a temporary drain formed by two walls of soft red brick (individually 0.21m × 0.1m × 0.05m), unmortared (but sampled bricks had mortar on them, implying they were reused), survived five courses high, running E–W for a recorded distance of 1.2m (Fig. 25). There were traces of timber boarding which originally formed a cover or top. The drain was later put out of use: pebbles and sand had either fallen or been pushed into the drain, over the board, marking its disuse. Similar sand and gravel and then dark grey silt lay above. Above this lay a spread of grey-yellow mortar over the whole small excavation (ie going off in all directions), and then traces of a series of timbers, of which five showed in the excavation, laid horizontally E–W (Fig. 26). These were covered by compact mixed yellow sandy mortar. This is interpreted as a temporary mixing area for mortar.

A branch of the main Wren drain system (ie not a temporary run on the construction site) lies under the corridor which is N of the SW tower and the adjacent crypt to the E; like the other branches, the drain runs from E to W. The top of this drain was exposed during the Site C excavation, but was not broken open.

The tunnel through the foundation between the SW tower and the main chamber at crypt level to the E produced 77 fragments of moulded stone, including at least 45 identified as being from the portico of Inigo Jones (1635–42), reused as rubble (*SPCBW*, 201–5). A small part of the inner core of the tower foundation may be seen behind a hinged panel on the N side of the new passage. A shallow trench along the passage from the W end of area B to the domed chamber beneath the SW tower, excavated to a depth of about 200mm, uncovered backfilled testpits dug here in 1932, Site 58. The pits had revealed three lengths of the foundations beneath the circular Wren basement wall, and had excavated a previous pit which is interpreted as the removal by Wren's workmen of a Roman kiln.

In the trench along the corridor on the N side of the main chamber, part of a truncated foundation of ragstone and chalk fragments in a yellow sandy mortar lay roughly N–S (though at right-angles to the general line of the medieval cathedral, not the Wren building), and protruded S into the narrow trench from the N side (see Fig. 24; context [74]). The length showing was 1.8m N–S by about 1.5m E–W. Within it were two parallel slots evidently formerly containing timbers, later covered by crushed chalk presumably when the structure was destroyed or removed. It may be the base of a raking timber support used in the demolition.

Site D

Corridor from N transept to Works Department, 1997

This comprised a single E–W trench in the E–W arm of the corridor leading N out of the crypt beneath the N transept, and removal of a small section of the foundation of the W side of the N transept of the Wren building; the foundation wall had been pierced previously for the passage (in 1909), but the lower part of the Wren foundation had been left below the floor of the passage as a slight hump. This was to be removed to make the passage level, and the new drain would cross it. The observed trench was 20m long, varying between 0.8m and 1m wide, and the cut was a maximum of 1.3m deep from the floor of the passage (*SPCBW*, 308, with plan of the trench, fig G7). The trench was dug by workmen but observed by T Thomas of MoLAS. In recording, Site D shared and continued the context numbers of Site C after number 250, so the records and finds have context numbers such as C[251] (Schofield 2014). Some clay tobacco pipes and pottery sherds are reported here; they include a piece of Chinese blue and white porcelain (above, Fig. 27). The records are deficient, but it seems likely that this sherd, in context C[340], came from the Wren construction layer immediately beneath the corridor floor; it is unlikely to be a later intrusion (eg of 1910).

Site E

Crypt beneath St Dunstan's Chapel, 1998

Observations in the crypt beneath St Dunstan's Chapel, immediately E of the NW tower, during refurbishment of the underlying Wren drain and the walls of the crypt in this area were made by Robin Wroe-Brown of MoLAS (*SPCBW*, 309–10 with plan, fig G8; site code SPV98; Wroe-Brown 1999a). The previous (19th-century) floor level was generally at 13.59m OD, and archaeological deposits survived to 13.3m OD. The Wren drain crossed the site from E to W and continued beyond both limits of the excavation area. It consisted of a rounded arched culvert, with a modern sewer pipe running its length along the base (probably inserted by Penrose or possibly Macartney). Pieces of marble columns were seen here buried beneath the floor at an unknown time; they are perhaps fragments of the columns originally beneath the Wren-period choir screen, supporting the organ, which were reused in the N transept internal porch, destroyed in 1941, and buried here.

Site F

Drain shaft W of St Paul's Cathedral, 2000

Work to insert a new connection between the Wren drain and the 19th-century sewer running down Ludgate Hill was preceded by excavation in February and March 2000 (PWT00, supervised by Robin Wroe-Brown: Schofield 1999; Wroe-Brown 2000; Fig. 197, Fig. 198; *SPCBW*, 310–11, location plan fig. G10).

The major part of the trench was occupied by a massive cut, context F[39], which truncated the pre-Fire archaeology in all but the northern side. The S side of the cut was only observed at 2.8m below ground surface (13.00m OD) in the extreme SW corner of the trench. It was 1.9m wide at this point and would have been considerably wider at the top. It was observed to be 3.2m in depth but extended deeper than the excavation.

The base of the cut was occupied by the Wren drain F[38], which consisted of a rounded arch with straight vertical sides supported externally by small brick buttresses at intervals. In plan it measured 1.66m across externally and lm internally and was built with a double thickness of bricks. They were all laid with their long axis parallel with the culvert and a long edge facing into it. At the level from where the arch sprang there was a 0.2m ledge on the N side which was probably also present to the S but was not exposed. The top of the arch was at 12.92m OD, sloping down slightly to the W.

After the backfilling surrounding the Wren culvert was finished the surface within the cut F[39] was trampled or compacted flat. The material above this mainly comprised closely packed disarticulated or semiarticulated human bone with some soil and fragments of coffin. The trench was separated into two halves. To the W (F[22]), the bones were mainly skull fragments, upper torso and arm bones, although all other bones were present in smaller quantities. The bones tended to be E–W in orientation. To the E (F[24]), the bones were almost without exception pelvis, leg and foot bones, very closely packed and orientated E–W, and in some cases whole legs were articulated. It was impractical to attempt to excavate separate individuals in most instances.

Fig. 197 *(left)*
Site F: the top of the drain being excavated (Andy Chopping, MOLA)

Fig. 198 *(below)*
Site F: plan and section of Wren drain (Carlos Lemos, MOLA)

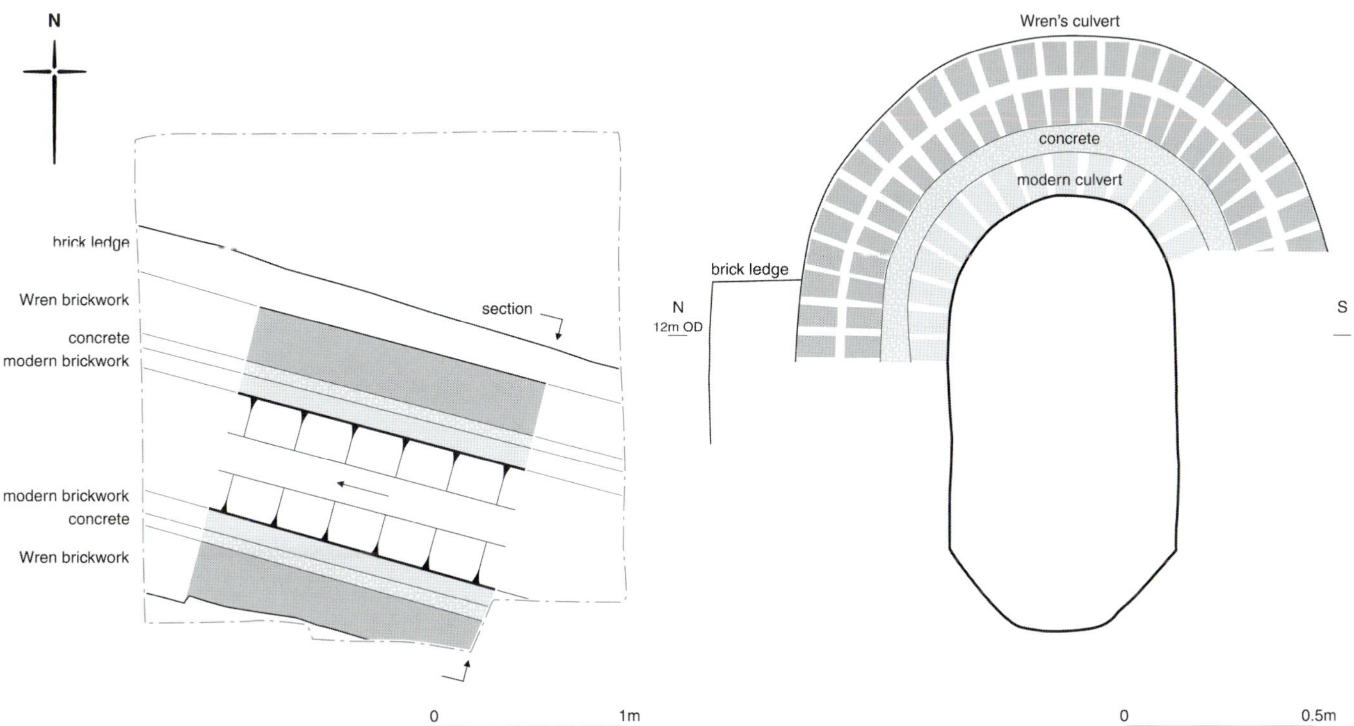

Layers F[22] and F[24] were up to 0.3m thick. Above them was F[5], a similar soil type but with much less disarticulated bone. It was up to 0.8m thick and contained the remainder of the burials numbered F[6]–[20]; as well as two fragments of decorated medieval floor tile. All of the burials were laid in supine extended fashion, with the head at the W end but many of them were disturbed to a greater or lesser extent by subsidence from beneath or above. Most were adults with the exception of F[9] and F[17] which were juveniles, and F[10] and F[16] which were collections of neonate burials in the NW corner of the trench against the edge of cut F[39]. All were associated with wood staining and fittings from coffins including decayed plates, handles and studs. One burial F[13] had a patch of plaster surrounding the left arm and pelvis.

In the main the burials tended to be in rows and stacked with the skull of the upper body being immediately above the skull of the next body down. Two of the stacks were five skeletons deep. There is little doubt that these burials in the cut for the culvert were repositioned, either from the culvert work or from elsewhere on the site of St Paul's during the rebuilding of the cathedral after the Great Fire. It is possible that some of the top examples, F[6]–[9] inclusive and [11], were new burials as they were much less disturbed. If so, use was being made of the culvert cut already filled with relocated remains. A considerable effort had been made to rebury the bodies in as decent a fashion as possible. All were still in coffins, laid E–W with the head at the W end and even the semi-articulated bones at the bottom of the grave sequence were given this treatment. Some were probably disturbed prior to their reburial during transport. Most, if not all, of the intact bodies were probably post-medieval in origin. Many possessed coffin fitments consistent with the 16th or early 17th century (Adrian Miles, pers. comm.) and earlier burials are not likely to have been transportable as complete units within their original coffins. The final fills to the culvert cut were two dumped deposits F[1] and [2]. They were not horizontally laid but sloped down to the W. Both contained quantities of building material including brick, tile and mortar. They also contained fragments of clay tobacco pipe.

Site G

Crypt below S transept, 2000

Refurbishment of the post-War arrangements for the choir practice rooms in the crypt beneath the S transept required the excavation of a trench about 4m N–S by 2m E–W beneath the floor of the E aisle of the transept crypt, for the insertion of toilet facilities, and refurbishment of several conduits for cables in the rooms and passages beneath the transept. Excavation here was undertaken by Robin Wroe-Brown of MoLAS (site code SAT00: Wroe-Brown 2001). This has been reported in *SPCBW*, 312–14 (with plan, fig. G12), and only the Wren-period and later features will be summarised here.

The W (internal) side of the foundation of the E wall of the Wren S transept, G[24] in cut G[25], was recorded. It was composed of reused masonry from the destroyed cathedral roughly coursed in a hard mortar matrix. Several of the stones were dressed and some examples were moulded architectural fragments, including parts of a moulded column and a window mullion, but these were not removed. Examples of Kentish ragstone, Caen, Reigate stone, Taynton and Portland were identified. The large cut for this foundation was backfilled by G[21], a loose fill of building debris. From G[21] came a fragment of a copper-alloy portable sundial (see Fig. 28 and report in Chapter 6). The N–S masonry formed a corner with another section of foundation, G[53] in cut G[56], part of the grillage supporting the internal walls. It was very similar to G[24], constructed with reused masonry from the pre-Fire cathedral and further architectural fragments were observed.

The majority of the deposits in this trench were truncated by two post-medieval graves (Fig. 121), which contained two burials each, with respective fills and coffins. The first contained two skeletons which had been interred together, an adult woman and an infant, both in coffins. They were laid supine and extended with the infant coffin beside the shoulder of the adult. The adult was identified by the ledger slab above as Dorathy Spencer née Bradshaw, wife of Lawrence Spencer senior, who died in 1687. There was no mention of the child. The second grave held the coffins and skeletons of two adult men laid supine and extended and facing E. They were identified by the inscription as Lawrence Spencer, Clerk of Works during the construction of the cathedral, and his son, also Lawrence. They died within five months of each other in 1719–20 and were buried together, with the elder Lawrence on top. Their skeletons only partly survived, but are reported in Chapter 6; where there is also a biography of Spencer and some details of his family.

Site H

SW churchyard: medieval chapter house and cloister, S of Wren nave, 2004–6

In 2004 the Cathedral began a project to improve the landscaping of the 'south churchyard', the area actually forming the SW part of the churchyard between the S transept and the SW tower of the Wren building. This was to be landscaped as part of the improvement of access for disabled people to the door into the present cathedral in the corner of the S transept and the nave. The path for disabled access from the public pavement to the S was to be rerouted along the line of the E walk of the 14th-century cloister, which had been located by Penrose in 1878. He left the SE corner of the cloister and two buttress bases for the octagonal chapter house exposed but by 2004 these had been almost totally obscured by the backfilling of the corner in 1937 and an accumulation since of soil, bushes and trees. Recording was by Robin Wroe-Brown of MoLAS (site code SPC04; Wroe-Brown 2005). The fragments found and conserved by Penrose were uncovered and recorded. They were then backfilled carefully with geotextile and iron-free sand. The design of the chapter house bases and the cloister, as far as this complex lay outside the nave of the present building, was then laid out in replica above the buried remains in 2006–8 (Fig. 36). During this landscaping, further fragments of the cloister, evidence of its post-Fire use, the Wren drain, a brick foundation near the Dean's Door, evidence of Penrose's work associated with the provision of gas to the cathedral in the 19th century and his conservation of the medieval fragments were recorded (Sankey 2007). The post-Fire elements are described here; for the medieval, see *SPCBW*, 23–4, 147–57.

A tentative and speculative reconstruction of the Wren site office, built out of the ruins of the medieval chapter house and S walk of the cloister, is given in the main text, Figure 32. The remains recorded on this site comprise a small open brick drain probably connected to drain pipes for the new offices (Fig. 199); from their survival, all the S walk and the S halves of the E and W cloister walks must have been reused, probably to support the new site office buildings of 1671 and later which probably functioned mainly at first-floor level.

Fig. 199 *Site H: Trench 8 looking north (Andy Chopping, MOLA)*

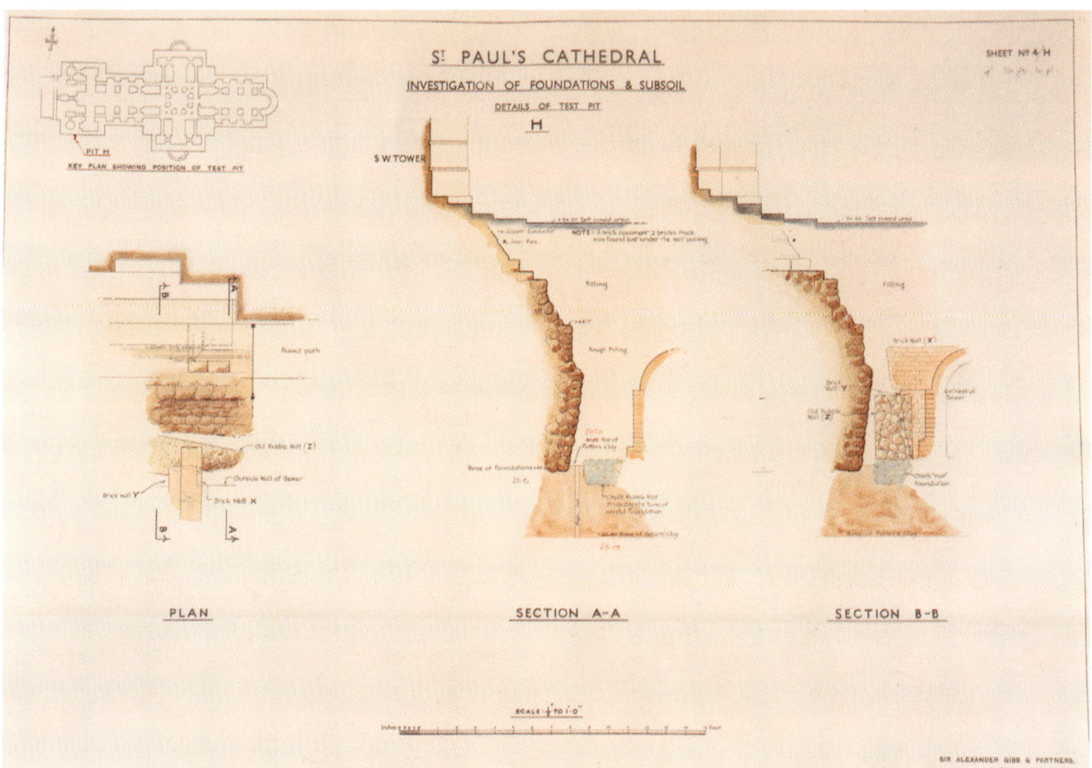

Fig. 200 *Gibb-Freeman testpit H, showing the foundation of the cathedral immediately east of the Dean's Door, and the north side of the Wren drain (SPCAA D/24/5/4H)*

The drain system for the cathedral was dug round the S side of the building starting in 1688. The plan of the drains can be taken from the drain plan of 1710 (Fig. 92). On Site H the drain has been recorded at three points. In 1932, two of the Gibb-Freeman testpits found it. Testpit H was dug against the wall of the cathedral immediately E of the Dean's Door, and found the N side of the drain, apparently reinforced with rubble (Fig. 200). A second testpit, M, was dug a few metres to the E, and also found the N side of the drain (drawing in SPCAA). This testpit lay on the site of the W walk of the medieval cloister, but all trace of that here had been removed by the trench for the Wren drain. Third, the works in 2006 required a connection with the drain and it was exposed again, roughly half way between the two 1932 observations. Here, as also shown in the testpit drawings, the vault of the drain survived. The sides of the drain were buttressed to the edges of its enclosing trench with brick projections.

In the NE part of the site against the nave wall, a circular chamber had been dug by Penrose to accommodate a 'gas meter' below ground, approached by a curving passage from a new doorway cut in the wall of the crypt (the metal door is still visible in the cathedral, shop, but obscured by fittings). The exterior chamber was uncovered in 2006 and after recording it was filled with gravel. Penrose's conservation measures for the 14th-century fragments included capping with bitumen or occasionally slate, and a system of thin lead pipes to drain rainwater into a channel outside the cloister to the W. The brackets holding the pipes were stamped with the arms of the Dean and Chapter (Fig. 154). Small gaps in the medieval stonework were occasionally filled with a new hard mortar.

At the W end of the site, during the landscaping, a brick foundation [93] was recorded (not illustrated). The foundation formed a curve (best explained as 'from 12 o'clock to 4 o'clock'). The E side was intact brickwork, but the W side was indented. The N end would have met the cathedral wall about 5m E of the Dean's Door. The bricks were laid in a hard cream-coloured mortar. This wall foundation is at present unexplained. Perhaps it represents the base of railings as they curved in towards the Dean's Door; but the curve is the reverse of what might be expected if this were the case, and the intact, better side is on the E.

Site M

W end, the W steps and the Geometric Stair, 2003–2005 (with a note on Penrose's recording here 1873)

This project comprised: (i) cleaning of the exterior of the W end; (ii) taking up and relaying of the W steps; (iii) repairs to the Geometric Stair in the SW tower (site code SWG03; Schofield 2005; 2006). The documentary evidence for construction of the W end and towers in 1688–1711 is given in the main text, Chapter 2.

Fig. 201 The central section of the W front revealed after cleaning, June 2004 (John Schofield)

In 2003 the cleaning of the exterior of the W façade and W towers was monitored. Here the project included the possibility of some local repairs (though in the event none were necessary), conservation of the statues and pediment, and there were many 18th-century graffiti, some incised but others in ink, on the stonework around the W door. The cleaned façade was revealed in stages in summer 2004 (Fig. 201).

Part of the archaeological brief was to record by photography, before cleaning took place, as many as possible of the historic graffiti to be seen all over the exterior walls of the ground floor of the W front vestibule, especially around the doors. The archive report on the recording (Schofield 2005) contains a plan showing their locations around the central and northern doors. The first five graffiti groups are illustrated above in Fig. 131–Fig. 135. Most of the others are shown here in Fig. 202–Fig. 229; with the exceptions of Graffito groups 18 and 19, which are too faint (photographs of them, with the others, are held in the archaeological archive). There are many other marks and graffiti in this area which were not photographed.

Proposals for repair of the W steps were made by Martin Stancliffe in 2002. Some of the black marble blocks forming the steps were not level, forming a hazard, and there was a need to insert new railings and lights in the steps to improve access and visiblility. The

Fig. 202 Graffito 6

Fig. 205 Graffito 9 group

Fig. 203 Graffito 7 group

Fig. 204 Graffito 8 group

Fig. 206 Graffito 10

Fig. 207 Graffito 11 group

Fig. 208 Graffito 12 group

(Images: Andy Chopping, MOLA)

Fig. 209 Graffito 13 group

Fig. 210 Graffito 14 group

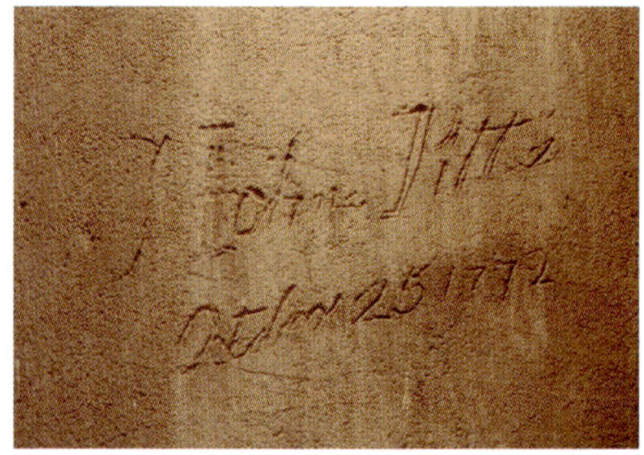

Fig. 211 Graffito 15

Fig. 212 Graffito 16

Fig. 213 Graffito 17 group

Fig. 215 Graffito 21 group

Fig. 216 Graffito 22

Fig. 214 Graffito 20 group

Fig. 217 Graffito 23

(Images: Andy Chopping, MOLA)

Fig. 218 Graffito 24 group

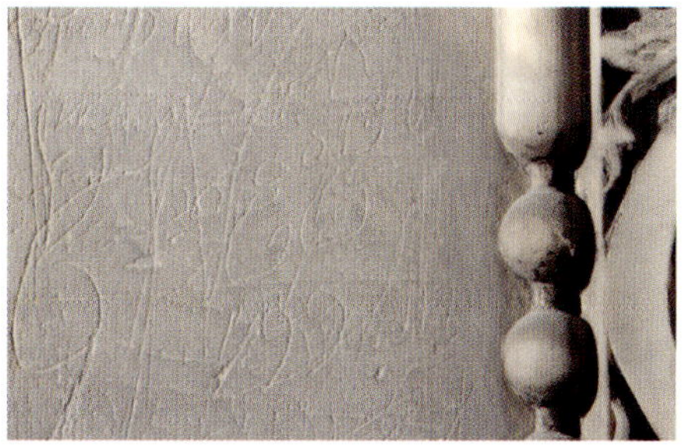

Fig. 219 Graffito 25 group

Fig. 221 Graffito 27

Fig. 220 Graffito 26 group

Fig. 222 Graffito 28

Fig. 223 Graffito 29

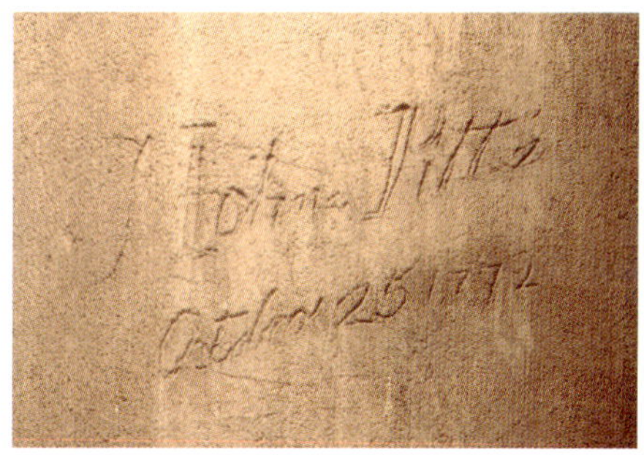

Fig. 224 Graffito 30

Fig. 225 Graffito 31

Fig. 226 Graffito 32

Fig. 227 Graffito 33 group

Fig. 228 Graffito 34

Fig. 229 Graffito 35

(Images: Andy Chopping, MOLA)

documentary evidence for construction of the W steps in 1708–12 is given in the main text, Chapter 2. In 1873 Penrose replaced the existing design, with flared sides, with the present squared lower flight, which he thought to have been Wren's original intention, as part of his major alterations to the area outside the W end.

The archaeological recording comprised recording of the brick substructure of the steps, including evidence of the original curved outer edges of the lower section (Figs 45–7). During his rebuilding of the steps in 1873, Penrose had noted brick and stone foundations for a curving wall on the south side of the steps, later superseded by the Wren railings which went round the atrium, evidently that shown in a plan by Dickinson (Fig. 98, Fig. 99).

The documentary evidence for construction of the Geometric Stair (Fig. 42) in 1701–5 is given in the main text, Chapter 2. In 2004 conservation and repair was proposed along with cleaning of the stair wall. In the event, no substantial repairs were necessary. Investigation into the side wall of the stair revealed one of the iron shims which were used to tighten the joint of each tread of the stair within its seating in the wall (Fig. 43).

Site N

Replacement of lift in the main stair and external cleaning apart from the west end, 2006–10

This entry covers two separate projects: (i) the replacement of the lift within the core of the stair at the junction of the nave and south transept, along with renewal of stair treads; (ii) external cleaning of the cathedral, during which there was photographic recording of decorations above some of the main windows and the panels carved by Gibbons below the windows (both using a single MoL site code, PUF06; Schofield 2011).

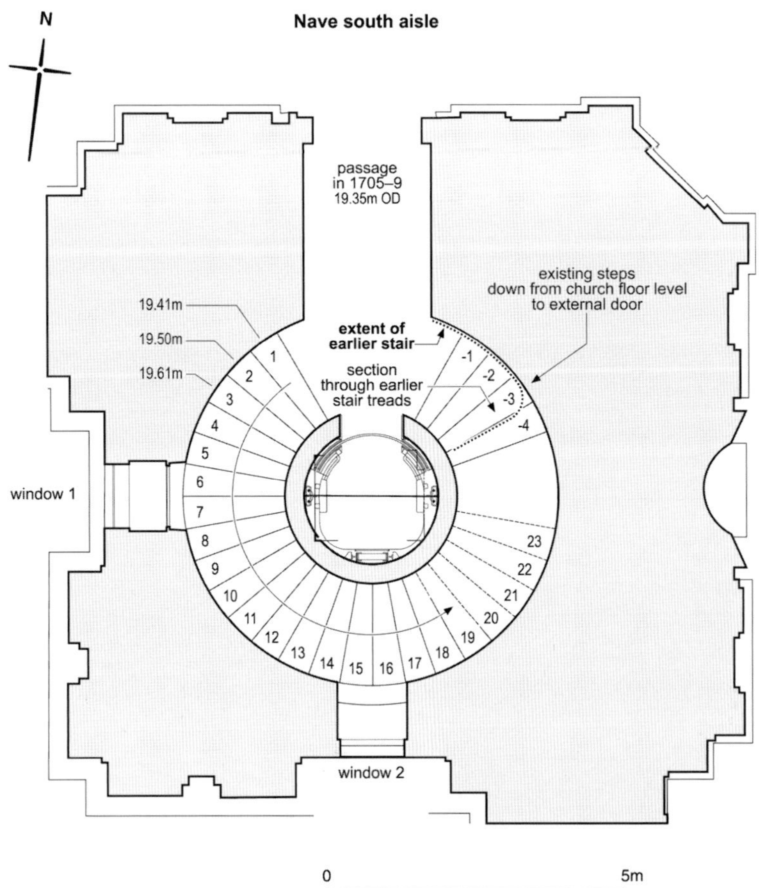

Fig. 230 Site N: plan of the main stair at church floor level, showing the lines of the ashlar wall found below, and the approximate line of the observed section through the first-phase stair (from Purcell Miller Tritton drawing SP170 5168 by Clara Verdegaal)

The replacement of the existing lift within the main stair at St Paul's with a larger one suitable for disabled people (e.g. large enough for the turning circle of a wheelchair) took place over a two-year period in 2006–8. The present landing on the stair which marks the passage into the nave of the cathedral, i.e. church floor, is at 19.35m OD. This is the same level as the passage leading to the main church floor, paved with black and white marble. One floor below, the churchyard entry landing level is at 16.6m OD. One further storey down, the crypt floor is generally at 13.48m OD. As part of the refurbishment, the lift pit was to be deepened to a new depth, including any foundation matter, of about 11.4m OD. At basement level, which the lift would reach, there was to be a new passage excavated through the wall of the nave crypt. The works are shown in a plan (Fig. 230) and a section of the stair and adjacent fabric looking west (Fig. 231).

The removal of the landing and excavation of the core of the south wall of the nave beneath the passage revealed the courses of the core itself, of rubble of several kinds of stone (Reigate; Caen; flint) with occasional brick in rough courses, in a similar pink mortar with charcoal flecks. Masonry was also removed for a short distance to the east of the landing at church floor level, approximating to the first two steps down to the crypt; these two steps were removed. This excavation disclosed two things: four rows of ashlar masonry continuing down the inside of the exterior wall of the stair (not illustrated, but still visible after the refurbishment), and above that but within the rubble masonry of the wall, the line of several former steps marked as dirty soil (Fig. 232). The line indicated three steps before disappearing into the masonry as a horizontal stretch. Above this line was a layer or dump of fine gray mortar including chips of chalk and brick, with charcoal flecks. This infill was approximately 0.6m thick where seen at the south end (the right hand side of Fig. 232) and 0.57m thick below what had been the first step down from the landing. The dark line was clearly the trace of a former or temporary

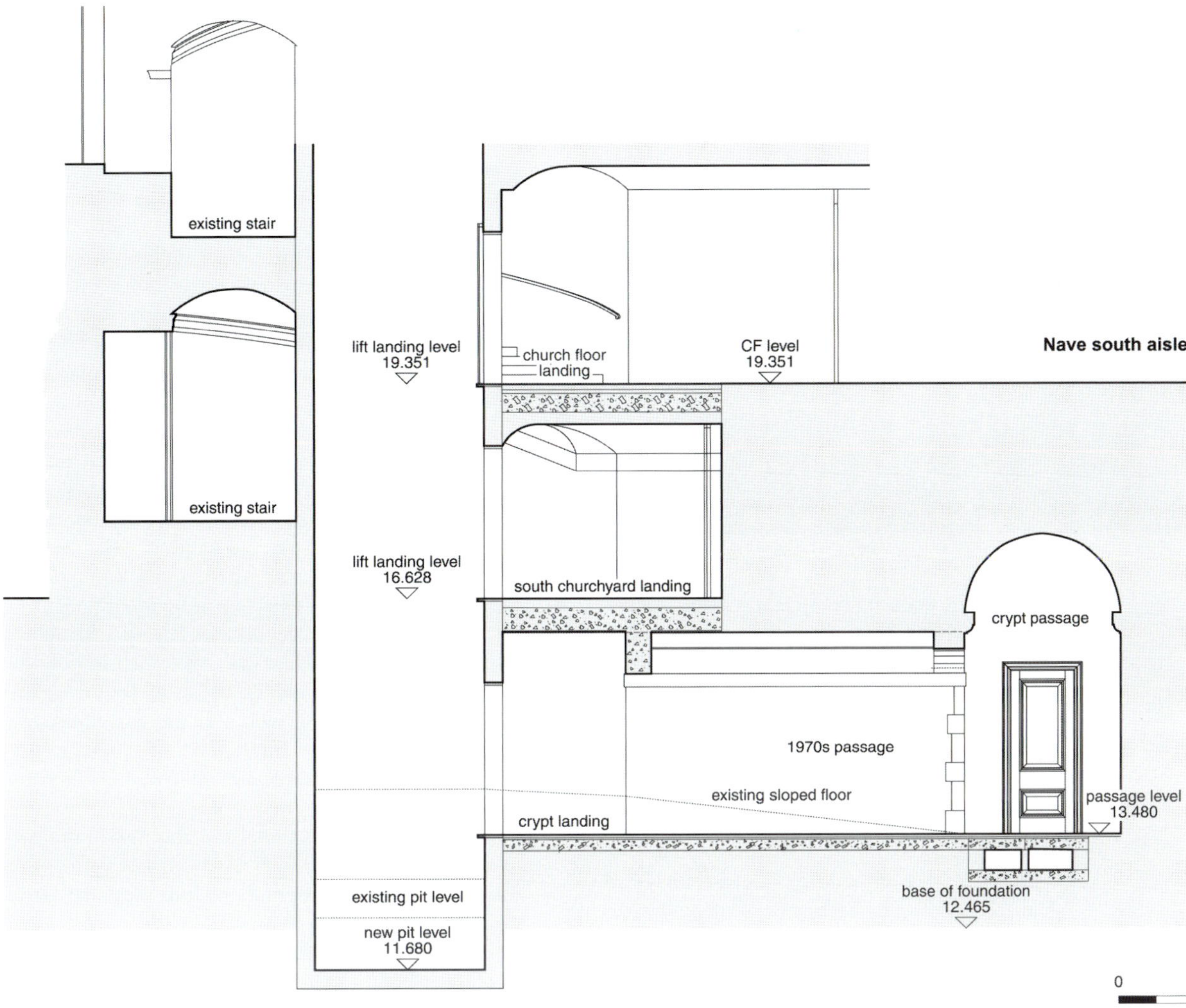

Fig. 231 Site N: section looking west, showing the lower part of the lift, the main stair which wraps around it, and the intended new floors at three levels (toned areas) (from Purcell Miller Tritton drawing SP170 5177 by Clara Verdegaal)

stair. The sharp corners of the three outlines of risers indicates that steps or timber boards were formerly in place, but were later removed.

There is clearly a slight 'error' in that the first step after the landing, now, is only 60mm high (steps above are 120mm high). But it seems to be original, and so is the height of the passage at 19.35m OD, which is at the same level as the church floor.

There seem to be two ways of explaining these construction 'events':

1. The first phase stair, of 1677–81, continued round below the future landing, to meet the existing steps which start after the landing. It would be possible to have six steps of the normal depth of 120mm between the first phase step at 18.65m OD and the first step after the present landing, at 19.41m OD. But this can only be a rough estimate; in fact the height of 18.65m OD on the first phase step is of the dark soil scar left by it, not by its top surface, which cannot be reconstructed. The difference in height between 18.65m OD and 19.41m OD is 0.76m. If the original step below step -1 was also, like the eventual steps, about 120mm deep or high, then there might have been five steps to bring it up to the first step after the landing.

This interpretation, with no original landing in 1677, would mean that the passage from church floor level, from 1677 to 1705–9, ended by butting against the edges of several steps. Then, in 1705–9, the landing was created when the marble paving of the passage was laid; and this required the steps

Fig. 232 Evidence of first phase stair line showing in the masonry beneath the stair (Maggie Cox, MOLA). The stepped line of dark silt is interpreted as a trace of a temporary stair with either boards or stone steps originally, later removed. The underside of step -3 (see Fig. 230 for its position) appears immediately left of the top of the brace

Fig. 233 Site N: recording the royal arms in the pediment of the north transept, 18 August 2009 (John Schofield)

from church floor down to churchyard level to be modified. But it would mean all the steps from church floor to churchyard level would have to be modified, since they now have uniform amounts of rising. This interpretation therefore seems extremely unlikely. I have been through the published building accounts for 1705–9 several times, and cannot find any reference in those years to rebuilding or relaying of the steps from church floor level to churchyard level.

2. The second interpretation suggests that the first phase stair was a transitory arrangement during the construction of the steps from churchyard level up to church floor level, in 1677–81, and that it was quickly overtaken by the existing stair from churchyard level to church floor level, in the same years. When the cathedral was paved in 1705–9, the passage was paved, and here as elsewhere some small adjustments were needed to level up the paving. These presumably carried on to the existing landing, thus slightly obscuring the first step after the landing (which is now only 60mm high). This is clearly a preferable interpretation.

The steps leading down from church floor level to the external door were much decayed and some renewal was proposed. The lowest section of steps of the main stair also required repair. A first intention was to replace the treads of all the steps from churchyard level to church floor level, but this was later modified to local repairs. The British Geological Survey was engaged to sample one of the stair treads. The step which was sampled was fourth up from churchyard level (i.e. 18 steps below church floor level). The sample was declared to be 'pale greenish-grey, sandy, glauconitic limestone, i.e. Kentish ragstone (Report in SPCAA by Dr Graham Lott, 28 November 2006). After investigation and discussion, the solution was to replace some of the most decayed examples with pieces taken from near the top of the stair near the Whispering Gallery. Most steps seemed to be of wedge-shaped pieces at the rear, but a front edge of rectangular slabs, of varying lengths. They were not keyed into the outer wall; whether they keyed into the inner wall of the stair could not be identified.

The stonework repair, weatherproofing and cleaning of the exterior (with the exception of work to the Stone Gallery which began in 1996) began at the same time as the works in the SW churchyard (Site H) and on the lift in 2006–7, and extended until 2011. Photographic recording of the decorations above the main windows took place before and after cleaning on nave, transepts and choir, with the main emphasis being on the N side and N transept (Fig. 233). At the same time, a number of the panels carved by Grinling Gibbons below the windows, all on the N side of the building, were also photographed both before and after cleaning.

The swags around the upper parts of the windows were recorded by photography, both before they were cleaned (their 'dirty' state) and afterwards ('clean'). Some of the photographs are given above; the rest are in archive, pending further and appropriate study of the swags. The panels below the windows, carved by Grinling Gibbons, were also to be cleaned and were photographed similarly in 'dirty' and 'clean' states. This photographic survey is also retained in archive.

Site O

Crypt, at east end of south aisle: creation of Knights Bachelor Chapel, 2007

In 2006 the Order of the Knights Bachelor approached St Paul's Cathedral with the suggestion that a chapel for the Knights Bachelor should be made by adapting and refurbishing the E-most bay of the S aisle of the crypt of the cathedral. This was at the time fitted up as a chapel to designs by Martin Stancliffe, with screens containing doors on both W and N sides. It communicated on the N side with the existing OBE Chapel. Fragments of original Tijou ironwork had been incorporated in the screens, probably by Lord Mottistone after World War II (MoL site code PKB07; Schofield 2009).

There were nine ledgers (this term will be used though one of them, no. 2 Foley, is a memorial plaque) within or on the borders of the proposed scheme. As far as could be ascertained, no. 1 Mrs Holman Hunt of 1931 and no. 2 Foley of 1874 were in their original position; but the others had all been brought from elsewhere in the cathedral (probably from places in the crypt) since it was known that a broad duct for the heating system lay beneath them, running N–S. This comprised concrete walls about 1m apart and is a trench about 1.1m deep, with working heating pipes within it. They are part of the system inserted by Macartney around 1909. This would then be the date of laying ledgers over the duct. The ledgers are listed in Table 8 and five are shown individually as Figs 125–9. They are illustrated here as a group of ledgers from the cathedral, as examples of their general character.

1	Marion Holman Hunt, 1931
2	John Henry Foley, 1874
3	M Jasper Waters, 1774 and Deborah Waters 1788*
4	Edward Roth, 1696*
5	John Taylor, 1766
6	Edmund George Wilson, 1781
7	George Dunt, 1706*
8	Barbara Comyn, 1750*
9	Thomas Jackson, 1797*

Table 8 *Ledgers in the floor of the chamber at the south-east corner of the crypt, refurbished as a chapel of the Knights Bachelor, 2006. Those marked * are illustrated in Fig. 125–Fig. 129*

Site P

Relaying of ledger of 1883 in centre of crypt, 2008

In 2008 the construction of a ramp to connect two levels of the crypt floor, part of the programme to make the crypt accessible to wheelchairs, involved the moving and turning through 90° of a ledger in the south part of the crypt, and the associated slight movement (only a few inches) of the burial casket, within a coffin, which lay beneath it. Thus the ledger has been moved, but the casket and coffin not (MoL site code also PKB07; Schofield 2009) (Fig. 123).

The removal of the ledger revealed the expected brick burial chamber beneath (context [10], including York slabs on top of it but beneath the ledger). This was 2.14m E–W by 0.98m N–S externally, one brick thick, with no brick floor, and 0.72m deep. Within, placed at the W end, was a lead box within the traces of a wooden coffin [11]. Handles and other coffin furniture were found, but they have been placed back in the grave and were not recorded. The lead box was 0.69m long E–W by 0.37m wide N–S and 0.42m high. The coffin, much decayed, survived for a length of 1.62m long and 0.52m wide. Originally on the top of the coffin, probably originally attached, was a lead inscription or name plate (Fig. 124).

The nameplate read:

Professor E H Palmer
Captain William Gill
Royal Engineers
Lieutenant Harold Charrington
Royal Navy
Killed 11th August 1882

Edward Henry Palmer (1840–82) was an Arabic scholar, professor of Arabic at the University of Cambridge. His death was noted in the house of Commons, as First Lord of the Treasury Gladstone concluded that 'Professor Palmer has fallen a victim to his patriotism and courage' (Hansard 2 November 1882). A portrait of Palmer is in the hall of St John's College Cambridge.

The date of the burial in St Paul's, as stated on the adjacent plaque on the wall E of the grave, was 6 April 1883. The inscription on the plaque relates the story of the deaths of the three men, but adds that two others also died in the incident, a Syrian and a Hebrew, 'whose remains lie with theirs'. Thus it seems likely that the casket contains the collected bones of up to five men, but only the British have their names on the coffin. The ledger was moved to its new position a short distance to the S, but the coffin and casket were not affected by the construction of the new ramp along the east side of the passage.

Site Q

N aisle of choir crypt, 2008

Excavation for alterations to the drainage system revealed two post-medieval coffins beneath the crypt floor; they were recorded but not removed (also site code PKB07; Wroe-Brown 2008). The first coffin was in a lead coffin shell. The coffin and skeleton were severely decayed. The decorated coffin breast plate named the individual as Mrs Martha Brigden, who died in 1785 aged 48. Above this was a second coffin, with a breast plate identifying the occupant as Edward Brigden, who died in 1787 aged 67. Edward Brigden (1721–85) was a London merchant with interests in North Carolina who supported the American revolution (letters to and from Benjamin Franklin survive). At the time of his death he lived in Lovell Court, in the parish of St Faith's; hence probably the place of burial, which is at the W end of the notional St Faith's section. His second wife was Martha Richardson (1736–85), daughter of the English novelist Samuel Richardson; after his death in 1761 she edited, with her sister Anne, later editions of the novel *Pamela* (Wroe-Brown 2008).

Site R

S transept steps, 2007

Repair and cleaning of the walls, portico and steps of the S transept was proposed in 2003 (Stancliffe 2003b). An engineering analysis of the stability of the transept was made at the time (see R Bowles, Chapter 7). The archaeological component concerned the steps. The black marble steps of the south portico were those laid by Penrose in 1875–6, using 'the best of the old marble collected from the two porticoes'. In 2007 they were replaced by new steps in a similar Chinese stone, cut into the required shapes and sizes in China. During preparation for this work a small archaeological evaluation trench was made in the steps by removing three of the treads (Fig. 48; Fig. 234). They were found to be built on a brick foundation which must underlie the entire set of steps, though only the top was revealed (Fig. 235). Three types of mortar were sampled for analysis (MoL site code PXL07; Wroe-Brown 2007, with mortar report by Alan Vince, online at htttp://archaeologydataservice.ac.uk/catalogue/adsdata/arch-1000-1/dissemination/pdf/AVAC_reports/2007/avac2007076.pdf.

Fig. 234 Site R: examination of the mortar layers below the steps of the south portico, 2007 (Andy Chopping, MOLA)

Fig. 235 Site R: the brick base of the portico podium, with the steps above, looking north-west (John Schofield)

Three contexts were sampled: from the lowest upwards, a hard mortar containing fragments of brick [6], above the mass of mortared brickwork which lay beneath (presumably Marshall's rubble work foundation of 1677); a second or intermediate layer of mortar with fragments of marble in it; and above the insertion cut for the steps, a fairly hard grey fine-grained mortar with pebbles and fragments of brick or tile [3]. The archaeologist was of the opinion that the original portico steps were set into this. A fourth layer of mortar [2] found only at the south end of the small trench was harder and different in character from the other three; it is taken as part of the 19th-century relaying.

Vince concluded that layer [6] was made from lime mortar mixed with a local, Thames valley quartz sand and that the sample has been contaminated after burial both with calcium phosphate and local sediment. The intermediate mortar [5] was another lime mortar, containing a higher proportion of quartz sand than the raft. The sand is, however, probably of local origin. Sparse chips of Irish Black Marble are present, indicating that the steps were on site and being prepared when this layer was laid down. The mortar nearest the step [3] was not a lime mortar but a hydraulic cement. The resulting compound will set under water and is resistant to sulphate corrosion. The materials used in this case were volcanic tuff, crushed flint and a small admixture of Thames valley sand.

The above sites given letters A–R were investigations and observations of 1969–2014. The following site entries are numbered; they repeat the numbering of the gazetteer entries in *St Paul's Cathedral before Wren* (2011), with the addition of new sites.

Site 8

Paternoster Row, E end, 1997

In December 1997 an existing telecommunications inspection manhole at the E end of Paternoster Row, in the street, was enlarged, and this excavation was observed by Gina Porter of MoLAS (MoL site code PRN97). The excavated shaft measured 3.8m × 4.4m × 5.2m deep from street level. The top 2m of deposits comprised services and utilities (a sewer and cables), but below this level 3.9m of strata were recorded in the sides of the shaft. At the base, at around 11.9m OD, were Roman pits; in the NE corner was gravel metalling 0.4m thick, which may represent a courtyard or minor street. Several medieval burials were sealed by gravel metallings, up to 0.6m thick, which were then overlaid by further burials, of the 17th and 18th centuries, which raised the ground surface to 15.89m OD (Porter 1998). No Great Fire deposits were noted.

The E end of Paternoster Row in 1997 was S of its medieval alignment, and the site falls inside the NE corner of the medieval and post-medieval precinct, though just outside the present railings.

Site 17

St Paul's Chapter House, St Paul's Churchyard

The present building (Fig. 101; Fig. 103) was built in 1712–14 by Edward Strong junior, mason, Richard Jennings, carpenter, and Richard Billinghurst, bricklayer, to the design of Wren (building accounts transcribed in WS XV, 211–20). An attic storey was added in 1885. By the time of the RCHME survey in 1929 only a few internal fittings remained, and it was then let for commercial purposes (RCHME 1929, 118). The building was badly damaged in World War II (Fig. 102) and restored by Godfrey Allen in 1957; the attic storey was omitted. The foundation of the E side was observed by Robert Crayford on Site A (*SPCBW*, 304, fig G4; records in SPCAA). Refurbishment, the insertion of a lift and the second addition of an attic storey in 2013–15 resulted in a small amount of archaeological recording of strata before 1712, but no new information on the Wren building (Langthorne 2014).

Site 18

St Faith's parish pump, St Paul's Churchyard (now in Paul's Alley)

In Paul's Alley, of which only a short section remains at the W end of the present Chapter House, stands an iron pump of St Faith's parish, dated 1819 by an inscription. It was moved to the present position in 1973. It presumably stood further E against the outside of the churchyard railings, where a predecessor is shown on a plan of 1710 (Fig. 92) and on Malton's view of the N side of the cathedral around 1800 (Fig. 95), though he has apparently moved it a few yards to the W of the position shown on the plan.

Site 20

'St Paul's Cross', NE churchyard, c. 1910

In a paper of 1913–14, Macartney describes excavations at 'St Paul's Cross'. This is taken here to be excavation required for the erection of the monument called St Paul's Cross, by Sir Reginald Blomfield of 1910, which still stands in the NE churchyard. It replaced the earlier fountain here by Penrose and Horace Jones. Macartney reported that the excavation for the Cross revealed numerous remains of [human] bones, the upper layer laid uniformly E–W, the lower without any apparent order. He published an outline plan of the new Cross (though it does not accord with the plan above ground) and a W–E section of the strata beneath it, the section running through the middle of the Cross site and looking N (Macartney 1913–14, fig 7). This shows two general layers of burials, the upper arranged E-W and about 9ft 6in (2.9m) deep, the lower with bones more haphazard, 10ft 6in (3.2m) deep.

Site 34

E end of choir crypt, before 1914 (possibly in 1911), Pits A to C

'Pit A' was dug in the present N aisle of the crypt below the choir when Macartney examined the foundations 'on behalf of the London County Council' (Macartney 1913–14). This was in 1911 when:

> 'a tram subway was proposed along the east end of the building and it was thought necessary to examine the foundations at this end. The pit, against the N wall, was about 6ft (1.8m) E–W and 5ft (1.5m) N–S, and 13ft 6in (4.1m) deep. As it was in the NE corner of the choir, it recorded foundations both of the N wall and of the start of the foundation beneath the E wall which forms the chord of the apse. The base of the N wall foundation was just over 6ft (1.8m) below crypt floor level, on 'pot earth'. The underlying 'ballast' was at about 10ft (3.05m) below crypt floor level. Macartney drew the sides of the hole, thus providing elevations of the plinth and foundations of the N wall of the Wren choir, and of an internal cross-foundation beneath the floor (Macartney 1913–14, fig 2). This included 'part of a column of Old St Paul's'.

'Pit B' was dug outside the E end of the cathedral, against the north side of the corner buttress and against the E wall. The Wren foundations were recorded to a depth of 25ft 10in (7.9m) below ground level. 'Pit

C' was dug outside the E end of the cathedral, in line with the N wall of the choir, eastwards from the NE corner. It was a trench about 20ft (6.1m) long. It exposed the Wren foundation of the E end, deeper than elsewhere, to a depth of about 32ft (9.8m) below churchyard level.

Site 35

St Paul's School, post-Fire (site), now St Paul's Cathedral School

The school which had been re-established by Dean Colet in 1512 was rebuilt after the Fire in 1669–70 on the same site, with its W boundary slightly re-arranged so it was cut back on the N but gained a small amount of space at the S end (*Mills and Oliver Survey*, iv, 144), to designs of Edward Jerman (Colvin 1995, 546; McDonnell 1959, 238–42; elevation, Fig. 105); it is shown on Ogilby and Morgan's map in 1676 (Fig. 22). This building was demolished in 1822 and replaced by a Greek Corinthian design of George Smith in 1823–4 (Colvin 1995, 891; illustrated in Elmes 1827, 124). In his brief description, Elmes (1827, 126–8) mentions its 'hexastyle portico of the Tivoli-Corinthian order' which stood above the footway which ran beneath it. The school moved to Hammersmith in 1884, and the site became a block of offices. The original site is now within the outline of the post-War St Paul's Cathedral Choir School (now called St Paul's Cathedral School), and is probably destroyed.

Site 37

The wall around the medieval churchyard: history after 1666

Parts of the 'Dean's wall', evidently remains of the precinct wall, survived the Fire (eg *Mills and Oliver Survey*, ii, 60, 113v); in 1669 a note on the wall records it as 540ft (164.7m) long in Paternoster Row, and 3ft 3in (1.0m) thick; and 182ft (55.5m) long in Old Change, where it was '2 foot thick beside the 9 inches allowed by the Deane for the party wall' (*Mills and Oliver Survey*, iii, 66). On the E side of St Paul's School, the wall was 4ft 6in (1.4m) thick after the Fire (*Mills and Oliver Survey*, iv, 144). The wall along the N side of the Churchyard is also mentioned in records. In 1671 the surveyor Oliver could still note that one building owner wanting to establish his foundations held 21ft 4in (6.5m) of the 'churchyard wall', which was 4ft 6in (1.4m) thick, on a site probably within the former bishop's palace NW of the cathedral (*Mills and Oliver Survey* i, 61; ii, 120v; v, 84v; Jones 1970, 184). The wall between Paul's Alley E to the main pre-Fire gate into the churchyard at the NE corner also largely survived until after the Great Fire, when its site was sold to the City by the Dean and Chapter; this strip was 4ft (1.2m) wide (Blayney 1990, 8). The foundation of the wall was probably reused in post-Fire building all round the Churchyard when property boundaries coincided, but it had probably slipped from view above ground by 1700. The line of the railings of the Wren cathedral bore no resemblance to that of the medieval precinct wall; it enclosed the new building with a considerably tighter perimeter on all four sides, and had a different purpose.

Site 39

St Gregory's parish burial vault, SE of Wren choir

The entrance to this brick burial vault survives above ground, with the vault below ground (Fig. 152). A vault is shown in this place on Dickinson's plan of the churchyard of May 1710 (Fig. 151), where the external drain takes special account of the entrance. As the outline of the vault is only dotted in, perhaps this was an intended construction and not one standing in 1710. In 1715 John James was instructed to 'set labourers about breaking up ground for a Vault for the Parish of St Gregory', and in October 1716 the 'new vault' was to be paid with tiles (WS XVI, 120, 128). Its outline is shown in a plan of 1753, drawn up to indicate also the extent of the burial ground for St Faith's parish in the N aisle of the crypt (LMA Prints and Drawings, Pr. 221/FAI). The vault was adapted and partly rebuilt in the 19th century as part of the heating system. The N wall of the later rebuilding is on the line of the N wall of the original vault, as shown in one of the Gibb-Freeman testpits, testpit L (not illustrated; SPCAA D/24/5/4L). This would make the vault quite deep, the likely internal floor level being (from this section alone) 4.75m (15ft) below the churchyard level.

Site 41

Gibb-Freeman testpit 10, 1932

This testpit lay at the W end of the crypt, in the central bay but S of the centre-line of the crypt, between the foundation for the W end and one of the piers to the E (not illustrated; SPCAA D/24/5/4C; see Fig. 24 for location). Here the top of the natural brickearth ('potter's clay') was at 12.37m OD. Besides local Wren-period foundations, the testpit revealed one of the central branches of the Wren drainage system. This drain, which had been backfilled with loose rubble before 1932, had lost its top. It was of brick with a single brick floor whose top surface lay at 12.14m OD, exactly the depth of the bottom of the adjacent foundation for the W end of the cathedral. The sides of brick survived about 0.38m high. A note on the plan says that the bricks were not mortared, and that 'indications of a timber roof were found'; presumably collapsed fragments of timber among the filling rubble. A second note says that the drain was cleared of its loose rubble for a distance of about 9ft (2.75m) either side of the pit (ie a length of about 6.4m, as shown on the plan) by the testpit engineers, and then backfilled with mortared rubble.

Site 43

Gibb-Freeman testpit G, 1932

This testpit was dug against the outside of the N wall of the nave, about 2m E of the NW door which leads down into the crypt (*SPCBW*, fig 3.21). The surviving top of brickearth lay at 12.09m OD, and an augur drilled through it found the interface with the gravel at 11.02m OD. Laid on to the brickearth was a 'chalk raft' comprising three base layers separated by gravel, a total of about 0.46m thick, and then packed chalk in a single layer a further 0.86m thick. The surviving top lay at 13.88m OD. The raft had been cut neatly on its S side by the Wren foundation, the N edge of which curved inwards slightly at the junction as though the chalk were sufficient support (section B-B). The raft was recorded for a distance of 1.5m to the N, and 1.3m E–W; its N side or edge, on a slightly different alignment from that of the Wren building, was seen in the pit for a length of about 2.4 m. The E edge of this raft was an original edge or end. From its character the raft appears to be a Saxon or early medieval foundation rather than a temporary work for the Wren building, but it could be either.

Site 45

Removal of unexploded bomb, S of the W steps, 1940

In the early morning of 12 September 1940 a high explosive bomb fell near the SW tower of the Wren cathedral and pierced the roadway, but did not explode. Efforts to remove it were complicated by a gas main in the hole having broken, and by the slipperiness of 'the clay soil', which was presumably disturbed graveyard soil (Fig. 172). The depth to which the bomb slipped or had penetrated was in estimated at 27ft 6in (8.4m) below ground level (Matthews 1946, 36–7); a remarkable depth, but probably to be partly explained by this being the site of one of Penrose's excavations. The bomb was removed and taken to Hackney Marshes for a controlled explosion. A map of where high explosive bombs fell around the cathedral (Fig. 171; from Matthews 1946) shows the site of the hole, a few metres SW of the SW Wren tower. This would be on or near the site of the SW corner of St Gregory's church, but perhaps understandably no note of seeing this was made. The commanding officer of the party of Royal Engineers which removed the bomb, Lieutenant Robert Davies, was awarded the George Cross. The aluminium impact fuse of the bomb was engraved with his name and retained as a souvenir; it is now in the Museum of London (MoL 25102).

Site 47

Gibb-Freeman testpit F, 1932

This testpit was dug against the N side of the N transept of the Wren building, at the NW corner (not illustrated; SPCAA D/24/5/4F). The surviving top of the brickearth, 'very rough and variable', lay at 11.02m OD. An augur was drilled through the brickearth and its bottom (ie the gravel stratum) found at 10.38m OD. This pit is noteworthy for the character of the Wren foundation at this point. The plan and sections together show that the foundation for the N transept at its NW corner went at least 2.14m (7ft) N of the wall line, and possibly further. This broad foundation lies only 0.46m below the ground surface, and has up to three ledges on the W side as it broadens with depth. The fill to its W was noted as 'Loose Filling (Rubble, earth, rubbish etc some pottery was found near the base of this Pit)'. The total depth of stratigraphy here is 5.73m to the top of the 'potter's clay'. With the matching record at Gibb-Freeman testpit K (Site 85), at the NE corner of the N transept, this indicates that the foundation for the terminal wall of the transept extends for an unknown distance to the north, presumably as a base for the steps of the portico.

Site 51

Gibb-Freeman testpit A, 1932

This testpit was sunk on the outside of the S wall of the Wren choir, against the SW corner of the S buttress for the SE corner (*SPCBW*, fig G18; SPCAA D/24/5/4A). The surviving top of the brickearth here was at 12.19m OD. The battered Wren foundation for the S wall of the choir was recorded; at its base, in the brickearth, was a fragment of mortared masonry which was probably a remnant of the foundation of the S wall of the medieval choir.The total depth of stratigraphy here was about 5.5m to ground level.

Site 58

Gibb-Freeman testpit 9, 1932

This testpit record described three separate holes, each small in plan but deep, within the circular room at crypt level beneath the SW Wren tower (SPCAA D/24/5/4/9). The level of the crypt floor was at 13.52m OD, and 'natural ballast' was reached at a depth of 14ft (4.27m). A full description of the strata and foundations observed is given in *SPCBW*, 337–9 and fig G19; here only those of relevance to the Wren building are mentioned. To fully understand the following note the reader should consult that figure.

In the S of the three holes, and seen in sections L-L and M-M, was the E edge of a 'chalk mat'. The observed edge ran SW–NE for at least 1.14 m; the mat was laid directly on the brickearth, and was 0.53m deep and at least 0.84m wide E–W. It lay beneath the foundation of the S wall of the tower (section M-M), but also protruded into the centre of the tower area for its length of 1.14m. This is possibly a chalk mat put down by Wren's workmen; but it also coincides with the likely line of the E end of the church of St Gregory. The foundations of the walls of the SW tower of the Wren building are shown in all the sections. The foundations evidently presaged the curved outline of the walls. On the W side, shown in section G-G and on the sectional plan Z-Z, there was an apparent join between two sections of foundation. This occurred a quarter of the way round the curve when viewed from the S, and presumably reflects a butt joint between two pieces of work.

Site 60

St Paul's Churchyard (S side), 1980

In 1980, a trench 2m square and 1.3m deep was cut for tree planting 10m S of the S facade of the SW chapel and 20m E of the line of the W front. In the W half of the trench a brick structure at least 0.8m wide, possibly a burial vault, was observed running on a NNW–SSW axis about 0.45m below the present ground surface. A blocked round arch of four orders was found in its E face. Limestone blocks were used in the blocking and in the main structure itself, which was overlaid by demolition debris including limestone, mortar, brick, tile and ash containing no finds (recording by Richard Lea; MoL site code SPC80, Schofield with Maloney 1998, 166).

Site 61

Gibb-Freeman testpit H, 1932

This testpit was dug against the S wall of the SW tower, immediately E of the Dean's door (Fig. 200). The N half of the Wren drain in section was recorded. In the testpit, a brick wall or strengthening lay above the arched brick vault and bonded with the rubble wall. The top of the arch and its strengthening lay at 14.18m OD. The rubble wall lies about 6m SE of the proposed SE corner of St Gregory's church, and is running E–W. Its function remains unknown. It is probably of medieval date, and is on the alignment of the medieval cathedral. It must be in St Gregory's churchyard. The Wren drain running round the S side of the cathedral probably dates from 1696 (WS XV, 7).

Site 63

Gibb-Freeman testpit M, 1932

This testpit (not illustrated; SPCAA D/24/5/4M) was dug S of the E end of the foundation of the S side of the SW tower, about 1m away from the wall line because of an intervening path. The N edge of the Wren drain running round the S side of the cathedral, with part of one of its buttresses, was also recorded. The top of the brick buttress lay at 14.6m OD.

Site 65

Gibb-Freeman testpit C, 1932

This testpit was dug against the outside of the present nave wall, halfway between the SW chapel and the W side of the S transept (Fig. 33); its dimensions in area were about 12ft (3.66m) N–S by 6ft (1.83m) E–W. A layer of 'Purbeck marble paving' was found about 4ft (1.22m) below the ground surface, that is at about 15.4m OD. The marble extended for at least 7ft 6in (2.29m) N–S. On it was a small rectangular chamber, of later date, made of three walls of brick and stone. From its position the marble paving would seem to be the flooring of the chamber or open space beneath the chapter house (from plotting in this study, between the E buttresses and the central four columns), and the brick and stone wall above it from the post-Fire period when the chapter house above was converted into Wren's site office. A note beneath the drawing reads 'The Purbeck marble Tiling is probably part of the Undercroft of the Chapter House of the Old Cathedral. A further excavation to the S of the present pit disclosed the well preserved base to a column belonging to the Old Chapter House.' The best candidate for this would be one of the four central piers below the chapter house, but there are no further records. The diverging alignment of what was recorded as the lowest part of the foundation of the Wren nave S wall is notable. The alignment is that of the medieval cloister and chapter house which although partly removed would have been standing immediately to the S. A note on the drawing says the trial hole was backfilled with concrete.

Site 67

Gibb-Freeman testpit D, 1932

This testpit was dug immediately S of the SW bastion (main pier of the dome) (*SPCBW*, fig. G20; SPCAA D/24/5/4D). A fragment of medieval foundation was seen cutting into the natural brickearth. It probably ran N–S, and was cut off at the N end by the Wren foundation of the S side of the bastion. The Wren foundation had a sloping, battered external side which protruded almost exactly 10ft (3.05m). From the drawing it comprised layers of random mortared rubble, not ashlar.

Site 68

Gibb-Freeman testpit E, 1932

This testpit was dug against the W wall of the S transept, towards the S end (*SPCBW*, fig. G21; SPCAA D/24/5/4E). The surviving top of brickearth here lay at 12.35m OD. This was also the depth of the underside of a piece of 'mortar bound rubble, probably work left in from the Old Cathedral'. A W face was seen, and although only a length of 1.2m was observed, it had a slightly different alignment from the Wren building. A note on the section adds 'Exactly where the New Work [*sic*; presumably the Wren work is meant] joins with the Old Work is somewhat doubtful, but it seems probable that the New Work was built over the Old Work'. A second note on the plan reads: 'A number of holes about 3ft dia. and 2ft 0in deep were found in the surface of the Potter's Clay. Generally these holes were nearly vertical but one ran nearly horizontally under the Old Work. An inspection manhole was constructed in the pit using the Old work as its E side.' The section shows that the surviving top of the pre-Fire masonry was only 0.6m below the present churchyard level, and that the total depth of stratigraphy here is 4.27m to the top of the 'Potter's Clay'. The slab covering this excavation was lifted in November 2001, but it was clear that all strata and old foundations were covered in brickwork of drains, presumably in 1932 or shortly after.

Site 70

Wren period Churchyard railings (general note)

This entry revises the gazetteer entry for the railings (Site 70) in *SPCBW*. The cast-iron railings were made in 1710–14 by Richard Jones at Lamberhurst, Kent (WS XVI, 108–15; though Jones seems to have subcontracted the work to a Mr Gott: Campbell 2007, 155–6). The railings around the cathedral are shown in a plan of 1710 (Fig. 92); this has not yet been tested against what is known of the original line of the wall and the original gates. The supporting wall, which seems to have been always of stone above ground, was on foundations of two kinds. In some sections, and around the E end of the cathedral, rubble was used (WS XV, 193–4); but on the N side, between the N portico and the W end, brick was used (182,500 place bricks specifically for the fence wall foundation were delivered in 1711: WS XV, 200). In this section brick arches were observed by Robert Crayford on the 1969 works department site (Site A). Where the new fence crossed the site of the medieval chapter house, it was also borne on brick arches by the bricklayer Richard Billingshurst; this required more removal of old foundations, as late as 1713 (WS XV, 208). The base of the wall, in each case a short distance outside the present railings, has been seen twice in recent years, S of the nave and near the NE corner (see Site 86 and Site 87 below).

Penrose removed the railings around the W end in 1873, replacing them with the present arrangement of Shap granite bollards which marks a line inside the previous line, as the ground was given up to the highway. The two lines are shown in Penrose's plan of the completed works, Figure 144; the bollards are up to 40ft (12.2m) inside the railings. A length of the railings was transported to Canada in the 1870s and is now in front of the tomb of J G Harper and his wife in High Park, Toronto.

Site 85

Gibb-Freeman testpit K, 1932

This exploration comprised two adjacent testpits dug against the N side of the N transept, at the NE corner, and matching testpit F (Site 47) at the NW corner (not illustrated; SPCAA D/24/5/4K). One pit was adjacent to the N side of the transept, and found that the top of the Wren foundation extended for at least 10ft (3.05m) to the N; it lay 3ft 6in (1.07m) below the present surface. The second pit, at right angles to the first and a little to the N, found the E edge of this foundation. This was 13ft (4.12m) deep and lay directly on brickearth.

Site 86

Pavement outside railings, SW churchyard, 2009

Archaeological monitoring of replacement by Thames Water of water mains in the streets around the cathedral comprised several small excavations in the pavement or highway from 2006. These were by Compass Archaeology, and two are reported here (this site and the next). They were undertaken between April and May 2009 and share the Museum of London sitecode PYK08 (information from Geoff Potter, Compass Archaeology).

A trench about 3m N–S and 1.5m E–W was dug in the pavement outside the railings of the south-west churchyard, about 3m south of the laid out design of the medieval cloister and chapter house. An arch of brick on stone bases was found, about 1.5m wide and spanning an E–W distance of 1.2m. The arch was apparently built in a cellar that was backfilled when the arch was inserted. Part of the S wall of the cellar was also recorded. It seems possible, even likely, that the cellar formed part of the Wren site offices.

Site 87

St Paul's Churchyard [pathway] N of railings near NE gate, 2009

For the circumstances of this excavation, see Site 86. A trench about 16m long E–W, 0.65m wide and up to 2m deep was monitored. Two differing but contemporary forms of wall foundation were exposed: to the W a brick relieving arch, and to the E solid stone construction. The wall line itself was about 4m outside the present line of railings.

The exposed arch was about 1.35m wide and spanned 1.88m E–W. The solid masonry foundation was 1.35m–1.6m wide, although the base was not established. The masonry retained some evidence for the overlying wall, which about 0.6m narrower and located somewhat off-centre to the N. To the S, two localised blocks of masonry were also recorded, each about 0.3m × 0.4m in plan and 2.8m apart. These were probably bases for back bracing of the original overlying railing, similar to the present-day arrangement.

Site 88

Shafts dug around S transept, 1831

At least two and possibly three shafts dug in 1831 to test the ground ahead of a proposed Corporation of London sewer along the S side of the cathedral are described in the main text, Chapter 3. The source is Hollingshead 1862, 117–29. There is no detailed information on the strata exposed, or the depth reached. The sites of these shafts remain unknown.

NOTES

Foreword

1 For example, Geraghty 2007; Higgott 2004b, 2008, 2013.
2 'The conservation architect is the generalist in the whole building conservation process' (Feilden 1994, 13).

Chapter 1

1 For brief analyses of *Parentalia*, see Harris 1990, 503–8; Soo 1998, 8–17. In terms of immediate sales, its publication was a disappointing flop. The conventional publication date of 1750 is used here, but Harris notes that the proposals for printing it by subscription date to February 1750 and the publication was actually in 1751. References in the main text here are to the original edition; the facsimile edition of 1965 is also mentioned in the specialist reports.
2 Keene *et al.* (eds) 2004, with the largest bibliography of any study of the cathedral, both before and after the Great Fire. One of its objectives was 'to capture the quirky distinctiveness of the most prominent of England's cathedrals' (editor's preface, p. x). Histories of the Wren building useful for the 19th century, written by members of the cathedral clergy, are Milman 1868 and Sinclair 1909.
3 Campbell 2007, Saunders 2012 respectively.
4 Downes 1988a, 1988b; Geraghty 2007. From the large scholarship on Wren's life and work, studies I have found useful include Dutton 1951; Summerson 1953 (9th ed., 1993); Whinney 1971; Beard 1982; Downes 1971, 1988b, 2004; Colvin 1995, 1083–97.
5 Higgott 2004b, 539; Geraghty 2007, 66. The sale of a large proportion of Wren's drawings in 1749 included Lot 41, a large portfolio of drawings of Les Invalides; its fate and present whereabouts are unknown (Geraghty 2007, 7).
6 WS XIII deals with the period 1 October 1675 to 30 September 1685; WS XIV with the period October 1 1685 to 30 September 1695; WS XV with the period 1 October 1695 to 24 June 1713; and WS XVI publishes the accounts for 1668 to 1674. Only the first month, October 1675, is given in full.
7 I am grateful to Jo Wisdom for the following concordance. WS XV and XVI edit much of LMA CLC/313/I/B/001/MS 25471/1–59 (formerly GL MS 25471/1–59); WS XIII to XV edit much of CLC/313/I/B/003/MS 25473/1–43 (formerly GL MS 25473/1–43). Hereafter only the new catalogue numbering of Guildhall Library (GL) manuscripts within London Metropolitan Archives (LMA) will be used.
8 LMA CLC/313/I/B/012/MS 25481/1–8.
9 Poley 1927, xii–xiii.
10 Brown's drawings, which are still kept at the cathedral, were published in WS XVI, pls xxxiv–xxxvi.
11 SPCAA D/24/5/1–32. The work of Gibb and Freeman is also briefly described in Allen 1936. Plaster models were made of all the testpits, for future engineering reference, and are kept by the present cathedral.
12 All of them have heights above sea-level in feet; but as this refers to the Liverpool Datum then in use, 1.3ft has to be subtracted from each measurement to correspond with the present Newlyn Datum (signified by OD or Ordnance Datum). This has been done in the text when measurements, usually also converted to metric, are cited.
13 The great majority of the surviving artefacts from Site A in 1969, and all artefacts and human bones from excavations of 1994–2010, together with their records, are held at the London Archaeological Archive and Research Centre (LAARC) in the Museum of London; copies of the archaeological reports are in SPCAA. A small number of objects are still at the cathedral. The architectural project records of Martin Stancliffe during his time as Surveyor (1990–2011) are housed at SPCAA.

Chapter 2

1 Downes 1988a, 50–1.
2 In some literature about St Paul's, the term 'quire' is used, but 'choir' is preferred here. In 1691 the spelling was 'Choire', as shown in Fig. 7.
3 Higgott 2008, 2009.
4 Higgott 2013 and in prep.
5 Campbell 2007, pl. 7.
6 For discussions of this period of construction, see also Higgott 2004a; Geraghty 2007; Campbell 2007.
7 Bodleian Library, Tanner MSS 145, f.129; WS XIII, 20–2; transcribed in Tindal Hart 1957, 194–6.
8 WS XIII, 22–3, 25, 46–7.
9 Geraghty 2007, no. 51 (AS, II.42), attributing the drawing to Edward Woodroofe. More or less, the proposed plan fits inside both the plan of the medieval building in Wren's pre-Fire scheme

of 1666, and the outline of the building currently proposed by archaeological work. The entrance to the choir in the proposed new building is roughly where the entrance to the medieval choir lay. The scale is not marked on the drawing but can be deduced as 16ft to 1in from comparisons with Wren's pre-Fire plan. This indicates that the west portico on the plan was intended as a replica of Inigo Jones's in the ruined pre-Fire cathedral, but at a slightly smaller size, the columns scaling at roughly 3ft 6in in diameter rather than 4ft as built. I am grateful to Gordon Higgott for discussion of these correspondences, which may be the subject of detailed research in the future.

10 WS XIII, xii–xiv and photographs and measured drawings of it between p xiv and xv; it was brought to light by Godfrey Allen in 1936.

11 WS XVI, 190–1; Higgott 2004a, 186–9, and fig. 110 demonstrating the overlay of the model on the pre-Fire building. Gordon Higgott is the source of the suggestion about Vicenza.

12 WS XV, viii.

13 Geraghty 2007, 50–1.

14 LMA P69/FAI/A/001/MS 08882, f.77–79v.

15 LMA P69/FAI/A/001/MS 08882, f.66, 69v, 70v.

16 *VCH* i, 340–1.

17 LMA P69/GRE/A/003/MS 10233, f.114–16.

18 WS XIV, 22–3.

19 Strype 1720, I, 228–9.

20 Pers. comm., 2014.

21 WS XIII, 57, 61, 73; WS XVI, 190–1.

22 WS XIII, 24, 59; WS XVI, 194.

23 WS XIII, 60–1; WS XVI, 199.

24 WS XVI, 186.

25 Crayford 2001. Downes (1988, 13, 71) says that Wren had the extent of the Great Model staked out on the ground at some point between 1673 and 1675, when it was rejected by the clergy. The famous incident when Wren was laying out the church and used a fragment of gravestone inscribed RESURGAM is in *Parentalia*, but this is only said to be 'in the Beginning of the new Works' (p. 292).

26 Crayford 2001, 243–4. On Crayford's reconstruction maps, it is possible to turn the plan of the Great Model a couple of degrees either way, but his proposal that the alignment of the present building is inherited from intentions over the Great Model is accepted.

27 WS XVI, 204–7; Downes 1991, 17, 52; 2004, 190. For drawings of the Model and the detailed story of its construction and reception, Higgott 2013, section 1.

28 Millon 1999, 544, in a catalogue of an exhibition which features many models from European sites of 1650–1750.

29 Rodwell 2010, fig. 34.

30 Downes 1988, xvi; WS XIII, 73–4, 76–7, 85. It is now thought there was no formal foundation ceremony, though the laying of the first stone on 21 June 1675 by Strong is mentioned by Hatton in 1707–8 (i, 456). Hatton does not say there was a ceremony; perhaps the story just grew.

31 WS XIII, 6.

32 *SPCBW*, 219–20.

33 WS XIII, 64; WS XVI, 9.

34 WS XIII, 79, 199.

35 WS XIII, 89, 94, 122.

36 WS XIII, 178, 180; WS XV, 72, 101; WS XVI, 209.

37 WS XIII, 83; WS XV, 3.

38 WS XIV, 4.

39 WS XIII, 90, 104; WS XVI, 62–3.

40 WS XIII, 71–2.

41 WS XIII, 57 for both references.

42 WS XIII, 73–5, 147; WS XV, 81; WS XVI, 199, 202.

43 WS XIV, 45.

44 WS XVI, 201, 206; WS XIII, 83.

45 WS XIII, 206; WS XIV, 41; WS XV, 206.

46 Mills and Oliver *Survey*, i, 61; Jones 1970, ii, 322–3.

47 LMA CLC/313/I/B/012/MS 25481/1.

48 WS XVI, 65, 99, 107. For Wren's own account of the purchase, WS IX, 17–18. A site plan of 1710 of the whole Wren building, overlaid on the medieval cathedral, also incorporates an outline plan of the buildings to be demolished: AS III, 45 (Geraghty 2007, 83, no. 109).

49 Higgott 2013, discussion of drawing WRE/7/2/2.

50 WS XV, 186, 191.

51 Some of this section has already appeared in *SPCBW*, 221–2.

52 WS XIII, 58; LMA CLC/313/I/B/012/MS 25481/1 is the relevant Acquittance Book.

53 WS XVI, 196–200. Several maps of the devastated and the rebuilt City were published in 1666–1671, but most are small (Darlington and Howgego 1964, 59–65). One is that by John Leake of 1667, known only in the form of two sheets each 520mm by 410mm, but which mentions a larger form in six sheets, of which no known example survives (*ibid.*, 62, no. 21).

54 WS XIII, 51.

55 Geraghty 2007, 51–4 (nos 55–60).

56 In the guidebook by F. Colsoni (1693), edited by Godfrey 1951, 13.

57 WS XVI, 206.

58 WS XVI, 207.

59 WS XIII, 75; WS XVI, 10, 207, 209.

60 WS XIII, 71; WS XVI, 207.

61 WS XIII, 79, 81.

62 WS XIV, 4.

63 WS XIII, 94, 101; XVI, 192.

64 WS XIII, 114, 136.

65 WS XIII, 106.

66 Martin Stancliffe suggests that since drawings were at that time called 'models', the 'Model room' might signify what we would call a drawing office.

67 *Parentalia*, 282.

68 WS XIII, 114, 160–2, 166.

69 WS XIII, 200; XIV, 23, 25–7.

70 WS XIV, 75; XV, 14.

71 WS XIV, 72.

72 WS XIV, 75.

73 WS XIV, 79.

74 WS XIV, 87.

75 *SPCBW*, fig. 4.14

76 WS XV, 190.

77 WS XVI, 174; WS XV, 206, 218–19.

78 Detailed further in *SPCBW*, 147–57.

79 Observation by Gordon Higgott.

80 Adams 1983, 27, 29–30; WS XIV, pls ix–xlv. A section drawing in this group is dated for its engraving to 1702–3 but using an earlier drawing. Downes (1998, no. 94) suggested the drawing was 'no later than 1675'; Higgott (2013, discussion of the drawing as WRE/5/1/2) suggests the late 1680s.

81 Eg WS XVI, 198, of 1672.

82 WS XIII, 84–5.

83 WS XIV, 93.
84 Wilkinson 1991, 274–5.
85 WS XIV, 5. Lifting mechanisms known to or used by Jones and Webb are discussed in Hart 2011, 241–6 and Bold 1989, 168–70 respectively.
86 Campbell 2007; Higgott 2004b, 2008, 2013.
87 *Parentalia*, 284.
88 Testpit A, on the outside of the choir near its south-east corner, gives the best profile of the foundation at the east end; *SPCBW*, fig. G18. Testpit G, immediately east of the north-west door into the crypt, also on the outside, found that the Wren foundation cut into remains of the chapel of the medieval bishop's palace; *SPCBW*, fig. 3.21.
89 At about 12m–12.8m OD. The Purbeck flooring below the medieval chapter house was recorded in 1932 at 14.9m OD and immediately to the south in a small excavation of 2003 (Site H) at 15.1m OD.
90 A drawing of 1675 containing a section through the walls of the crypt at the south-east corner sketches the stepped courses on the outside of the foundation (Downes 1988, no. 59; Higgott 2013, WRE/2/1/1).
91 *SPCBW*, 223.
92 *SPCBW* gazetteer, sites 29, 33, 34.
93 WS XVI, 14.
94 WS XVI, 52.
95 WS XIV, 31; XV, 178; XVI, 14, 22.
96 *SPCBW*, figs G18, G20, G21.
97 *SPCBW*, 117–18.
98 WS XIV, 21–2, 29, 32, 49, 63.
99 WS XIV, 27, 29.
100 WS XIV, 45, 47.
101 *SPCBW*, Site 10 and fig. 1.6.
102 WS XIII, 77–80, 96–7; WS XVI, 14–16.
103 WS XIII, 97, 101.
104 WS XIII, 85; as an example of the 'caseing', WS XIII, 103, of 1678.
105 WS XIII, 108.
106 WS XIII, 114, 135.
107 Kentish steps were used in other stairs besides the main stair. Seventeen 'Circular Kentish steps' were used in the two round stairs of the vestries (ie within the north-east and south-east bastions) in September 1678 (WS XIII, 108). Kentish steps were supplied in November 1679 for the work of Edward Pearce, then employed on the south transept and south-east bastion (WS XIII, 124, 142–3). In August 1681 Jasper Latham was paid for setting 29 steps of Kentish rag in his work on the north side of the cathedral (WS XIII, 153).
108 WS XIII, 146, 180.
109 WS XIV, 82.
110 WS XIV, 38, 82; WS XV, xiv, 23.
111 Ward 1740, 105; Bennett 1982, 42.
112 A detailed building history of the west end is provided by Higgott 2008.
113 Wren's report of 30 March 1697 and recommendations are in WS XVI, 84–6.
114 The detailed history of these years is in Higgott 2008, ch. 5. The phases of design of the towers have been elucidated from study of the drawings and the works accounts, see the online catalogue of drawings, Higgott 2013, especially section 6.
115 WS XV, xv, 49, 60–1.
116 WS XV, 109, 124–5, 140.
117 WS XV, xiv.
118 WS XV, 133–4; 203, 206, 219; XVI, 169–70. The panels were also photographed before cleaning in 2003.
119 WS XV, 146. Ward-Jackson 2003, 361–73 is a summary of the histories and present state of all the external statuary and the west end panels by Bird, but not of the Gibbons panels below the windows.
120 WS XV, 62, 74.
121 WS XV, 77–8, 153.
122 WS XV, 152, 163, 171.
123 WS XV, 65, 79, 114.
124 WS XV, 146, 152, 154, 165, 186.
125 WS XVI, 175.
126 WS XV, 80, 104.
127 WS XV, 122–4. The process of design of the stair, with one drawing by Dickinson in 1703–4 showing a stair with half-landings, is studied by Higgott 2008, 77–81. The circular stair with a void in the middle, not a column, was a type of stair shown by Palladio in 1570 (Ware 1738 (ed Placzek 1965), 34–5); he had built one which survives in the Accademia, Venice (originally the monastery of La Carita).
128 Stancliffe 1993, 2.
129 This summary of the analysis is from Stancliffe 2004b.
130 WS XV, 167, 171, 175.
131 WS XV, 174; 180.
132 WS XV, 205, 189.
133 Geraghty 2007, nos 79, 80; Higgott 2013, drawings WRE 3/4/3, 3/3/5, 3/3/7.
134 WS XIII, 96, 144.
135 WS XIII, 180–1; Higgott 2013, WRE/2/4/20.
136 WS XIII, 170–1; XV, xxvi, 29; XV, xvii, 38.
137 WS XV, 8, 40, 43.
138 WS XV, xvii, n2.
139 WS XV, 113, 115, 121, 135.
140 Unpublished analysis of the accounts by Robert Crayford; Campbell 2007, plan on p. 127; dates modified slightly here.
141 WS XV, xix.
142 WS XIV, 100, 104, 119, 125.
143 WS XV, xlvi.
144 WS XV, 28.
145 WS XV, 45–6.
146 WS XV, 145.
147 WS XIV, 72, 76.
148 WS XV, 129, 156.
149 WS XV, 114.
150 WS XV, 134.
151 WS XV 6–9, 95, 145; XVI, 103.
152 Rackham 1976, 75.
153 Shown by timber framing of the 1690s at Middle Temple Lane: Goodburn and Minkin 1996a. Samuel Pepys noted 'New-England masts' being measured in the dockyard at Deptford in 1662 (Latham and Matthews 1971, 274).
154 Millett and McGrail 1987, 106.
155 Eaton 1998; Smith 1997.
156 Yeomans 1992, 30–1, 34–43.
157 Geraghty 2007, 25, fig. 12.
158 Richards 1676, 223; American examples in Maryland, Virginia and Charleston (S Carolina). Houses in Annapolis (Maryland) could employ king-post trusses on tiebeams up to 43ft (15.05m) long, but these were presumably scarfed (Carson and Lounsbury 2013, 231–3).

159 Plott 1677. I am grateful to Julian Munby for discussion of this point.
160 Soo 1998, 74–6 and fig. 24.
161 Campbell 1999, 189–90.
162 Hewett 1985, 71, 76. Hewett's assertion (ibid, 66) that a roof at Lichfield Cathedral with forelock bolts is from a reroofing of 1661–6 is doubted by Yeomans (1992, 6) on the grounds that existing records fail to support this and the structure looks later.
163 Hewett 1985, 70, 80–1.
164 Campbell and Bowles 2004, 211, 215–17. This includes details of ironwork and masonry jointing in the peristyle, observed in 1997; and reproduction (on p. 211) of the isometric projection of the construction of the cathedral, including the dome, by R B Brook-Greaves in collaboration with W Godfrey Allen, of 1923–8.
165 Higgott 2009; 2013, section 5.
166 *Parentalia*, 291.
167 WS XV, 57, 155. The evolving design of the dome with changes and revisions during 1687–1708 is analysed by Higgott 2013, section 5.
168 Hyde 2004, fig. 275. A possibly related survey drawing of a section through the dome, perhaps by Gwynn, also survives: Campbell and Bowles 2004, fig. 137; comments by Gordon Higgott. Gwynn produced several architectural tracts in the middle of the 18th century, but the St Paul's engraving appears to have been published without any accompanying text (for Gwynn, see Harris 1990, 214–17).
169 A fifth unmeasured sketch of the timbers is provided by Hewett 1985, 154, fig. 148.
170 WS XVI, 124–7, 148.
171 WS XV, 220; for Wren's objections and the ensuing contracts, WS XVI, 130–3.
172 WS XVI, 135.
173 WS XIV, passim; analysis mapped on plans of the fabric by Campbell 2007, pl. 7.
174 Eg WS XIV, 10 (1686).
175 A set of 12 engravings by Edward Pearce or Pierce senior, originally produced in 1640 and reprinted three times up to ?1668, comprise scroll and swag designs (Jervis 1986). They might be relevant, but there are only general similarities to the styles of swags and cornucopiae at St Paul's. I am grateful to Gordon Higgott for this reference.
176 WS XV, 188–90.
177 WS XIV, 157.
178 WS XV, 181.
179 Though in the case of the 1st-century AD Ara Pacis, the swags or garlands are only on the inside of the temple structure, and have more affinity with contemporary painted decorations in houses. Green (1964, 24, n2) suggests that 'the swag originated in Rome as a garland hung about the neck of beasts to be sacrificed.'
180 Whinney and Millar (1957, 114) suggest there was a 'clear intention' to bind the architectural units of the façade into a larger whole by their decoration, which is a baroque as opposed to a Palladian thought.
181 Bradley and Pevsner 1997, 164.
182 Harris and Higgott 1989, 241.
183 Gibbons' work at the cathedral is summarised (from the accounts) in WS XV, xxii–xxiii. Most scholarship on Gibbons concerns his work in wood: eg Esterly 1998. For his work in stone, Green 1964.
184 WS XIV, 138, 143, 148; XV, pl. 30 for sketch plan.
185 WS XV, 72.
186 Green 1964, 89. Whinney and Millar (1957, 329) includes the surprising statement that the flowers and fruit of Gibbons's carvings beneath the windows 'are so deeply undercut that many of the panels have almost perished'; presumably the grime gave that impression and discouraged examination.
187 WS XV, 45.
188 WS XVI, 175.
189 Ward-Jackson 2003, 361–81.
190 LMA CLC/313/I/E/014/MS 25809/2, 104.
191 Analyses of paint have been undertaken by Ian Bristow; reports in SPCAA. An area of old paintwork, about 2m by 1.8m, has recently been identified in the south nave triforium, where it may have escaped removal by being behind fittings. Future analysis may show if the layers of paint include the original three coats in oil. There are traces of paint elsewhere at triforium level.
192 WS XV, 35; Sladen 2004. William Thompson painted the interior 'three times in oil', for which he was paid in 1710: WS XV, 188, 190. His son Joseph, also a painter, recalled that according to his father, areas of softer stone were given several coats of oil to harden them before the three main layers: WS XVI, 169.
193 WS XV, 31.
194 Watkin 1974, 116.
195 de Beer 1959, 1025.
196 Newman 2004.
197 Higgott 2013, section 4; Geraghty 2007, 75–80. Penrose produced several drawings of the choir stalls before he moved them, for instance SPCAA D/1/14/29.
198 Newman 2004.
199 Higgott 2013, section 7, catalogue entry for the drawing, WRE/7/27.
200 WS XV, 181.
201 Geraghty 2007, no. 103.
202 WS XIV, pls 18, 19. The Trevitt view is also Newman 2004, fig. 154. This paragraph is a comment by Gordon Higgott.
203 WS XV, 27.
204 Summarised in WS XV, xxxiii. Drawings by Penrose of the altar rail and of part of the choir screen by Tijou are reproduced in WS XVI, pls xiv, xv.
205 RCHME 1929, 51. The Bodley and Garner screen on the north side is drawn by Poley 1927, pl. xxxi.
206 WS XV, 152.
207 Eg a view from the west end of the nave of about 1725: Jacob 2004, 73, fig. 33.
208 WS XV passim; for the windows, ibid 50, 59, 84, 88–9, 100.
209 WS XV, 157, 165.
210 WS XV, 182; XVI, x.
211 This is the suggestion of Robert Bowles.
212 Geraghty 2007, 67, no. 79. I do not think that the drain running under the Morning Prayer chapel at the north-west corner of the building was 'pre-existing': it was part of the system dug after 1687, and was recorded on Site E in 1998. This plan also shows the lower western steps with a square plan, not flared; what is presumably an early proposal for the line of the railings; and steps down on both sides of both transepts.
213 WS XIV, 22–3, 25–7.
214 WS XIV, 30.
215 WS XIV, 61–2, 77, 79, 88; XV, 5, 50.
216 WS XIV, 49, 51, 59. In SPCAA are photographs, with a plan of locations, forming a survey of the interior of branches A to D from the junctions to about the east sides of the Wren towers, by Robert Crayford in 1971.

217 WS XIV, 30.
218 The top of the brick buttress lay at 14.6m OD, ie this run of the drain is higher than those which have to run below the crypts of the building.
219 RCHME 1930, 107; Hill *et al.* 1980, 20–2, figs 9–10, 12; Tatton-Brown 2000, 67.
220 Colvin and Newman 1981, 41; WS VII, 113.
221 WS XV, 50.
222 WS XV, 62 [1700].
223 WS XIV, 108, 110, 115; the payment, WS XV, 219. Jones was employed at the same time, in 1715, to make the casements for the windows in the dome, under the direction of the Assistant Surveyor John James (WS XIV, 119).
224 WS XVI, 157.
225 WS XVI, 155.
226 Jackson-Stops 1988, 58.
227 In his study of English decorative ironwork, Harris includes a smith's trade card showing a railing in front of a house, possibly Monmouth House, Soho, attributed to Thomas Archer about 1717–18 (Harris 1960, fig. iv; date modified from Colvin 1995, 77). From the second decade of the 18th century the gardens in some of the West End squares also had iron railings, or of wood imitating iron.
228 WS XV, 186, 191, 193, 200, 208.
229 Gloag and Bridgwater 1948, 47.
230 Wolffe 2004, figs 315–16.
231 Higgott 2007, 112, figs 144–5.
232 WS XIV, pls v–viii.
233 WS XV, 211–20.
234 SPCAA D/1/9/27.
235 Langthorne 2014 (site SPP13).
236 Mills and Oliver *Survey*, ii, 98v, 136, 137, 137v, 165v (a large piece 96ft (29.3m) by 22ft 6in (6.9m)); iii, 76; iv, 144.
237 Blayney (1990, map opp p. 9) reconstructs the north side of the churchyard from Canon Alley east to Paul's Gate, which he shows was completely rebuilt by 1671.
238 Mills and Oliver *Survey*, i, 61–2; for cutting back the frontage, ii, 14v; v, 111, 141v; v, 56v.
239 It may be useful to differentiate the two schools at St Paul's. The medieval grammar school was run by the chancellor of the cathedral and was refounded by Dean Colet in 1510. This is the St Paul's School referred to here. The medieval choir school, first mentioned in 1127 and run by the almoner, was distinct. Its site in the medieval period is not certain. In the 19th century the choir school was in Carter Lane (where the building of 1874–5 by Penrose survives), and it moved to the present site in New Change after World War II. Now it is called St Paul's Cathedral School, and is an independent preparatory school.
240 Howgego 1978, 61.
241 More could also be said about the construction of the Wren building from records not drawn on by the Wren Society: for instance, LMA CLC/313/I/D/001/MS 25494 is four volumes of accounts which describe when each consignment of materials (stone, brick, ironmongery, timber, ropes) arrived on the site between 1679 and 1702. Some paragraphs of this section have already appeared in *SPCBW*, 222–4.
242 *SPCBW*, 143, figs 4.89–90.
243 In January 1677 labourers were paid specifically for 'sorting Portland ashler from rubble stones, pileing up same' (WS XIII, 84). Whether the Jones Portland ashlar was reused for anything specific is not yet known.
244 Keay with Harris 2008, 175–7.
245 WS XIII, 108–9.
246 WS XIII, 23–4.
247 WS XIII, 159, 163.
248 It would be useful to know the source of the 187 tons of rubble brought from 'Lambeth' in 1685; WS XIII, 197. The other references are WS XV, 43; WS XIII, 59–61; WS XV, 116, 129.
249 For archaeological work on the parish churches of the City of London, including those of the Wren period, see Schofield 1994.
250 Bettey 1971; Campbell 2007, 91–6.
251 Calculations by the editors in WS XV, xvi. For a study of all the stone types used, Campbell 2013.
252 WS XV, 142, 144.
253 WS XIII, 14, 90.
254 WS XIV, 6.
255 WS XIV, 28.
256 Information from Martin Stancliffe, who suggests the Beer stone was perhaps chosen for its ease of carving for the coffered work.
257 WS XV, xvi.
258 In his catalogue entry for this drawing, Gordon Higgott (2013, drawing WRE/5/3/3) writes: 'In pencil, Hawksmoor noted brickwork and types of stone to be used. Inscribed from top to bottom, inside to out, these are: 'Bear' (four times, for Beer stone), 'Brick', 'portland'; 'H[eadington]', 'Hedingt[on]' 'K[etton]' (five times), 'Kett[on]', and 'Port[land]'. Beer stone was to be used for carved elements of the internal peristyle, Portland for its pilasters, Headington for the levelling courses in the radial walls, Ketton stone for the external pier masses, and Portland for the external columns. Ketton and Portland are used in this way in the fabric. Beer stone was probably used for the internal peristyle (now painted), as supplies were delivered from 1699, when construction reached this level (see WS XV, 50, 61).'
259 WS XIV, 35, 38–9, 97. A step in the great stair, sampled in 2006 ahead of repairs, was of Maidstone stone (i.e. Kentish ragstone): see Gazetteer, Site N.
260 WS XIV, 10.
261 WS XIII, 156, 178, 197.
262 F Dimes in Ashurst and Dimes 1998, i, 109.
263 In his reflection on his work at Westminster Abbey: Soo 1998, 85.
264 For a summary of the various marbles in the floor, WS XV, xxiv–xxviii.
265 WS XV, 178.
266 Wilson 2008.
267 WS XIII, 114.
268 From the index to the Wren Society volumes, WS XX.
269 WS XV, xvi.
270 WS XIII, 75, 78; XV, xlviii.
271 Lloyd 1925, 24–5, 33–7; Campbell and Saint 2002; Cruikshank and Burton 1990, 104–6; Gunther 1928, 229.
272 WS XIV, 30–1.
273 WS XV, 57, 62, 115, 138.
274 WS XV, 200, 216.
275 E.g. WS XIII, 84, of January 1677.
276 WS XV, 147, 157; Price 1733, 30.
277 Reddaway 1951, 128.
278 WS XIII, 79; WS XV, 39; WS XVI, 25. GL MS 25585 is a bundle of paper tallies for bricks supplied to the cathedral in 1709.
279 Brett-James 1935, 155; Smith 2002, 274–5. For records of imports of pantiles in 1669, indicating moderate quantities, Reddaway 1951, 127, n2.
280 WS XIV, 70; XV, 145.

281 Neve 1703, 271.
282 Feilden 1994, 199, fig. 13.12.
283 Feilden 1994, 64, fig. 5.3.
284 WS XIII, 73.
285 A summary of the provision of timber, both foreign imports and native oak, from 1689 to 1710 is in the introduction to WS XV, xli–xlvi.
286 WS XIII–XVI, passim. Slyford also delivered stone to Wren's work at Hampton Court and at least two City churches (WS IV, 33; X, 47, 49).

Chapter 3

1 Friedman 2011, 356. For a review of the illustrations of St Paul's from before and after its completion, Hyde 2004.
2 Gwynn 1766, 13.
3 Hyde 2004, 330–1.
4 Malcolm 1803–7, iii, 109.
5 Elmes 1827, 2, 6.
6 Ralph 1783, 54–5 (a guide originally published in 1743).
7 Friedman 2011, 52.
8 Gwynn 1766, 37–41.
9 Moritz 1886, 75–80.
10 Hitchcock 1987, 16, 593.
11 Malcolm 1803–7, iii, 128; the flags detailed by Ralph 1783, 54–5.
12 Poley 1927, xiv.
13 Introduction by Sir Bannister Fletcher to the report about the restoration given to the RIBA by Peach and Allen 1930.
14 Allen 1936, 120.
15 For a summary of their work, Stancliffe 2004a.
16 WS XVI, 134.
17 Downes 1988, 184, no. 209; Higgott 2013, drawing WRE/7/3/4.
18 Stancliffe 2004a, 294–5.
19 WS XV, xv.
20 Illustrated in Aston 2004, fig. 308.
21 Eg Hyde 2004, fig. 279.
22 Hyde 2004, 328.
23 Ward 2007, 172–3.
24 Aston 2004, 366–7.
25 John Physic in the Bell Guide to Westminster Abbey (Wilson *et al.* 1986, 145) says that 'Criticism and alarm at the number of monuments [in the Abbey], as well as their destruction of the fabric, first voiced in the mid-eighteenth century, increased in volume. Thus it was decided that memorials to those killed (including Nelson) in the wars with the French should be placed in St Paul's Cathedral'.
26 Bowdler and Saunders 2004; Saunders 2012, 82–99. The present furnishings and monuments of St Paul's up to the 1990s are summarised by Bradley and Pevsner 1997, 168–82.
27 Wolffe 2004; Cherry 2013.
28 In his biography of Robert Mylne, Ward (2007, 178) says Mylne expanded the opening of a small brass grating already at the centre of the dome floor, but I do not know what the evidence for this is, and such a grating does not show on 18th-century engravings of the floor. I think Mylne dug the first hole.
29 Matthews and Atkin 1957, 257.
30 Prestige 1955, 41.
31 For example the monument to Lord Collingwood by Westmacott (1813–17) in the south transept, a photograph not dated but probably late 19th century (Courtauld Institute 191960).
32 Quoted in Sinclair 1909, 308.
33 Esdaile 1946, 69–70; Bowdler and Saunders 2004.
34 Hollingshead 1862, 117–29.
35 Other internal works during the surveyorship of Penrose not discussed here include new windows in the dome, 1857–77; the design and introduction of Wellington's tomb 1858; removal of the choir screen and division of the organ 1860–1; new windows of Munich glass inserted 1866–7; replacement of timber stairs in the dome with the present iron ones, 1868–9; internal cleaning which removed any surviving traces of Wren's original paint scheme 1872–4; lowering of the floor around Nelson's tomb in the crypt and a new floor there 1874; insertion of a new peal of bells in the north-west tower 1887; a new bell (Great Paul) inserted in the south-west tower 1882; a new reredos 1886–8; a spiral stair leading from the north choir aisle down into the crypt, piercing the fabric 1888–9 (perhaps the source of some of the medieval carved stones stored in the present south nave triforium); mosaics in the crossing by Watts, finished *c.* 1891; placing statues of saints in niches in the drum of the inner dome 1892–4; mosaics in the choir and choir aisles by Richmond 1892–1904. For some of these projects, Hyde 2004; Sladen 2004; Stancliffe 2004a. The mosaics and related models and art works are being studied by Dr Heike Zech.
36 Wolffe 2004, fig. 316.
37 Matthews and Atkin 1955, 262; Wolffe 2004, 383, fig. 317. A plan of the seating throughout the cathedral, including the temporary works, is in LMA, along with drawings of the platform and machinery used in lowering the coffin.
38 Prestige 1955, 75–7.
39 Virger Green's diary, quoted in Sinclair 1909, 313, says the Duke's coffin was removed off Nelson's tomb on 22 November 1853. The Duke's tomb was not ready until 1858.
40 Ward-Jackson 2004; the Invalides-like excavation, proposed by T L Donaldson, is illustrated in fig. 7.
41 LMA CLC/313/I/E/014/MS 25809/1, 104.
42 Sinclair 1909, 318.
43 Hyde 2004, 332 and fig. 290.
44 Sinclair 1909, 320.
45 Sladen 2004.
46 LMA CLC/313/I/E/014/MS 25809/1, 3.
47 Sinclair 1909, 378–90 with description of the subject matter; Bradley and Pevsner 1997, 172, 176–7.
48 Addleshaw and Etchells 1948, 213–14.
49 This period of religious reform and change at the cathedral is described in Burns 2004.
50 Sladen 2004, 243–5.
51 Penrose drew elevations of the stalls 'as they originally stood', SPCAA D/1/14/29 and /30. His plan of the choir before the alterations is redrawn in WS XVI, pl. x; the original shown in Newman 2004, fig. 156.
52 Sinclair 1909, 313.
53 Matthews and Atkins 1957, 261–2.
54 Prestige 1955, 42–3; Sinclair 1909, 312.
55 Prestige 1955, 2–3, 42. The Penrose plan is SPCAA D/1/2/2.
56 LMA CLC/313/I/E/015/MS 25808, 3–4.
57 Sinclair 1909, 325, 329. The monuments to Samuel Johnson and John Howard are shown with railings in front of them in 1828: WS XIV, pl. xlviii.
58 LMA CLC/313/I/E/014 MS 25809/1, 10r; *Parentalia*, 318–21; transcribed in WS IX, 15–18 and Soo 1998, 112–18.
59 SPCAA D/1/2/13.

60 The pulpits of Mylne and Penrose are now preserved as relics at the west end of the north triforium of the nave.
61 *Parentalia*, 319.
62 Hatton 1707–8, ii, 472. Burials beneath the floor of a church crypt are found at St Philip's Birmingham (now Birmingham Cathedral) in 1709–15; quite possibly St Paul's started the practice (information from Julian Litten).
63 WS XVI, 122.
64 LMA P69/AUG/B/013/MS 8916 is an agreement of the cathedral with united parishes of St Augustine and St Faith, that the parishes can use the 'cathedral vaults' and parts of St Paul's Churchyard, with an attached plan of 1753 by James Dodson, Vestry Clerk of the parish of St Faith's, showing that the parish of St Faith 'have been accustomed to bury in' the north aisle of the choir crypt.
65 Register of burials, LMA CLC/313/F/002/MS 25741; Clay 1899, 180.
66 So later than the interment of Earl Beatty near Nelson in 1938, said to be the last by Bradley and Pevsner 1997, 180.
67 LMA CLC/256/MS 2480/004; RCHME 1929, 50.
68 SPCAA D/1/2/2.
69 Bradley and Pevsner 1997, 179.
70 Wroe-Brown 2001.
71 WS XIII, 71; XIV, 5.
72 Edward Palmer (1840–82) was a professor of Arabic at the University of Cambridge; a portrait of him is in the hall of St John's College Cambridge.
73 Schofield 2009.
74 For a drawing of intentions with the paving in the portico, SPCAA D/1/7/3.
75 Called Howard apparently in error by Simpson (1894, 258–9).
76 Drawing in SPCAA D/1/7/10 dated 1874.
77 The design by Penrose is SPCAA D/1/17/12 of 1873.
78 From notes made by Christine Faunch from transcriptions of Penrose's annual reports, held in SPCAA.
79 Barman 1930.
80 LMA P69/GRE/B/001/MS 1336/1; for Evelyn, de Beer 1959, 1025; WS XIV, 105.
81 LMA P69/FAI/B/016/MSS 00622–7.
82 LMA P69/FAI/B/016/MS 00622 is a plan of the north-east churchyard before its landscaping in 1879; LMA P69/FAI/B/017/MS 00623 is a plan of the relocated ledger slabs in the north aisle of the choir crypt.
83 A design of 1879 by Penrose for a fountain in granite for the north-east churchyard is in SPCAA D/1/9/11.
84 Sinclair 1909, 336.
85 They are probably the four now to be found in a north–south row outside the north transept, where the ground was much excavated for the underground Works Department and garage in 1970.
86 *SPCBW*, 116–18.
87 LMA CLC/313/I/E/015/MS 25808, 96.
88 WS XVI, 98. A coach and a cart can be seen trying to take the route along the north side in Canaletto's painting of about 1754 (Fig. 1).
89 Jackson 2002, 132–3. Tallis does not name the occupant at this time, as he does for nearly all the other shops and premises.
90 Raven 2004. Paternoster Row before World War II, including at least one late 17th-century house, is shown in several photographs in Davies 2009, 92–3.
91 Clarke 2014, 217, 219, fig. 11.31.
92 Summerson 1976, 18; 1990, 212. A pen and ink drawing of the ground-floor elevation of this building, and the plan of its front, was made by Richard Kelsey as part of his work on street frontages and sewers: LMA, CLA/016/PL/01/082, p12. For the grave marker, *SPCBW*, 48–9, 254–64.
93 Bradley 2004.
94 Friedman 2011, 180.
95 Roach Bed is used on the St Paul's Choir School in New Change (1962–7). It was not much used before the Second World War, but had an increasing popularity thereafter (Ashurst and Dimes 1998, i, 112).
96 Elsden and Howe 1923, 37–9.
97 Simpson 1894, 278–9 (information given to him by Penrose); confirmed by geologists Ashurst and Dimes 1998, i, 43, 95.

Chapter 4

1 LMA CLC/313/I/E/015/MS 25808, 94; Prestige 1955, 241.
2 LMA CLC/313/I/E/015/MS 25808, 59.
3 LMA CLC/313/I/E/015/MS 25808, 77–8; Bradley and Pevsner 1997, 171.
4 LMA CLC/313/I/E/015/MS 25808, 112, 123, 125.
5 LMA CLC/313/I/E/015/MS 25808, 133.
6 For these medieval features see *SPCBW*, 299–302, 322.
7 *SPCBW*, 322, Site 20; the section drawings are in Macartney 1913–14.
8 Matthews and Atkins 1957, 288–9.
9 SPCAA SPW/2/1: plan by R C A French of 1916, amended 1939.
10 RCHME 1929, 44–56.
11 Robert Bowles suggests (pers. comm., 2014) that 'with the benefit of hindsight, it is extremely unlikely that the dome tilted by an extra 35mm between 1901 and 1913 as inferred by these figures'.
12 This account is from Fox's autobiography, Fox 1924, 188–200; for one report by Somers Clarke to the Dean and Chapter, LMA CLC/313/I/E/015/25808, 88. The fissuring of the stone of the piers had begun during Wren's lifetime.
13 Peach and Allen 1930; Briggs 1957, 353–4; Feilden 1994, 64; Stancliffe 2004a, 299–300. Robert Bowles suggests that damage was being caused by corrosion of the iron cramps used to attach facing stones which were part of the Mylne repairs and not by fresh movements in the underlying structure.
14 Stancliffe 2003b, 17.
15 Bradley and Pevsner 1997, 343. This paragraph has profited from improvements suggested by Kathryn Stubbs.
16 The proposals are outlined in a paper for the London Society, Allen 1936.
17 Atkinson 1985, 58; *City of London: Protected Views, Supplementary Planning Document* (Corporation of London, 2012); information from Kathryn Stubbs. An area somewhat larger than that within the boundary governed by the Cathedrals Fabric Commission for England (CFCE), as regards planning and archaeological matters, is protected by the Depths at the level of 13.716m OD. The present crypt floor is at about 13.45m OD.
18 Matthews 1946, 20, 84; Gibbs 1939, v.
19 Matthews 1946, 47.
20 Briggs 1957, 358.
21 Matthews 1946, 38–9, 48.
22 Godfrey Allen concluded that the stone inscription could not be restored, and the Dean and Chapter decided to replace it with the current inscription let into a circle of stone below the dome (Ward 2007, 173).

23 Contribution by Alan Baxter and Associates to Stancliffe 2003b, 27–8.
24 Matthews 1946, 16.
25 This view of the work of the St Paul's Watch is contributed by Martin Stancliffe.
26 Bradley 2004, 444.
27 For instance in *Night and the City*, an example of American *film noir* in 1950, Richard Widmark is chased across the west atrium in the middle of the night, dramatically illuminated by a single large spotlight on the roof of an adjacent building.
28 Clun n.d. [*c.* 1957], 17: [around Fore Street and around St Paul's] most of the property which has been razed to the ground was very little less than a hundred years old and much of it would have been rebuilt within the next quarter of a century ... thus is may well prove that the ravages of war.. have their compensations in the extensive sites becoming available for the construction of fine new streets and buildings.'
29 Bradley 2004.
30 The views of the Corporation of London and their consultants in 1947, C H Holden and W G Holford, are chronicled in *the City of London: a record of destruction and survival*, Corporation of London Improvements and Town Planning Committee, 1951. This contains a useful survey of the damaged areas of the City. As a further comment on the buildings destroyed in the war, it mapped them and said 'it was the districts of old-fashioned buildings which suffered most' (p. 149).
31 Bringing back Temple Bar was part of the Corporation's proposals in 1947. Two other sites were suggested in 1951, either next to Wren's church of St Anne and St Agnes in Gresham Street, or on a site within the Temple, which was thought the more fitting of the two (Corporation of London 1951, 264).
32 Pevsner and Cherry 1973, 185–6.
33 Bradley and Pevsner 1997, 598.
34 Stancliffe 2004a. One can only regret that post-War Surveyors from Lord Mottistone to Bernard Feilden did not undertake archaeological recording of the fabric or strata they altered or destroyed, as Penrose had 80 years before.
35 For the small amount recorded by Robert Crayford and its interpretation, see *SPCBW*, 299–304, Site A.
36 Nairn 1966 [2014], 19.
37 Feilden 1994, 19, 235. Placing a lift within the hollow core of the main stair had been suggested by Mervyn Macartney in 1926, but not undertaken.
38 Feilden 1994, 153, 162.
39 Inkpen *et al.* 2012.
40 Work by Robert Potter to renew the upper part of the cornice on one of the western towers is illustrated and commended by Ashurst and Dimes in their study of stone conservation practices (1998, 11; chapter written by Ian Bristow).
41 Stancliffe 1993.
42 City of London Corporation, Department of the Built Environment, 2013 *St Paul's Conservation Area: character summary & management strategy*, City of London Corporation.
43 Corporation of London, report to Planning and Communications Committee, 26 November 1991.

Chapter 5

1 Bowsher *et al.* 2007; Impey 2010.
2 Thurley 1999.
3 Schofield 1994.
4 Campbell 2013.
5 Newman 2004; Sladen 2004; Bowdler and Saunders 2004; Wolffe 2004; Raven 2004; Bradley 2004 and Saint 2004 respectively.
6 Wren's building of new Queen's Privy Lodgings at Whitehall Palace, partly revealed in 1939, is studied by Thurley 1999, 137–42; for Wren's work at Westminster Abbey Cocke 1995, Rodwell 2010. For Wren's reflections on his work at the Abbey, WS XI, 15–20, and comments in Soo 1998, 79–92.

Chapter 6

1 Schofield with Maloney 1998, 121.
2 Blackmore 1998.
3 Jeffries 2000; Wroe-Brown 2001
4 Cf Pearce 1992, fig. 24, no. 88.
5 Cf *ibid.*, 18.
6 Pearce 1992, 32–3.
7 Cf Noel Hume 1977, 45–6, pls 45–8; Orton 1988, fig. 137, no. 1368.
8 For discussions of mercury jars, Cotter 2000, 307–8 and Brown 1995, 321.
9 Hurst and Clarke 1979, 53, fig. 12, no. 222a.
10 For a discussion of the form, Cotter 1992.
11 Cyril Beecher pers. comm.
12 Sheaf and Kilburn 1988, 115.
13 Godden 1979, 119.
14 Jean Martin pers. comm.
15 Macintosh 1994, 105, 112.
16 Hobson 1915, 128.
17 Macintosh 1994, 113.
18 Watney Collection Part 1, no. 269.
19 Watney 1997, 29, 58.
20 Watney 1973, pl 56a; Adams and Redstone 1981, pl. 86a–b.
21 Godden 1979, 340.
22 Adams and Redstone 1981, 161.
23 Godden 1979, 119.
24 Cox 1989, 4, citing Lambeth Palace Library MS 2723, fols 21v–22
25 Smith 2000, 14–16.
26 Campbell and Saint 2002, 172–8.
27 Cox 1989, 4–5.
28 *Parentalia*, 319.
29 Reddaway 1951, 127.
30 At the extreme west end a pair of modest scantling oak beams served as rafters (Truss 25), set on stone corbels protruding from the east face of the portico gable instead of a framed truss. Two half trusses (22a, and 22b) also exist now between Trusses 22 and 23 but from the tool marks surviving on some of the timbers used these appear to be of 19th–early 20th century date (possibly part of the repairs of 1903). These additional trusses include old oak second-hand timbers, at least one of which appears to derive from a common purlin roof.
31 Goodburn 1998.
32 Rackham 1972.
33 Goodburn 1991, 1992.
34 Goodburn 1992, 1998.
35 Goodburn 2009, and archive reports on 17th-carpentry at Middle Temple Lane and St Ethelburga Bishopsgate: Goodburn and Minkin 1996a, 1996b.
36 Litten 1991, 99.

37 Campbell 2007, 75–6; information from G Higgott.
38 WS XVI, 210; XIII, 84.
39 WS XIII, 71, 199.
40 WS XVI, 54; XIV, 4–5.
41 WS XVI, 111.
42 WS XVI, 120.
43 WS XV, 222.
44 WS XVI, 132–5.

Chapter 7

1 For a recent summary, Campbell and Bowles 2004.
2 See p. 80 above.
3 The repairs of 1925–30 are described in detail in Peach and Allen 1930.

BIBLIOGRAPHY AND ABBREVIATIONS

Abbreviations

AS Codrington Library, All Souls College, Oxford
BL British Library
BM British Museum
CFCE Cathedrals Fabric Commission for England
DUA Department of Urban Archaeology, Museum of London (active 1973 to 1991)
EH English Heritage
EVE Estimated Vessel Equivalent
GL Guildhall Library
GLC Greater London Council
GM Guildhall Museum
ILN *Illustrated London News*
LAARC London Archaeological Archive Research Centre, MoL
LMA London Metropolitan Archives
Mills and Oliver Survey: P E Jones and T F Reddaway (eds), 1962–7 *The survey of building sites in the City of London after the Great Fire of 1666*, 4 vols, London: London Topographical Soc
MoL Museum of London
MoLAS Museum of London Archaeology Service (active from 1991 to 2008)
MOLA Museum of London Archaeology (active from 2008)
Parentalia: C. Wren, 1750 *Parentalia; or, memoirs of the family of the Wrens… chiefly of Sir C. Wren .. compiled by his son Christopher; now published by his grandson Stephen Wren*, London
PCA Pre-Construct Archaeology
RCHME Royal Commission on Historical Monuments (England)
RIBA Royal Institute of British Architects
SL Survey of London, formerly of GLC, now of University College, London
SPCAA St Paul's Cathedral Architectural Archive, at the Cathedral
SPCBW J. Schofield 2011, *St Paul's Cathedral before Wren*, London
VCH W. Page (ed.) 1909, *Victoria County History of London, I*
WS Wren Society volumes I-XX, 1923–42

Copies of reports noted as 'for the Dean and Chapter' in the bibliography are held in the St Paul's Architectural Archive (SPCAA); archaeological reports, for instance those of the Museum of London Archaeology Service (MoLAS) and its successor Museum of London Archaeology (MOLA) are held at the London Archaeological Archive and Research Centre (LAARC), Museum of London.

Bibliography

Adams, B., 1983. *London illustrated 1604–1851: a survey and index of topographical books and their plates*. London.

Addleshaw, G. W. O., and Etchells, F., 1948. *The architectural setting of Anglican worship*. London.

Aston, N., 2004. 'St Paul's and the public culture of eighteenth-century Britain', in Keene *et al.* (eds), 363–71.

Atkinson, D., and Oswald, A., 1969. 'London clay tobacco pipes', *Journal of the British Archaeological Association* 3rd ser 32, 171–227.

Atkinson, F., 1985. *St Paul's & the City*. London.

Barman, C., 1925. *The danger to St Paul's*. London.

Beard, G., 1982. *The work of Sir Christopher Wren*. London.

Bennett, J. A., 1982. *The mathematical science of Christopher Wren*. Cambridge.

Bettey, J. H., 1971. 'The supply of stone for rebuilding St Paul's Cathedral', *Archaeological Journal* 128, 176–85.

Betts, I. M., and Weinstein, R. I., 2010. *Tin-glazed tiles from London*, MoL. London.

Birch, G. H., 1896. *London churches of the XVIIth and XVIIIth centuries: a selection of the most remarkable ecclesiastical buildings, including St Paul's Cathedral, erected within and around the ancient city walls between the years 1630 and 1730, from the designs of Inigo Jones, Sir Christopher Wren, Nicholas Hawksmoor, and James Gibbs*. London.

Bold, J., 1989. *John Webb: architectural theory and practice*. Oxford.

Bowdler, R., and Saunders, A., 2004. 'The post-Reformation monuments', in Keene *et al.* (eds), 269–92.

Bowsher, D., Dyson, T., Holder, N., and Howell, I., 2007. *The London Guildhall: an archaeological history of a neighbourhood from early medieval to modern times*, MoLAS Monograph 36. London.

Bradley, S., 2004. 'The precinct and setting of St Paul's from the nineteenth century', in Keene *et al.* (eds), 439–50.

Bradley, S., and Pevsner, N., 1997. *London 1: The City of London*, Buildings of England series. Harmondsworth.

Bradley, S., and Pevsner, N., 2003. *London 6: Westminster*, Buildings of England series. London.

Brett-James, N. G., 1935. *The growth of Stuart London*. London.

Briggs, M. S., 1957. 'A brief history of the fabric', in Matthews and Atkins, 326–59.

Brown, D., 1995. 'Iberian pottery excavated in medieval Southampton', in C. M. Gerrard, A. Gutiérrez and A. G. Vince (eds), *Spanish medieval ceramics in Spain and the British Isles*, British Archaeological Reports S610. Oxford, 319–28.

Burns, A., 2004. 'From 1830 to the present', in Keene *et al.* (eds), 85–110.

Campbell, J. W. P., 1999. 'Sir Christopher Wren, the Royal Society, and the development of structural carpentry 1660–1710', Ph D thesis, University of Cambridge.

Campbell, J. W. P., 2007. *Building St Paul's*. London.

Campbell, J. W. P., 2013. 'The supply of stone for the rebuilding of St Paul's Cathedral 1675–1710', *Construction History* 28, 23–49.

Campbell, J. W. P., and Bowles, R., 2004. 'The construction of the new cathedral', in Keene *et al.* (eds), 207–19.

Campbell, J. W. P., and Saint, A., 2002. 'The manufacture and dating of English brickwork 1600–1720', *Archaeological Journal* 159, 170–93.

Carson, C., and Lounsbury, C. (eds), 2013. *The Chesapeake house: architectural investigation by Colonial Williamsburg*. Chapel Hill.

Casson, L., Drummond-Murray, J., and Francis, A., 2014. *Romano-British round houses to medieval parish: excavations at 10 Gresham Street, City of London, 1999–2002*. MOLA Monograph 67. London.

Cherry, B., 2013. 'London's public events and ceremonies: an overview through three centuries', *Architectural History* 56, 1–28.

Clarke, J., 2014. *Early structural steel in London buildings*. London.

Clay, J. W. (ed.) 1899. *The Registers of St Paul's Cathedral*, Harleian Society Registers 26. London.

Cocke, T., 1995. *900 years: the restorations of Westminster Abbey*. London.

Colvin, H., 1995. *A biographical dictionary of British architects*, 3rd ed. London.

Colvin, H., and Newman, J. (eds), 1981 *Of Building: Roger North's writings on architecture*. Oxford.

Corporation of London, Improvements and Town Planning Committee, 1951 *The City of London: a record of destruction and survival*. London.

Cotter, J. P., 1992. 'The mystery of the Hessian wares: post-medieval triangular crucibles', in D. Gaimster and M. Redknap (eds) *Every-day and exotic pottery from Europe c. 650–1900*, Oxford, 256–72.

Cox, A., 1989. 'Bricks to build a capital', in H. Hobhouse and A. Saunders (eds), *Good and proper materials: the fabric of London since the Great Fire*. London Topographical Socociety Publication 140. London.

Crayford, R., 2001. 'The setting-out of St Paul's Cathedral', *Architectural History* 44, 237–48.

Darlington, I., and Howgego, J., 1964. *Printed maps of London circa 1553–1850*. London.

Davies, P., 2009. *Lost London 1870–1945*. London.

Doran, S., with Blyth, R. J., and Starkey, D., 2012. *Royal river: power, pageantry and the Thames*. London.

Downes, K., 1971. *Christopher Wren*. London.

Downes, K., 1988a. *Sir Christopher Wren: the design of St Paul's Cathedral*. London.

Downes, K., 1988b (1982). *The architecture of Wren*, rev edn, privately printed [Redhedge].

Downes, K., 1991. 'Wren and the Cathedral of London', in *Sir Christopher Wren and the making of St Paul's*, Royal Academy of Arts Exhbition Catalogue. London, 7–56.

Downes, K., 2004. 'Wren and the new cathedral', in Keene *et al.* (eds), 191–206.

Downes, K., 2007. *Christopher Wren*. Oxford.

Dugdale, W., 1658. *The history of St Paul's Cathedral in London*; 2nd ed with a continuation by Edward Maynard, 1716; 3rd ed with a continuation and additions by Henry Ellis, 1818. London.

Dutton, R., 1951. *The Age of Wren*. London.

Easton, T., 1998. 'Ritual marks on historic timber', *The Mortise and Tenon* [no volume number], 7–9.

Elmes, J., 1827 *Metropolitan improvements: London in the nineteenth century*. London.

Elsden, J .V., and Howe, J. A., 1923. *The stones of London*. London.

Esdaile, K. A., 1946. *English church monuments 1510–1840*. London.

Feilden, B. M., 1994. *Conservation of historic buildings*, 2nd ed. Oxford.

Fox, Sir F., 1924. *Sixty-three years of engineering: scientific and social work*. London.

Friedman, T., 2011. *The eighteenth-century church in Britain*. London.

Geraghty, A., 2007. *The architectural drawings of Sir Christopher Wren at All Souls, College. Oxford: a complete catalogue*. Aldershot.

Gloag, J., and Bridgwater, D., 1948. *A history of cast iron in architecture*. London.

Godfrey, W. H. (ed.), 1951. *Le Guide le Londres (1693)*. London Topographical Society. Cambridge.

Goodburn, D., 1991. 'Wet sites as archives of ancient landscapes', in J. Coles and D. Goodburn (eds), *Wet Site Excavation and Survey*, Exeter, 51–3.

Goodburn, D., 1992. 'Woods and woodland: carpenters and carpentry', in Milne 1992, 106–31.

Goodburn, D., 1998. 'New lights on aspects of the Roman woodwork at the Regis House site (KWS94)', MoLAS archive report.

Goodburn, D., 2009. 'Woodwork from Southwark', in Blatherwick, S., and Bluer, R., *Great houses, moats and mills on the south bank of the Thames; Medieval and Tudor Southwark and Rotherhithe*, MoLAS Monograph 47, 200–21.

Goodburn, D., and Minkin, J., 1996a. 'Woodworking evidence recorded at 1–4 Middle Temple Lane, City of London (MTE96)', MoLAS archive report.

Goodburn, D., and Minkin, J., 1996b. 'St Ethelburga The Virgin Bishopsgate, EC2, City of London: Report on the third phase of the work on the salvaged Woodwork (SEH94)', MoLAS archive report.

Green, D., 1964. *Grinling Gibbons: his work as a carver and statuary 1648–1721*. London.

Gwynn, J., 1776. *London and Westminster improved, illustrated by plans*. London.

Harris, E., 1990. *British architectural books and writers 1556–1785*. Cambridge.

Harris, J., 1960. *English decorative ironwork 1610–1836*. London.

Hart, V., 2011. *Inigo Jones, architect of kings*. London.

Harvey, W., 1925. *The preservation of St Paul's Cathedral and other famous buildings*. London.

Hatton, E., 1707–8. *A new view of London*, 2 vols. London.

Heard, K., and Goodburn, D., 2000. *Investigating the maritime history of Rotherhithe*. MOLAS Archaeology Study Series 11. London.

Henderson, A. E., 1937. *Saint Paul's Cathedral. London, then and now*. London.

Hewett, C. A., 1974. *English cathedral carpentry*. Chichester.

Hewett, C. A., 1985. *English cathedral and monastic carpentry*. Chichester.

Higgott, G., 2004a. 'The fabric to 1670', in Keene *et al.* (eds), 171–90.

Higgott, G., 2004b. 'The revised design for St Paul's Cathedral, 1685–90: Wren, Hawksmoor and Les Invalides', *Burlington Magazine* 146, 534–47.

Higgott, G., 2008. 'The west end of St Paul's Cathedral: design and construction history', Report for Dean and Chapter.

Higgott, G., 2009. 'Geometry and structure in the dome of St Paul's', in B Gerbino and S Johnson *Compass and rule: architecture as mathematical practice in England 1500–1700*. London, 154–69.

Higgott, G., 2013. *Wren Office Drawings*, online catalogue at http://www.stpauls.co.uk/Cathedral-History/The-Collections/Architectural-Archive/Wren-Office-Drawings.

Higgott, G., in prep. 'Wren's interventions in the fabric of St Paul's Cathedral during construction'.

Hitchcock, H-R., 1987. *Architecture: nineteenth and twentieth centuries*. Pelican History of Art. London.

Holford, W., 1956. *Report to the Court of Common Council of the Corporation of the City of London on The Precincts of St Paul's*, privately printed [MoL Library].

Hollingshead, J., 1862. *Underground London*. London: Groombridge, Paternoster Row.

Hyde, R., 2004. 'Images of St Paul's', in Keene *et al.* (eds), 317–34.

Impey, E. (ed.), 2008. *The White Tower*. London.

Inkpen, R. J., Viles, H. A., Moses, C., Baily, B., Collier, P., Trudgill, S. T., and Cooke, R. U., 2012. 'Thirty years of erosion and declining atmospheric pollution at St Paul's Cathedral. London', *Atmospheric Environment* 62, 521–9.

Jackson, P. (ed.), 2002. *John Tallis's London street views 1838–1840*, 2nd rev edn. London Topographical Society Publication 160. London.

Jackson-Stops, G., 1988. 'The court Style in Britain', in Baarsen, R., Johnston, P. M., Jackson-Stops, G., and Evans Dee, E., *Courts and Colonies: the William and Mary Style in holland, England, and America*, Smithsonian Institution, New York, 36–61.

Jacob, W. M., 2004. 'History, 1714–1830', in Keene *et al.* (eds), 71–83.

Jervis, S., 1986 'A seventeenth-century book of engraved ornament', *Burlington Magazine* 128 (December 1986), 898–903.

Keay, A., with Harris, R. B., 2008. 'The White Tower, 1642–1855', in Impey (ed.), 179–208.

Keene, D., Burns, A., and Saint, A. (eds), 2004. *St Paul's: the cathedral church of London 604–2004*. London.

Kuyper, W., 1980. *Dutch classicist architecture: a survey of Dutch architecture, gardens and Anglo-Dutch relations from 1625 to 1700*, Delft.

Lang, J., 1956. *Rebuilding St Paul's after the Great Fire of London*. London.

Langthorne, J., 2014. 'Wren's Chapter House, St Paul's Cathedral, City of London: assessment of an archaeological investigation (SPP13)', PCA archive report.

Latham, R., and Matthews, W., 1971. *The diary of Samuel Pepys: III, 1662*. London.

Litten, J., 1991. *The English way of death: the common funeral since 1450*. London.

Longman, W., 1873. *A history of the three cathedrals dedicated to St Paul in London*. London.

Lloyd, N., 1983 [reprint of edition of 1925]. *A history of English brickwork*. London.

Macartney, M., 1913–14. 'Some investigations into the soil in and around St Paul's Cathedral, and comparison with data in *Parentalia*', *Proceedings of the Society of Antiquaries of London* 2nd ser. 26, 218–28.

Malcolm, J. P., 1803–7. *London Redivivum: or an ancient history and modern description of London*, 3 vols. London.

Matthews, W. R., 1946. *Saint Paul's Cathedral in wartime 1939–1945*. London.

Matthews, W. R., and Atkins, W. M. (eds), 1957. *A history of St Paul's Cathedral and the men associated with it*. London.

Miles, D., and Russell, H., 1995. 'Plumb and level marks', *Vernacular Architecture* 26, 33–8.

Millett, M., and McGrail, S., 1987. 'The archaeology of the Hasholme Logboat', *Archaeological Journal* 144, 69–155

Millon, H. A. (ed.), 1999. *The triumph of the Baroque: architecture in Europe 1600–1750*. New York.

Milman, H. H., 1868. *Annals of St Paul's Cathedral*. London.

Milne, G., 1992. *Timber building techniques in London c. 900–1400*. London & Middlesex Archaeological Society Special Paper 15. London.

Milne, G., and Milne, C., 1982. *Medieval waterfront development at Trig Lane*. London & Middlesex Archaeological Society Special Paper 5. London.

Moritz, C. P., 1886. *Travels in England in 1782*. London.

Nairn, I., 1966. (with an afterword by Gavin Stamp, 2014) *Nairn's London*. London.

Neve, R., 1703. *The City and Country Purchaser and Builders' Dictionary*. London.

Newman, J., 2004. 'Fittings and liturgy in Post-Fire St Paul's', in Keene *et al.* (eds), 220–32.

Peach, F. C., and Allen, W. G., 1930 'The preservation of St Paul's Cathedral', *Journal of the Royal Institute of British Architects* 37, 655–76.

Pearce, J. E., 1992. *Post-medieval pottery in London, 1500–1700: 1, Border wares*. London.

Penrose, F. C., 1851. *An investigation of the principles of Athenian architecture*, Macmillan for The Society of Dilettanti, rev edn, 1888. London.

Penrose, F. C., 1879. 'Notes on St Paul's Cathedral', *RIBA Transactions* 29, 93–104.

Penrose, F. C., 1883. 'On the recent discoveries of portions of old St Paul's cathedral', *Archaeologia* 47, 381–92.

Pevsner, N., and Cherry, B., 1973. *London 1: the Cities of London and Westminster*, rev edn. London.

Plot, R., 1677. *The natural history of Oxfordshire*. Oxford.

Pluis, J., 1997. *The Dutch tile: designs and names*. Leiden.

Poley, A. F. E., 1927. *St Paul's Cathedral, measured, drawn and described*. London.

Prestige, G L., 1955. *St Paul's in its glory: a candid history of the Cathedral 1831–1911*. London.

Price, F., 1733. *A treatise on carpentry*. London.

Rackham, O., 1972. 'Grundle House: On the quantities of timber in certain East Anglian buildings in relation to local supplies', *Vernacular Achitecture* 3, 3–8.

Rackham, O., 1976. *Trees and woodland in the British landscape*. London.

Ralph, J., 1783. *A critical review of the publick buildings, statues, and ornaments in, and about London and Westminster*. London.

Ramsey, N., 2004. 'The Library and archives to 1897', in Keene *et al.* (eds), 413–26.

Raven, J., 2004. 'St Paul's precinct and the book trade to 1800', in Keene *et al.* (eds), 430–8.

RCHME, 1929. *London IV: The City of London*. London.

Reddaway, T. F., 1951. *The rebuilding of London after the Great Fire*, rev edn. London.

Richards, G. ('G R'), 1676. *The first book of architecture by Andrea Palladio translated out of the Italian*. London.

Rodwell, W., 2010. *The Lantern Tower of Westminster Abbey 1060–2010*. Oxford.

Saint, A., 2004. 'The reputation of St Paul's', in Keene *et al.* (eds), 451–63.

Sankey, D., 2007. 'St Paul's Cathedral South Churchyard London EC4: an archaeological watching brief report', MoLAS archive report.

Saunders, A., 2012. *St Paul's Cathedral: 1400 years at the heart of London*. London.

Schofield, J., 1994. 'Saxon and medieval parish churches in the City of London: a review', *Transactions of the London & Middlesex Archaeological Society* 45, 23–146.

Schofield, J., 2005. 'St Paul's Cathedral: cleaning and refurbishment projects 2003–5 (SWG03)', report for Dean and Chapter.

Schofield, J., 2006. 'Graffiti at St Paul's: the cleaning and repair of the west end of the cathedral, 2003–5'. *London Archaeologist* 11, 151–6.

Schofield, J., 2009. 'Archaeological recording in the crypt of St Paul's Cathedral, 2007–8 (PKB07)', report for Dean and Chapter.

Schofield, J., 2011. 'St Paul's Cathedral: archaeological recording of installation of new lift and external cleaning, 2006–11 (PUF06)', report for Dean and Chapter.

Schofield, J., 2014. 'Excavations in the crypt of St Paul's Cathedral (SPU96)', report for Dean and Chapter.

Schofield, J., with Maloney, C. (eds), 1998. *Archaeology in the City of London, 1907–91: a guide to records of excavations by the Museum of London and its predecessors*. London.

Simpson, W. S., 1894. *St Paul's and old City life*. London.

Sinclair, W. M., 1909 *Memorials of St Paul's Cathedral*. London.

Sladen, T., 2004. 'Embellishment and decoration, 1696–1900', in Keene *et al.* (eds), 233–56.

Smith, L., 1997. 'Compass, Cut Circle and Daisy Wheel', *The Mortise and Tenon* 5, 3–5.

Smith, T. P., 1999. 'London pantiles: use and status – a cautionary tale'. *London & Middlesex Archaeological Society Newsletter* 96, 7–9.

Smith, T. P., 2000. 'The church of Saint Benet, Paul's Wharf, City of London, and its brickwork', *British Brick Society Information* 79, 9–18.

Smith, T. P., 2002. 'The Flemish Connection: cautions regarding some building materials terminology', *Journal of the British Archaeological Association* 155, 272–7.

Soo, L. M., 1998. *Wren's 'Tracts' on architecture and other writings*. Cambridge.

Stancliffe, M., 1993. 'St Paul's Cathedral London Quinquennial Report', report for Dean and Chapter.

Stancliffe, M., 2003a. 'St Paul's Cathedral Framework Conservation Plan', report for Dean and Chapter.

Stancliffe, M., 2003b. 'The Cathedral Church of St Paul. London: South transept structural stonework repair and cleaning', report for Dean and Chapter.

Stancliffe, M., 2004a. 'Conservation of the fabric', in Keene *et al.* (eds), 293–303.

Stancliffe, M., 2004b. 'The Cathedral Church of St Paul. London: Detailed proposals for the conservation and repair of the Geometric Stair following access', report for Dean and Chapter.

Stevenson, C., 2013. *The City and the King*. London.

Strype, J., 1720. *A survey of the Cities of London and Westminster*. London.

Summerson, J., 1965. *Sir Christopher Wren*. London.

Summerson, J., 1993. *Architecture in Britain 1530–1830*, 9th ed. London.

Tatton-Brown, T., 2000. *Lambeth Palace: a history of the Archbishops of Canterbury and their houses*. London.

Thomas, T., 1995. 'West crypt, St Paul's Cathedral. London EC4: an archaeological investigation', MoLAS archive report.

Thurley, S., 1999. *Whitehall Palace: an architectural history of the Royal Apartments, 1240–1698*. London.

Vince, A., 2007. 'Analysis of mortar from the south portico of Wren's cathedral, St Paul's Cathedral. London', Report AVAC2007.076, SPCAA.

Ward, J., 1740. *The lives of the professors of Gresham College*. London.

Ward, R., 2007. *The man who buried Nelson: the surprising life of Robert Mylne*, Stroud.

Ward-Jackson, P., 2003. *Public sculpture of the City of London* (Public Sculpture of Britain Volume Seven). Liverpool.

Ward-Jackson, P., 2004. 'Carlo Marochetti and the tombs of Napoleon at the Dôme des Invalides, Paris, and the Duke of Wellington at St Paul's Cathedral. London', *Church Monuments* 19, 115–29.

Ware, I., 1738. *The four books of Andrea Palladio's architecture* (repr with an introduction by A. K. Placzek, 1965). New York.

Watkin, D., 1974. *The life and work of C. R. Cockerell*. London.

Watson, S., 2012. 'St Paul's Cathedral: evidence for a Saxon ditch and medieval activity from excavations at Paternoster Square 2000–2001', *Transactions of the London & Middlesex Archaeological Society* 63, 33–66.

Watson, S., and Heard, K., 2007. *Development on Roman London's western hill: excavations at Paternoster Square, City of London*, MoLAS Monograph 32. London.

Weaver, L., 1915. 'The complete building accounts of the City churches (parochial) designed by Sir Christopher Wren', *Archaeologia* 66, 1–60.

Wheatley, H. B., and Cunningham, P., 1891. *London past and present: its history, associations and traditions*. London.

Whinney, M., 1971. *Wren*. London.

Wilkinson, C., 1991. 'Building from drawings at the Escorial', in J. Guillaume (ed.), *Les Chantiers de la Renaissance*, Paris, 263–78.

Wilson, C., Gem, R., Tudor-Craig, P., and Physick, J., 1986. *Westminster Abbey*. London.

Wilson, E., 2008. 'Bishop Wilson and the steps of St Paul's', *Isle of Man Natural History & Antiquarian Society Proceedings* 12, 133–46.

Wolffe, J., 2004. 'National occasions at St Paul's since 1800', in Keene *et al.* (eds), 381–91.

Wroe-Brown, R., 1999. 'St Paul's Cathedral Crypt Phase IV, London EC4: an archaeological watching brief', MoLAS archive report.

Wroe-Brown, R., 2000. 'St Paul's Churchyard West End, Post-excavation assessment', MoLAS archive report.

Wroe-Brown, R., 2001. 'St Paul's Cathedral Choir Practice Facilities. London EC4: post-excavation assessment and updated project design', MoLAS archive report.

Wroe-Brown, R., 2005. 'St Paul's Cathedral South Churchyard. London EC4, An archaeological evaluation (phases 1 and 2) report', MoLAS archive report.

Wroe-Brown, R., 2006. 'St Paul's Cathedral Educational Facility. London EC4, An archaeological excavation and watching brief report', MoLAS archive report.

Wroe-Brown, R., 2007. 'St Paul's Cathedral South Portico steps. London EC4, An archaeological evaluation report', MoLAS archive report.

Wroe-Brown, R., 2008. 'St Paul's Cathedral Crypt Access Project, EC4, Archaeological watching brief report', MoLAS archive report.

WS IX: Bolton, A. T., and Hendry, H. D. (eds), 1932. *The parochial churches of Sir Christopher Wren 1666–1718 Part 1.*

WS XIII: Bolton, A. T., and Hendry, H. D. (eds), 1936. *Designs and drawings by Sir Christopher Wren for St Paul's Cathedral, the residentiaries' houses, and the Deanery.*

WS XIV: Bolton, A. T., and Hendry, H. D. (eds), 1937. *Engravings of St Paul's Cathedral and Part II of the building accounts for the years 1685–95.*

WS XV: Bolton, A. T., and Hendry, H. D. (eds), 1938. *Photographic supplement of St Paul's Cathedral, part III of building accounts 1695–1713, Chapter House accounts 1712–14 and Cathedral accounts 1714–25.*

WS XVI: Bolton, A. T., and Hendry, H. D. (eds), 1939. *Drawings and models of the construction of St Paul's Cathedral, Contract Book and accounts 1668–75.*

WS XX: Bolton, A. T., and Hendry, H. D. (eds), 1943. *Catalogue of Sir Chr. Wren's drawings.*

Yeomans, D., 1989. Structural Carpentry in London Building, in H. Hobhouse and A. Saunders (eds), *Good and proper materials; the fabric of London since the Great Fire.* London Topographical Society Publication 140, 38–47. London.

Yeomans, D., 1992. *The trussed roof: its history and development.* Aldershot.

INDEX

Numbers in italics denote pages with illustrations, numbers underlined denote pages with tables